NOBBY'S LADS

EDWARD SKINGSLEY

ISBN: 9798639247477

DEDICATION

To all of my family

CONTENTS

<u>FOREWORD</u> **JOHN STILES**

The morning of May 1st 1978 was not a happy one in the Stiles household.

Later that day Third Division champions Wrexham had to prevent Peterborough winning in the final game of the season in order for Preston North End to be promoted.

Around 9am the telephone rang. Dad quickly answered it – the call was brief. I heard dad inform my mum that Wrexham were leaving out a large number of regular first teamers that day.

In overhearing this news, and – considering the circumstances – some of dad's reasonably chosen profanities, I laid on my bed devastated. It seemed all hope had gone and that my dad's first season as a manager would end in disappointment after such a fantastic campaign.

At that time I was 13, Peter was 11 and Robert was nine so obviously we had not been able to share in dad's great achievements as a player, but that 1977/78 season we can all remember vividly.

Dad would take us to Deepdale during school holidays, and it was magical. We met real characters like Harry Hubbick the bow-legged physio and George Warr the kitman, who maintained he had met Rommel in the desert during his days as a Desert Rat. We played for hours in the wooden floored gymnasium and roamed around to the café and shop over the road and the chippy around the corner.

Being able to watch the players was the big treat. These players were like gods to us, and like any fan we all had our favourites. Peter's was Alex Bruce (Brucie), an unbelievable goalscorer and Robert's was Gordon Coleman (Coley). I didn't really have a favourite, to me they were all legends, but I have to say Mike Elwiss was outstanding that year.

The telephone rang once more that May morning. Again, dad quickly answered. It was another fleeting call with dad ending the conversation with, "thank you for letting me know." Dad told my mum that it had been

Arfon Griffiths, the Wrexham manager reassuring him that the injury absentees were all genuine and had said, "We're going to give it a real go."

The hope was back.

The rest of May 1st remains much of a blur. Dad went to the game of course, but we didn't. We listened to the match on the radio in the kitchen with mum. Dai Davies seemed to be making miracle save after miracle save to keep Peterborough out. It was the longest last ten minutes ever, but when the final whistle went, we all erupted!

My uncle and cousins went to Wrexham that day and told me about the scenes as Wrexham and Preston fans embraced on the pitch after it was all over. Dad celebrated with Arfon and the Wrexham players in their dressing room.

Dad had put his heart and soul into the job and had succeeded along with his superb team and staff.

Everyone who can remember that time will enjoy this book that warmly and accurately recalls a memorable time for the players and people of Preston, and the happiest of times for our family.

John Stiles, April 2020.

INTRODUCTION

There is an episode of the fast paced 1970's television series 'The Sweeney' in which a Turkish police captain is seconded to the Flying Squad to help shut down a stolen car exporting racket.

He embroiders tales about himself and his position to whoever will listen, and then eventually messes up the whole operation.

This results in Detective Inspector Jack Regan having to hurriedly drive him away at speed from a crime scene with a dire warning ringing in his ears from a helicopter's megaphone.

The pair had unwittingly wandered into and ruined a security services operation. Their last scene together takes place in the car.

Regan is musing upon his probable carpeting and suspension when Captain Shebbeq breaks the tense silence. He tells Regan that the authorities in Turkey will crucify him over the destroyed mission.

"You'll be alright," says Regan. "Remember... you've still got your three pensions, one for each wife."

Shebbeq comes clean. "I have a confession to make... I am not a Muslim; I am a Christian like yourself."

He then nervously explains, "In my flat I have three pictures on the wall. One of St. Anthony, one of the Virgin...... and one of... Nobby Stiles," he adds, his voice quivering with emotion.

As he pulls the car up at a set of traffic lights, Regan now staring straight ahead, reflects on this revelation for a few seconds before agreeing, "Ah well... he was a great footballer."

"A name to conjure with," replies the humbled Shebbeq. "A man of determination and guts... if we could but emulate him."

Regan nods his head in agreement. "Where are you now Nobby, when we most need you?" he sighs as the scene comes to a close.

The episode was first aired in September 1976, so to answer DI Regan's lament, Nobby was at Deepdale in his second season as chief coach under manager Harry Catterick – less than a year away from assuming the top role himself.

If I have learnt anything from putting this book together, it is the esteem in which Nobby is held by the people he worked with. The words of admiration roll off the tongues of the players he coached at Deepdale – passionate, humble, lovely man, brilliant, excellent manager.

As a player Nobby had seen and done it all. His knowledge of how the game worked was conveyed to him over the years by Sir Matt Busby and Sir Alf Ramsey – was there ever a better footballing *alma mater*?

This is the story of Nobby Stiles' first season as a manager – a name to conjure with, a man of determination and guts... impossible to dislike.

'I loved my time being coached by Nobby - a special human being' – *Mark Lawrenson*

ACKNOWLEDGMENTS

I am so very grateful to the following for all their help

John Stiles, Alan Kelly Jr

John Smith, Ricky Thomson, Roy Tunks, Mike Elwiss, Alex Bruce

Kevin Williamson, John Steinson, Mike Thorpe, Gary Mounsey

Ian Rigby, Mike Payne, Ben Rhodes of PNE FC

Mike Hill and Dave Seddon of the Lancashire Post

Photographs are from the archives of the Lancashire Post, PNE FC, Ian Rigby, and the private collections of former players.

CHAPTER I

CLOSE SEASON DRAMA

As North End's 1976/77 season stuttered to a close, a crowd of just over 5,000 turned up at Deepdale to witness the last home game of the season.

The opponents, a Portsmouth team who had rather fittingly already 'dropped anchor' earlier in the season, occupied 20th position. However, they proved able to easily frustrate their hosts and take a point back to the south coast. The headline in that evening's edition of the Football Post summed up that match, and the North End's season perfectly – "PNE LACK KILLER PUNCH."

A final league position of sixth was attained with a last day victory at Shrewsbury Town which suggested there was absolutely no imminent danger to the clubs standing. A team that was still blessed with the bounding youthful ability of Mike Elwiss, Alex Bruce, Mark Lawrenson, Mick Baxter and Gary Williams should really have shown more of an improvement on the previous season's placing of eighth, instead of really just marking time.

There was however, no prospect at all of strengthening any of the other positions in the team without selling first – and the great Preston North End sale of the Seventies was still to reach its peak.

Despite a story – which many fans thought was deliberately planted to placate them – that North End were trying to lure Howard Kendall back to Deepdale, the hope of any exciting prospects arriving in time for the 1977/78 season would only be possible if one or two of our exciting prospects mentioned above departed!

During the close season, news coming out of a club is typically very thinly spread until it ramps up again as the new dawn approaches. The close season that was the summer of 1977 never really happened at Deepdale. It was a soap opera from start to finish.

A litany of back page headlines almost daily kept this fan at least very intrigued. Here are some of the more important items of interest.

It began just as season 1976/77 was being signed off, when we read that David Sadler, the most professional of professional footballers, had been advised to quit the game by medics at the age of 31. A troublesome knee would only get worse it was suggested, and now was the time to finally hang up his boots. In recognition of his contribution and approach while at Deepdale, the board rewarded the European Cup winner with a testimonial match – hopefully against his former club Manchester United – to be played at some point during the forthcoming season.

Then there was the news of an admission price increase for the forthcoming season. Adult 'Ground' prices at Deepdale were to be hiked up to 90p (value £5.49 in 2019), but it was possible to save 20% by buying a season ticket and pay just 72p per game (£4.39)!

News of a more serious nature broke a couple of days later when it was revealed that six North End players were still locked in a pay dispute with the club which had begun before the end of the previous season and they were still refusing to sign new contracts. The players involved - Alex Bruce, John McMahon, Jimmy Brown, Ricky Thomson, Roy Tunks and Francis Burns – were the players out of the 17 strong retained list whose contracts desperately needed renewing.

The complication? In the middle years of the strike ridden Seventies, the country was in a dire state and was borrowing huge amounts of money from the International Monetary Fund to balance the books. The club were consequently only legally allowed to sanction a maximum £4 per week wage increase, (current value £24) due to the government imposed 'Pay Code.' Employers had to strictly apply this rule or face huge fines.

It was the very same time as Kerry Packer, the Australian magnate, was signing up Test cricketers from all over the world to play in his World Series Cricket venture. The English players that had signed for him were rewarded with contracts of as much as £50,000 for two winters work in some cases, and here the North End 'rebels' were holding out for a better offer than £4 per week!

Manager Harry Catterick didn't think the situation was serious. He said that the club could not offer any more money even if they had it, due to government legislation. "The terms offered are very good for the Division Three. There is not an unhealthy situation developing, and it's only polite that the players put forward their views. Their letters don't mean they will refuse to sign."

The saga only ended in mid July when Thomson, the last rebel standing, finally signed up after returning from honeymoon. McMahon had by now progressed to the transfer list and wasn't for staying and neither was Mike Elwiss, who was very ambitious to succeed at a higher level. Clubs had been circulated as to their availability, with the newspaper speculation being that North End would listen to offers of £20,000 for McMahon, and £100,000 for Elwiss.

By this time almost a month had passed since North End had wished bon voyage to both Mark Lawrenson and Gary Williams; the pair both signing for go-ahead Brighton & Hove Albion during June. Brighton had just won promotion from Division Three and with Alan Mullery at the managerial helm had an ambitious plan to keep moving forward by continually improving their squad. They were in Division One within two years.

Preston born Lawrenson left a fortnight before Williams in a straight cash transaction, North End profiting by around £100,000. Williams then followed, leaving as part of a three player deal also involving Graham Cross and Harry Wilson and around £20,000 cash in North End's favour.

Straight after the Lawrenson deal, manager Harry Catterick made an enquiry about the availability of John Bird at Newcastle, but the £50,000 swing ticket around his neck drew gasps from the North End board. "We apparently can't afford that kind of money," lamented Catterick. This dead end obviously spurred the North End directors in to factoring in Cross with any deal for Williams.

Cross was a very experienced central defender who had spent most of his career in Division One with Leicester City and Wilson was a decent full back – a commodity that North End would be short of; as besides Williams' departure it was becoming highly likely McMahon would soon be on his way.

Chief coach Nobby Stiles was delighted with the two signings. He had played against Cross many times as a player and saw him as a straight replacement for Sadler. "Obviously I didn't want to lose Lawrenson and Williams but these are the facts of life at Preston. We are fortunate that we have been able to produce so many good young players.

"Sadler was the man in defence who did all the talking and he certainly helped Lawrenson to develop. I see Cross doing a similar thing alongside young Mick Baxter."

Cross and Wilson joined Steve Uzelac, (a young centre half signed at the end of the previous season from Doncaster Rovers), and the new boys were introduced to the existing North End squad for the first time upon the commencement of pre-season training at Willow Farm on July 14th. Alan Jones welcomed the squad and said he hoped they could go a step further than the previous season where they just fell short of promotion.

Catterick was also present after returning from a holiday and told the Lancashire Evening Post (LEP) that although the new signings were the best North End could do in the circumstances, Lawrenson and Williams would be missed. "We have had to meet a difficult financial situation. Now I still happen to think that the team will need further strengthening but whether I can sign anyone or not depends on economics."

The following day it was announced that local building company owner Tom Croft had been co-opted to the North End board upon the retirement of the long serving Bob Bolton. This was the second such board appointment of the close season; Gerald Brown had retired due to health issues in mid June and had been replaced by Keith Leeming.

During the following week, Catterick reported that all the players had settled back into the training routine well, and various combinations were being tried out in defence before the first of the three pre-season games was due to kick off on July 30th. This was an away fixture at Clyde, to be followed by a visit to Queen of the South before ending the friendly season with a home fixture against Luton Town.

All seemed on course as we approached the weekend, the water was calm with no hint of the commotion that was about to unfold.

Then, on Friday, July 22nd the final bombshell exploded in this summer of high activity at Deepdale. Suddenly, Stiles and Alan Kelly were to handle all affairs on the pitch, with Catterick being asked to move upstairs into a consultancy role.

This didn't seem to have sat well with Catterick following his summoning to the boardroom. After being informed of the board's plans, he hurriedly drove off to his Ainsdale home in his new PNE company car after telling his employers that they would be hearing from his solicitor!

As the dust settled over the weekend, it was left to LEP reporter Norman Shakeshaft to fill in some of the gaps and help the bewildered ordinary fan understand exactly what had happened.

To Shakeshaft at least, the events had not come as a complete surprise. Apparently, the moves had been planned for some time; it was just a matter of 'when.' Catterick had been offered a consultancy role to enable him to continue to collect his salary until his contract expired in 1979. A condition of this was that he made no comments at all to the media – an effective gagging order. He left the club a bitter man, totally disappointed with the new proposal.

Apparently, Catterick had been neither a board man nor a players' man, and there had been dissatisfaction all around Deepdale for quite a while. His management style was to delegate responsibility to those below him in order to hopefully bring out the best in them. He rarely got involved in coaching the players directly, but could however demoralise a player quite easily with the sharpness of his tongue.

Make no mistake, in the Sixties and early Seventies Catterick was highly regarded as a manager. He had led Everton to League Championships in 1963 and 1970 and to the FA Cup in 1966. At Everton there was always cash in his pocket to wheel and deal with, and he was very adept at buying and selling at just the right time in the transfer market. He was able to buy the best around, backed all the way by the Everton chairman and Littlewoods Pools owner, John Moores – a far cry from the Deepdale scenario.

If the North End directors hired Catterick back in 1975 with a view to him being able to continue this aspect of his management with a fiver and a reel of cotton in his coat pocket, they were sadly mistaken. Not able to go into the market and bring in some decent stock frustrated Catterick continually – even though he knew the financial score at Deepdale when he took over.

He had been allowed to bring in one signing of his own at the start of his tenure – Jimmy Brown from Aston Villa for £10,000 but that was as much latitude he got with transfers at Deepdale. The default button was pressed by the directors after that recruit. At Preston North End, the directors sold and bought, when they wanted.

Chasing down free transfer and budget targets after the directors had sold off yet another starlet for big money was always going to cause an eventual rift, and it seems that after Lawrenson and Williams were sold while Catterick was away on holiday, his frustration finally boiled over.

Catterick towed the official line to the press, but was obviously unhappy. He had also angered the directors previously by not denying football gossip in the national press that he would take up a general manager's role at Everton if approached.

For Stiles this was a big opportunity, unlike two years previously when his close friend Bobby Charlton resigned over the issue of captain John Bird being sold by the board without his knowledge. In 1975, he had walked away from the club two days after Charlton, disgusted at his friend's treatment and refusing to take over as manager.

Ironically, it was the then new manager Catterick who smoothed matters over with Stiles, installing him as chief coach upon his return to the

Deepdale fold.

Now with two years coaching experience behind him, Stiles didn't hesitate to take on the job.

Kelly, a much liked and admired cornerstone of the club and more than worthy of a shot at management, seemingly had no hesitation either. The idea was sold to the fans that Stiles and Kelly were very much a team and would work hard together to bring success to Deepdale. Both had swathes of football experience to draw on. Between them they had seen highs and lows at every level of the game, and it wasn't just this fan that was happy about the appointment.

Season ticket sales improved dramatically at the news, and there was hope in the air – along with a seemingly happier bunch of players.

Francis Burns, another longtime colleague of Stiles at Manchester United said, "I'm sure everyone will give them their full support and work very hard. Last season, Nobby and Alan did all of the coaching with Harry Catterick more of a father figure." These sentiments were backed up by other members of the first team squad. Roy Tunks: "I'm very happy with the situation," Gordon Coleman: "The players could not get on better with Nobby and 'Kel'," Alex Bruce: "Both of them are well respected and that is the main thing. The team spirit is excellent," John McMahon: "Nobby did well with us last season and I can't see any problems with the new set up" Jimmy Brown: "The big difference now is that Nobby will be picking the team. We are very optimistic."

The first pre-season friendly took place on Saturday, July 30th away at Clyde. This would be the first time the North End club had crossed the path of Clyde's new manager, (and future North End manager) Craig Brown, who was also starting his first football managerial job...along with being a headmaster at a primary school!

The result was a 1-1 draw with the Clyde part-timers putting up a determined show. It was only in the last few minutes that Bruce levelled matters after a poor back pass from Baxter had led to the home side opening the scoring. This performance saw North End far from their best but on a positive note the performances of Wilson and Cross were very encouraging.

There were a few changes for the trip to Dumfries to take on Queen of the South on Wednesday August 3rd, the most notable being Uzelac replacing Baxter. The match ended 2-2, but it was an improved performance from North End, who created well but failed to convert many chances. The two goals that did go in were scored by Brown and Uzelac. Still frustrated by the defensive errors, Stiles commented that, "Alan Kelly and myself are both still open minded about what our best line-up will be."

PNE FC

The new management team, Nobby and 'Kel' flanked by trusted sidekicks - kit man George Warr (left) and trainer Harry Hubbick (July 1977).

News then broke the following day that Sammy Morgan, Brighton's Northern Ireland international centre forward was due at Deepdale for initial talks with Stiles about a possible move to Deepdale. By the following Tuesday however, Morgan had decided to keep his domestic upheaval to a minimum and sign for Cambridge United – despite agreeing terms with Stiles.

Amongst all this, North End played their last friendly on Saturday, August 6th at Deepdale against Luton Town. This resulted in a 0-1 defeat, the only goal being swept home by Phil Boersma, the lively former Liverpool player who had joined the 'Hatters' for just £35,000. Again, North End created but failed to convert in front of a crowd of 2306 and Stiles agreed that North End's attack generally lacked bite.

"We created a few real chances but they were at full strength and are a good second division side. They passed the ball better and taught us a lesson but I'm generally pleased with the way things have gone and there's no reason why we can't improve."

The next match was the League Cup first round encounter at Port Vale on Saturday, August 13th and thus the close season of 1977 had come to an end. What a roller coaster it had been...would the new season be just as enthralling?

CHAPTER 2

AUGUST

Port Vale (LC 1, two legs) – Plymouth Argyle (away) – Port Vale (LC replay) – Rotherham Utd (home) – Walsall (LC 2, away)

The 1977/78 season started in earnest on August 13th. During the close season, North End had been drawn to play Third Division Port Vale in the League Cup first round – a two-legged affair with the first contest to be played at Vale Park.

Team selection had proved difficult; Francis Burns and Danny Cameron were ruled out with nagging injuries so Nobby Stiles and Alan Kelly selected what looked like the most experienced side possible in the circumstances with Mike Elwiss continuing as captain:-

Tunks, McMahon, Wilson, Doyle, Baxter, Cross, Coleman, Brown, Smith, Elwiss and Bruce. Substitute: Thomson.

Vale had spent some brass in the months before, signing Alan Lamb from North End and Blackpool defenders Bill Bentley and Terry Alcock. *"They have more strength and experience now,"* said Stiles, adding *"I'm expecting a very tough midfield battle."* The manager asked for a bit of patience from the fans with regard to John Smith too. *"John is a good young player who just needs a little more confidence."*

As so often happens in games of high expectation, disappointment was the order of the day. North End went down 2-1, with the result being a fair reflection of proceedings. Indeed, during the first half, life for the Lilywhites was very difficult. The only attempt on Vale's goal was a solitary high and wide effort from Mike Elwiss before Vale took the lead just before half time with a Ken Beech header.

Life worsened for the 500 enthusiastic and noisy North End fans just after the half time break when Terry Alcock nodded the home side into a 2-0 lead following an Alan Lamb cross. Just a minute later however, Alex Bruce finally lifted North End hopes by delivering a back post header that found its way past the pawing grasp of 'keeper John Connaughton following Steve Doyle's centre.

Unfortunately, Doyle's love affair with the referee's book continued, roly-poly showman ref Mr Kirkpatrick bringing laughter to the crowd by demonstrating the offence in a mime. A Ken Beamish attempt for Vale then went just wide of the post with the North End fans holding their breath, but North End manufactured the odd half chance too. Bruce went close on two further occasions, Doyle shot over the bar and Gordon Coleman forced the keeper into a diving save from a snap shot.

"We have improved each time we have played and our new key defenders Harry Wilson and Graham Cross are settling in nicely into the back four," said Stiles who went on to wax lyrical about Bruce and Elwiss, who were both returning to their lethal selves. *"Alex told me he didn't mind not scoring in the friendlies as he didn't want to dry up when it mattered."*

Before the second leg of the League Cup tie took place on the following Tuesday evening, there was good, (for the North End fans, great) news coming out of Deepdale. Mike Elwiss had been taken off the transfer list at his own request and had signed a new two year deal.

Placed on the list at a price of £100,000 during the close season after declaring his ambition to play at a higher level, North End didn't receive any offers. That was a massive miss by other clubs in the market for a striker. Elwiss was a unique, plundering high tempo forward. At that asking price North End were ridiculously contenting themselves with just a negligible profit on their outlay to Doncaster Rovers.

Stiles had been straight with North End's 'want away' hero. *"I have persuaded Mike to sign a new contract for a pay increase which is in his own best interests. I have also assured Mike that North End will not stand in his way if an offer comes in from a good club."* That outcome was surely the best for both Elwiss and the management. The player could now concentrate fully on his game and regain his form, while those burning ambition issues would take care of themselves.

North End kept named exactly the same 12 as they had done for the trip to Vale Park. *"We want to progress in this competition because the club needs a good cup run from a financial point of view,"* said Stiles.

"The result will be in our own hands. If we can start the game as we finished the second half at Vale Park, we will be good enough to turn the tables.

"That's why I have decided to give all the lads another chance."

Unfortunately, North End's performance was akin to that in the first leg; a poor first half followed by a much improved display in the second. The first half was a very lean affair in terms of entertainment and chances, and the less said about it, the better! With the score still at 0-0, North End walked into their dressing room to see Stiles at his furious best.

"I gave the players a real roasting at half time and told them it was no good thinking they were a 'good team' – they had to prove it out on the field. We were just not good enough and that's why I sent on substitute Ricky Thomson for John Smith straight after the interval."

It was captain Elwiss, turning in a fine second half performance, who won North End the game. He gave North End the lead in the 56th minute when he crashed home a low left footed shot from about eight yards out. With the Lilywhites chasing the winner on aggregate, a defensive lapse by Roy Tunks who was deemed to have fouled Vale striker Ken Beamish in the penalty area, resulted in Vale bringing the scores level on the night but edging ahead again over the two legs.

There were just 14 minutes left to save this tie, and with just four of them remaining it was Elwiss who finally found the net giving North End a 2-1 lead to level up the aggregate scores again at 3-3.

The second half had seen a great captain's knock by Elwiss, much to the satisfaction of his manager. Describing it as a *"fine display"* Stiles added the names of Alex Bruce, Stephen Doyle, Harry Wilson and John McMahon to that of Elwiss, as those who were now allowed to jump off the half time 'naughty step.'

Back in 1977, the rules were such that there had to be a replay at a neutral ground. North End wanted to play at Tranmere, Vale wanted to go to Stockport. A coin was tossed and Vale won.

This meant that North End's first home league game of the season at

PNE FC

Mike Elwiss rifles home North End's winner in the League Cup tie against Port Vale at Deepdale

home to Tranmere Rovers on Tuesday, August 23rd now had to be postponed and re-arranged for a later date. Meanwhile the draw for the second round of the League Cup was made and saw North End or Port Vale drawn away to Third Division Walsall.

The preparations continued for the first league match of the season at Plymouth Argyle on Saturday, August 20th. Behind the scenes, Stiles and Kelly were desperate to get Francis Burns fit and ready. He would hopefully bring his calm professionalism to the North End team that appeared to be lacking in their outings to date.

On the eve of the match it was announced that Ricky Thomson would replace John Smith, who would be in contention for the substitute spot along with Burns. Stiles said that Smith was suffering from a lack of confidence and the break would do him good. *"Being dropped may well bring the best out of him later and it certainly doesn't mean he's out of my plans. I was pleased with Thomson on Tuesday night and the competition between him and Smith is good for them both."*

As far as the match itself was concerned, Stiles requirements were simple. *"We need to work harder from the start. We have got to be more positive, be really competitive and play for two halves instead of one as we did in the League Cup matches. I'm looking for more of a will to win and I want us to get a good start to the campaign."*

Freshly relegated Plymouth Argyle were a young team, with an average age in the mid 20's. As well as being determined to bounce back to Division Two they would want to impress their new manager, former Queens Park Rangers goalkeeper Mike Kelly, who came in promising the Home Park faithful attractive football through the extensive use of wingers. Thus, North End had an idea what to expect and the scene was set.

The long journey down to Home Park, Plymouth didn't prove a fruitless one. North End's performance was a good one considering Stephen Doyle had to leave the pitch with an injury after 27 minutes. Francis Burns replaced him and more than adequately covered his teammate's position.

Argyle could consider themselves unfortunate that not one of four excellent chances they created managed to cross the North End goal line.

The North End team was:-

Tunks, McMahon, Wilson, Doyle, Baxter, Cross, Coleman, Brown, Thomson, Elwiss, Bruce. Substitute: Burns.

Burns was given the nod as substitute ahead of John Smith, who had travelled with the squad.

The home side began all guns blazing, and North End were in 'scramble mode' for the first 15 minutes. The first breach of the North End defence was after just three minutes when midfielder Mike Trusson put the ball past Roy Tunks, but the referee silenced the delighted home crowd by disallowing the goal for offside after noting the linesman's raised flag.

Soon afterwards, a corner from the right was floated into the North End box where it was met powerfully by the charging full back, John Uzzell. The ball flew like lightening towards the bottom corner of the net, only to be stopped by John McMahon who earned the back-slaps of his fellow defenders after he cleared the ball off the goal line.

The home side were certainly performing true to their manager's promise that they would play entertaining football, and in the eighth minute all but took the lead when striker Terry Austin – the 'make weight' in the deal that had taken Paul Mariner to Ipswich Town during the previous season – slammed a close range shot against the North End bar. The ball made its way to the left and was crossed back into the North End box instantly where again Austin met the ball, this time with a good header, which flew just over Tunks' still wobbling crossbar.

North End eventually managed to retain enough of the ball and poke their noses out into the Plymouth half. Two corners were won in quick succession on the Argyle left, thanks mainly to the diligence of Alex Bruce. The ball was eventually cleared, but at least the visiting back four had time to catch their breath.

Possession was a little more even by the 20th minute, and Doyle demonstrated his class with a magnificent 20 yard forward pass into the path of the rampaging Bruce whose shot was hurried and thus placed wide.

Bruce, Doyle, Gordon Coleman and Ricky Thomson all had shots blocked or saved in the next few minutes or so, which the few hundred away followers appreciated with increasing volume. Any thoughts that Argyle were done however were misplaced.

Trusson, attacking from midfield shot past the diving Tunks only to see the ball glide past the outside of the post. From the goal kick, the ball found its way to midfield where Doyle and Argyle's John Delve clashed in a tackle, with the North Ender coming off worst. He had to be helped off the pitch, being replaced by Burns – fortuitously named as substitute earlier.

After a spell of North End pressure that didn't really produce any clear goal chances, it was Argyle who turned the screw as the first half came to its conclusion.

This time North End had Jimmy Brown to thank as he cleared off the line to prevent Trusson's diving header putting Argyle ahead following a corner from the right. Shortly afterwards, more held breaths from the North End fans as another shot at Tunks' goal resulted in the ball pinging around the goalmouth begging to be hammered in. It was eventually hoofed clear for a corner, but this wasn't the end of the danger.

With just seconds of the first half remaining, the flag kick was launched into the North End penalty area by winger Brian Johnson, and met low down by Austin whose diving header struck the post with the ball thankfully for North End, bouncing to safety.

The start of the second half replicated the first. Argyle were swarming all over, and North End were then caught asleep as ex Sunderland and Manchester City star, Mickey Horswill, took a quick free kick that resulted in panic stations in the North End area. It needed McMahon to demonstrate great composure by intercepting a pass and allowing his keeper time and space to smother the ball at his feet.

Stiles was using the tactic of dropping Brown deeper and deeper to assist his overworked back four, but there was much consternation in the North End goalmouth after McMahon conceded a free kick on the right, the ball eventually being hoofed away almost clearing the adjacent stand.

Bruce then almost created a goal from nowhere when he intercepted a back pass to the Argyle keeper Paul Barron, who was next tested by a long shot from Burns after the midfielder gained possession some 20 yards out.

In the latter stages, both teams were trading blows in search of a winner to get their season off to the perfect start. Johnson hooked a Horswill free kick over the North End crossbar, Bruce tenaciously won the ball back in the Argyle area but saw his snap shot saved, Austin then headed past Tunks but wide of the post. Mike Elwiss now came more into the game, roaming all over the Plymouth half heading wide on one occasion, then having a stinging shot saved.

The game ended as a goalless draw, but both teams had created enough chances to give their fans hope for the future.

In their new roles as the men paid to live and breathe North End, Stiles and Kelly must have had one name prominent in their minds as they reviewed matters on the team bus travelling back up the motorway to Preston – John McMahon.

Here was a player who any manager would have loved to inherit; a strong and skilful defender with a flair for rampaging forward to join the attack whenever he spotted the opportunity – indeed, he had been chosen in the 'PFA Division Three Team of 1976/77' for such exploits during the previous season.

He had begun this campaign very well, against a backdrop of refusing to sign a new contract and being placed on the transfer list at his own request.

The management team would have known full well that it wouldn't be long before clubs would come along knocking at the door to prise their star full back away. It was a slightly worrying matter for Nobby and Kel.

Danny Cameron, another of North End's experienced full backs was still out of action recovering from a muscle injury sustained at Clyde during the pre-season friendly, but it was hoped he would be available for selection again soon after a run out or two in the Reserves. He was the obvious choice to replace McMahon should the worst happen and the board decide to accept an offer for him.

Stiles was happy enough though with North End's performance in their first league outing season.

"Plymouth came at us very strongly at the start of the match as we expected, but held out with that little bit of luck every team needs. They played two wingers in a 4-2-4 formation and although we had anticipated it, they still gave us some problems.

"We dropped Jimmy Brown deeper in the second half which eventually calmed things down. I didn't think we were in much danger after that.

"I was very pleased to pick up our first league point. Our back four are looking better with each game they play but all the players worked tremendously hard and Mike Elwiss set a tremendous example as captain. Ricky Thomson had a very good first half – one of his best performances for the club so far. We created three clear-cut chances and although we didn't score, it's good to see us making the openings away from home.

"In fact, we could actually have nicked it had Alex Bruce converted a great opportunity. That doesn't worry me particularly because the really important thing about his play is that he is always in the opposing penalty area when it matters and is not afraid to have a go."

As sure as night follows day, the inevitable happened and the first matter Stiles had to deal with on the following Monday morning was a message from the board that a telephone call from Gerry Summers the Gillingham manager had been received, formally offering £10,000 to secure the services of McMahon. *"I promised John I would tell him about any offer that was made for him, and I did just that – but he told me that he didn't want to go to Gillingham, so I have refused the bid."*

WEEKEND

Leisure and Football POST

Lancashire Evening Post

No. 28,128 SATURDAY AUGUST 20, 1977 7p

INSIDE

What does the future hold at Deepdale — See pages 3 & 4

PLUS

LENA'S Fashion Problem

Dalglish on target for Liverpool —page 10

● Blackpool's Paul Hart jumps to head the ball away, only to put it over his own bar in today's game against Oldham at Bloomfield Road. Match report — page 16.

NO GOALS...BUT PNE EARN THEIR POINT

PRESTON North End began their Third Division campaign by gaining a point from a goalless draw with Plymouth Argyle in front of a crowd of 7,154 at Home Park today.

Point for

By NORMAN SHAKESHAFT

Preston's performance was a good one especially in view of the fact that midfield man Stephen Doyle was injured and had to leave the field after 27 minutes.

Fortunately for North End, Francis Burns came on and

Preston's line-up was as announced yesterday with Francis Burns preferred as the substitute to John Smith who travelled in the squad.

Plymouth manager Mike Kelly kept the same team that drew with Exeter in the League Cup first round second leg this week.

John Peddelty was named as the sub in preference to former Preston schoolboy Brian Hall who joined the club from Liverpool [illegible]

The visitors had to thank Brown for clearing off the line to prevent Trusson scoring with a diving header following a right wing corner, and there were a few other anxious moments.

Seconds before the interval, Austin was desperately unlucky with a diving header which hit the post and bounced to safety following a Johnson centre.

Half time: Plymouth 0, Preston 0.

SCOREBOARD

DIVISION ONE

B'm'gh'm	1	Man U	4
Bristol C	2	Wolves	3
Coventry	3	Derby C	1
Everton	1	Notm F	3
Ipswich	★	Arsenal	★
Man C	0	Leicester	0
Midd'bro'	1	Liverpool	1
N'wcastle	3	Leeds U	2
QPR	1	Aston V	2
WBA	3	Chelsea	0
West Ham	1	Norwich	3

DIVISION TWO

Blackpool	1	Oldham	1
Burnley	0	Bolton	1
Cardiff	1	Bristol R	1
Fulham	1	Charlton	1
Hull	3	Sund'land	0
Luton	1	Orient	0
Mansfield	2	Stoke	1
Millwall	0	Crystal P	3
Notts C	1	Blackburn	1
S'th'pton	1	Brighton	1
Tott'ham	4	Sheff U	2

TV soccer

● BBC Match of the Day tonight: IPSWICH v ARSENAL and MANCHESTER CITY v LEICESTER CITY.
Tomorrow — BURNLEY v BOLTON.

DIVISION THREE

Bradf'd C	4	Cambr'ge	0
Bury	★	Lincoln	★
Chester	4	Hereford	1
Gill'gham	1	C'chester	3
Oxford U	2	Roth'ham	3
Peterboro	0	Portsm'th	0
Plymouth	0	Preston	0
Port Vale	1	Chest'f'ld	3
Sheff W	1	Swindon	1
Shrewsb'y	2	Wrexham	1

DIVISION FOUR

Barnsley	4	Rochdale	0
Brentford	3	N'th'pt'n	0
Crewe	L	B'nem th	L
Doncaster	2	Newport	2
Grimsby	2	Darl'gton	0
Hartlep'l	1	Torquay	2
Hudd'f'ld	0	Swansea	0
Reading	0	Southend	1
Southport	L	Scunth'pe	L
Stockport	1	Watford	3
Wimb'd'n	3	Halifax	3

SCOTTISH PREMIER DIVISION

Ayr	2	Celtic	1
Clydeb'k	1	Aberdeen	3
Dundee U	2	St Mirren	1
Moth'well	3	Partick T	0
Rangers	0	Hibernian	2

SCOTTISH DIVISION ONE

Airdrie	0	Montrose	3
Arbroath	2	D'barton	2
Hearts	2	Dundee	1
Morton	4	Alloa	2
Qu'n of S	2	Hamilton	1
St J'nst'ne	3	East Fife	0
Stirling A	2	Kilm'nock	1

SCOTTISH DIVISION TWO

Brechin C	1	Albion R	2
Clyde	3	S'h'muir	0
D'f'mline	4	Qu'n's Pk	0

From this, it could be deduced that McMahon wanted a move to a club in a higher division, or a club nearer his Manchester home...or he might even be having second thoughts about leaving at all. Any which way, it was good news that he would be staying at Deepdale at least for the time being.

There was another phone call for Stiles a couple of days later, from Wrexham. They wanted to offer £75,000 for Mike Elwiss.

Elwiss didn't want to go to Wrexham however, and the offer was well short of the North End board's trigger valuation of £100,000.

"Mike wants a higher grade of football if he is to leave Deepdale. The main thing as far as I'm concerned is to keep Mike happy here," Stiles told the LEP.

The League Cup first round replay against Port Vale at neutral venue Edgeley Park, Stockport took place on Tuesday, August 23rd.

Gordon Coleman had now joined Stephen Doyle in the treatment room at Deepdale following the Plymouth encounter. It was thought initially that Doyle had maybe sustained knee ligament damage, while Coleman, although just about lasting the duration of the match, had suffered severe bruising to both legs along with an injured ankle.

In the event, Doyle made the cut but Coleman couldn't recover in time, enabling Francis Burns to get his first start of the season. North End's line up was:-

Tunks, McMahon, Wilson, Doyle, Baxter, Cross, Burns, Brown, Thomson, Elwiss and Bruce. Substitute: Smith.

After a quite rousing second half performance North End triumphed 2-1, turning the tables on Port Vale who had strode in for their half time cuppa heads held high, holding a 1-0 lead.

The hangover from Plymouth had threatened to continue for a time in the first half. After a flurry of early activity North End appeared to relax, the game becoming a more even contest with the crowd treated to goalmouth incidents at both ends. The 'Valiants' took the lead just three minutes before the interval, when former Blackpool duo Terry Alcock and Bill Bentley exposed North End's defensive weakness in the air and the former powered in an unchallenged header from the latter's corner.

The second half was a different story however, as North End determinedly set out to settle the tie once and for all in their favour. Skipper Mike Elwiss set the ball rolling with the equaliser in the 48th minute, poking home a shot from a Jimmy Brown free kick into the bottom left corner of the net from a tight angle.

From that moment on, the pressure on the Vale penalty area was never relaxed. Ricky Thomson shot wide from a good position; Alex Bruce had a shot desperately saved by Vale keeper John Connaughton and Mick Baxter, thrown forward at every opportunity, saw a header bounce just the wrong side of the unattended right post. It was unrelenting as Bruce, fastening himself onto a through ball on the run, launched a cannonball shot from the inside left position which slammed into the post before bouncing behind to safety.

Vale manager, Roy Sporson, amidst much arm waving as he tried to re-organise his fatigued defence brought on substitute Terry Bailey for ex North Ender Alan Lamb. However, almost immediately Bruce forced the winning goal when his fiercely struck shot was deflected into the Vale net by right back Graham McGifford. He simply couldn't get his head out of the way in time!

"During the interval I told the lads to keep their heads and if they kept playing good football they would win," said the delighted Stiles after the game.

"They then went out and showed everyone just how well they can play. They were on a mission. They had fire and aggression and all in all it was a great performance. All the players did well and were hungry for the ball, and the goal from Mike Elwiss that was pulled out of nowhere demonstrated their determination.

"I'm crediting the second goal to Alex Bruce by the way and I'm not going to single anyone out for their goal. John McMahon and Mick Baxter performed very well, and no, I don't want to sell anyone. I'm in a good mood tonight!"

As Stiles prepared his team for the first home league game of the season against Rotherham United, North End invited the fans to join their latest idea for raising funds – the *'Sponsor A Goal'* scheme.

In fact, Stiles was happy to underscore the scheme with an insert message in his name which was eventually included with the official programme during the last week of August.

"The idea is basically very simple. You simply decide how much you would like to donate to PNE every time we score a league goal.

"The amount per goal can be tailored to suit your pocket from 1p upwards. If you decide to donate 10p per league goal and at the end of the season, we have scored 60 for instance, your sponsorship would amount to £6.

"At the end of the season, you simply make out a cheque to PNE for the appropriate amount."

The initiative was the first from a newly formed 'commercial committee,' assembled by North End chairman Alan Jones. There would be more ideas as the season progressed.

While we look back and marvel at such 'quaint ingenuity,' in many ways it demonstrates just how desperate for funds the club were back in 1977. Yes, North End were technically in the 'black' after the latest round of summer sales, but funds would rapidly diminish as the season progressed if they failed to meet their calculation that home crowds needed to be at least 7,000 in size.

Around that time football attendances right across the spectrum were suffering severely from the media coverage of hooliganism both at home and abroad and it was singularly the major issue for clubs the size of

North End.

Excepting the usual festive boost to the turnouts at Deepdale, it is worth noting that by the end of 1977, the 7,000 attendance break-even figure had only been achieved on a handful of occasions.

There was rain all morning on Saturday, August 27th – the day of Deepdale's first league contest of the season – against Rotherham United. It had stopped by lunchtime, but had left the Deepdale surface slippery.

Stiles and Kelly were obviously loath to change the team that had played well to overcome Port Vale in midweek – so the only change was the substitute, with Gordon Coleman warming the bench instead of John Smith. The team was:-

Tunks, McMahon, Wilson, Doyle, Baxter, Cross, Burns, Brown, Thomson, Elwiss and Bruce. Substitute: Coleman.

'The Millers' were beginning the new season with away games on the first two Saturdays. They had been promotion contenders during the previous season, and had won their season opener at Oxford United by 3-2.

North End were boosted with the news that the free scoring David Gwyther was missing from the visitor's line up through suspension.

The ball was certainly zipping off the wet surface when the match started and in the first couple of minutes passes from both teams flew astray because of the extra speed. It didn't take North End long to settle down however, and after four minutes they took the lead after some enterprising play.

Ricky Thomson moved forward down the left side and fired a long hard shot at goal, which Rotherham goalkeeper Tom McAllister fumbled. Whether it was the late awkward bounce from the pitch or surprise at Thomson's snap shot we will never know, but the ball went spinning out of his hands and towards the goal line.

Mike Elwiss was alert as ever and as he pounced forward, his right leg extended towards McAllister, the loose ball needed just a prod from his boot to help it roll over the line.

It was a great start to the Deepdale season, but the home fans delight was to last for only three very short minutes. That's how long it took for the Millers to draw level with a neatly taken goal.

Mike Elwiss pounces and slides the loose ball into the Rotherham United net.

PNE FC

Winger Alan Crawford progressed down the left and crossed the ball. Stephen Doyle got into a tangle and failed to clear the ball, enabling Richard Finney to drive a low shot into the back of the net despite Roy Tunks getting his fingertips on the ball as he dived.

Rotherham continued to press after the equaliser and North End were forced onto the back foot for a spell, Tunks pulling off two essential saves to deny Dick Habbin and Tommy Spencer increasing the visitor's lead. It didn't end there either, as in the 19th minute forward Jimmy Goodfellow thumped a shot against the North End cross bar, the rebound eventually being hustled out for a corner. From this, Tunks pulled off a spectacularly dramatic save under the bar from a bullet-like header from midfielder

Spencer.

Things were certainly not going as planned, but when North End did get the ball they were moving forward with menace. In fact, Thomson looked at the top of his game. His speed was proving a handful and he displayed the confidence to repeatedly run at and leave behind the United defenders.

He had a thunderbolt shot blocked, and a mazy run past three defenders towards the visitors' goalmouth was only halted by the sheer desperation of right back Gerry Forrest.

Ricky Thomson proved a real handful for the Rotherham United defence.

<u>Top</u>: Ricky leaves two defenders in his wake as he races towards goal

<u>Bottom</u>: Striking one of his many shots at goal

PNE FC

It was during this period of North End pressure that they regained the lead through Doyle. Another pacey move down the left by the charging Elwiss resulted in a centre that found Doyle on the right-hand side of the penalty area who was able to deftly slot the ball home past McAllister.

The game remained even in terms of chances – North End almost scoring when Mick Baxter, joining the attack for a corner, hung around for the follow up cross and saw his header fly just over. Rotherham then almost equalised seconds later when Tunks tipped away a dangerous swirling cross from the left that was heading for the top corner.

It was North End who struck again though, with just seven minutes remaining of the first half.

A corner from the right was headed on towards Alex Bruce who hammered a snap shot at goal which dramatically pinged downwards off the crossbar but remained in play. Full back John Breckin and Bruce moved towards the ball but it was the Northender who won the challenge, prodding the ball home to the delight of the crowd.

North End went in at half time somewhat flattered to be 3-1 up, as Rotherham had certainly played their part too in an exciting first half.

The second half began with North End launching aggressive attacking raids and Bruce was unlucky not to put the game beyond all reasonable doubt in the 54th minute when his piledriver shot from the right side of the penalty area was acrobatically tipped over the bar by McAllister.

Jimmy Brown then tried a long shot when North End next probed forward, rising just inches over the bar. Thomson nearly etched his name on the scoresheet for the second time but his chase ended when McAllister got to the ball first and hoofed it forward to set Rotherham off on the break; Finney's centre thankfully landing on the roof of Tunks' net.

The game was still pretty much end to end.

Bruce headed narrowly wide from a nicely flighted Harry Wilson centre before the redoubtable McAllister was once again called into action, plucking a dangerous free kick from John McMahon out of the air before watching another Thomson shot fly past the face of goal.

Rotherham manager Jimmy McGuigan then sent on substitute Trevor Womble for Habbin with around 20 minutes left.

WEEKEND

Leisure and Football POST

Lancashire Evening Post

No. 28,134 SATURDAY AUGUST 27, 1977 7p

INSIDE

Save Our Soccer

TOM FINNEY — on the urgent need to stamp out hooliganism — PAGE 3

PLUS

WIN with Junior Post Plus

Travel Desk

— Morocco Bound

Rovers win in style, but 'Pool crash—P10

● Mike Elwiss challenges Rotherham goalkeeper Tom McAllister, but Ricky Thompson's shot squirmed over the line for Preston's first at Deepdale today.

PNE POWER TO 3-2 VICTORY

PRESTON won their first home League match of the season when they beat Rotherham 3-2 in front of 5,964 spectators at Deepdale today.

By NORMAN SHAKESHAFT

The game was a thriller and Preston had to play well to win.

Rotherham, who missed promotion to Division 2 on goal average last season, put up a terrific fight and both their goals were ... by ...

Ricky Thompson opened the scoring after four minutes and Stephen Doyle got North End's second goal in the 32nd minute before Alex Bruce ...

... through pass.

It looked for a moment as though Finney had an opportunity to score, but Baxter moved across to stop him on the edge of the penalty area.

Rotherham gained the first corner but the flag kick was cleared without any trouble.

North End took the lead soon afterwards. THOMSON tried a ... the ball.

Preston: Tunks, McMahon, ...

● Ricky Thompson breaks through between Rotherham defenders Tommy Spencer and John Breckin ...

SCOREBOARD

DIVISION ONE

Aston V	1	Everton	2
Chelsea	1	Coventry	2
Leeds U	1	B'm'gh'm	0
Leicester	0	Bristol C	0
Liverpool	3	WBA	0
Man U	0	Ipswich	0
Midd'bro'	2	N'wcastle	0
Norwich	1	QPR	1
Nottm F	3	Derby C	0
West Ham	0	Man C	1
Wolves	1	Arsenal	1

DIVISION TWO

Blackburn	3	Cardiff	0
Bolton	2	Sheff U	1
Brighton	3	Millwall	2
Bristol R	0	Fulham	0
Charlton	3	Blackpool	1
Crystal P	0	Hull	1
Oldham	1	Luton	0
S'th'pton	1	Mansfield	0
Stoke	2	Burnley	1
Sund'land	1	Orient	1
Tott'ham	2	Notts C	1

DIVISION THREE

Bradf'd C	2	Oxford U	3
Cambr'ge	2	Gill'gham	3
Carlisle	0	Plymouth	0
Chest'f'ld	★	Peterboro	★
C'chester	2	Chester	0
Exeter	2	Bury	2
Hereford	L	Tranmere	L
Lincoln	1	Shrewsb'y (PLAYED LAST NIGHT)	3
Preston	3	Roth'ham	2
Sheff W	0	Walsall	0

DIVISION FOUR

Aldershot	1	Doncaster	0
Brentford	1	Reading	1
Halifax	0	N'th'pt'n	1
Newport	2	Hudd'f'ld	0
Rochdale	2	Darl'gton	0
Scunth'pe	0	B'nem'th (PLAYED LAST NIGHT)	0
Southend	1	Crewe (PLAYED LAST NIGHT)	0
Southport	1	Hartlep'l	1
Stockport	2	Grimsby (PLAYED LAST NIGHT)	0

SCOTTISH PREMIER DIVISION

Aberdeen	0	Dundee U	0
Celtic	0	Moth'well	1
Hibernian	2	Clydeb'k	0
Partick T	0	Rangers	4
St Mirren	2	Ayr	0

SCOTTISH DIVISION ONE

Alloa	1	St J'nst'ne	3
D'barton	2	Qu'n of S	0
Dundee	0	Stirling A	1
East Fife	2	Airdrie	3
Hamilton	3	Arbroath	1
Kilm'nock	1	Hearts	1
Montrose	0	Morton	1

SCOTTISH DIVISION TWO

Albion R	1	Stranraer	2
Berwick	2	M'd'wb'k	1
C'd'nb'th	3	D'f'mline	1
E Stirling	0	Falkirk	2
Forfar	4	Brechin C	1
Qu'n's Pk	1	Clyde	1
S'h'muir	1	Raith	1

Bolton v Sheff U

(Continued)

Late scorer for Bolton, WHATMORE.

Result.—Bolton 2, Sheffield United 1.

TV soccer

● GRANADA tomorrow: MANCHESTER UNITED v IPSWICH

● BBC Match of the Day tonight: WEST HAM v MAN...

It paid immediate dividends as Finney scored for the Millers to reduce their goal deficit to just one.

Racing down the middle towards the penalty area, Finney latched on to a Trevor Phillips through ball in his stride, and gave Tunks no chance with a well placed shot.

Despite the setback, North End took the game back to their opponents and remained on top during the final stages. The pack of Thomson, Bruce and Elwiss continued to roam dangerously, with Bruce unlucky not to score on two occasions and Elwiss appearing to be fouled in the penalty area but going unrewarded from the referee.

The whistle finally blew on an afternoon of excellent entertainment. The win lifted North End to seventh in the table, albeit after only two games.

After the game, North End manager Stiles paid homage to his players.

"The players are working very hard, and that is what I promised everybody. The back four played particularly well but I'm delighted with the team work all round.

"If we had got a goal early in the second half the game could have been sealed. But Rotherham are a very good team. I expected a hard game and they gave it to us."

There was injury news however. Both Elwiss and Brown were doubtful for the last game of the month, the League Cup tie at Walsall.

"Mike has strained a calf muscle and will hopefully respond to treatment, but Jimmy has had a recurrence of back trouble and is more of a problem. Mike has a chance of being fit, but Jimmy will be ruled out. Their performances on Saturday did them great credit as both were in pain for most of the second half."

Tuesday, August 30th, saw North End roll up at Fellows Park, Walsall hoping to progress in the League Cup by seeing off their hosts in this second round tie. After the difficulties encountered in beating Port Vale in the first round, everyone was hoping this would be a lot more straightforward – alas, they were to be disappointed.

The contest ended goalless, meaning yet another game had to be shoehorned into an already bulging fixture list. Indeed, when the replay took place – September 6th – it would be the first team's eighth outing in the three weeks and three days since the season began!

Stiles brought in Gordon Coleman to start in place of the injured Jimmy Brown, and reserved the seat on the bench for John Smith. Mike Elwiss was fit to play after his calf strain responded to Harry Hubbick's magic touch. North End lined up:-

Tunks, McMahon, Wilson, Doyle, Baxter, Cross, Coleman, Burns, Thomson, Elwiss and Bruce. Substitute: Smith.

Despite the lack of goals at Fellows Park, there was no shortage of incident; the game was far away from the typical bore-draw. The early exchanges were dominated by North End, cheered on by a healthy contingent of followers, numbering in excess of 500.

Francis Burns with a rather hopeful long shot got North End underway, and then Bruce went close when his shot from a tight angle was saved by Walsall 'keeper Mick Kearns.

Walsall warmed to their task, and dominated play for the next 20 minutes. Stalwart 'Saddlers' striker Alan Buckley was at his best, and almost embarrassed the visitors by deftly intercepting a woeful back pass from North End left back Harry Wilson – his shot forcing Roy Tunks into a superb fingertip save.

Midfielder Alan Birch then shot over, before testing Tunks again with a low drive. At the other end of the pitch, Alex Bruce ended a good run with a good shot... but then frustratingly saw full back Dave Seralla clear the ball off the line to safety.

The second half was different in that North End dominated proceedings completely for the first 30 minutes. Following a disallowed header from Elwiss on 50 mins, possession was seemingly easily retained, and a string of chances created.

Ricky Thomson shot wide, Stephen Doyle shot over, Elwiss shot inches wide and although a rasping shot from Bruce was on target, Kearns palmed the ball over the bar.

A team of North End's ability should have won this contest with ease, but the ball just wouldn't go in. Walsall rallied in the last 15 minutes and it was a slightly nervy time for those travelling fans.

It didn't help that some of this was self-inflicted, as when Doyle lost possession and placed the defence under immediate pressure. In the event Alf Wood's effort was grasped by Tunks and North End breathed again.

Walsall went close again a few minutes later when it looked like Buckley had turned a cross into a wide open goal, but Mick Baxter appeared from nowhere to head the ball off the line.

A replay it was then, and Stiles once again spoke positively of his team after the game.

"We were very unlucky not to win this game. Walsall didn't get a touch for a long period in the second half as we attacked continuously.

"The lads played very positive stuff and it was a great team performance with everyone working hard.

"Mike Elwiss came through very well and covered every blade of grass but I don't want to single any players out because it was nice to see them all showing confidence in going about their tasks."

The following day, the draw for the third round of the League Cup took place and spat out the possibility of a trip to the seaside – IF – North End could beat Walsall at home in the replay, and Second Division Blackpool managed to defeat Sheffield Wednesday at Hillsborough...

Preston North End Football Club Limited

Dear Supporter,

As you are no doubt well aware, Football Clubs these days cannot exist solely on gate receipts and Clubs have to look at every angle to raise money from off the field activities.

This season, one of our keen supporters, Neville Bolton, has come up with a scheme aimed at raising money each time we score a league goal, and we are writing to you in the hope that you a genuine North Ender, will give your support to our new 'SPONSOR A GOAL' scheme.

The idea is basically very simple and this is how it works :-

1. You simply decide how much you would like to donate to P.N.E. everytime we score a league goal.

2. The amount per goal can be tailored to suit your pocket, from 1p upwards. E.G. If you decide to donate 10p per league goal and at the end of the season we have scored 60 league goals, your sponsorship would amount to £6.00.

3. At the end of the season you simply make out a cheque to P.N.E. F.C. for the appropriate amount.

Please support your Club and help make this scheme a success. All amounts no matter large or small will be very greatly appreciated and help towards the solvency and running of Preston North End Football Club.

Yours in sport,

Nobby Stiles

NOBBY STILES
Team Manager

....

TO: "SPONSOR A GOAL" P.N.E. F.C., DEEPDALE, PRESTON.

I WISH TO HELP P.N.E. BY SPONSORING EACH LEAGUE GOAL AT £....p.... per goal.

NAME ....

ADDRESS ....

....

TEL. NO. ....

The Preston North End 'Sponsor A Goal' scheme details. It signaled the start of one of the club's most barren spells in front of goal for years!

CHAPTER 3

SEPTEMBER

Oxford Utd (away) – Walsall (LC 2 replay) – Carlisle Utd (away) – Swindon Town (home) – Hereford Utd (home) – Colchester Utd (away) – Walsall (away)

The first weekend of September saw North End suffer their first league defeat of the season at the hands of Oxford United at the Manor Ground. The match was a scrappy affair, but one North End certainly didn't deserve to lose. The recurring ailment of not turning superiority into goals reared its head once again, and North End were left with nothing to show for their endeavours.

With Jimmy Brown still suffering back issues, and John McMahon feeling the effects of an upset stomach, Nobby Stiles and Alan Kelly were forced into making changes to the team that drew at Walsall. Therefore, Steve Uzelac and Danny Cameron were added to the coach party for the Friday night sleepover in *'the city of dreaming spires.'*

After due deliberation, the North End line up was confirmed as:-

Tunks, Cameron, Wilson, Doyle, Baxter, Cross, Coleman, Burns, Thomson, Elwiss and Bruce. Substitute: Smith.

Free scoring centre forward Hugh Curran, back at the Manor Ground for a second spell would be on the bench for Oxford after recovering from injury.

The home side were quick out of the blocks and took the game to North End in the early stages. In this time, the best efforts came from promising youngster Jason Seacole who saw a well hit drive go over the North End crossbar and Hugh McGrogan who headed a dangerous Brian Drysdale cross towards goal but not past Mick Baxter, who firmly cleared North End's lines.

North End eventually poked their noses out, and started to play. Ricky Thomson caught the eye, working hard down the right and Mike Elwiss was just an inch or two offside from one good move initiated by the young Scot.

Elwiss and Alex Bruce were marked men, with the home defence attempting to stop their forward progress at all costs. The itinerant Elwiss suffered the most, and the fact that the referee booked Billy Jeffrey just 10 minutes into the game for his overzealous attentions, demonstrates how the powerful forward worried opponents.

Oxford pushed forward again and came as close to scoring as they possibly could when Peter Foley slammed the ball against the North End crossbar with a powerful header following good work by Drysdale and Colin Duncan.

The game became dogged, with most of the spade work occurring in midfield. In fact, the only North End bright spot before half time was a run and shot from Thomson that drifted wide of the post.

A sluggish restart to the game after the half time refreshments didn't improve matters, with North End's forwards still shackled by the home defence. Elwiss however was determined to attack and break free and in the 55th minute he did just that, wriggling clear of a plethora of gold shirts on the left to launch a stinging 20 yard drive that goalkeeper Roy Burton did very well to tip around the post for a corner.

This buoyed the visitors, and again Elwiss broke free – this time down the right – but his curling cross for Alex Bruce was headed wide of the post.

North End's control of the game in terms of possession was causing the home fans to barrack their team, such was their frustration.

This prompted Oxford manager Mick Brown to introduce Curran into the proceedings for the remaining 15 minutes. Within five, he had decided the game.

Speculatively back heading a cross into the middle of the penalty area, the ball bounced back into his path off Danny Cameron and Harry Wilson. Curran swung around and volleyed a shot which managed to thread its way through the defence and evade Tunks' dive before nestling into the bottom left corner of the net.

Credit: Oxford United FC

Danny Cameron (right) looks on as Hugh Curran smashes the ball past Roy Tunks

North End threw everything forward and created three more chances in the last 10 minutes.

Elwiss was unlucky when a goal bound shot bounced to safety off the fortunate Burton, then Cameron drove in a fierce drive which was scrambled away to the cheers of the home fans. Graham Cross then ventured forward; his drive being cleared off the line by Les Taylor with Burton well beaten.

And that was that. A disappointing result but surely North End would learn from this – goal chances must be converted!

Nobby was philosophical after the match.

"It was poor all round before half time, but we played much better in the

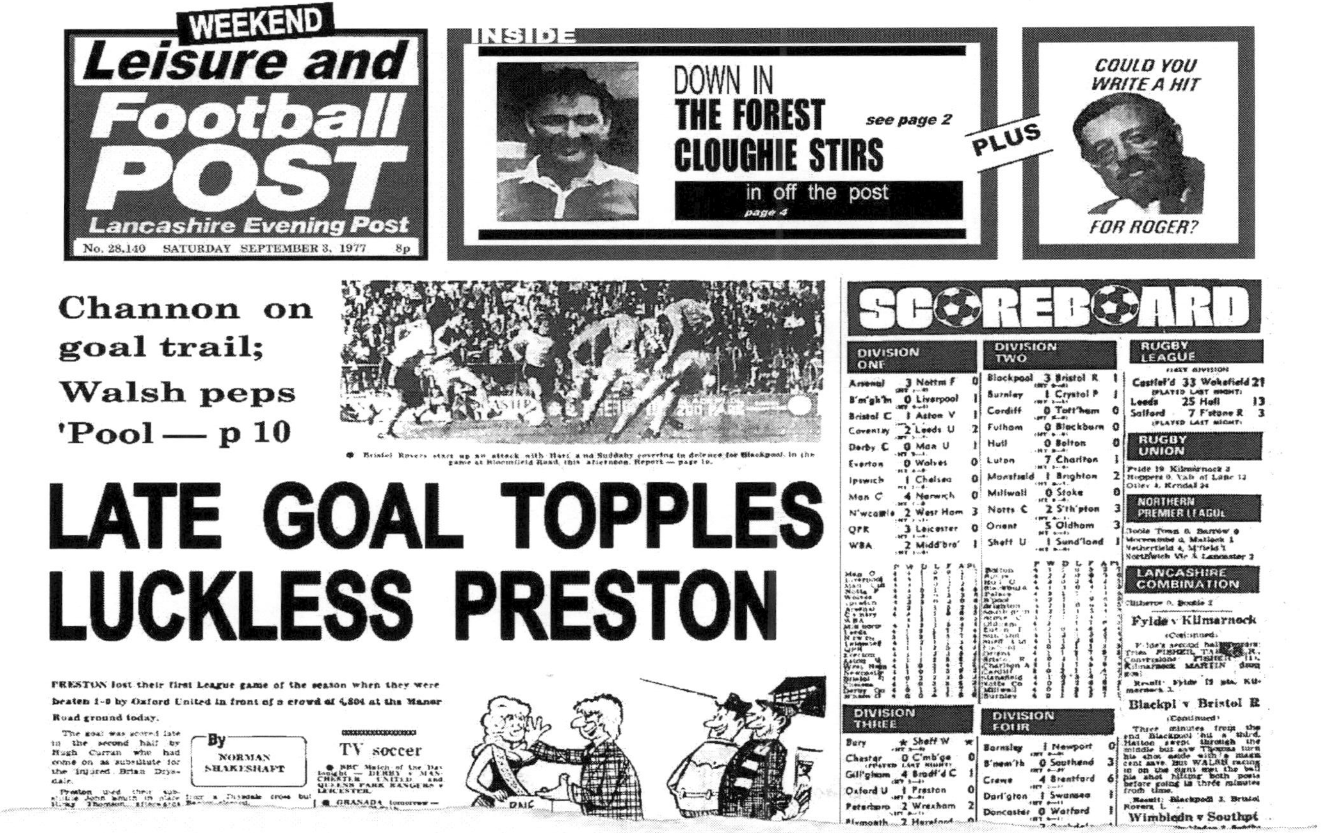
WEEKEND
Leisure and
Football
POST
Lancashire Evening Post
No. 28,140 SATURDAY SEPTEMBER 3, 1977 8p

INSIDE

DOWN IN
THE FOREST
CLOUGHIE STIRS
see page 2
in off the post
page 4

PLUS

COULD YOU
WRITE A HIT
FOR ROGER?

Channon on
goal trail;
Walsh peps
'Pool — p 10

● Bristol Rovers start up an attack with Hart and Suddaby covering in defence for Blackpool in the game at Bloomfield Road this afternoon. Report — page 10.

LATE GOAL TOPPLES
LUCKLESS PRESTON

PRESTON lost their first League game of the season when they were beaten 1-0 by Oxford United in front of a crowd of 4,804 at the Manor Road ground today.

By
NORMAN
SHAKESHAFT

The goal was scored late in the second half by Hugh Curran who had come on as substitute for the injured Brian Drysdale.

TV soccer

● BBC Match of the Day tonight — DERBY v MANCHESTER UNITED and QUEENS PARK RANGERS v LEICESTER.

SCOREBOARD

DIVISION ONE

Arsenal	3	Nottm F	0
B'm'gh'm	0	Liverpool	1
Bristol C	1	Aston V	1
Coventry	2	Leeds U	2
Derby C	0	Man U	1
Everton	0	Wolves	0
Ipswich	1	Chelsea	0
Man C	4	Norwich	0
N'wcastle	2	West Ham	3
QPR	3	Leicester	0
WBA	2	Midd'bro'	1

DIVISION TWO

Blackpool	3	Bristol R	1
Burnley	1	Crystal P	1
Cardiff	0	Tott'ham	0
Fulham	0	Blackburn	0
Hull	0	Bolton	0
Luton	7	Charlton	1
Mansfield	1	Brighton	2
Millwall	0	Stoke	0
Notts C	2	S'th'pton	3
Orient	5	Oldham	3
Sheff U	1	Sund'land	1

DIVISION THREE

Bury	★	Sheff W	★
Chester	0	C'mb'ge	0
Gill'gham	4	Bradf'd C	1
Oxford U	1	Preston	0
Peterboro	2	Wrexham	2
Plymouth	2	Hereford	0

DIVISION FOUR

Barnsley	1	Newport	0
B'mem'th	0	Southend	3
Crewe	4	Brentford	6
Darl'gton	1	Swansea	1
Doncaster	0	Watford	1

RUGBY LEAGUE

FIRST DIVISION

Castlef'd 33 Wakefield 21
(PLAYED LAST NIGHT)
Leeds 25 Hull 13
Salford 7 F'stone R 3
(PLAYED LAST NIGHT)

RUGBY UNION

Fylde 19 Kilmarnock 3
Hoppers 0, Vale of Lune 12
Otley 4, Kendal 24

NORTHERN PREMIER LEAGUE

Goole Town 0, Barrow 0
Morecambe 0, Matlock 1
Netherfield 4, M'field 1
Northwich Vic 3, Lancaster 2

LANCASHIRE COMBINATION

Clitheroe 0, Bootle 2

Fylde v Kilmarnock

(Continued)

Result: Fylde 19 pts, Kilmarnock 3.

Blackpl v Bristol R

(Continued)

Three minutes from the end Blackpool hit a third. Hatton swept through the middle but saw Thomas turn his shot aside with a magnificent save. But WALSH racing in on the sight met the ball, his shot hitting both posts before going in three minutes from time.

Result: Blackpool 3, Bristol Rovers 1.

Wimbledn v Southpt

second half. We created the chances but the ball would just not go into the net," he lamented.

"The important thing now is that the lads should not let their heads go down. They must want the ball and want to win. The more we have the ball, and the more we are in the opposing penalty area the more likely we are to score."

Reaction to the 'Sponsor A Goal' competition amongst the fans hadn't gone down too well if the letters section of the Football Post was anything to go by.

Opinion canvassed by LEP reporter Norman Shakeshaft suggested the scheme wouldn't go far.

To be fair to North End, it would have been easier to launch such a scheme in a town where the local football club hadn't enjoyed any success at all, rather than in one where the game had been played at its best in the past, and nothing less than the best being really appreciated by those still around who witnessed it.

Shakeshaft noted that mention of the scheme had brought forth loud guffaws from the fans he had spoken to.

"If the players were playing in front of my house, I'd shift them," said one. Another added, *"I tell my young lad that if he does owt wrong, I'll take him to Deepdale,"* while an older fan mused, *"There are so few goals they'll soon be giving prizes for corners."*

Amongst other suggestions made to the intrepid reporter were to use the ground for growing potatoes, or to even build flats on it.

"What will the directors ask for next?" said one man. *"I don't get paid extra for doing my job after I've arrived at work to collect my wages. Why should I pay extra to see the players doing their job by scoring a few goals after I've already paid to go through the turnstiles?"*

It didn't bode well.

There was some good news for Nobby Stiles and Alan Kelly before the League Cup replay against Walsall on Tuesday, September 6th.

There had been some concern over Alex Bruce after he reported a thigh injury at Oxford, but once more Harry Hubbick had pummelled a worrisome strain into submission and Bruce would start.

John McMahon would return too replacing Danny Cameron; otherwise the team was unchanged.

Tunks, McMahon, Wilson, Doyle, Baxter, Cross, Coleman, Burns, Thomson, Elwiss and Bruce. Substitute: Smith.

The visitors were now able to include Jimmy Robertson, a player of note in the Seventies who had turned out on the wing with success for Spurs, Arsenal, Ipswich and Stoke City. He had just returned from a successful summer stint in the United States and was 'raring to go.'

Stiles warned in his programme notes that he felt that the game would be far from easy. *"...I know we didn't see Walsall at their best last week, and our players will have to give 100 per cent."*

Falling out of the programme that night was a 'Sponsor A Goal' enrolment form...but there would have been no dues to pay on this contest; North End exiting the League Cup after conceding a goal three minutes from the end of extra time.

The first half is barely worth a mention, apart from the fact that Mike Elwiss insisted on talking himself into a booking after Gordon Coleman had come off second best in a tackle.

Walsall set their stall out at the start and were going to absorb North End pressure and break forward when possible. Their solid rearguard certainly produced the goods. The only real piece of excitement for North End was a magnificent and powerful shot on the turn from Bruce which was spectacularly dealt with by Saddlers keeper, Mick Kearns.

With the tepid first half over and done with, North End were on a mission after the interval. They were the better team by far; the defence was barely troubled, they won the ball well, moved it forward positively but then labored; unbearably so, to find a way through a resolute defence.

There was no shortage of opportunities. Bruce had a piledriver shot blocked at the near post by Kearns chest; Ricky Thomson saw Kearns turn aside two shots with 'goal' written all over them, Elwiss turned a first time shot over the bar and then mishit a great opportunity on the edge of the six yard box, watching the grateful Kearns collect the ball easily.

And so it came to pass that after a goalless 90 minutes, and deep into the second half of extra time, the formidable Alan Buckley – lower league goalscoring specialist – pounced with just his second shot of the night.

PNE FC

A powerful shot from Ricky Thomson is palmed away by the acrobatic Walsall goalkeeper, Mick Kearns

Robertson latched onto a through ball on the right, moved forward and curled a centre across North End's six yard box. North End's chasing defence, hesitant and trying to find their bearings, watched on as in the blink of an eye, Buckley steadied himself and hammered a fierce shot into the back of the net past the helpless Roy Tunks. It was a brilliant strike and just what North End were badly missing of late – which made the bitter pill even harder to swallow. This was now the third match in a row that North End had failed to find the net, despite not really playing poorly.

Stiles was pragmatic after the game, and backed his team.

"It was just one of those things. The result was very disappointing, but this is precisely what happens when the ball isn't running for you.

"In the first half we didn't push up enough. I told the players what I wanted at half time and was pleased with our display in the second half and extra time, even though we obviously didn't score.

"The lads really battled and I felt gutted for them when they were punished on the one occasion Walsall got through. Our shots hit legs and came off the keeper – we had no luck and one mistake made all the difference."

This was very true, and it was worth noting that North End had only conceded two goals in the last three games – so the 'problems' were not at the back. Goalscoring chances were somehow not being taken although by the same token, nobody could fault the effort up front.

It appeared that both Stiles and Alan Kelly had identified the problem area as the midfield, and it was reported that Brian Hall, the diminutive ex-Liverpool midfielder now plying his trade at Plymouth had been watched by Jimmie Scott, the renowned North End scout. The indifferent run of results coincided exactly with Jimmy Brown's absence from the team, and it was now likely he would be out of action for some time.

Whatever Scott's report had detailed, no immediate action was taken and Stiles named an unchanged team for the long range 'derby' match at Carlisle on Saturday, September 10th. The one change was at substitute where youngster Ian Cochrane was favoured ahead of John Smith:-

Tunks, McMahon, Wilson, Doyle, Baxter, Cross, Coleman, Burns, Thomson, Elwiss and Bruce. Substitute: Cochrane.

Heavy morning rain had relented in Carlisle by lunchtime, leaving the pitch in a sort of 'playable quagmire' state. For some ancient unknown reason, I never fancy North End away at Carlisle, and this would be yet another day that bolstered my gut feeling.

Despite the 3-1 defeat, a score uneven largely due to North End being caught piling forward in search of a winner, and then a late equaliser, this game replicated many of the maladies of their recent outings. Defence solid, attack very mobile, chances not being taken.

North End were quick out of the traps, and forced two corners within the first few minutes. Nothing was forthcoming but the early trend had been set with Carlisle scrambling a little to keep up.

They were certainly scrambling when the ever-alert Alex Bruce all but intercepted a back pass from full back Mike McCartney to goalkeeper Trevor Swinburne; Bruce receiving applause and cheers from the contingent of North End fans.

Carlisle's first probe into the visitor's half via centre forward Billy Rafferty was coolly stifled by Harry Wilson, the clearance turning quickly to attack as Mike Elwiss picked up the ball and drove forward. His centre found Bruce but his shot veered wide of Swinburne's left post.

John McMahon's turn next, as he broke out of midfield hurtling down the right wing. Mick Baxter moved forward in tandem down the middle and met the right back's cross only to see the header go over the bar. It was all Preston, and they were looking a class act.

Then, unbelievably, the Cumbrians went down the pitch for the first time with any intent and scored. 'The Curse of Brunton' had struck again!

Winger George McVitie moved down the right, cut infield and passed forward to Rafferty on the left of the penalty area. The trigger was pulled and the shot flew past Roy Tunks into the back of the North End net.

While the North End fans were still thinking, 'why wasn't it happening for North End like that?' the Lilywhites had restarted and were moving forward again. Another glut of chances to score was produced – and squandered.

Francis Burns managed to reach the ball from a tight angle and shoot, but Swinburne tipped the ball away for a corner, Gordon Coleman's 20 yard screamer was palmed away in similar fashion, Bruce played Elwiss in but his shot was too high and Ricky Thomson drilled in a low elevation missile that was inches wide of the post.

After that lot, Carlisle finally laid claim to the ball, went down the field and unbelievably... almost scored!

A McCartney centre from the left found the head of Rafferty, the ball flying towards the unguarded net before Graham Cross appeared from nowhere to head away to safety.

North End responded with more pressure and won three corners on the bounce, but alas the outcome was unproductive. The lads didn't have long to wait however, and the long overdue goal finally materialised in the 40th minute.

The ball was passed out to the right for Elwiss who progressed a few yards before crossing the ball for Bruce to hurl himself forward and meet, glancing his header past the stranded Swinburne. The teams went in for half time all square, when really North End should have been out of sight.

PNE FC

Alex Bruce draws North End level at Brunton Park

There must have been a stirring speech in the home dressing room from manager Bobby Moncur at the interval, as Carlisle started the second half ferociously. They had the ball in the North End net on 49 mins, when a screaming drive from midfielder Steve Ludlam evaded Tunks, but the referee pulled play back for offside against Mick Tait. Centre forward Rafferty then had a powerful shot saved brilliantly by Tunks, diving to his left.

North End weathered the storm and broke away when Baxter slid a long through pass to Bruce who was racing towards the Carlisle goal. Taking the ball in his stride, Bruce launched a great shot but once more Swinburne was able to tip the ball away.

North End were pressing now to take the lead, and Stephen Doyle saw a shot gathered at the second attempt by the home keeper, just before a Bruce header shaved the outside of the post.

A neat movement from the home side then saw them take the lead in the 71st minute. It was quite simple – consisting of three passes, two back and forth and the third the teeing up for Tait to punch the ball into the North End net from 20 yards.

I just knew we were never going to win this game no matter how well we played!

Credit: Carlisle United FC

Mick Tait hits a superb rising shot to put Carlisle United into the lead

North End were suddenly chasing an equaliser now instead of a winner, and to their credit gave it a go. Everything and everybody was thrown forward and we all thought Bruce had done it in the 85th minute with a header, but Swinburne somehow saved it, hugging the ball as he fell to the ground.

WEEKEND

Leisure and Football POST

Lancashire Evening Post

No. 28,146 SATURDAY SEPTEMBER 10, 1977 8p

INSIDE

Who was TOM FINNEY'S hero?

Find out by reading Tom's own life story — starting in the Post — ON MONDAY

AND DON'T FORGET HIS WEEKLY COLUMN - IT'S ON PAGE 3 TODAY

PLUS

AMATEUR ACTION

SEE PAGE 9

Derby joy for 'Pool, Kidd sinks United—p10

● Mick Walsh scores the opening goal for Blackpool, giving Rovers goalkeeper Paul Bradshaw no chance with his diving header, at Ewood today. See page 10

PNE CRASH AGAIN AFTER BRAVE FIGHT

CARLISLE United were flattered by a 3-1 scoreline in the Third Division game against Preston played in front of a crowd of 5,743 at Brunton Park today.

By NORMAN SHAKESHAFT

SCOREBOARD

DIVISION ONE			
Aston V	1	Arsenal	0
Chelsea	1	Derby C	1
Leeds U	2	Ipswich	1
Leicester	1	Everton	5
Liverpool	2	Coventry	0
Man C	3	Man U	1
Midd'bro'	1	B'm'gh'm	2
N'wcastle	0	WBA	3
Norwich	1	Bristol C	0
West Ham	2	QPR	2
Wolves	2	Nottm F	3

DIVISION TWO			
Blackburn	1	Blackpool	2
Bolton	1	Oldham	0
Brighton	2	Hull	1
Bristol R	1	Luton	2
Charlton	2	Orient	1
Crystal P	2	Sund'land	2
Mansfield	0	Millwall	0
Notts C	1	Cardiff	1
S'th'pton	3	Burnley	0
Stoke	4	Sheff U	0
Tott'ham	1	Fulham	0

CENTRAL LEAGUE			
Blackpool	1	B'ckb'n R	2
Preston	6	Burnley	1

RUGBY LEAGUE

Whiteh'v'n	5	Rochdale	7

RUGBY UNION

JUBILEE MATCH

Lions	23	B'barians	14

DIVISION THREE			
Bradf'd C	2	Chester	2
C'mb'ge	1	Tranmere	0
Carlisle	3	Preston	1
C'lchester	3	Plymouth	1
Exeter	4	Port Vale	1
Gill'gham	2	Oxford U	1

DIVISION FOUR			
Aldershot	0	Barnsley	0
Brentford	1	B'nem'th	1
Halifax	1	Crewe	1
Hartlep'l	2	Wimb'd'n	0
Newport	★	Darl'gton	★
Scunth'pe	★	Southend	★

LANCASHIRE COMBINATION

CHESHIRE LEAGUE

NORTHERN PREMIER LEAGUE

Just to rub salt into the gaping wound that was this game, Rafferty then ran across the face of the North End goal to glance a McVitie cross past Tunks to make it 3-1. Incredible.

As always, Stiles was very supportive of his team and confident that the tactics he and Kelly had devised for them were correct. Those expecting panic and doom were going to have to wait for a very long time. Nobby explained the management's position in some detail after the Carlisle game.

"Despite three defeats in a row, there is no crisis to report. What particularly pleased me about the game was that we made a lot of chances. We got the wrong result but if we keep playing as well as that, the goals and the wins will come.

"There is no way that I am going to change our tactics. People said last season that we defended too much and could have won more games if we had attacked more often. The lads think this is right too, so we are going to continue to play attacking football. When you have got Elwiss and Bruce at the front, you have to give them plenty of the ball. I am sure we are a better proposition going forward than playing tight to close up games.

"Nobody was at fault in the game today. Nobody. The midfield gave the forwards plenty of support. It may be that we left some gaps at the back, but this is the risk that you have to take.

"Their first goal came from their first shot, but we kept plugging away and the heads of the lads never went down, even though the Carlisle keeper had a brilliant day and we had no luck at all."

Asked for an update on the Brian Hall situation, Stiles indicated he was well primed about the player and also about how important a decision it was for the club.

"I was disappointed with what I saw of him the other day playing for Plymouth at Colchester, and would like to watch him again. I have to be sure that I get this right for the team and the club and until I am sure and

satisfied, nothing will be happening.

"And before you ask, there is no truth in the rumour that Burnley have offered £75,000 for Mike Elwiss."

The rumour had apparently started after the Burnley chairman Bob Lord was spotted watching the Burnley Reserve team in the Central League fixture at Deepdale. News that John Smith and Michael Robinson had scored six goals between them in that game while the first team were in action at Carlisle was music to Stiles' ears.

He immediately told them both that they were in contention for the midweek game against Swindon Town at Deepdale and organised a special shooting training session for them along with Elwiss, Bruce, Thomson and Cochrane.

Just to complicate matters, the first team on duty at Carlisle had reported no aches or strains so the management duo had to consider the matter of team selection very carefully on this occasion.

Swindon had started the season well in contrast to the misfiring North End. They stood fifth in the table with seven points, while North End languished in 18th place with just three points. This would be a stern test for North End in front of their own fans.

The match took place on Tuesday, September 13th and after leaving it to the last minute, Nobby handed referee Mr Ashley of Nantwitch the names of the following 12 players:-

Tunks, McMahon, Wilson, Doyle, Baxter, Cross, Coleman, Burns, Thomson, Elwiss and Bruce. Substitute: Robinson.

Just the one change – Mick Robinson on the bench, replacing Ian Cochrane. The hidden message here was the management's continued faith in the established first team despite the lack of goals and points that quite frankly, the team had deserved.

The Robins started the game in powerful fashion, rapid movement combined with zipping the ball along the ground quickly and to feet.

North End had hardly touched the ball before they went behind in the fourth minute. And to be fair to the visitors, the early strike wasn't a surprise. They had shown enough to the North End fans already to leave a feeling of inevitability lingering over the proceedings.

When Swindon winger Dave Moss fired a turf hugging pass down the left wing into the path of the sprinting full back John Trollope, inevitability quickly morphed into grim reality. Trollope sped across into the penalty area as the North End back line tried to keep up. Near the by-line he drew North End keeper Roy Tunks to the near post before whistling a crisp ball past him along the six yard line that was met by the onrushing Trevor Anderson who smashed the ball into the gaping net. Two passes and a shot starting from their own penalty area and Swindon were one up. The whole process at most took no more than 20 seconds.

Having unlocked North End with such ease, Swindon smelled blood and continued their lesson in swift movement and passing that seemingly paralyses the opposition.

Full back John McLaughlin, teed up to perfection, crashed a drive against the North End crossbar with Tunks caught off his line a couple of minutes after Anderson's opener.

The torment continued with North End's usually capable defence unable to cope with the speed and ingenuity of the electric attack. A header by Steve Aizlewood grazed the top of the North End cross bar following a centre from the right by Dave Moss, this just one in a regular series of crosses that fizzed menacingly across the face of the North End goal.

The assault lasted for all but the first 20 minutes before North End finally poked their noses out of their half actually in control of possession.

Confidence grew and soon North End were knocking on the door. An Alex Bruce header that left Swindon keeper Jimmy Allen flat footed, agonisingly hit the inside of the post then sat up perfectly for Trollope to hack the attempt clear.

This summed up Preston's long lasting bad fortune perfectly. Just when would the Lilywhites get a break?

North End tried to keep the pressure up but were making elementary mistakes in their approach play. Too many passes went astray, forward movement was haphazard and more often than not their play was predictable. This all added to the frustration of the crowd.

Mike Elwiss dwelt too long when about to shoot and lost the ball, and Gordon Coleman after regaining possession well, fired in a snap shot that went over the bar.

Half time arrived and there was time to reflect that despite continuing bad luck, this was a contest between a well-oiled machine and a car badly in need of a service!

It was obvious that Stiles and Kelly had read the riot act during the interval.

North End's play seemed more structured, and was being applied with much more thought. Indeed, the crowd thought that Coleman, always willing to try his luck from distance, had struck the equaliser with a shot from the edge of the box but Allen somehow managed to fist away the strike for a corner.

On the hour Stiles gambled, withdrew Francis Burns, dropped Ricky Thomson deeper and introduced Robinson into the North End attack. It took five minutes for North End to draw level.

Elwiss, storming up the left flank centred towards Bruce, competing with Town defender Colin Prophett. The ball glanced off the pair towards Robinson, who deftly turned the ball home firmly with a low shot before Allen could position himself. Something at last to cheer about!

The noise level was turned up again within a few minutes when Robinson almost got a second – his attempt hitting the crossbar and then frustratingly bouncing to safety.

The sobering sight of Moss playing another intelligent ball through the middle to put Andy Ford completely in the clear – and bearing down on

Roy Tunks – soon silenced the North End fans, but Tunks pulled off an excellent save by blocking the ball with his body.

North End's late flurry resumed and there was time for a magnificent Bruce volley to be blocked en-route to the Swindon onion bag, and another blistering low drive from Coleman flashed inches wide of the post.

PNE FC

Mick Robinson turns the ball into the net past Swindon Town 'keeper Jimmy Allen

In the end, a draw seemed a fair result. Swindon didn't deserve to lose, and after getting their act together in the second half, neither did North End.

Stiles openly admitted after the match that North End were *"awful"* in the first half in a very honest and open session with the press.

"But this is the kind of thing that happens in football," he added. *"We had played so well at Carlisle for no reward that the lads thought they would just have to go out and wait for their luck to turn.*

"They forgot that you have to make things happen on the field, they didn't do this, were too relaxed and couldn't find their rhythm. As a result, we were very ragged and sloppy and made several defensive mistakes."

Stiles wouldn't say what was said during half time to the players, but was pleased with the second half display.

"We started to play, we made a lot of chances and we were unlucky not to win in the end. I was delighted for young Mick Robinson.

"Frannie Burns is a very honest player but he was tiring after three games in a week and I felt we needed to push another player into the attack. Mick was able to play at the front and although Ricky Thomson dropped back a bit to make way for him, we could switch from 4-3-3 to 4-2-4 when necessary. I was also pleased with both Gordon Coleman and Steve Doyle's displays in the second half too."

Friday's press conference saw Nobby in a positive mood. After revealing that Danny Cameron had put in a formal transfer request because of lack of first team opportunities, he appealed to the fans not to 'give up' on the team after their recent string of poor results.

"We have had a few bad results in the last couple of weeks but overall I think the lads have been playing well. They have been producing attractive attacking football and have been creating many chances. I believe firmly that if they can keep on playing well the results will start to change."

The honesty became 'brutal' when Stiles revealed, *"I was disgusted with our first half display Tuesday night and that performance was the worst we have put in so far this season. Yet, ironically, we got a point from the match and should have won in the end. On the other hand, we went down at Oxford where we played well enough to win and again at Carlisle where we gave our best display so far.*

"We were caught sleeping when Swindon went ahead, but when the ball hit our crossbar a few minutes later instead of putting them two up, I think our luck changed at last. I have told the lads that the ball will break for them sooner or later and then all the shots that have just missed or have been unbelievably saved will start going in.

"I made a promise to the Preston supporters when I became manager that

the staff and players would all work hard this season. No one can accuse us of not doing this, but I realised there would be setbacks.

"While asking the lads for more concentration and discipline I am also asking our supporters to keep faith. They have been terrific and helped us tremendously in the second half against Swindon. I thought they might have given us the slow handclap and buried us, but instead they urged us on and nearly enabled us to force a win."

Well, you can't say fairer than that! Compared to some of today's over hyped, self promoting and basically ridiculous 'manager press conference events', that was so very refreshing. The North End fans knew where Nobby stood, and exactly what he wanted. Brilliantly done!

By the time the home game against Hereford United came around on Saturday, September 17th, Stiles and his 'oppo' Alan Kelly had tinkered with the team slightly, moving Ricky Thomson to the substitute's bench to accommodate Mick Robinson. Wilson had recovered from illness and started. The team was:-

Tunks, McMahon, Wilson, Doyle, Baxter, Cross, Coleman, Burns, Robinson, Elwiss and Bruce. Substitute: Thomson.

It certainly was another thin shanked day of meagre reward at Deepdale as North End were held to a goalless draw by a struggling Hereford United team; a team who would be boarding the Division Four bus at the end of the season. This day was the nadir of North End's 1977/78 campaign.

A glance at the opposition team revealed a couple of lower division names prominent in the Seventies – centre forward Dixie McNeil and inside forward Peter Spiring, while a youngster called Kevin Sheedy was named as substitute. McNeil was in fact due to sign for Wrexham on the following Monday morning barring any last minute hitches, leaving 'the Bulls' with a rich legacy of 85 goals in 129 appearances.

The visitors got the game underway, kicking towards the Kop. It was North End though who were providing what attacks there were, with attempts from Mike Elwiss, Alex Bruce and Mick Robinson all going wide.

The classy Francis Burns lends a hand to the North End attack, but even he couldn't spark the team into scoring

The game was flat but North End continued to move forward hopefully, with Gordon Coleman adding to the 'misses' list with a snap shot from 15 yards. Coleman was involved in most North End play and in the 20th minute instead of shooting, intelligently rolled the ball back into the path of John McMahon whose thunderbolt drive went just over the bar from 25 yards.

This 'domination with no end result' lasted until the half hour mark, when Hereford finally plucked up enough courage to attack. McNeil was provided with two opportunities in quick succession, the first ending with a weak shot straight at Roy Tunks, the second a header – which Tunks again saved without any problems.

More shots and misses from Bruce (twice) and Stephen Doyle brought groans from the crowd which turned to howls of anguish just before half time when Elwiss plundered his way up the left flank and launched a terrific cross from which Coleman shot wide when well placed.

There was little improvement after the interval, with Francis Burns, Coleman, and Bruce all striking shots that went wide or were saved by Tommy Hughes in the Hereford goal.

It was Andy Proudlove, the Hereford winger who put the North End fans even more on edge when he broke down the left, moved infield and launched a shot that beat Tunks then glanced off the top of the crossbar as it flew into the crowd.

Hereford became 'the side most likely to' around this point in the proceedings and Colin Sinclair went close with a header following a centre from the right.

Stiles swapped Burns for Thomson on 65 minutes, but Hereford continued to dominate; Tunks saving well from a McNeil shot five minutes later.

The action swung around to the Hereford end again, as Bruce volleyed over from around 15 yards. North End's luck remained out when Coleman drove a low shot that hit the base of the post, the ball bouncing directly to Bruce whose first time effort was blocked and cleared.

Hereford's McNeil and Steve Ritchie traded wide efforts with Elwiss and Robinson, and as the game entered its last throes, barracking started form the home fans.

Played out before the lowest Deepdale crowd of the season to date, this was the sixth consecutive outing without a win. Lots of possession, lots of wasted opportunities. Lots of work still to do.

An apology to the fans was quick to arrive via the pages of Monday's LEP. Nobby could never be accused of hiding behind excuses or using smoke and mirrors. Once again, he levelled with the fans.

"The fact is we were rubbish. Our supporters have been terrific and they were still good during the game with Hereford, so I'm not blaming them for booing at the end.

"Alan Kelly and I both stressed when we took over that we would be

WEEKEND

Leisure and Football POST

Lancashire Evening Post

No. 28,152 SATURDAY SEPTEMBER 17, 1977 8p

INSIDE

Bob Paisley

SHRUGS OFF ANFIELD PRESSURES

— Page 3

Blackpool Chairman

SPEAKS OUT ON THE CONTRACT ROW

— Page 3

PLUS

A Lakeland Panorama and PRIZES with Womanpost

Blackpool lose their Spurs, but Rovers hang on for point — page 10

CHANCES GO BEGGING AS PNE LABOUR

THE Preston players were barracked by some of the North End followers in a crowd of 5,447 at Deepdale today when Preston could only share a goalless draw with Hereford United.

By NORMAN SHAKESHAFT

The gate was the lowest of the season at Deepdale and Preston have now gone six games without a victory.

They deserved no more than a point today after giving a laboured performance.

They had most of the possession and did a lot of attacking but Hereford, who are also struggling near the foot of Division Three, made just as many scoring chances.

Ricky Thomson substituted for Francis Burns in the late stages and Hereford's Peter Spiring was booked for dissent just before Mike Elwiss...

Preston: Tunks; McMahon, Wilson, Doyle, Baxter, Cross, Coleman, Burns, Robinson, Elwiss, Bruce. Sub: Thomson.

Hereford: Hughes; Emery, Ritchie, Marshall, Layton, Proudlove, Briley, Carter, Sinclair, McNeil, Spiring. Sub: Sheedy.

Ref: John Hough (Macclesfield).

Preston manager Nobby Stiles gave Mick Robinson his first full League home game. Robinson, who scored Preston's...

...ing the 3-1 defeat at Chesterfield in midweek. Steve Emery returned to right back after recovering from injury in place of Phil Burrows and Andy Proudlove made his league debut for the club after being signed from Norwich in the summer. He replaced Kevin Sheedy who was named a sub.

The game was likely to be Dixie McNeil's last appearance for Hereford for he is set to sign for Wrexham on Monday for £?,000.

Conditions were good at the start and Hereford kicked off towards the Fulwood end.

Preston were soon on the attack and Elwiss just failed to reach a Bruce centre. North End's next attack ended when Robinson headed wide.

● Mike Elwiss has the ball kicked away from his feet in today's game against Hereford at Deepdale.

SCOREBOARD

DIVISION ONE

Arsenal	2	Leicester	1
B'm'gh'm	3	N'wcastle	0
Bristol C	3	West Ham	2
Coventry	2	Midd'bro'	1
Derby C	2	Leeds U	2
Everton	3	Norwich	0
Ipswich	1	Liverpool	1
Man U	★	Chelsea	★
Nottm F	2	Aston V	0
QPR	1	Man C	1
WBA	2	Wolves	2

★ Today's result not included

DIVISION TWO

Blackpool	0	Tott'ham	2
Burnley	0	Brighton	0
Cardiff	1	Mansfield	1
Fulham	5	Notts C	1
Hull	0	Stoke	0
Luton	0	Blackburn	0
Millwall	3	S'th'pton	0
Oldham	1	Charlton	1
Orient	2	Bristol R	1
Sheff U	0	Crystal P	2
Sund'land	0	Bolton	2

DIVISION THREE

Carlisle	2	Oxford U	2
Chester	2	Gill'gham	2
Chest'f'ld	★	Wrexham	★
Peterboro	1	Exeter	1
Plymouth	0	C'mb'ge	1
Portsm'th	0	Lincoln	2
Port Vale	0	Sheff W	0
Preston	0	Hereford	0
Roth'ham	1	C'lchester	0

DIVISION FOUR

Barnsley	1	Watford	0
B'nem'th	0	Halifax	0
Crewe	2	Torquay	0
Darl'gton	1	Aldershot	1
Doncaster	3	Brentford	1
Hudd'f'ld	0	Stockport	0
N'th'pt'n	5	Hartlep'l	3
Reading	3	Southport	1
Rochdale	0	Newport	1
Scunth'pe	★	Wimb'd'n	★

RUGBY UNION

Fylde 12, Gloucester 20

Roundhay 24, Hoppers 11

NORTHERN PREMIER LEAGUE

RUGBY LEAGUE

ESSO YORKS CUP (Semi-Final)

Keighley 4 Castlef'd 14

Nethrfld v Willngtn

(Continued)

Chorley v Clitheroe

(Continued)

judged by results on the park. We know that the performance on Saturday was just not good enough, and I'm not making any excuses.

"But...we have been playing well in some games and our lads are still good players. I have to make them believe that and get them concentrating on doing the right things. They have lost confidence and they are sick of the way results have gone. Some players are now trying to do the difficult things when it's the simple things that are needed. They are going to have to get that confidence back and work even harder on the field to make things happen. We just didn't put it together on Saturday as a team."

Stiles then added that Preston had missed midfielder Jimmy Brown, whose absence from the team coincided with the bad run. He wasn't due to start training for at least another two months following an operation on his back.

"Jimmy is a different type of player to Frannie Burns for instance, and the balance of the team has been upset. The problem needs addressing and I know I have to strengthen my squad."

The manager was under no illusion about getting exactly the right player for the vacancy.

"I knew that finances were tight when I accepted the position. I know and understand that I have to spend the money wisely. If I went out and bought a player just to please other people and it happened that he wasn't the right fit, I would be in a real mess. Yes, it's taking time but it will be the right signing for the club and the fans. The search will go on."

Another, wider football issue was being discussed at this time in 1977. The 92 Football League clubs were voting on the prickly issue of players' 'freedom of contract.' During the season there were several votes and amendments to the proposals, club camps of 'yes' and 'no', but during 1978 after a couple of 'fudged' attempts, contractual freedom and better earning conditions finally became tangible for the footballer.

The Independent Tribunal System was established to deal with out-of-contract professional players who sought to move to a new club having declined a retaining contract from their current club. The 'marketplace' was further lubricated in 1995 with the outcome of the Bosman case; the players now being provided with total contractual freedom – as we recognise the system today.

For the record, North End always voted 'for' the freedom of contract proposals back in 1977/78.

Meanwhile, Alan Kelly was considering whether to ask former club captain Alan Spavin to return to Deepdale to assist in bringing on the young players in North End's reserve team. Spavin had spent the summer in the United States acting as player/coach for Washington Diplomats.

As weekend approached with North End due to appear at Layer Road, home of table topping Colchester United, Stiles had a 'softly-softly' tone about him.

"My main concern this week was to build up the confidence of the players. I haven't finally decided on the line-up for Saturday's game, but there is no crisis.

"Every one of the players was disappointed about the Hereford game – but the positive in all that is that they didn't lose. In recent years we would have, and a home defeat would have compounded the issues further. The reality is that we have picked up two draws from two poor performances in two poor home games. That's better than no points.

"The players are still in good spirits, and looking forward to the game at Colchester."

North End's travails didn't seem to be fooling Colchester United manager Bobby Roberts.

"Preston have stuttered and been disappointing, but they have some experienced players and will be wanting to get back among the good results again. I admire Mike Elwiss and Alex Bruce, as do many others in this division. This will be a hard match alright."

The clash with Colchester took place on September 24th. Stiles and Kelly finally settled on the following team after a week of cajoling, confidence building and hard work.

Tunks, McMahon, Wilson, Doyle, Baxter, Cross, Coleman, Burns, Smith, Elwiss and Bruce. Substitute: Robinson.

John Smith was recalled for his first league start of the season, Mick Robinson would now warm the bench and Ricky Thomson was 13th man, having travelled down with the team as cover.

Although the match was goalless, this was a vastly improved performance by North End. For large spells of the game they were the better team, despite the 17 places between the teams on the Division Three ladder. The real value for North End and their fans in this particular goalless game was that they negated a rampant Colchester attack that had plundered 16 goals in their five previous home games.

The conditions were fair and North End kicked off in their alternative yellow strip, and patiently asserted control to such an extent that table toppers Colchester only gained their first corner in the 25th minute.

In that time, North End had roamed forward with Mike Elwiss heading just wide of the post, Alex Bruce shooting past the uprights on a couple of occasions and Stephen Doyle driving a blistering shot inches over the bar. Smith had the ball in the net too, but was deemed offside after successfully converting a Gordon Coleman centre.

Despite the continued 'misses', there was a better air about the team and they were playing a dominating, straightforward, brisk passing game.

The Colchester corner in the 25th minute came to nothing, and the action returned to the home end when Smith's long shot was palmed away for a corner.

The best opportunity of the half however was created by the home team. A Colin Garwood centre was perfectly met by John Frogatt but the centre forward saw his effort brilliantly tipped over the bar by North End keeper Roy Tunks with a twisting save.

WEEKEND

Leisure and Football POST

Lancashire Evening Post

No. 28,158 SATURDAY SEPTEMBER 24, 1977 8p

INSIDE

FOREST'S McGOVERN PLAYS IT COOL Page 2

ANDREW HOYLE'S TURF TOPICS page 2

PLUS

Blackpool's Grand old days

AND PRIZES WITH JUNIOR POST

Blackburn grab late winner! —Page 10

● The ball glances off Blackburn's Noel Brotherst on while colleague Glen Keeley goes in to collect during a midfield tussle in the game against Orient at Ewood Park today.

NORTH END KEEP A REARGUARD GRIP

PRESTON NORTH END improved on their last two displays and gained a valuable point from a goalless draw with Colchester United at the Layer Road ground today.

By NORMAN SHAKESHAFT

Although Preston are in the bottom half of the Third Division table and Colchester are among the division's leaders, it was North End who were the better side in the first half.

TV soccer

SCOREBOARD

DIVISION ONE

Aston V 2 Wolves 0
Leeds U 1 Man U 1
Leicester 0 Nottm F 3
Liverpool 1 Derby C 0
Man C 2 Bristol C 0
Midd'bro' 1 Ipswich 1
N'wcastle 1 Coventry 2
Norwich 1 Arsenal 0
QPR 1 Chelsea 1
WBA 3 B'm'gh'm 1
West Ham 1 Everton 1

DIVISION TWO

Blackburn 1 Orient 0
Brighton 2 Sheff U 1
Bristol R 0 Oldham 0
Cardiff 3 Fulham 1
Crystal P 2 Bolton 1
Mansfield 4 Burnley 1
Millwall 1 Charlton 1
Notts C 1 Blackpool 1
S'th'pton 1 Hull 0
Stoke 0 Sund'land 0
Tott'ham 2 Luton 0

RUGBY LEAGUE

FIRST DIVISION

B North'n 26 Hull KR 14
Leeds 40 Dewsbury 11
Salford 21 Warr'g'n 10

SECOND DIVISION

W'haven 11 York 11

DIVISION THREE

Bradf'd C 0 Plymouth 1
Bury ★ Shrewsb'y ★
C'mb'ge 1 Roth'ham 1
C'lchester 0 Preston 0
Exeter 0 Portsm'th 1

DIVISION FOUR

Aldershot 2 Rochdale 0
Brentford 2 Scunth'pe 0
Grimsby 0 Doncaster 0
Halifax 0 Southend 1
Hartlep'l 2 Reading 1
Newport ★ Swansea ★

RUGBY UNION

NORTHERN PREMIER LEAGUE

CHESHIRE LEAGUE

Kevin makes

The home side were resorting to petty fouls chiefly in the middle of the pitch when they lost possession. Bruce was well shackled too, and a half chance just inside the penalty area was lost as the Preston striker was converged upon by two home defenders.

Two more efforts on the fly by Elwiss ended the first half; a vast improvement on recent outings.

A tactical change by the 'U's' manager Bobby Roberts saw him replace Steve Leslie with Paul Dyer at the start of the second half. Dyer certainly made a difference, and the home side commenced a spell of domination.

The North End defence responded well to this examination, with Graham Cross and Mick Baxter both pillars of reliability at the back. The only time that the smattering of North End fans present held their breath was when Francis Burns headed the ball clear from near the goal line following a shot by Steve Dowman.

Whilst this home assault restricted North End somewhat in terms of attack, Elwiss, mainly operating on the right side, put in an outstanding shift – a fine display.

In fact, all the North End players performed well. John Smith, recalled for the first time since the League Cup ties against Port Vale at the start of the season was lively and linked up play well. Bruce, though heavily chaperoned, was always a danger and the midfield of Coleman, Burns and Doyle were more of a unit than at any time in the previous half a dozen outings.

At the bottom of the front page of that evening's 'Football Post' was a small piece of late news. *'PNE eye Haselgrave'* was the intriguing header, the small article describing how Archie Gemmill's move from Derby County to Nottingham Forest would mean that Forest's Sean Haselgrave was now available for transfer. Haselgrave was a stylish midfielder who had played over 100 times for Stoke City in Division One before being transferred to Forest in 1976/77.

If Haselgrave was to be Nobby's choice, and he could get this deal over the line, this would be a massive feather in his cap. Haselgrave could play!

On Monday, the banner headline on the back of the LEP proclaimed, 'PRESTON OFFER £20,000 FOR HASELGRAVE' along with the news that the player was to meet Nobby Stiles in the evening to discuss terms.

It was Jimmie Scott, the North End chief scout who had set the ball rolling while North End were busy at Colchester. Having turned up at Leicester, who were entertaining Forest that afternoon, Scott put in North End's £20,000 bid directly to the Forest hierarchy, and was immediately told that it was accepted and the discussing of terms with Haselgrave could commence.

With nothing much to add on the Haselgrave situation until after their imminent meeting, Stiles reflected on the North End performance at Colchester.

"I was delighted with the performance and the result was a good one for us. I thought we could have been leading 4-0 at the end of the first half after having nearly all the play. We didn't get the run of the ball in their penalty area though – same old story."

"Their best attempt by the centre forward looked offside to us."

"Despite heavy knocks to John McMahon and Coleman, we still played well and gave a much better display than of late. The reason for that was the players applied themselves to their task much better. After all the hard work in training, they all put in a terrific amount of effort."

By Tuesday, September 27th, matters with Sean Haselgrave were progressing frustratingly slowly. The player was still considering whether or not to accept North End's terms after protracted talks with Stiles – his main concerns were reported to be wages and a reluctance to drop down two divisions.

Meanwhile North End had yet another midweek league fixture to contest on this day, away at Fellows Park, Walsall.

Stiles was leaving the selection of his team until the very last minute, due to the weekend injuries to McMahon and Coleman. Transfer listed Danny Cameron was added to the squad.

"Neither have trained properly and I'm adding Cameron to the 13 as a defensive option. I prefer a forward for the role of substitute but considering the overall position I may use a defender this time.

"Although Walsall knocked us out of the League Cup recently, we looked the better team that night. It's a fresh game tonight, and I'm confident."

Amazingly, North End would be seeking their first win in eight League and League Cup games, and would be hoping to improve their sixth-from-bottom league position. Walsall, seven places above the Lilywhites, were lying in wait with manager Dave Mackay quietly confident.

It was an evenly matched and entertaining game, the only downside being... it was yet another goalless draw – North End's third in succession. They had only found the net twice in their last eight outings and hadn't scratched out a win in any of them. They hadn't found the Walsall net in 300 minutes of football this season either, but on the whole this result was thankfully another step forward. The football was good, and if one flipped the North End form dilemma on its head, the negatives turned a little more positive. North End, although remaining sixth from bottom had only been beaten twice and had only conceded seven goals, so the fans could content themselves that their team was very hard to beat.

There was just one change to the starting line-up, McMahon failing to make the cut after being unable to shake off his knock at Colchester.

Tunks, Cameron, Wilson, Doyle, Baxter, Cross, Coleman, Burns, Smith, Elwiss and Bruce. Substitute: Robinson.

Both teams settled well from the off, and there were signs in the bright Preston opening that this could even be the night when North End announced a comeback to winning form.

John Smith miscued a shot from a Cameron centre and then Mike Elwiss had a shot brilliantly saved by the Walsall Keeper, Mick Kearns when he ran on smartly to a Mick Baxter free kick. Stephen Doyle then shot wide before Walsall carved out two glorious opportunities to take the lead.

The experienced defender Roger Hynd split the North End defence twice with through balls directly into the path of the surging Miah Dennehy, leaving the Irish international in the clear on both occasions.

North End keeper Roy Tunks was quick to narrow the angle and then spread himself to block Dennehy's first opportunity, and although the striker managed to round Tunks with the second chance, he reckoned without Baxter haring back and clearing away his goal bound shot.

Goal attempts from Elwiss (four shots), Coleman (two shots) and Smith (shot and header) were registered by North End before the interval while Alan Birch saw a thunderbolt shot palmed away by Tunks for a corner at the other end.

The ante was upped in the second half as both teams tried to establish a lead.

It was North End who seemed the likeliest bet at this stage, when a surging run by Elwiss was topped off with a blistering strike that Kearns had to twist acrobatically in the air to prevent entering the top right corner of the net. Cameron then kept the pressure up with a mazy run and shot which went just wide.

The introduction of former Wolves and Liverpool striker Alun Evans for the tiring midfielder Henry Newton, saw the tide change direction and suddenly it was the North End rearguard who were under examination.

In a blistering 15 minutes of tested nerves, North End saw off a Hynd drive, an Alan Buckley bicycle kick, survived two penalty appeals, two shots from Birch and another Buckley attempt that was blazed over the crossbar when seemingly easier to score. Evans then shot wide, prompting manager Stiles to and register his disgust with the referee from the dugout over what he obviously considered a blatant offside.

In all this time, Graham Cross and Baxter looked remarkably sound and unflappable as had the full backs, Cameron and Harry Wilson. It was as though they knew that Walsall wouldn't score.

Nobby backed his lads once again after the game.

"We played well and the confidence is slowly coming back. We still need to find consistently good form but I am convinced that we will soon start to score a few goals if we continue to play as well as in the last couple of games."

A point from this game was certainly no disgrace as Walsall were a team of experienced ex-higher division pro's.

Every North End fan was now waiting impatiently to see if Sean Haselgrave would sign to give that edge to North End that was sadly missing despite the hard work and application of the existing team.

Wednesday brought news that there were no further developments to report, but the LEP back page headline on Thursday read, **"SEAN AGREES TO JOIN NORTH END,"** a message that brought both delight and a certain amount of relief to all Deepdale disciples.

Drilling down into the story, the news got even better. Haselgrave had completed his medicals, signed a three year deal and had been registered in time to make his debut at home against Cambridge United on the coming Saturday.

"We have sorted out all the problems, and Sean agreed terms when I spoke to him on the phone last night. He is the type of player who will fit in well with the other lads here. I'm sure he will do a good job for us," declared a clearly happy Stiles.

"I was delighted when he signed. The deal was the first major one I have completed in the transfer market since I took over as team manager.

"We think we have a got a good deal, and I hope the fans well give Sean a little time to settle in as he has to get used to a whole new style of play after playing with two wingers at Forest.

"Everybody involved in the deal from our side – Alan Kelly, Jimmie Scott and myself – all agree he is sharp, skilful footballer. 'Cloughie' was excellent to deal with too, and there was no messing about."

Like the other North End fans, I couldn't wait for Saturday to come around. However, with all the comings and goings over Haslegrave, it was left to the brilliant LEP cartoonist Ken Wignall to sum it all up rather well...

You can put that away now - he's signed!

Credit: Lancashire Post

CHAPTER 4

OCTOBER

Cambridge Utd (home) – Sheffield Wed (home) – Bradford City (away) – Swindon Town (home) – Hereford United (home) – Colchester Utd (away) – Walsall (away)

Although we didn't realise it at the time, Saturday, 1st October was the day that North End's 1977/78 campaign was effectively re-launched.

No loud music and fireworks, just a solid 2-0 win over Cambridge United and the comfort that North End were very likely over the unproductive run that had seemed to persist for an eternity. Oh, and for good measure, Sean Haslegrave made a very promising debut!

Fitting the new man in meant that someone would have to draw the short straw; the 'unlucky' winner on this occasion was utility man, Francis Burns.

Nobby explained, *"This decision must not detract from the displays of Frannie, for he has been playing well for us and leaving him out of the starting line-up was a very difficult decision.*

"I know Frannie very well, and can tell you he will be battling for his place because he is such a good pro."

John McMahon had still not recovered from the knock he had sustained at Colchester. The North End team was:-

Tunks, Cameron, Wilson, Doyle, Baxter, Cross, Coleman, Haslegrave, Smith, Elwiss and Bruce. Substitute: Burns.

Cambridge United, the previous season's Division Four champions were managed by the young 'Big Ron' Atkinson and had made a decent start to the higher life, sitting comfortably in tenth place. This was their first visit to Deepdale.

Atkinson had gone to lengths of re-introducing the yellow and black striped shirts used in the club's early days, with a newly designed club crest which did seem to have inspired the team.

Befitting such an occasion, Tom Finney took part in this game – the international forward wearing the number ten shirt – for Cambridge United. This was of course the 24 year old Northern Ireland player, not Sir Tom... in fact, definitely not Sir Tom!

Haslegrave positioned himself on the left side at the kick-off, with Stephen Doyle switching to the central midfield role.

The start of the match was very quiet, but it was noticeable that Haslegrave was receiving a healthy amount of the ball early on.

It was Finney who had the first real scoring chance of the afternoon, following a free kick from winger Graham Watson. His shot was blocked however – the ball being deflected for a corner. This yielded another flag kick at the opposite side, but Roy Tunks rose unchallenged catching the ball safely to set North End into play once again.

Alex Bruce and Mike Elwiss were being well marshalled, with two Cambridge companions at their sides most of the time.

After intercepting and clearing a possibly dangerous situation, the ever mobile Danny Cameron launched a ball forward that Haslegrave picked up, quickly making space for a long shot at goal which went wide.

North End were trying to camp in the visitor's half as the interval approached. Harry Wilson broke down the left but his cross was cut out by Malcolm Webster, the 'U's' keeper. This was quickly followed another

Haslegrave shot that earned a corner on the left.

This led to an almighty goalmouth scramble following Gordon Coleman's centre, but centre half Steve Fallon eventually hoofed the ball clear.

Bruce wriggled free of his guards to fire in a hard low drive that required an equally good diving save from Webster to keep the score goalless. Two more North End corners just before the mugs of tea and oranges were served in the dressing room came to naught, and North End walked off to polite applause from the home crowd.

Most loyal North End fans had probably by now downgraded their high hopes during the first half, but in reality the team now had a new vital part that was from a higher spec engine. It needed to learn how the other parts around it functioned. When all was said and done, although the first half had produced no goals, it was better fare than the previous six outings.

The tempo from the home team was much faster following the half time break.

Haslegrave split the defence with a great through ball for Elwiss to charge onto, but his cross aimed at Bruce was cleared.

Coleman then sped down the right, cut infield and curled a cross to the left side of the penalty area which Elwiss just failed to reach. John Smith then provided the same service, but from the right wing, and although Elwiss failed to connect, Coleman did – but shot high and wide.

Cambridge were pinned in their own half for the next few minutes as North End were rewarded with three successive corners and a free kick about 20 yards from goal for a foul on Coleman. The midfielder flicked the ball backwards for Cameron to try his luck but the attempt was too high.

Finally, finally it happened! After three goalless draws, North End actually found the net!

Coleman burrowed his way down the right and curled in a centre which

PNE FC

PNE FC

Top: Stephen Doyle heads goalward from a Gordon Coleman centre

Bottom: The lurking Alex Bruce bundles the loose ball into the net

Doyle headed the ball down into the goalmouth. Webster could only parry the ball, enabling Bruce to kick it over the line from close range. It was a typical 'Brucie' goal and one we all hoped would reintroduce him to his happy knack of finding the net.

Three minutes later, and Webster was picking the ball out of the net as North End went two up. Haslegrave curled a free kick from just outside the box into the goalmouth for Mick Baxter to outjump the defence and plant his header firmly into the back of the net.

PNE FC

Mick Baxter makes no mistake, heading home from a Sean Haslegrave cross

It was all North End now, as they romped forward looking to increase their lead still further.

Bruce had a shot blocked, Elwiss had a shot hacked clear in desperation, Smith headed over and Cameron shot just wide as the pressure was piled on.

A penalty appeal for a foul on Bruce was waved away, and he went down again in the box a few minutes later but the referee ignored the frantically waving linesman – again inviting the players to 'play-on.'

A long forward ball by Elwiss for Bruce was frustratingly just too long, as

WEEKEND

Leisure and

Football POST

Lancashire Evening Post

No. 28,164 SATURDAY OCTOBER 1, 1977 8p

INSIDE

BURKINSHAW wins back his Spurs

SEE PAGE 2

John Morrell's PREMIER LEAGUE COLUMN PAGE 3

PLUS

T.V. Sagas BY ERIC PORTER

AND

MORE PRIZES WITH JUNIOR POST

PRESTON END FAMINE WITH A 2-0 WIN

● A tussle for the ball, won by PNE defenders who foiled this Cambridge attack at Deepdale today.

● Gordon Coleman fails to intercept this shot from Cambridge's Graham Watson, at Deepdale today.

PRESTON NORTH END gained their first victory since August 27 when they beat Cambridge United 2-0 at Deepdale today.

The win stretched Preston's unbeaten run to five matches but was their first victory in seven League and two League Cup fixtures.

The goal scored by Alex Bruce soon after the interval was also Preston's first in four games.

Defender Mick Baxter then got another soon afterwards and Preston fully deserved the two points for a bright attacking display after a poor first half.

Sean Haslegrave, who made his Preston debut after being signed from Nottingham Forest on Thursday, gave a promising display in front of a crowd of 5,216, and North End's position in Division Three is now a little healthier.

Preston: Tunks, Cameron, Wilson, Doyle, Baxter, Cross, Coleman, Haslegrave, Smith, Elwiss, Bruce ...

SCOREBOARD

DIVISION ONE

Arsenal	3	West Ham	0
Aston V	0	B'm'gh'm	1
Bristol C	2	QPR	2
Chelsea	1	Leeds U	2
Coventry	1	WBA	2
Derby C	4	Midd'bro'	1
Everton	1	Man C	1
Ipswich	2	N'wcastle	1
Man U	2	Liverpool	0
Nottm F	1	Norwich	1
Wolves	3	Leicester	0

DIVISION TWO

Bolton	1	Stoke	1
Blackpool	3	Cardiff	0
Burnley	0	Millwall	2
Charlton	3	Bristol R (PLAYED LAST NIGHT)	1
Crystal P	2	Fulham	3
Hull	0	Mansfield	2
Luton	2	Notts C	0
Oldham	0	Blackburn	2
Orient	1	Tott'ham	1
Sheff U	3	S'th'pton	2
Sund'land	0	Brighton	2

DIVISION THREE

Carlisle	1	C'lchester	3
Chest'f'ld	★	Exeter	★
Hereford	2	Oxford U	1
Peterboro	0	Walsall	0
Plymouth	1	Gill'gham	3
Portsm'th	2	Sheff W	2
Port Vale	1	Bury	2
Preston	2	C'mb'ge	0
Roth'ham	2	Bradf'd C	1

DIVISION FOUR

Barnsley	2	York	1
B'nem'th	3	Southport	1
Brentford	4	Halifax	1
Crewe	1	Hartlep'l	0
Darl'gton	2	Stockport	2
Hudd'f'ld	4	Doncaster	1
Newport	★	Grimsby	★
Reading	2	Wimb'd'n	2
Rochdale	2	Watford	3
Scunth'pe	★		

RUGBY LEAGUE

FIRST DIVISION

Castlef'd	26	Bramley	2
Warr'gt'n	22	St Helens	10

RUGBY UNION

Hoppers 18, Wrexham 3

Fylde 5, Gosforth 19

Ashton v Chorley

Fylde v Gosforth

Carlisle v Colchester

were two good swerving crosses from Haslegrave.

The newcomer wasn't finished there and was unfortunate not to score just before the end with a tremendous long shot that Webster just managed to tip over the bar.

It was a much better performance by North End, the second half in particular giving the fans some real hope at last.

"I was pleased with the way Sean Haslegrave played declared Stiles. *He hadn't trained all week, it was the first time he had actually met the other players and the first time he had played in Division Three, so obviously there was a lot to take in."*

Cambridge manager Ron Atkinson said his team got what they deserved after a poor showing.

"I knew it was going to be hard for us after half time, but never thought that Preston would score the way they did from crosses. They played very well."

The final note on the Cambridge game concerns the dropped Francis Burns who went out of his way after the match to praise the performance of newcomer Haslegrave. Even if confidence in their own play was sometimes lacking, team spirit at North End obviously wasn't. A classy gesture.

There was hardly time to catch breath as yet another midweek league fixture loomed into view. Sheffield Wednesday were due to visit Deepdale on Tuesday, October 4th. The Owls were having a rough time of it, anchored to the bottom of the section with just five points from nine games played.

"Wednesday are in a completely false position," warned Stiles. "I watched them beat Blackpool 3-1 in the League Cup and they played some excellent football. Their league position gives the wrong picture."

There were no changes to the North End team, except that Mick Robinson replaced Francis Burns on the bench. North End lined up:-

Tunks, Cameron, Wilson, Doyle, Baxter, Cross, Coleman, Haslegrave, Smith, Elwiss and Bruce. Substitute: Robinson.

North End continued their run of improved results with a hard fought win. The attendance of 7,627 was the best of the season to date and saw the Lilywhites stretch their unbeaten run to six league games. Their play was a little 'clunky' at times, but as the saying goes, 'they were getting there'.

In fact, if anybody wasn't paying full attention at the kick off they would have missed the opening goal of the game! Clocked at just 25 seconds, North End took the lead with a quite superb goal by Mike Elwiss.

The quickest goal seen at Deepdale for many years began when Gordon Coleman passed down the right wing for Stephen Doyle to collect the ball. Without any hesitation he delivered a cross into the box whereupon the galloping Elwiss lunged forward and sent his diving header past Wednesday keeper Chris Turner.

What a great start, and a moment when Nobby's words about the ball 'will start to bounce for us if we keep working hard' were proved correct.

North End kept up the early pressure and Harry Wilson and Elwiss both had decent attempts saved by the spectacular Turner.

Wednesday retaliated, looking swift and dangerous on the counter attack. It was not really a surprise when they equalised after 18 minutes, with a move down the right that produced a cross for centre half Dave Cusack to leap and head powerfully downwards. The ball bounced up and towards the corner of the net, eventually crossing the line when Mick Baxter's desperate attempt to head clear deflected the ball into the net.

It was the first goal North End had conceded in five games, and stirred them into action.

More possession, two near misses by Elwiss, a goalbound Alex Bruce shot that took a deflection for a corner, a denied North End penalty claim along with the occasional Wednesday forage forward accounted for the next 20 minutes or so. It was then that North End deservedly regained the lead.

Following a cross into a crowded Wednesday penalty area, the ball has hacked clear but only as far as Doyle, a good 25 yards from goal. He returned a low speculative drive that was destined to go wide but Graham Cross was on hand to deflect the ball back onto target, past a gallant sprawling effort from Turner as his flatfooted defences looked on.

It was well a deserved reward for Cross, and the big quiet defender who just got on with his task efficiently every week was mobbed by his teammates.

North End kept the domination going when the second half commenced. A veritable catalogue of chances were manufactured but not converted. Two Doyle shots went just wide, Cross headed wide, Coleman had a low drive saved, Bruce had two chances but was swamped by defenders, John Smith headed just over, Elwiss had a shot parried away, and Doyle rose high only to see Turner tip over his tremendous header when it seemed destined for the top corner.

Substituting Hugh Dowd for Bobby Hope with just over ten minutes left saw Wednesday suddenly launch a late offensive that saw North End fingernails being bitten down to the quick.

Winger Roger Wylde forced Roy Tunks into a fingertip save to keep North End ahead, and nerves were really stretched when Danny Cameron, playing against his old club, cleared shots by Tynan and Jeff Johnson off the North End line when all hope looked lost.

The whistles for full time from the home fans began early. There was still time to ponder North End's luck as a superb low drive from Johnson scraped the paint from the outside of North End's right post.

A collective sigh of relief from the home fans accompanied the final whistle.

While Wednesday manager Len Ashurst believed his team had been worthy of a point, Stiles was very pleased with the win.

"We played some good stuff – ok, it was in spells – but now we must concentrate on keeping that standard up for the entire game.

"There may have been more goals if their keeper hadn't been in such good form, but they proved that they are a much better team than their position suggests. They won't be at the bottom of the table at the end of the season.

"We went to pieces a little bit at the end, but give them some credit for fighting back so well."

The win hoisted North End up to 11th, and they certainly now looked to be treading a different path than the one they were on a couple of games ago.

On Wednesday, it was confirmed that Alan Spavin would be returning to Deepdale to help Alan Kelly develop the younger members of the staff, initially for a month's trial.

'Spav' was now 35, and had been playing for Washington Diplomats in the North American Soccer League for the previous few seasons. He was still fully fit, and just a few weeks previously had played against a New York Cosmos team sporting Franz Beckenbauer and Pele.

"I joined North End when I was 14. I didn't need asking twice when I was told that I could make a contribution again," said Spavin. "I have no plans for returning to America and just want to help the club in any way I can."

The midfielder trained at Deepdale and then travelled with the reserves to see them in action in the Central League fixture against Derby County at the Baseball Ground.

Shrewdly, Stiles also registered Spavin as a player, predominately with the reserve team in mind.

It was 'as you were' for the North End squad named to contest the next league fixture on Saturday, October 8th at Valley Parade, Bradford. Just as for the previous game, the only change was on the bench, were Francis Burns returned, seen as a better option for the away fixture.

Both Nobby Stiles and Alan Kelly were busy preparing for the club's annual meeting of the shareholders, so Jimmie Scott stepped in to cover the press interviews on Friday.

"Alan Kelly and I watched Bradford when they beat Peterborough 1-0 recently. They are a hard working side, aggressive and direct and their pitch is narrow. It will be a tough game as some of their players are very physical.

"There is nothing much to choose between any of the teams in the division and we must aim for consistently good performances because the three sides that do achieve this will win promotion."

Scott added that John McMahon was having a run out in the reserves after missing three first team games through injury.

The shareholder's Annual General Meeting didn't produce any real bombshell news, but there was reassurance, (if any were still needed) that Stiles and Kelly were exactly the right men for the job.

If the manager wanted to strengthen the team at any time, the directors would take each case on its merits, said chairman Alan Jones. *"If I said that a certain sum was available the LEP would be telling us how to spend it every night,"* he added.

About fears that skipper Mike Elwiss would soon be sold, both chairman and manager said that Elwiss was very ambitious and North End could not stand in his way if the right offer came along as this would only create bad feeling.

Stiles then had to defend the 'signing' of former captain Alan Spavin.

"We have some promising kids who are out of their depth in the reserve team. They have no old head to help them, to encourage them and to tell them where they are going wrong. Kel is in charge of the reserves but there are times we have to be together with regard to the first team. The danger is that if they keep getting hammered in the Central League they will not come through. It's as simple as that.

"He is a good pro whose heart is in Preston plus we can call upon his experience if it's needed in the first team to avoid putting a youngster in too soon."

The manager then agreed with one shareholder that not enough goals had been scored.

"We have been creating chances but they haven't been going in. I would be a lot more worried if the chances weren't being made, and I'm sure that the goals will come soon.

"There are no wingers at Deepdale so I can't play 4-2-4. One of the many reasons for signing Sean Haslegrave was to give the team a bit of width at the front. He will add to the team."

Stiles then added that another reason why the first team results had improved lately was the contribution of John Smith since his recall.

"People just don't or won't see the graft John puts in. He gets a lot of criticism but I don't care who scores our goals and I will defend any of my players.

"They are as good or better than any in Division Three and it is my job to make them believe it."

The timing of Nobby's public appreciation of John Smith would prove to be perfection itself!

Conditions were good at Valley Parade as the teams ran out. The North End team was confirmed as:-

Tunks, Cameron, Wilson, Doyle, Baxter, Cross, Coleman, Haslegrave, Smith, Elwiss and Bruce. Substitute: Burns.

Former North End stalwart Alex Spark occupied the left back position for Bradford City, and chatted to a few of his old teammates on the pitch during the kick-about.

The home side made the early running, with Roy Tunks well occupied for the first half hour. It was winger Don Hutchins who was the conduit for most of City's moves, and the former Blackburn Rovers player was giving North End's Danny Cameron a hard time.

Tunks had to fist out a Hutchins cross from under the crossbar that had swerved in menacingly at the last moment, before Hutchins' follow up fell short, enabling the keeper to shepherd the ball out of play at the near post.

Bradford worked the ball over to Hutchins again and Cameron could only halt progress by felling the winger. Spark curled in a good centre from the free kick which Bernie Wright got his head to, but Tunks was again on hand to save with ease.

After Joe Cooke had put in a powerful header following a corner, Graham Cross took control of the loose ball when more danger threatened, calmly flicking the ball back to Tunks.

North End eventually started to probe City's defence and Alex Bruce had a low drive blocked following a pass from Elwiss. Gordon Coleman then shot wide, and a 20 yard drive from Elwiss was finally cleared at the second attempt.

Mick Baxter then tracked a developing attack, and was unlucky when his powerful header was eventually held by City keeper Peter Downsborough.

City went back on attack. Hutchins left Cameron behind and sent over a centre and North End were fortunate that no other City attacker had the pace to keep up with the winger, thus enabling Tunks to collect unchallenged.

After Bruce couldn't cash in with a couple of half chances, attention turned to Hutchins and Cameron once more after they clashed in midfield, resulting in a protracted lecture by the referee to both players.

The half ended just after Bruce collected a through ball, made progress, but ultimately denied the opening goal by Downsborough who managed to get his outstretched leg to the ball as the striker was in the process of rounding him.

An early long shot from Bruce was the first intent of the second half, and the striker was in the thick of it a few minutes later after Elwiss headed on a Tunks clearance into his path in the Bradford penalty area. Racing forward, he lobbed the ball over the head of Downsborough and into the net, only to turn and see the linesman's flag raised for offside. North End argued, but it got them nowhere.

Downsborough hadn't got up after a collision with Bruce that followed the lobbed shot and had to leave the field after lengthy stoppage. Centre half John Middleton took over in goal, but the City substitute was told to 'stay-put' on the bench while a thorough check was made on the ailing keeper.

Unfortunately, in the eight minutes North End had a numerical advantage they couldn't profit. Middleton had raised the cheers of the home fans when called upon to cut out the couple of crosses North End managed to muster, and was applauded loudly as he returned the green jersey to Downsborough in the 61st minute.

Ironically, North End struck gold just two minutes after the keepers return when John Smith headed his first goal of the season.

Home appeals for a foul by Elwiss on defender Brian Smith were waved away as the Northender progressed down the right. After taking on and passing Spark, he crossed the ball for Smith to pick his spot with a header from around ten yards out.

North End turned up the heat and piled forward looking to seal the game with a further strike. Bruce had a goalbound shot blocked from ten yards and Elwiss had a header saved – but they couldn't break through.

Cameron had locked out Hutchins completely in the second half and with this main outlet closed, City were looking resigned to their fate. North End were steadily closing off all avenues to Tunks' goal, but then out of the blue Bradford were level with 15 mins left on the clock.

There seemed little danger as defender Dave Fretwell moved forward looking for someone to pass the ball onto after receiving it from Wright. With every option closed the defender simply looked up, pushed the ball forward a couple of feet and proceeded to launch an incredible shot from 30 yards distance that left Tunks totally disarmed as it ripped into the Preston net.

Credit: Bradford City FC

Bradford City's Dave Fretwell ruins North End's day with an unstoppable equaliser

Neither side could claim a winner in the remaining time, Nobby however was pleased enough with the outcome.

"The lads all worked hard against a team who are difficult to beat at home. These are the sort of games we used to go away to and lose.

"I was delighted when John Smith scored because he played very well. 'Smudger' deserved his goal for his hard work and honest endeavour.

"I've said before that this player is very underrated by some people. He works very hard at his game and is an important link with Alex Bruce and Mike Elwiss.

"It's worth noting too that we haven't lost since he returned to the side.

"I was disappointed for the team though as I thought they did enough to

WEEKEND

Leisure and Football POST

Lancashire Evening Post

No. 28,170 SATURDAY OCTOBER 8, 1977 8p

INSIDE

Why Ward must get his chance page 3

SOCCER ABROAD Page 4

AMATEUR ROUND-UP Page 9

PLUS

WIN A RADIO

LEISURE POST

MEET MR MEN

Rovers, Burnley and Bolton all triumph —page 10

PNE KEEP UP THE RUN WITH 1-1 DRAW

PRESTON NORTH END stretched their unbeaten run to seven Third Division games when they drew 1-1 with struggling Bradford City in front of a crowd of 8,813 which was the best of the season so far at Valley Parade ground.

By NORMAN SHAKESHAFT

TV soccer

SCOREBOARD

DIVISION ONE

B'ngh'm	1	Coventry	1
Bristol C	3	Leeds U	2
Leicester	0	Aston V	2
Liverpool	2	Chelsea	0
Man C	2	Arsenal	1
Midd'bro	2	Man U	1
N'castle	1	Derby C	2
Norwich	2	Wolves	1
QPR	1	Everton	5
WBA	1	Ipswich	0
West Ham	0	Nott'm F	0

DIVISION TWO

Blackburn	2	Charlton	1
Brighton	1	Bolton	2
Burnley	3	Bristol R	2
Cardiff	1	Luton	4
Fulham	1	Blackpool	1
Mansfield	1	Sheff U	1
Millwall	[illegible]	Hull	[illegible]
Notts C	1	Orient	1
S'th'pton	4	Sund'land	2
Stoke	0	Crystal P	2
Tott'ham	5	Oldham	1

DIVISION THREE

Bradf'd C	1	Preston	1
Bury	[illegible]	Peterboro	[illegible]
C'mb'ge	2	Carlisle	0
Chester	1	Plymouth	1
C'chester	0	Hereford	0

DIVISION FOUR

Aldershot	2	Newport	2
Doncaster	2	Barnsley	1
Grimsby	0	Scunth'pe	0
Halifax	0	Hudd'f'ld	0
Hartlep'l	0	B'nem'th	1

SCOTTISH PREMIER DIVISION

Clydeb'k	2	Moth'well	1
Dundee U	0	Rangers	1
Hibernian	1	Ayr	2
Partick T	1	Celtic	0
St Mirren	0	Aberdeen	4

SCOTTISH DIVISION ONE

East Fife	1	Qu'n of S	0
Hamilton	4	Alloa	1
Kilm'nock	2	D'barton	2
Montrose	1	Dundee	2
Morton	5	Hearts	3
St J'nst'ne	2	Airdrie	1
Stirling A	0	Arbroath	0

SCOTTISH DIVISION TWO

Albion R	3	D'f'mline	0
Brechin C	2	Berwick	3
Clyde	0	Raith	0
C'denb'th	4	Qu'n's P	3
Forfar	3	Stranraer	2
M'f'nb'k	1	Falkirk	2
S'h'muir	4	E Stirling	1

CENTRAL LEAGUE

win and would have had both points with a bit of luck. I couldn't see them scoring after we took control of the game but Fretwell's goal pulled it out of the fire for them.

"He looked to see if he could pass and then just decided to have a dip which gave Roy no chance to save."

He then added that he wasn't blaming Bruce for missing chances at the other end.

"He is bound to make some mistakes because he is forever getting in positions to try and score. I want him to do this."

Asked about rumours North End were looking to bring in Wolves reserve centre forward Bobby Gould, Stiles admitted that the player had been watched previously, but North End were now *"not interested."*

By midweek North End had broken new ground by becoming the first professional football club in the country to launch their own lottery.

This opportunity to raise big funds had come about as a result of a change to the Lotteries and Amusements Act, which would now allow sporting organisations, local authorities and charities to raise money in this way.

A jackpot of £1,000 (value £6260 in 2019) and prize money totalling £4,000 was promised when the fortnightly draw was due to be launched towards the end of November.

"Winning tickets will be at the ratio of one in every 12, and there will be instant payment of £5, £1 and 50p prizes", said Alan Jones, the North End chairman.

"The much bigger prizes of £500, £100 and £50 will be paid by cheque on presentation of the winning tickets at the North End office and the chance of winning the £1,000 jackpot will be open to everyone who has won one of the smaller prizes," adding, "All winning tickets bearing names and addresses will go into a drum and a public draw will be made in the town centre."

The North End board had at last started to use their imagination to raise funds rather than just sit on their hands as in the first half of the decade.

They deserved praise for the initiative, which had wider public appeal by offering the prospect of big prize money rather than the parochial "Sponsor a Goal" donation scheme. North End had only scored two goals since the scheme's launch and it was considered a 'jinx' in some circles.

Friday arrived, the eve of the of the biggest game of the season to date – a home fixture against league leaders Gillingham.

After losing their first two games, the 'Gills' had embarked on a run of ten unbeaten league games and sat proudly atop Division Three.

Manager Gerry Summers was expecting a good game. "Preston will give us a severe test but I'm looking for a clear indication that we're good enough to win promotion. We've gone ten games without defeat and they are having a good run too, so this should be a cracker. We need a good result which would set us up nicely for our next two games which are at home."

Nobby meanwhile delivered a vote of confidence to the North End team that had turned out in the previous three league fixtures. They were all named again, leaving the choice of Francis Burns or Mick Robinson the only issue to be decided later.

"The lads are playing well and have now regained confidence," said Stiles. *"If they treat tomorrow's game in the same way as they have their other recent matches, I see no reason why they shouldn't win.*

"It will be a good hard game because they are a useful side. We will have to remember that we have got to be patient because we could have problems if we over commit ourselves."

On the injury front Stiles added that although John McMahon was now fully fit again, Danny Cameron had played well enough to be retained in the first team.

Saturday, October 15th dawned dry and bright with a light breeze. I always felt on edge on days like this and couldn't wait to get into Deepdale to see – and hopefully – enjoy the game.

If there ever really is such a game as a 'four pointer' this was it. If North End could win, table toppers Gillingham would have 16 points while North End would have 14 – difference just two. If an away win transpired it would take Gillingham up to 18 points, and we would be left on 12 – difference six. Yes, it was only mid-October, but just four points separated the top 11 teams in the division. This could well turn out to be a season when every single point mattered.

When the teams ran out, it was Mick Robinson who was wearing the number 12 shirt:-

Tunks, Cameron, Wilson, Doyle, Baxter, Cross, Coleman, Haslegrave, Smith, Elwiss and Bruce. Substitute: Robinson.

An excellent performance from North End, especially in the second half, knocked Gillingham off the top spot and hoisted the Lilywhites up to tenth More importantly they were now just two points off the summit themselves.

After early but unproductive pressure on the Gillingham goal, North End were made to understand just why the Kent side had gone ten league games unbeaten.

They should have taken the lead as Damien Richardson split the North End defence with an incisive pass to Terry Nichol in the penalty area.

Roy Tunks was out towards the striker in a flash, blocking his shot. Cries of anguish from the crowd were audible above the stunned crowd as calamity engulfed the North End box. The ball bounced away into the path of Peter Hunt whose shot was also blocked by Tunks, incredibly regaining enough posture in the fraction of a second that was available to him.

Again, the ball ran loose and Danny Westwood looked certain to score from this third opportunity, but Graham Cross suddenly appeared from nowhere to relieve him of possession and restore calm to both the North End defence and fans.

It wasn't long before North End took the lead – the spectacular execution of which went a long way towards erasing memories of the commotion of just five minutes previously.

A gentle lobbed pass from Danny Cameron found Mike Elwiss free in the inside right position just outside the box. In an instant he pulled the ball down and launched a 20 yard 'special' that left Gillingham keeper Ron Hillyard pawing at thin air as it rocketed past him into the top right corner of his net.

The visitors retaliated, and North End were in turmoil again as Tunks somehow failed to collect a cross cleanly from the right. John Crabbe managed to drill the loose ball goalwards which Mick Baxter blocked before Tunks redeemed himself by tipping visiting captain Dave Shipperley's follow up spectacularly over the bar.

The corner was punched away and North End broke rapidly down the left, Alex Bruce unlucky as his shot flashed past Hillyard, across the face of goal and just wide of the far post.

A flying header from Baxter went well wide following a Cameron free kick just before Gillingham passed up a golden opportunity to level the scores.

A good run by Hunt produced a corner for the 'Gills' and Richardson, free at North End's back post, hung his head while sloping away from his teammates in shame after ballooning the ball over the crossbar from all of two yards.

There was still time before the interval for Bruce to see a low shot saved after a neat Sean Haslegrave through ball, and headers from Baxter and John Smith both drift wide.

Half time duly arrived, and although North End held the lead, Gillingham had looked a smooth, efficient unit.

It was to be a different story in the second half, however.

North End returned to the field of play with a lot more gusto and determination about them. They took control, and it's fair to say never let go of the scruff of Gillingham's neck. They set the tempo straight away.

A Cameron shot was deflected for a corner just after the restart. The flag kick was directed away from the crowded penalty area to Haslegrave lurking on the edge of the penalty area. His powerful low drive led to a scramble before the ball was eventually cleared. Back the ball came, but Smith's header from Harry Wilson's centre was saved by Hillyard.

Stephen Doyle then found Elwiss with a neat pass, Bruce just failing to connect with the charging forwards cross from the left which followed.

Just five minutes into the second half, North End doubled their lead.

Coleman progressed down the middle and slipped the ball to Smith on the left when the Gillingham defenders expected him to pass to Bruce on the right.

Smith fired in a powerful shot from the edge of the penalty area which Hillyard failed to hold and then ran through to hammer the rebound into the back of the net.

Gillingham tried vainly to get back into the game, but their attacks had been reduced to occasional at best as the Lilywhites stormed forward, cheered on by the home fans.

North End were playing their best football of the season and the confident and wholly dominant midfield was operating efficiently and effectively.

Haslegrave, Elwiss (twice), Doyle and Smith (twice) were all unlucky not to make the score 3-0.

In the 84th minute a limping Bruce left the field to loud applause to be replaced by Robinson. Bruce was usually a 90 minute man, so it was obviously an injury of note.

There was nothing on offer for the visitors as North End closed the game

John Smith follows up his blocked shot to score North End's second goal against Gillingham, deservedly enjoying the moment

"WHAT WAS IT LIKE TO SCORE A GOAL AT DEEPDALE FOR NORTH END?"

"IT'S ONE OF THE BEST FEELINGS EVER…" – **JOHN SMITH**

out. The defence had now only conceded three goals in their last eight league matches and continued to be a real bedrock.

Although the players probably don't realise it, it is something quite uplifting making your way back home after such a game has been won in style. The nervous start, the brilliant goals and the powerful end are all replayed in the mind of the loyal fan, as they were in mine on that day.

The effect is that it pulls the knot that binds a fan and his club together even tighter. Frustrations are forgotten, misplaced passes and missed chances forgiven. North End forever!

Nobby summed this pivotal game up perfectly.

"As a whole the game was not our best performance of the season as we were anxious at the start against a team that were on top of the table.

"But...having said that, we put things together well in the second half and showed everybody what we can do.

"The goal by Mike Elwiss was a great strike and was the sort that were going in against us earlier in the season. I was also delighted by John Smith's goal because he is a lad who always works hard."

Stiles also said that he was pleased with Sean Haslegrave's display and how he switched on occasions with Gordon Coleman to play on the left as well as the right.

"Seven points out of a possible eight in the four games since Sean signed...can't be bad!" said the beaming North End manager, adding *"But he's just one member of the team and everyone worked hard today".*

Alex Bruce was already being rated as a major doubt for the long trip to Exeter – North End's next league fixture in a week's time.

Bruce had suffered a recurrence of a knee injury and would not be asked to train for the next few days.

"He has not been fully fit and playing so many games in such a short space of time hasn't exactly helped.

WEEKEND

Leisure and Football POST

Lancashire Evening Post

No. 28,176 SATURDAY OCTOBER 15, 1977 8p

INSIDE

Why the young ones scorn soccer —

Charlton boss ANDY NELSON speaks out on page 2.

IN OFF THE POST — *Page 4*

PLUS

WIN tickets for the BALLET

PLUS TRAVEL DESK IN BAVARIA

Gould hat-trick stuns Rovers — p10

PNE TOPPLE LEADERS IN 2 - GOAL WIN

● Mike Elwiss' shot enters the top corner of the net to open the scoring against Gillingham at Deepdale, today.

GOALS by skipper Mike Elwiss and John Smith gave Preston a 2-0 win over Gillingham in front of a crowd of 7,212 at Deepdale today.

By NORMAN SHAKESHAFT

Gillingham, who had started the match as the Third Division leaders were well beaten after looking good in the first half.

The defeat was their first in nine matches and they have still never won or even scored at Deepdale — a ground they consider very unlucky.

Preston's win was their third in succession at home and stretched their unbeaten run to eight League games.

Their performance after the interval was excellent and

Preston manager Nobby Stiles kept an unchanged team for the fourth successive match although Mick Robinson was named as the substitute instead of Francis

● Hillyard the Gillingham goalkeeper, safely gathers the ball from marauding Preston forward Alex Bruce, at Deepdale today.

SCOREBOARD

DIVISION ONE

Arsenal	1	QPR	0
Aston V	3	Norwich	0
Chelsea	0	Midd'bro'	0
Derby C	1	WBA	1
Everton	1	Bristol C	0
Ipswich	5	B'm'gh'm	2
Leeds U	1	Liverpool	2
Leicester	1	Coventry	2
Man U	3	N'wcastle	2
Nottm F	2	Man C	1
Wolves	2	West Ham	2

DIVISION TWO

Bolton	2	Mansfield	0
Bristol R	4	Blackburn	1
Charlton	4	Tott'ham	1
Crystal P	1	S'th'pton	2
Hull	2	Blackpool	0
Luton	1	Fulham	0
Oldham	2	Notts C	1
Orient	2	Cardiff	1
Sheff U	2	Burnley	1
Stoke	1	Brighton	0
Sund'land	2	Millwall	0

DIVISION THREE

Carlisle	1	Bradf'd C	1
Chest'f'ld	★	Walsall	★
C'chester	1	Oxford U	1
Hereford	0	C'mb'ge	0
Lincoln	1	Exeter	2
Peterboro	2	Shrewsb'y	1
Plymouth	0	Tranmere	1
Portsm'th	1	Bury	1
Preston	2	Gill'gham	0

(C'chester v Oxford U: PLAYED LAST NIGHT)

DIVISION FOUR

Aldershot	1	Watford	0
Barnsley	1	Grimsby	2
B'nem'th	1	Wimb'd'n	2
Brentford	0	Southport	0
Crewe	3	N'th'pt'n	2
Darl'gton	2	Hudd'f'ld	2
Halifax	0	Torquay	0
Newport	★	Stockport	★
Rochdale	3	Doncaster	1
Scunth'pe	★	Reading	★

(Barnsley v Grimsby and Crewe v N'th'pt'n: PLAYED LAST NIGHT)

SCOTTISH PREMIER DIVISION

Aberdeen	1	Hibernian	2
Ayr	2	Clydeb'k	0
Celtic	1	St Mirren	2
Moth'well	1	Rangers	4
Partick T	2	Dundee U	1

SCOTTISH DIVISION ONE

Alloa	1	Kilm'nock	2
Arbroath	1	Morton	2
D'barton	1	Hamilton	0
Dundee	2	East Fife	1
Hearts	3	Airdrie	2
Montrose	2	Stirling A	2
Qu'n of S	2	St J'nst'ne	2

SCOTTISH DIVISION TWO

Albion R	0	Falkirk	2
C'd'nb'th	1	M'd'wb'k	1
E Stirling	0	Forfar	1
Qu'n's Pk	0	Berwick	0
Raith	2	D'f'mline	1
S'h'smuir	2	Brechin C	2
Stranraer	2	Clyde	1

★ — Result Delayed
L — Late Kick-Off
P — Postponed

CENTRAL LEAGUE

Burnley	0	Everton	1

NORTHERN PREMIER LEAGUE

"But he is an important member of the team and he has been keen to play. I don't want to change a winning team but we will just have to see how he is later in the week."

A midweek update on Bruce's condition in the LEP didn't bear any really positive news. He was still being monitored, hadn't trained and remained a doubt.

Other club news surrounded the resignation of North End's secretary, Chris Hassell. He was quoted as saying that he was moving on to concentrate on the running of the family newsagents in Liverpool but that wasn't to be.

It was generally accepted that he had done a good job with North End, arriving at Deepdale from Everton after a long association with Crystal Palace. He soon returned to football however, as assistant secretary at Arsenal. Subsequently, he spent many years as Lancashire County Cricket Club secretary before landing the role of Yorkshire CCC chief executive.

Friday arrived, and with it the North End team news. Bruce had only partaken in a light training session on Thursday and was now a 'serious doubt' according to Stiles. Mick Robinson, Ricky Thomson or Francis Burns would deputise, and all were travelling down to Exeter with the eleven starters from the Gillingham game.

North End had high hopes going into this game, the main one being able to stretch their unbeaten run to nine games. Stiles was hoping the players would forget about the previous eight games, however. *"Yes, I want them to approach the game in the same way, but thinking of it as a fresh start,"* he explained.

A glance at the league table showed Exeter in 11th position, right under North End just one point behind. *"They are a very attractive, attacking side who were unlucky to lose their last home game against Wrexham, conceding a late goal,"* said Stiles. *"We are looking forward to a good game."*

The 200 or so fans who had trekked down the M5 on Saturday, October

22nd were to be left as disappointed as they were elated just seven days previously. Such is the fortune of the North End fan over the years, but even now in 2019 I just don't quite 'get' how they often swing from sugar to – well you know what I mean!

The first bad news of the afternoon was that Alex Bruce was definitely out of contention, with Nobby opting to bring Ricky Thomson back into the first team 'scene' after a five match absence. Francis Burns was named as substitute, leaving Mick Robinson to tidy up the dressing room.

Tunks, Cameron, Wilson, Doyle, Baxter, Cross, Coleman, Haslegrave, Smith, Elwiss and Thomson. Substitute: Burns.

The 'Grecians' player manager Bobby Saxton, who later in his career would play a crucial behind-the- scenes roll at Deepdale under John McGrath, made one change to the Exeter line-up. He recalled the former long serving Brighton defender John Templeman.

Conditions were good as North End kicked off in their alternative yellow shirts, blue shorts and yellow socks.

The home team were quick out of the blocks with Roy Tunks pulling off a fine save in the second minute to deny winger Nicky Jennings, whose shot was pushed around the post. Tunks was in action again shortly after, having to be quick off his line to beat Harry Holman to a through pass. Templeman then made room and rammed in a fierce drive which flew just over North End's crossbar.

Eventually North End moved forward, their first real attack of any enterprise ending when John Smith's bicycle kick was saved by Exeter keeper Richard Key following a centre by Thomson.

When North End had the ball, their football looked neat and attractive, however it was the home teams' determination all over the field to be first to the ball that was guaranteeing them a huge amount of possession.

In the 26th minute Exeter duly took the lead, a reward for their continual dominance. Jennings slid the ball home from short range after a long throw-in on the right had been back headed to him by fellow forward Tony Kellow.

Back came the home team, going for the jugular. Holman had a header cleared off the line by the alert Graham Cross before Peter Hatch had a 'goal' disallowed for a foul on Tunks.

Holman then robbed Mick Baxter of possession and was moving forward looking certain to score when he was fouled by the desperate centre half. The offence cost Baxter a booking.

As half time approached, Exeter won three corners in succession, one of which led to a scramble in the goalmouth after Tunks mishandled as he leapt to catch the ball.

Half time came as a relief to North End, who had created little and had been hustled out of the contest so far. The constant movement up front of Alex Bruce was patently the Lilywhites' big miss so far. Paradoxically, even though the young Scot wasn't actually on the pitch, appreciation of his contribution was enhanced.

With Stiles' words of advice no doubt still ringing in their ears, North End looked a little sharper in the early stages of the second half.

Stephen Doyle had a good effort saved, as did Gordon Coleman but the home side were not suppressed for long, with centre forward Colin Randall leading the charge, shooting just wide from the edge of the penalty area.

Harry Wilson then cleared his lines well after being cornered inside the Preston penalty area just before Stiles brought on Burns for Thomson on the hour. Before North End could sort themselves out following the exchange, they went two goals down.

Doyle conceded a free kick in midfield for a foul on Holman and Saxton floated an accurately measured free kick into the box that saw Kellow leap and head the ball over the flat footed Tunks into the back of the net.

WEEKEND

Leisure and Football POST

Lancashire Evening Post

No. 28,182 SATURDAY OCTOBER 22, 1977 8p

INSIDE

Will P.N.E.'s £4000 Lottery be a Winner? PAGE 4

The simple way to success — see page 3

England coach furious over World Cup defeatists — Page 2

PLUS

Blackpool and Rovers hit back to clinch victories —— see p 10

EXETER PUSH KNOCKS PNE OFF BALANCE

● Blackburn's John Waddington climbs above a Stoke defender, but his header was saved by the goalkeeper at Ewood today.

PRESTON'S run of eight League games without defeat was ended when Exeter City beat them 2-0 in front of a crowd of 5,444 at the St James Park ground today.

By NORMAN SHAKESHAFT

Ick Jennings gave Exeter the lead after 26 minutes and Tony Kellow scored Exeter's second goal with a header after 52 minutes.

Preston's Ick Baxter and Stephen Doyle were both booked and North End never looked like extending their run of success.

Francis Burns substituted for Ricky Thomson after 60 minutes but the pattern of the game did not change, and Exeter were worthy winners who are now in the top half of the Third Division table after ...

... which went inches over the bar.

Preston's first real attack ended with Smith having a bicycle kick saved by Key following a centre from the right by Thomson.

Coleman had a similar effort saved two minutes later.

Randell shot over at the other end from just outside the penalty area.

Wilson did well to clear Preston's lines on one occasion and Baxter, Cross and Cameron were also defending with more assurance than in the first half.

Stiles sent Burns on to replace Thomson after 62 minutes. It was the first appearance by Burns in the senior side since the signing of Hasegrave.

Everton test the champs

No quarter in Mersey derby

SCOREBOARD

DIVISION ONE

B'm'gh'm	3	Derby C	1
Bristol C	0	Arsenal	2
Coventry	1	Ipswich	1
Liverpool	0	Everton	0
Man C	0	Wolves	2
Midd'bro'	2	Leeds U	1
N'wcastle	1	Chelsea	0
Norwich	2	Leicester	0
QPR	0	Nottm F	2
WBA	4	Man U	0
West Ham	2	Aston V	2

DIVISION TWO

Blackburn	2	Stoke	1
Brighton	1	Crystal P	1
Blackpool	2	Luton	1
Barnsley	1	Hull	1
Cardiff	1	Oldham	0
Fulham	1	Orient	2
Mansfield	1	Sund'land	2
Millwall	1	Sheff U	1
Notts C	2	Charlton	0
S'th'pton	2	Bolton	2
Tott'ham	9	Bristol R	0

RUGBY UNION

COUNTY CHAMPIONSHIP

Cheshire	18	Durham	3
Devon	18	Cornwall	12
Lancs	15	N'berland	6
Somerset	8	Gloucester	20
Yorks	25	Cumbria	6

Wigton 22, Hoppers 1.

RUGBY LEAGUE

JOHN PLAYER CUP (FIRST ROUND)

Leeds	22	Wigan	25
Salford	27	Rochdale	8
Dock L.B.	4	N Hunslet	18

DIVISION ONE

DIVISION TWO

DIVISION THREE

Bradf'd C	0	Hereford	0
Bury	★	Chest'f'ld	★
C'mb'ge	2	C'l'chester	0
Chester	1	Swindon	0
Exeter	2	Preston	0

DIVISION FOUR

Doncaster	1	Darl'gton	2
Grimsby	1	Aldershot	0
Hartlep'l	3	Brentford	1
Hudd'f'ld	2	Barnsley	0
N'th'pt'n	1	B'nem'th	0
Reading	2	Crewe	0

North End's rejigged formation saw Burns slot into Coleman's midfield place while Coleman now moved forward to support Mike Elwiss and Smith.

An Elwiss centre was met by Smith, but the shot went wide and Danny Cameron then shot over from 25 yards as North End desperately pushed forward in an attempt to salvage something from the game in the last half hour.

Exeter stood firm however, and a frustrated Doyle was booked for a foul on Holman on 73 minutes.

Enterprise from Elwiss saw him carve open a great opening, but his shot was too high. In the closing stages, Coleman fired a drive in from close range but even that was scrambled away as the more than competent home team crossed the winning line.

A dismal day all round then, especially for those fans who now had to make the long journey home, North End having given them precious little to cheer at St. James Park. Exeter thus moved up to ninth position, while North End dropped to 11th.

With a game against the new league leaders Tranmere Rovers due on Tuesday evening at Deepdale, the general feeling now was one of nerves and dread instead of confidence and anticipation.

Stiles lamented the fact Bruce didn't make the cut for the game.

"We missed his running and his penetration and I hope he is OK for Tuesday. None of the other players have injuries, I pulled Thomson off because I just wanted to try something different but we just didn't play at all in the game.

"It was a very disappointing performance after our long run without defeat and now we will have to put the game behind us and start to build up another good sequence."

Fast forward to Monday, and there were more hopeful noises about Bruce emanating from Deepdale. Apparently, those gifted healing hands of trainer Harry Hubbick were now at work on the troublesome right knee, but even that uplifting update didn't come with any guarantees.

Tuesday October 25th, and a match day announcement from Preston North End.

'Alex Bruce will return to the North End team tonight for the league game against Division Three leaders Tranmere Rovers at Deepdale. He has been undergoing intensive treatment from trainer Harry Hubbick over the last two days and was declared fit after training this morning.'

One Harry Hubbick, there's only one Harry Hubbick...

Stiles was delighted with developments, and added, *"John McMahon is now fully fit again too after a couple of reserve games following recovery from his injury, but I can't find room for him at the moment. I will decide the final line-up for tonight just before kick off.*

"The players were terribly disappointed with their performance at Exeter...but...we have an early chance to put things right in the match tonight.

"The team had an off day on Saturday, two or three of them gave decent displays but I'm not going to single them out. It's our team work that matters. Our consistency went on Saturday but it must be remembered that there were two teams and Exeter went about their task very well.

"We never looked like beating Exeter, but we have been doing well and won three of our previous four games. I have stressed to my players that when we go to places like Bradford and Exeter our attitude must be right. We have got to approach the match tonight in the right way as we had been doing up to last Saturday.

"We need to be patient and keep the right attitude whatever happens in the game."

The contest with Tranmere Rovers drew the best crowd of the season to date – 7,906 – despite North End's poor showing in the south west a just few days before, and as the Lilywhite's ran out the crowd was buzzing.

After all the dilemmas with selection over the past week, Stiles named the following team with Ricky Thomson and Francis Burns drawing the short straws:-

Tunks, Cameron, Wilson, Doyle, Baxter, Cross, Coleman, Haslegrave, Smith, Elwiss and Bruce. Substitute: Robinson.

It was a game that left the home fan with a feeling of pride at the final whistle, as surely the world and his dog could now plainly see North End's promotion credentials – but unfortunately not by just looking at the bare scoreline. That didn't do North End any justice at all.

With Stiles' words about attitude, effort and patience ringing in their ears, North End started well. All those virtues were present as they regularly pushed Tranmere back deep into their own half with a sustained passing-game type pressure. They had gone close on half a dozen times at least, the nearest being a goalmouth scramble that saw close range shots from both Alex Bruce and Mike Elwiss blocked in rapid succession.

While all this lent to the illusion that a breakthrough was inevitable at any moment for the Lilywhites, the reality in the 20th minute was head-in-hands silence for the home fans as the visitors took the lead totally and utterly against the run of play.

As Harry Wilson was getting into position to roll the ball back to keeper Roy Tunks following a failed Tranmere attack, he seemed unaware of the presence striker Ronnie Moore who stole the ball with precision and speed as he ghosted past the hapless full back and into the penalty area.

Looking up, he chipped the ball over the head of the advancing Tunks and it was as though time stood still as the ball gently fell to earth, taking one bounce forward before nestling in the far corner of the net.

As the home crowd pulled themselves together, they realised that they were not in the middle of a chilling torment, but probably witnessing yet another 'unlucky' North End defeat in the making.

This time however, when the Division Three gods rolled their dice again, it was deemed that justice was to be immediately dispensed.

North End moved forward from the kick off and won a corner on the right. Gordon Coleman pushed it back short to Danny Cameron who instantly swung the ball into the visitor's goalmouth where it was met powerfully by the soaring Mick Baxter, who directed an unstoppable header into the bottom left hand corner of the net giving keeper Dick Johnson no chance whatsoever.

Suddenly, Deepdale frowns had been inverted to smiles and every fan and North End shirt on the field felt an immediate lift. Things had gone *our* way for once!

Rovers were motivated enough too – swiftly creating a couple of chances over the next few minutes.

Striker Bobby Tynan manoeuvred his way through the middle, only for Tunks to bravely smother his effort when a goal seemed inevitable. The Merseysider's left back Eddie Flood then found himself in a position to drill a shot towards the North End goal, but Sean Haselgrave made sure he got his body in the way to deflect the ball away for a corner.

North End then took over and Bruce, looking as fit as a spring lamb again, almost played in Elwiss to score in a dynamic move after becoming the recipient of a poor headed clearance.

Racing forward to the by-line he twisted and smashed a low ball across the face of the Tranmere goal which eluded the captain's right footed lunge by inches.

With just a minute remaining of an engrossing first half, North End finally got their noses in front.

Elwiss was fouled just outside the visitor's penalty area, and after the Tranmere wall was formed, decided to take the free kick himself.

Struck low with immense power, the ball found a gap in the visitor's wall but could only be parried by the diving Johnson. The anticipation level rose as John Smith moved swiftly towards the loose ball, but sheer desperation saw Flood hurl himself feet-forward to somehow block his shot. With the active participants huddled around the left side of the goalmouth, the ball squeezed out of the melee and bobbled gently – and obligingly – towards the penalty spot. It was met there by another vicious swing of Elwiss's right boot, the ball buried into the back of the net at the speed of light.

What a way to end the half, and what great appreciation the crowd showed to the team as they walked off at half time. They had turned the game around, could they now go on and win?

PNE FC

Mike Elwiss hammers home North End's second goal against Tranmere Rovers

Just two minutes into the second half, you would have staked your life on it; a minute later you would have been opening negotiations with the grim reaper. That's how long it took for Bruce to be brought down in the box by the combined forces of Les Parry and Flood, line up the spot kick... and hit a surprisingly poor Bruce-type shot, that Johnson clung onto as though it was Christmas Day.

Still the Lilywhites flooded forward, and six minutes later Coleman, having made space on the left of the penalty area had a full-blooded drive beaten away by Johnson after being found by a Bruce pass.

Amongst all the North End pressing, there were two disallowed 'goals' – both headers by Mick Baxter – that were deemed to have included a push by Elwiss on the first occasion and an offside on the second.

Bruce, already irritated by the missed penalty was eager to score; his frustration there for all to see as his low right foot shot was cleared off the Tranmere line by Dave Philpotts. Stephen Doyle then saw his shot deflected, but heading for the corner of the net before the leaping Johnson recovered the situation.

Tranmere breathed again, and despite a final salvo in the dying minutes, they couldn't dent the North End defence, which had been outstanding in the second half.

Stiles was a happy, smiling man after the game. *"They played well, didn't they?"* he began proudly.

"The lads certainly responded to my demands for a big improvement on our Exeter performance.

"I don't like to single out players as I firmly believe this is a team game, but on this occasion, I must give special praise to Mick Baxter and Mike Elwiss who were both outstanding.

"Mick Baxter had an excellent match in defence, scored a great goal and could have gone on to score his first ever hat trick for the club. The referee disallowed his other two headers for alleged pushing by Mike Elwiss for one, and gave Alex Bruce offside for the other. Mick is the first to admit that the experience of Graham Cross has helped him to improve his game and given him added confidence.

"I'm not blaming Alex for the penalty miss, and he will continue to take them for us. Last night he was probably still feeling the knock he got from the foul that led to the penalty being given. That's probably why the Tranmere keeper was able to save. No one to my knowledge has a 100% record with penalties – I'm told even the great Tom Finney missed them on occasions – so let's hope he puts the next one in."

Wednesday brought news that Graham Cross was a serious injury doubt for the next game – at home against Chester on Saturday.

The ever-present had strained a calf muscle during the victory over

Tranmere Rovers, and was in pain for most of the second half.

"He did very well to carry on playing, but he's now very doubtful for the next game. He will have treatment for the remainder of the week, but is unable to train," said Nobby. *"Fortunately, Steve Uzelac has been playing very well in the reserves, and will be on stand-by to deputise if necessary,"* he added.

On Friday, Stiles updated the fans with the news that Cross was still rated as very doubtful for the visit of Chester.

"If we had scored another against Tranmere, I would have brought Graham off. But I just daren't take the risk while we were only leading by one goal.

"Sean Haselgrave and Harry Wilson also suffered knocks, but they are all right."

"We will treat the Chester match as just another game and continue to take each fixture as it comes. The lads showed the right attitude on Tuesday night and I want them to play in the same way. Alan Kelly and I have studied the reports on them, and we will treat them with respect."

Stiles also dismissed the theory amongst some fans that Chester were a bogey team for North End.

"There's no such thing! I know all about us never beating Chester and that we lost 4-3 against them here last season when we gave silly goals away. Those were different circumstances, and will not affect the result."

Saturday, 29th October. The North End fans look quizzically at each other as the Lilywhites enter the Deepdale arena.

It was at first thought by the fans that Harry Hubbick, skilfully swiping his cold wet sponge along Graham Cross's calf, was responsible for the big defender surprisingly trotting out as usual with the team for the pre-match kick in. Alas, Cross never benefitted from such delight.

As he commuted back and fro to Deepdale during the week from his home in Leicester, those kind Leicester City physios had taken care of the injury to save him the burden of travelling.

This enabled Nobby to name an unchanged team, with only the substitute's name changed – Steve Uzelac getting the nod over a forward as a precaution just in case of any breakdown by Cross.

Tunks, Cameron, Wilson, Doyle, Baxter, Cross, Coleman, Haslegrave, Smith, Elwiss and Bruce. Substitute: Uzelac.

In contrast to North End's Tuesday night start against Tranmere, the opening minutes of this contest were much more circumspect.

North End seemed clunky; movement wasn't smooth – indeed, the early questions were asked by Chester, their best effort coming from full back Jim Walker whose low drive, saved by Roy Tunks, ended an edgy few minutes for the home defence.

Quite out of the blue, North End took the lead after 16 minutes. Harry Wilson intercepted an Ian Edwards pass in midfield and passed forward to Alex Bruce.

The striker made progress forward and having reached the edge of the penalty area, put in a well struck low shot which appeared to deflect slightly off Mike Elwiss – enough to take the ball past the stranded Chester keeper Brian Lloyd and into the net.

Nobby's words in recent weeks about eventually getting the bounce of the ball sprang to mind, and while Bruce's goal certainly counted, it added a little overdue weight to the 'fortune' side of the North End scales.

Chester had a frustrated look about them after going behind, and following a series of overzealous challenges and fouls it came as no surprise when referee Colin Seel booked winger Ron Phillips for hacking down Elwiss as he drilled down the left flank.

John Smith and Gordon Coleman then shot over following another couple of home attacks, before a Chester sortie forward ended when Chester centre forward Mike Kearney had a shot blocked by Mick Baxter.

Kearney was unlucky a few moments later when he ran onto a long pass, cleverly lobbed Tunks, only to see the ball agonisingly finish inches wide of the unattended goal.

North End rallied in the last few minutes of the first half and went very close as Elwiss turned quickly on the edge of the Chester penalty area and shaved the outside of the right post with a snap shot.

A fairly even first half thus came to a close, with North End holding a rather delicate lead.

It was fun and games upon the resumption – with two goals within the first five minutes.

A neat, precisely played through ball from Stephen Doyle was picked up by Bruce in the penalty area who, in true Bruce tradition, rammed the ball past Lloyd mercilessly into the Kop goal.

The goal, far from opening any floodgates protecting the Chester box, had the opposite effect.

Far from sinking without trace the phlegmatic men from Cheshire took stock, settled down and within four minutes had reduced the deficit.

From a corner on the right, centre half Bob Delgado ran in and leaping in front of Tunks crashed a powerful header into the net with the minimum of fuss. The keeper was immobilised completely, unable to get anywhere near the ball to catch or punch it.

A few minutes later the visitors audaciously repeated the move, this time Delgado's header flying inches too high.

This was turning into being a real nail-biter of a game with incidents at both ends.

Lloyd did well to catch a centre when under challenge from Bruce and a Coleman header flashed across the Chester goalmouth, with Smith just unable reach the ball and glance it home.

Chester winger Paul Crossley, who started out at North End in the Sixties, came increasingly into the picture as the second half wore on. He began to torment the North End defence, and provided player/manager Alan Oakes with a solid gold opportunity to equalise after beating Wilson down the right.

With all the goal to aim at from near the edge of the box, Oakes produced something akin to a successful rugby league conversion – but without two points added to the score.

PNE FC

Sean Haslegrave assists the North End defence during the second half against Chester

As time started to run out more blocked shots at either end added to the tension, but the home fans' nerves were well and truly shredded in the 86th minute as Walker slung over a cross from the left near the North End by-line. Crossley met the ball perfectly and planted the header into the net.

As home hearts were sinking rapidly, the linesman was waving his flag furiously at the referee. This prompted a meeting, and after a few seconds the 'goal' was disallowed with the referee indicating that the cross from Walker had swerved out of play and then back in before Crossley had met it.

Those last few minutes that felt like an eternity eventually passed. Two more points in the bag, two wins in five days!

Stiles was pragmatic but pleased after the game.

"We had to work hard to beat them, and they were tackling and closing

us down quickly. They played hard and well, and possibly better than Tranmere a few days ago, so I am delighted with my lads for their determination in holding on to the points. I hope this now proves there is no such thing as a bogey club!

"I was particularly pleased with our second goal which was a real beauty, and was a great credit to Stephen Doyle and Alex Bruce."

Apparently, the patched-up players in the team were just about holding up.

"Graham Cross is about 90% fit which is good enough for me. But both he and Mick Baxter received knocks towards the end of the game and are very sore. Bruce is still feeling his knee injury and is receiving further treatment instead of training at the moment.

"Fortunately, there is no midweek game before next Saturday's trip to Port Vale, so there is plenty of time to get them fit."

Ex Manchester City stalwart Oakes was dissatisfied on several fronts.

"I'm very disappointed with the result. We were the better side in a good attacking game, but we gave two bad goals away. The first was a deflection and the second when we were caught cold at the start of the second half.

"When we pulled a goal back, I thought we could have had three or four more if we had taken our opportunities properly."

He was even more concerned about the Crossley 'goal.'

"There was absolutely nothing wrong with it! Jim Walker who had put over the centre assured me that the ball never went out of play.

The 'desperate-for-success' North End fan hasn't changed much over the years in their er, desperation for success! The DNA is obviously passed down through the generations...

Even after a run of eight unbeaten league games on the bounce, admittedly uneven in terms of performance but nevertheless all still

WEEKEND

Leisure and Football POST

Lancashire Evening Post

No. 28,188 SATURDAY OCTOBER 29, 1977 8p

INSIDE

SCOTS TAKE THE HIGH ROAD
— See Tom Finney on Page 3

and in Monday's Post

MATTHEWS v FINNEY
... AND THE COMPROMISE 'Sir Tom' didn't like

PLUS

WIN WITH 007

Blackpool, Blackburn win away

— Page 10

Attacking Preston forwards Mike Elwiss and Gordon Coleman chase a loose ball in the Chester penalty area at Deepdale today.

BRUCE DOUBLE LAYS BOGEY FOR PRESTON

PRESTON laid their Chester bogey when they won an exciting Third Division game 2-1 in front of a crowd of 7,550 at Deepdale today.

They had never beaten Chester in any of the previous League and Cup fixtures between the two clubs and Chester again played well.

But two goals by Alex Bruce gave North End their fifth successive home victory and two points which have put them firmly in contention for promotion.

Chester, who have not won away from home since beating Preston 4—2 at Deepdale in February, scored when Bob

TV SOCCER

BBC MATCH OF THE DAY — Derby v Norwich and Bolton v Luton.

GRANADA: Manchester City v Liverpool.

Phillips was booked for a foul on Elwiss and some of the Chester players appeared very frustrated at going behind after playing well in the first quarter

City rocked by super sub goal shock

SCOREBOARD

DIVISION ONE

Arsenal	1	B'm'gh'm	1
Aston V	2	Man U	1
Chelsea	1	Bristol C	0
Derby C	2	Norwich	2
Everton	4	N'castle	4
Ipswich	★	West Ham	★
Leicester	0	Leeds U	0
Man C	3	Liverpool	1
Nottm F	4	Midd'bro'	0
QPR	2	WBA	1
Wolves	1	Coventry	3

DIVISION TWO

Bolton	2	Luton	1
Brighton	4	Cardiff	0
Bristol R	0	S'th'pton	0
Burnley	0	Blackpool	1
Crystal P	1	Charlton	1
Hull	0	Blackburn	1
Mansfield	1	Notts C	3
Orient	0	Millwall	0
Sheff. U	2	Fulham	1
Stoke	1	Tott'ham	3

DIVISION THREE

Bradf'd C	3	Sheff W	2
C'mb'ge	2	Oxford U	1
Carlisle	2	Chest'f'ld	1
Gill'gham	1	Shrewsb'y	1
C'lchester	3	Peterboro	0
Hereford	1	Port Vale	1
Plymouth	3	Portsm'th	1
Preston	2	Chester	1
Roth'ham	0	Lincoln	0
Swindon	4	Exeter	0
Tranmere	0	Walsall	1
Wrexham	3	Bury	1

DIVISION FOUR

Aldershot	2	B'mth	0
Barnsley	3	Hartlep'l	2
Brentford	1	Southend	0
Darl'gton	3	Wimb'd'n	1
Hudd'f'ld	1	Grimsby	3
Newport	★	Torquay	★
Rochdale	1	N'th'pt'n	1
Scunth'pe	★	Halifax	★
Stockport	2	[illegible]	1

FA Youth Cup (1st round)

Tranmere 2 Preston 0

RUGBY UNION

COUNTY CHAMPIONSHIP

Cheshire	33	Cumbria	12
Cornwall	13	Gloucester	35
Devon	19	Somerset	13
Durham	7	N'berland	20
Yorks	12	Lancs	7

RUGBY LEAGUE
FORSHAWS LANCS CUP COMPETITION

Wigan 13 W'kingt'n 16

RUGBY LEAGUE

FIRST DIVISION

Leeds	27	N Hunslet	15
Salford	23	Hull KR	9

LANCASHIRE COMBINATION

unbeaten games, the first slip up at Exeter was a green light for some fans to immediately vent their ire.

There were no mobile phones back then to seek out a 'discussion group' to ping your quick carping text or tweet into like today; these devotees had to take the time and trouble to get angry, sit down with pen and paper, write the epistle, address the envelope, pay for a stamp and pop it into the pillar box, invariably walking back home in the rain.

For me, the anger would have worn off by then but here are three extracts, each from a different disgruntled fan from the October 29th 1977 edition of the Football Post letters page – a week after the Exeter defeat. I have to admit, they do make me smile...

'After the Lord Mayor's Show against Gillingham, we got the muck cart in the last Preston away display....the scoreline amazed me more than the spoken word can tell....North End were outclassed and were a poor disjointed team who suffered from inertia and were never in the hunt....I was aghast to say the least....'

'Having returned from the Exeter-North End match, I feel I must put pen to paper....I have never been so ashamed of my team until last Saturday....how so many so-called professionals playing in one team can lack the basic skills required is beyond me....apart from Cross, Wilson and Elwiss, the team was composed of just ordinary district league players (no offence meant to the district league players)....they could neither pass, trap or control the ball, and some of the attempts to head the ball were laughable....Instead of even attempting to beat the full back he tried to hit the defender's legs and gain a corner from the rebound. As you may have guessed he couldn't even do that and he put the ball miserably out of play for a goal kick. Hardly shades of Tom Finney or Jimmy Dougal!....if they haven't the skills they have no right to be professional footballers, least of all playing for North End....'

'We have lost three and drawn four of seven league games away from home and scored only two goals while conceding seven – these statistics are terrible. WHAT IS THE MATTER? Do Preston players not fight for the

ball away from home?....losing 2-0 against a side not rated among the promotion favourites is simply not good enough....It is time the players applied themselves much more in the away games....'

Looking back at that moment in time, the only really justifiable moan was about North End's general away form. There's no question that it wasn't the best, but a Nobby Stiles team was generally always difficult to beat. A draw back then was half of a win, not a third like today, so if a team could largely avoid defeat on the road and mainly win at home they would always be in contention near the top.

To prove the point, October had actually been a wonderful month for North End, although you wouldn't think it from the messages above! They started the month in 19th place, and after the Chester game sat in fourth position. In total, they had played 15 league games to date and lost only three.

Following the Chester match, Nobby was listed as one of the Division Three 'Manager of the Month' candidates, after engineering the October turnaround. Although he didn't win it, it was an acknowledgement from outside the club's confines that the 'little fella' had North End on the right track.

Yes, there had been frustrations so far, but certainly no catastrophes.

CHAPTER 5

NOVEMBER

Port Vale (away) – Wrexham (home) – Lincoln City (away) – Lincoln City (FAC 1, home)

The first day of the new month began with the North End fans having to endure that familiar, hollow feeling in the pit of their stomachs when rumours circulate that a bigger or more ambitious club is showing interest in one of their players.

The transfer market back in 1977 wasn't as controlled as it is today with the use of 'windows.' Clubs could prey upon one another at any stage of the season, and in an instant, fans of a club in a lower division often saw their promotion hopes disappear as a star player was plucked from their team.

The story had surfaced in the Sunday People and inferred Sheffield United were about to make a 'large' bid for the vastly improved North End defender Mick Baxter. It drew an interesting response from North End manager, Nobby Stiles.

"That's the way I like it. I'm delighted and would be disappointed if other managers did not come to look at the North End team."

He added that as yet he had not heard from the Division Two club.

"I don't want to sell any of my lads, but it is only natural for clubs to send

their managers or scouts to our games from time to time. We do the same thing, the purpose being to keep a check on as many players as possible.

"In Baxter's case he has been giving some great displays and he has shown tremendous improvement."

There was wasn't good news about Baxter's mentor either. Graham Cross had suffered a recurrence of the calf injury against Chester and would be staying in Leicester all week, nursed by the Filbert Street physios once again.

"We will have to wait until Friday before making any decisions. Alex Bruce will also be excused training to receive further treatment on his knee," reported Stiles.

That wasn't a bulletin the North End fans wanted to hear either – details were thin, and that wasn't usually a good sign.

On Wednesday, North End's commercial department learned that the they would have to dispense with their longstanding weekly 'bingo' fundraiser, meaning the 700 sellers at the sharp end bringing in the funds, would no longer be required.

This requirement had been pointed out to the club by their new lottery consultants as being the law if an organisation was to launch a lottery – as North End were fully intending to do following their announcement in mid-October.

The 700 were thanked for their efforts over the years, and 'their details would be kept on file in case they are needed' – a promise many of us have heard during the course of our working lives!

Sir Alf Ramsey also paid a visit to Preston, for the official opening of Visionhire's new Electronic House on Ringway (next to the Crest Hotel). He was also to present a £7,000 cheque to the Queen's Silver Jubilee Appeal Fund on behalf of the tv rental company for monies raised after they sponsored an international five-a-side competition that involved players from the 1966 World Cup.

Sir Alf had recently been appointed by Birmingham City as manager, and results had improved. Nobby Stiles was present to witness his very entertaining speech, in which he revealed that he had even offered Stiles a job at one stage, although Nobby had quickly said that he had plenty of work to do at Deepdale!

The big national news of the day however was a 'rebel' power workers dispute which had been escalated overnight from ongoing disagreements across the negotiating table to full scale blackouts across the nation. The escalation meant the power workers were now 'working to rule' at 60 major power stations across the country. This action was not backed by the TUC or its leader at the time, Len Murray.

A list of area 'zones' was hurriedly issued by Norweb during the day after their telephone lines were jammed by an anxious public. The day was split into six periods of four hours and each of those segments in an area zone would be either high or low risk on a rota basis.

It was reported that BAC factories at Warton and Preston could manage to continue with essential work by using their own generators to supply their workshops, but there were concerns at both British Leyland and BTR about laying workers off as neither company had this contingency to hand.

The situation didn't improve overnight and the LEP – where the presses ground to a halt on Tuesday afternoon following a power cut that accounted for the whole of the town centre – included a fantastic piece of Seventies scrapbook memorabilia in the Thursday editions entitled, "NORWEB'S NEW GUIDE TO YOUR POWER CUTS."

It affected football too. Port Vale promptly announced that the kick off time had been brought forward for their game with North End on the forthcoming Saturday from 3pm to 2:30pm, and North End announced that all Saturday Central League games at Deepdale would kick off at 2:00pm until further notice. Football League secretary, Alan Hardaker urged league clubs up and down the country to consult with their local electric boards and work around the swathe of planned Saturday power cuts.

Thursday also saw a big announcement by Preston North End. They had now formally re-signed 35 years old Alan Spavin on a two year deal, following his trial period over the previous four weeks.

"Spav has done very well and I am delighted to have him on a full time basis," said Stiles.

Alan Kelly added that Spavin had helped the young players in the reserve squad and proved himself in training. *"We don't regard him as someone just for the Central League, we are thinking of him as a member of the first team squad. Players like him can help youngsters, but they can also help experienced players too.*

He has shown us all that he can still play and his age doesn't bother us. He will play in the Central League against Leeds United reserves here at Deepdale this Saturday, but will now provide more competition for first team places as he is someone who can make other senior players look over their shoulders."

Alan Spavin pictured on the Lowthorpe Road training ground at work in his role as player/coach with the North End youngsters

PNE FC

By Friday, Stiles sounded even more doubtful about Cross's prospects of starting at Port Vale. Steve Uzelac had been added to the squad again as cover.

"Graham was 90% fit last week, he thought he was ok but this may have been a mistake. The calf muscle he had pulled was aggravated. He's been at Filbert Street all week, just as he was last week, but he remains very doubtful for the match tomorrow.

"I won't finalise the team until the morning after another check on Cross. Alex Bruce has responded to treatment on his knee, and he should be ok.

"Both teams know a lot about each other, and we must approach this game as though Vale are the division leaders."

Vale had sacked their manager Roy Sproson in the recent past and were under the temporary guidance of coach Colin Harper. They had floated down to 21st position in Division Three, but had drawn half their eight home league games so far, with two wins and two defeats. 'Dour' springs to mind...

The latest on the power strike was that it remained unresolved, and people were planning their lives around the Norweb rotas. A total power shut down loomed as electricity chiefs upped the ante by telling the workers they were in breach of contract and would not be paid until they returned to normal working. The power workers' response of 'if you are looking for a confrontation, that's fine by us,' didn't bode well.

Other trade unions were now willing to try their hand at a bit of disruption.

The broadcasting staff union, the ABS, had warned the BBC that industrial action was likely to intensify over the weekend because of their 'derisory' pay offer for the coming year – apparently 30% less than what the equivalent ITV employee was earning.

Blank screens had already been on display throughout the State opening of Parliament on Thursday, and the union warned they would be escalating the targeting of live programmes such as news bulletins, 'Nationwide,' 'Grandstand' and even 'Match of the Day.'

What an absolutely wonderful weekend this promised to be...

A dull, wet and windy day at Vale Park produced nothing in terms of bonfire day fireworks – just a 0-0 draw between two resolute teams determined not to lose.

For North End it was definitely an opportunity missed. They spurned the chance to rise into second spot behind Wrexham on goal difference; the single point gained keeping them in fourth spot.

While Vale named an unchanged team, Graham Cross's calf muscle wasn't risked again for the Lilywhites' cause, thus enabling Steve Uzelac to make his North End debut. The team was:-

Tunks, Cameron, Wilson, Doyle, Baxter, Uzelac, Coleman, Haslegrave, Smith, Elwiss, Bruce. Substitute: Burns.

North End actually had more than a fair share of the ball in the early stages, the best use of which was made when Stephen Doyle started a move on the left by passing to Sean Haslegrave. He found Harry Wilson galloping down the wing with an instantly played skimming pass, the full back driving on a few yards before centring the ball into the Vale box. Alex Bruce then managed to flick the ball onto Mike Elwiss whose snap shot from near the penalty spot was just too high.

North End were looking 'the real deal' at this stage, but it was the usual story of missed chances, as Bruce, Elwiss and Haslegrave all fired shots wide. A neatly flicked header by John Smith was cleverly placed directly into Bruce's path following an ultra long goal kick by Roy Tunks, but the resulting shot was again just wide of John Connaughton's post.

Elwiss provided a curling cross into the box that was headed goalward by Mick Baxter but blocked near the Vale goal line; Smith's instant riposte desperately shovelled out for a corner by the Vale defence.

Vale ventured forward, but any hopes of troubling Tunks from a centre by Peter Sutcliffe were shattered when Uzelac headed the ball away from the goalmouth with such power that the ball almost reached halfway. Former Northender Alan Lamb centred again, but the referee blew for an infringement on the North End keeper following a barge by Kenny Beech.

Shots at each goalkeeper were exchanged before the ref deemed it was half time. Sadly, North End had nothing to show for an enterprising half. They were once again squandering many chances, and it was on days like these you prayed that this wouldn't come back and bite them on the backside late in the game.

Ken Beamish, the prolific lower division goal scorer, had been anonymous in the first half, well marshalled by the provisional Baxter and Uzelac combination.

He was certainly at the coalface in the second half. Within the first five minutes he had rattled in two excellent drives at the North End goal, as Vale attempted to grab the initiative.

Vale then had a strong claim for a penalty denied, this enabling Bruce to race away, setting up a chance for Elwiss whose shot was blocked.

A disallowed 'goal' by Beamish for offside signaled the start of an onslaught by Vale on the North End goal. The defenders had to work extremely hard to withstand the pressure from the home team who now had a strong breeze in their favour.

North End chances were very few and far between for over 20 minutes as Vale continued to examine their defence, with Lamb prominent. He was pulling all the strings from his left sided midfield position.

The game eventually descended into a scrappy affair, becoming increasingly physical as time wore on, the point proved when Elwiss and Sutcliffe were lectured by the referee following a midfield clash, and Uzelac was booked for a robust challenge on Derek Brownbill as time was running out.

When it finally did, despite the popular belief among the away fans that it was a game that North End really should have won, the draw meant North End had only lost one league game in the last 12. This was clearly promotion form, which their league position of fourth duly indicated. It's just that only two goals in eight away fixtures was becoming a slightly ridiculous statistic considering the wealth of chances their football was

WEEKEND
Leisure and Football POST
Lancashire Evening Post
No. 28,194 SATURDAY NOVEMBER 5, 1977 8p

INSIDE
MILNE FINDS HIS FEET AT COVENTRY
— SEE PAGE TWO
INSIDE — WIN TICKETS FOR THE ENGLAND - ITALY MATCH

PLUS

ANOTHER SUPER 007 CONTEST

Two off, five booked as Saints go beserk—Page 10

PNE DESERVE POINT IN AWAY DEADLOCK

PRESTON North End gained a valuable point in their campaign for promotion to Division Two when they shared a goalless draw with Port Vale in front of a crowd of 4,208 at Vale Park today.

By NORMAN SHAKESHAFT

TV SOCCER

LIVERPOOL v ASTON VILLA and COVENTRY v WEST HAM.

GRANADA tomorrow. — OLDHAM v CRYSTAL PALACE.

● Southampton's Chris Nicholl clears the ball from Blackburn's Gordon ... at Ewood Park today. Match report — page 10.

SCOREBOARD

DIVISION ONE

B'm'gh'm	2	Wolves	1
Chelsea	1	Nottm F	0
Coventry	1	West Ham	0
Derby C	★	Everton	★
Ipswich	1	Man C	0
Leeds U	2	Norwich	2
Liverpool	1	Aston V	2
Man U	1	Arsenal	2
Midd'bro'	1	QPR	1
N'wcastle	1	Bristol C	1
WBA	2	Leicester	0

x Today's result not included

DIVISION TWO

Blackburn	2	S'th'pton	1
Blackpool	1	Sheff U	1
Bristol R	2	Millwall	0
Cardiff	2	Stoke	0

DIVISION THREE

Bury	1	Roth'ham	1
Chest'f'ld	2	Bradf'd C	0
Exeter	2	Oxford U	1
Lincoln	2	Chester	1
Peterboro	2	C'mb'ge	0
Portsm'th	2	Tranmere	5
Port Vale	0	Preston	0
Sheff W	3	Carlisle	1
Shrewsb'y	3	Hereford	0
Swindon	3	Gill'gham	2
Walsall	4	C'lchester	2
Wrexham	2	Plymouth	0

DIVISION FOUR

B'nem'th	1	Stockport	0
Brentford	1	York	0
Crewe	2	Rochdale	1

F.A. CUP

4th QUALIFYING ROUND
Burscough 0, Morecambe 0

NORTHERN PREMIER LEAGUE

Worksop 2, Lancaster 6
N'field 0 Scarborough 3

LANCASHIRE COMBINATION

Leyland M 4, B'pool Mechs 1

CHESHIRE LEAGUE

Referee injured

BIRMINGHAM referee Derek Civil injured an achilles tendon and was unable to continue for the second half of Peterborough v Cambridge. Resumption was delayed for ten minutes with senior linesman Brian Coxon taking over as referee and with Cambridge referee John Cozall answering a loudspeaker appeal to act as substitute linesman.

LATE NEWS
Editorial Telephones
PRESTON 54841
CHORLEY 79318

PARK PITCHES

Preston park pitches. Play only pitches 3, 4 and 5 ft. Sunday League games ON: Ashton and Grange NO PLAY: Haslam and ...

creating. The team were much, much better than that.

Nobby, as always, wanted to share the positives with the fans.

"Steve Uzelac did a very good professional job, and his display confirms what depth we have in our first team squad. I was delighted with his performance.

"Steve will be standing by for next Saturday's home game with Wrexham, as Graham Cross is staying down in Leicester as before, receiving continued treatment on his calf injury.

"Coming to Vale Park is always hard, but we gave a good all-round display and although nobody stood out, they all worked very well. They are disappointed that they didn't get two points and actually did enough to win it in the first half. The strong wind spoiled the game to a certain extent, but we were much better than in our last away outing at Exeter because our approach and attitude was right.

"An away win will come soon enough if we continue to play well enough to achieve consistently good displays."

The FA Cup first round draw was made on Monday, 7th November. North End were drawn at home to play Lincoln City on the 26th – the same team they would face at Sincil Bank the weekend before!

"We wanted a home tie against a team we knew – and we got it," said Stiles.

"They are a good team but being at home at Deepdale is much better than having to go away to play a fired-up Division Four or non-league club. Lincoln are a known quantity and we are at home, that's the important thing."

The weekend had seen very few power cuts, much less in fact than most had feared. However, Sunday's newspapers carried a warning for the new week ahead from an Electricity Council spokesman. He pointed out that after a very stable demand over the weekend, Monday through to Friday will be high risk days, and outages would be certain due to the masses returning to work and factories firing up from scratch. "The load increases considerably in a very short space of time," he cautioned.

The worst cut of the day was reserved for Preston town centre as people were making their way home in the evening rush hour.

"Traffic chaos hit Preston when the whole town centre was plunged into darkness by a power cut. Huge jams formed when traffic lights were blacked out and thousands of workers were delayed by up to an hour on their way home. Bus services were thrown into 'absolute chaos'," reported the LEP in its Tuesday editions.

This was quite an unnerving experience for all that were caught up in it by all accounts. Being suddenly hurled into deep darkness, the only light source being car headlights glaring into their faces was not fun, and nor was it safe. And that was before reaching their dark, paralysed homes.

A hostile public backlash began across the nation, and the rebel strikers with no official backing started to slowly drift back to work.

Meanwhile the big match build-up was beginning at Deepdale in preparation for the match against table toppers Wrexham.

Graham Cross had responded to the week's therapy on his calf muscle, and had been through a fitness test on Thursday morning with the Leicester City staff. This had gone well, but left Stiles with a case of deja-vu.

Last time, he had risked Cross he found himself back to square one by the end of the game against Chester. Should he continue with Steve Uzelac who hadn't put a foot wrong at Port Vale, giving Cross more time to thoroughly get back to fitness? He 'decided to decide' nearer the time.

Although the power cuts were diminishing, football clubs were still taking no chances. The big Division One game between Queens Park Rangers and Liverpool had been moved forward to 2:15pm as a precaution, however North End had spoken directly to Norweb and received an assurance that is was extremely unlikely there would be an interruption to their electricity supply. It was therefore decided to stick with the traditional 3:00pm kick off.

After a few days of fewer and fewer power shutdowns, Thursday brought news that the strike was crumbling as more and more power workers returned to normal working. By Friday it was virtually over, but even more national and community horrors lay just around the corner...

Meanwhile, at Deepdale the North End manager added Graham Cross, Francis Burns and Mick Robinson to the team that shared the points at Port Vale. 'New signing' Alan Spavin was also included, giving Stiles the option of strengthening the midfield with another body, after reviewing a scouting report from Francis Burns on Wrexham's recent 3-1 win over Bury.

"Besides us, Wrexham are in my opinion, the best side in Division Three. They have the class and experience necessary to gain promotion this season, and I have tremendous respect for them," said the North End manager.

"The lads won't need much motivation, as it always raises your own game when playing against good opposition. So, it is vital that we approach this with the right attitude. Patience, all-out effort, confidence and concentration will provide us with the right ingredients in this 'four-pointer'."

Friday evening and the early hours of Saturday morning brought a massive storm with accompanying 90 mph winds to the north west.

The storm hugged the coastline but tracked far enough inland to cause chaos. It was unusual in those days for such an event, but it certainly left its calling card.

"Raging seas, whipped up to a frenzy by the 90 mph gusts, literally ripped a section of Morecambe's West End pier from the sea-bed, twisting girders and smashing timbers beyond recognition," reported the LEP.

In Southport 60 people were left temporarily homeless due to widespread flooding and structural damage to their houses, the Preston area was also fell victim to structural damage, uprooted trees and partial flooding, as was Blackpool.

A relatively new amusement arcade sited in the middle of Morecambe's West End pier had disappeared completely, the only clue to its previous existence being discovered on Saturday morning – with the unearthing of a beach full of half buried and mangled one-arm bandits. In nearby Arnside, boats were ripped from their moorings, and converted in to matchsticks. The sea flooded the nearby land to a level deep enough for people to witness four unmanned yachts sailing away on what was previously a main road.

Miraculously, the Deepdale stadium was left intact, (unlike a few trees on Moor Park) and was able to attract 10,342 through its turnstiles for one of the big matches of the whole weekend football programme.

The weather was appalling. A very strong wind was still present, more often than not powerfully peppering the faces of the exposed fans with horizontal sleet.

It didn't help either that North End fell way short in this match, being taught a lesson by a confident Wrexham team to the delight of their healthy contingent of fans who had travelled north.

Tunks, Cameron, Wilson, Doyle, Baxter, Uzelac, Coleman, Haslegrave, Smith, Elwiss, Bruce. Substitute: Spavin.

Nobby ended up announcing an unchanged team, apart from Alan Spavin who replaced Francis Burns on the bench.

After early and confined midfield sparring, Graham Whittle was the first to break free of its shackles, moving forward, skipping past Danny Cameron and putting over a centre which Mick Baxter headed away.

In fact, Whittle was catching the eye. After he had fired in another cross that came to nothing, he was on hand to play a wall pass with Wrexham striker Bobby Shinton before unleashing a low shot that went narrowly wide.

North End were looking awkward in that they were unable to gain a foothold into the game.

Shinton then caused more anxiety for the home fans starting by quickly picking his way around the North End defence, but his centre, aimed at Dixie McNeil in the goalmouth was fortunately intercepted by Uzelac whose header cleared the area – and the pressure.

Despite the attention, Alex Bruce still manages to fire a shot in on target

Finally, after 10 long minutes, North End made a little headway when Alex Bruce after a long run down the left, cut into the Wrexham box only to blast the ball too high. A miss for sure, but at least it provided a much needed lift for the home fans.

Mike Elwiss then drove forward down the left, feeding a neat pass inside for Bruce to control and have another try at Dai Davies's goal. Davies could only parry the ball, but defender Alan Dwyer was on hand to hit it away. Gordon Coleman then weighed in with a powerful header from a

Harry Wilson cross, forcing Davies into making a brilliant save right under the crossbar.

The impetus started to swing again as Wrexham won their first corner. Les Cartwright's delivery almost led to the opening goal as Shinton cleverly back headed the ball beyond Roy Tunks, leaving Cameron to clear off the line. The ball went as far as McNeil, who attempted to prod the ball home but a full swing of Cameron's boot saw North End breathe easy again.

More Wrexham pressure followed and the tension was starting to take its toll on the home defence as Wilson heavily shanked the ball while attempting to clear a Shinton centre. No Wrexham player was on hand to take advantage, but the incident led to a full scale row between Wilson and goalkeeper Tunks. It looked for a moment like it was a case of 'seconds away, round one' but soon the pair were all smiles again.

After winning a couple of unproductive corners, North End fell behind to a smartly taken goal by Mel Sutton.

The North End defence was split following a pass by Mickey Thomas that found Shinton on the left. He centred the ball and McNeil's snap shot was blocked by Tunks, whereupon Thomas coolly picked up the rebound, slotting it across the box for Sutton to crash home an unstoppable shot.

Preston heads on the pitch and in the crowd dropped immediately. They just weren't firing on all cylinders and the visitors scented blood.

Back they came, and nearly doubled their lead just before the interval, when another move full of enterprise forced Tunks into making a brilliant point blank save from McNeil with the North End defence AWOL.

Lots of muttering at half time in the crowd about North End, the weather and trying to drink a brew in a tornado.

The second half got underway and it wasn't long before Doyle was booked for a late tackle on Thomas. North End were looking revived though, and Bruce was unlucky as his twisting header went just over the bar following a Cameron centre.

Shortly after McNeil was booked for a foul on Baxter, John Smith was unlucky – just failing as he attempted to turn and shoot following a low pass from the right.

None of this North End pressure seemingly bothered the visitors too much, as they regularly broke rapidly through midfield. It was on one such occasion that they went further ahead on the hour.

The ball was passed diagonally out to the left, Cartwright ran on to it, and passed immediately to Shinton on the edge of the box. The striker then confidently beat Tunks with a well placed shot then turning, arm raised, to greet his delighted teammates rushing towards him.

Before the restart Stiles hooked off Smith, which heralded the return of 'Spav' to first team football on the green, green grass of Deepdale. However, the oldest swinger in town could only stand and watch as less than three minutes later, the visitors went three clear to seal the win.

Following a long pass out of the Wrexham defence that Baxter somehow misjudged, the ball was collected by McNeil who sped into the North End penalty area before hammering the ball past the helpless Tunks, sending the away fans wild.

The visitors were full value for their lead, and had cut North End apart with intelligent passing, movement and clinical finishing.

North End weren't quite finished yet though, and following a Coleman centre from the right, Bruce belted the ball past Davies from short range to post North End's first of the afternoon. It made the score look a little more respectable at least, and the lads kept this new found spirit going.

Doyle had a long shot saved, and then Bruce was very unlucky not to further reduce the deficit with a brilliant shot that Davies did well to save. If only that had gone in...who knows how things may played out?

Wrexham remained dangerous despite their contentment having

WEEKEND

Leisure and Football POST

Lancashire Evening Post

No. 28,200 SATURDAY NOVEMBER 12, 1977 8p

INSIDE

WORLD CUP COUNTDOWN

ENGLAND v ITALY

"Post" Special — Page 4

PLUS

A CHANCE TO SEE KWACKERS IN PRESTON

Rovers' raid on The Den pays off with valuable point — See Page 10

PRESTON SLIP AS WREXHAM APPLY THE POLISH

PRESTON crashed to their first home defeat of the season when Third Division leaders Wrexham beat them 3—1 at Deepdale today.

The game was played in appalling conditions but Wrexham deserved their victory.

Mel Sutton gave them and interval lead and Bobby Shinton and Dixie McNeil added further goals in the second half before Alex Bruce pulled one back for North End.

Alan Spavin made his first Preston appearance for nearly four years as a substitute for John Smith, and Wrexham also sent John Lyons on in place of the injured Shinton towards the end.

Preston's Stephen Doyle and Wrexham's McNeil were

Wrexham 'keeper Dai Davies saves, despite the close attentions of Mike Elwiss, in the vital clash at Deepdale this afternoon.

Blackpool rocked by teenage dream!

TEENAGER Graham BAKER made a dream debut for Southampton by putting his side ahead after just 58 seconds.

SCOREBOARD

DIVISION ONE

Arsenal	1	Coventry	1
Aston V	0	Midd'bro'	1
Bristol C	3	Derby C	1
Everton	2	B'm'gh'm	1
Leicester	2	Ipswich	1
Man C	2	Leeds U	3
Norwich	0	Chelsea	0
Nottm F	2	Man U	1
QPR	2	Liverpool	0
West Ham	3	WBA	3
Wolves	1	N'castle	0

DIVISION TWO

Bolton	2	Charlton	1
Brighton	1	Orient	0
Burnley	3	Notts C	1
Crystal P	1	Tott'ham	2
Hull	4	Cardiff	1
Mansfield	3	Luton	1

DIVISION THREE

Bradf'd C	2	Bury	1
C'mb'ge	5	Lincoln	0
Carlisle	3	Portsm'th	1
Chester	2	Port Vale	1
C'lchester	2	Swindon (PLAYED LAST NIGHT)	0
Gill'gham	1	Exeter	0
Hereford	3	Walsall	2
Oxford U	1	Sheff W	0
Plymouth	2	Chest'f'ld	0
Preston	1	Wrexham	3
Roth'ham	0	Peterboro	1
Tranmere	2	Shrewsb'y	0

DIVISION FOUR

Aldershot	3	Torquay	0
Barnsley	0	Brentford	0
Darl'gton	2	Southend	0
Doncaster	4	N'th'pt'n	2

RUGBY UNION

COUNTY CHAMPIONSHIP

Cheshire	0	Yorks	12
Cumbria	0	N'berland	10
Durham	12	Lancs	33
Oxford	15	Gloucs	29

OTHER MATCHES

Cheltenham 4, Fylde 12

RUGBY LEAGUE

FIRST DIVISION

Castlef'd 14 Hull 14 (PLAYED LAST NIGHT)

SECOND DIVISION

Whiteh'v'n 26 Halifax 4

RUGBY LEAGUE

UNDER 24'S INTERNATIONAL

seemingly set in. However, there was so little time left for North End to recover the situation.

As the curtain was ready to come down on the match, thunder and lightning in the distance signaled one last salvo from North End, but the ensuing scramble in the Wrexham goalmouth that followed yet another Bruce shot went the way of the visitors.

There could be few complaints about the result. Wrexham had proved themselves worthy of being clear at the top of the table with, considering the conditions, a polished performance. North End slipped from fourth to eighth, and surely those fans who had recently complained bitterly about 'too many North End draws' would happily have taken one on this particularly horrible day!

Compared to some manager/coaches of today who profess not to see things, gloss over blatant cheating whilst living in a dreamland of truth spinning, it is refreshing to read the integrity in Nobby's take on the Wrexham defeat. He made no excuses for North End's first home reverse of the season, and began by saying he was sorry for the club's fans.

"I thought our supporters were terrific," he added.

"They turned up despite the shocking weather and kept urging us on, even when we were 3-0 down. They deserve better results and I hope we will not disappoint them again.

"I have to hold my hands up and say they were the better team. Their first goal was a beauty and all their players adapted well to the terrible conditions. You have got to give them credit for punishing us for our mistakes because that is the sign of a very good team.

"But these things happen and we will have to bounce back again, learn from the defeat and work even harder. Setbacks happen from time to time, and we have to put the game behind us and concentrate on the Lincoln game next weekend.

"The defeat was disappointing but it isn't a make or break result for the

season. There is a long way to go yet and I still think we are as good as any other team in Division Three – apart from Wrexham who have a tremendous amount of skill in their side."

Stiles praised the effort of Alex Bruce, and said none of his players gave up on the game. He was also pleased with Alan Spavin's display, who came on for the last half hour.

"I sent Alan on to strengthen our midfield because Wrexham were playing a 4-4-2 line-up and swamping us a little in midfield.

"He did well, and we were certainly not disgraced in the second half, after playing poorly in the first half when we looked tense and lacking in confidence.

"The 'clash' between Roy and Harry was just something in the heat of the moment and although I will be speaking to them both, I wouldn't read too much into it."

As honest as the day is long!

I seem to recall spending Sunday morning in the garden, roof tile gathering with my dad. November was only 13 days old and everybody felt shell shocked with what it had brought to the table so far – power cuts and an almighty storm. In our case it would now necessitate finding a roofer who was hopefully not booked up for the next six months, but a quick glance at the television news showed that for others it was much worse. Trees with trunks as wide as a garden gate had been toppled, some quite effectively slicing the nearest house in two.

What better then, on a bright and breezy Monday morning gamely attempting to put all of those woes behind you, being stopped dead in your tracks by news of another strike!

This time it was the firemen. Their union's demand for a 30% wage increase was way outside the imposed government 10% limit at the time, so there was nothing their employers could do, except sit back and watch the whole situation disintegrate rapidly before their eyes.

This strike, involving 30,000 firemen, would last until mid-January at a cost of 1.25 million working days. Emergency cover was provided by 10,000 servicemen using a fleet of 'Green Goddess' engines.

Unlike with the power workers strike, there was widespread public support for the strikers – and for the servicemen. The firemen were receiving no strike pay, but got plenty of donations from the public in the run up to Christmas. As with the power workers, the TUC refused to back the strike action, urging the FBU to agree a deal within the 10% guidelines. After nine weeks, the FBU finally agreed a 10% pay rise with the employers.

Back to November, and there was shock news coming out of Deepdale on Friday, the 18th.

It surrounded Steve Uzelac, who had deputised for the injured Graham Cross against Port Vale and Wrexham. He had been dropped by Nobby Stiles for 'disciplinary reasons.'

"He has broken the rules and we have also fined him, but the matter will stay within the club. It has nothing to do with the way he has been playing and the position will be reconsidered next week," added the manager.

Cross was still not fit enough to return to the side for the away fixture against Lincoln City the next day, and the new situation was now leaving Stiles and Alan Kelly with the headache of finding a partner for Mick Baxter at the back.

When the team was announced just before kick off at Sincil Bank, Stiles and Kelly had slightly re-jigged things. Francis Burns was recalled, and took Stephen Doyle's place in midfield, freeing Doyle to play alongside Baxter in the middle of the back four.

Alan Spavin was again named 12th man.

Tunks, Cameron, Wilson, Burns, Baxter, Doyle, Coleman, Haslegrave, Smith, Elwiss, Bruce. Substitute: Spavin.

Although Lincoln City had been trounced 5-0 at Cambridge the previous week, North End still couldn't manage to break their away duck despite leading twice.

The early sparring was dominated by North End. Alex Bruce fired in an early 'sighter' from the edge of the penalty area that went wide, and soon after Burns drove in a long shot which Lincoln keeper Peter Grotier, couldn't hold. John Smith followed up quickly and fired in the rebound from a narrow angle, from which Grotier was more than happy to concede a corner.

Mick Baxter deflects the ball away to safety during the match against Lincoln City at Sincil Bank

Credit: Lincoln City FC

The corner was cleared and Lincoln winger Alan Jones, broke quickly down the right but underestimated the strength of the stiff breeze, watching his centre sail high, wide and well beyond the North End goal.

North End's defence was tested when a shot from Glen Cockerill produced a goalmouth scramble following a Lincoln corner. The ball was fired low and hard across the six yard box, but Dean Crombie's goalbound deflection was well saved by the alert Roy Tunks on the goal line.

The match had now become very even, and following a Smith shot that was too high, Lincoln went forward and Phil Hubbard's header once again brought out the best in Tunks.

Mike Elwiss then combined well with Smith in a 'one-two' manoeuvre as he cut in from the right, curling in a magnificent shot on the run that was destined for the top corner until Grotier's outstretched left hand tipped it over the bar.

There was still time for the North End defence to hold its breath following a Lincoln penalty claim for handball that followed a Hubbard shot, before the teams retired for refreshments.

Out of the traps quickly and with the wind at their backs, North End took the lead after 47 minutes after Bruce – with back to goal – swiftly brought a pass from Gordon Coleman under control, turned quickly and slammed the ball into the net with a shot to the Grotier's right.

A few minutes later Harry Wilson, injured in the first half and now wearing a bandage to the knee had to retire. After much arm waving, Stiles moved Burns to left back and brought on Spavin to bolster the midfield.

Lincoln were putting North End under pressure and, although Bruce was unlucky to have one shot saved and another bounce just wide, Peter Graham and Alan Harding had decent chances saved by Tunks at the other end.

Out of nowhere, Harding then equalised when he cheekily back-heeled a centre from Graham past the flat footed Tunks to set off a chain of three goals in six minutes.

North End wasted no time in responding, and a couple of minutes later Bruce restored the Lilywhites lead when in true 'Elwiss style' he cut in from the right, went past two defenders and launched a terrific shot that flew past Grotier and into the net.

The Imps were soon back though, and Graham grabbed their second

WEEKEND

Leisure and Football POST

Lancashire Evening Post

No. 28,206 SATURDAY NOVEMBER 19, 1977 8p

INSIDE

THE Alan Kelly COLUMN PAGE FOUR

On Monday . . . Tom Finney recalls THE BIGGEST SHOCK IN SOCCER HISTORY

PLUS

LPs of Guys 'n' Dolls MUST BE WON

VIOLENCE ON TV

Rovers win to step up promotion bid—page 10

SO NEAR BUT PNE LET AWAY WIN SLIP

● Blackpool full back Steve Harrison tries an overlapping move past Millwall defender Hamilton at Bloomfield Road today.

TWO goals by leading scorer Alex Bruce, bringing his total for the season to nine, helped Preston to gain a deserved point from a 2-2 draw with Lincoln City at the Sincil Bank ground today.

By NORMAN SHAKESHAFT

The crowd of 3,894 saw Bruce give Preston the lead soon after the interval.

Alan Harding equalised after 84 minutes, but Bruce restored Preston's lead with a fine solo effort.

Lincoln refused to give in, however, and Peter Graham headed their second equaliser soon afterwards.

The result was a fair one but Preston, who had only scored two goals in their previous league games away from home this season, have still to gain an ...

... Hubbard, Dave Smith, Harding. Sub: Fleming.

North End: Tunks, Cameron, Wilson, Burns, Baxter, Doyle, Coleman, Haslegrave, John Smith, Elwiss, Bruce. Sub: Spavin.

Graham Cross, who was still ruled out because of calf strain.

Alan Spavin, who substituted for John Smith in the final 30 minutes of last week's game against Wrexham at Deepdale, was again named as the 12th man.

Lincoln manager George Kerr kept faith with the team beaten 5—0 at Cambridge last week, although John Fleming was named as the substitute instead of Dennis Leigh.

Lincoln skipper Clive Wigginton won the toss so John Smith kicked off for Preston ...

SCOREBOARD

DIVISION ONE

B'm'gh'm	1	Leicester	1
Chelsea	0	Aston V	0
Coventry	4	QPR	1
Derby C	2	West Ham	1
Ipswich	3	Everton	3
Leeds U	1	Nottm F	0
Liverpool	1	Bristol C	1
Man U	1	Norwich	0
Midd'bro'	0	Wolves	0
N'wcastle	1	Arsenal	2
WBA	0	Man C	0

x today's result not included

DIVISION TWO

Blackburn	3	Mansfield	1
Blackpool	2	Millwall	2
Bristol R	0	Bolton	1
Cardiff	2	Burnley	1
Charlton	3	Sheff U	0
Fulham	2	Hull	0
Luton	1	Stoke	2
Notts C	2	Sund'land	2
Oldham	1	S'th'pton	1
Orient	0	Crystal P	0
Tott'ham	0	Brighton	0

x today's result not included

DIVISION THREE

Bury	★	Chester	★
Chest'f'ld	★	C'mb'ge	★
Exeter	1	Bradf'd C	0
Lincoln	2	Preston	2
Peterboro	1	Plymouth	0
Portsm'th	2	Hereford	0

DIVISION FOUR

B'nem'th	2	Darl'gton	0
Brentford	0	Swansea	2
Crewe	0	Grimsby	2
Halifax	2	Aldershot	1
Hartlep'l	0	Doncaster	2
N'th'pt'n	1	Barnsley	1

RUGBY LEAGUE

JOHN PLAYER COMPETITION

(QUARTER FINAL)

Hudd'f'ld	0	Bradf'd N	11

FIRST DIVISION

Leeds	16	Castlef'd	28

RUGBY LEAGUE Second Division

Lloyd in final

JOHN Lloyd, the 23-year-old glamour boy of British tennis crushed the No 3 seed Raul Ramirez of Mexico in the semi finals of the Benson and Hedges £75,000 Tennis Championships at the Empire Pool, Wembley.

Lloyd was full value for his 6-1, 6-4, 6-3 victory in 95 minutes.

Out of hospital

ENGLAND Under-21 defender Paul Futcher was at Luton today to see his club play Stoke, having been released from hospital last night. Futcher had been treated for ...

equaliser four minutes later with a header following a centre by Jones.

Goalmouth incidents continued at both ends with Bruce going the closest, failing to make contact after a Coleman centre.

In the end a draw was a fair result, and had nicely set up the following weekend's encounter between the two clubs in the FA Cup first round at Deepdale. Jones, Graham and Harding would all have to be chaperoned very carefully by North End if they were to progress in the competition.

Stiles began his reflections on the game with injury updates on Graham Cross and Harry Wilson.

"We brought Harry off soon after the start of the second half to avoid him doing any further damage to a strain he developed in the back of his thigh. Graham still isn't fit enough and Harry Hubbick will be treating their injuries this week.

"I was pleased with the lads for getting their heads up after the Wrexham disappointment. Their attitude was good and we are back on the right lines. The performance was a good team effort and we will start winning away games soon if we keep working in the same way.

"The second half was very entertaining and all the goals were good ones. We did enough to win, but an away point isn't bad. We always looked like scoring, created plenty of chances and knocked the ball about well.

"Frannie Burns played well in midfield in the first half and his display when he covered for Wilson demonstrates that we have a bit of cover.

"The goals by Bruce were terrific. Mike Elwiss kept the defenders busy and made a bit of room for Alex. His second goal was the best of the season so far, and I'm only sorry it didn't win us the game."

The manager also said that Steve Uzelac, dropped and fined for disciplinary reasons during the previous week, was now back in contention and that the incident was now forgotten.

There was positive news on Tuesday for the North End fans when it was announced that Danny Cameron had asked to be removed from the transfer list which was circulated to other clubs.

"We have done this, and I am delighted that Danny wants to stay at Deepdale," said Stiles.

Team worries were building up with the news that besides Graham Cross, Harry Wilson and Alex Bruce being massaged back to fitness by Harry Hubbick, Roy Tunks had now gone down with a 'flu like illness and was staying at home for a few days.

"Of the four, I think only Bruce will be fit at this stage," lamented the manager.

The North End bright ideas panel, consisting of members of the North End board and commercial department, stole the headlines however with news of their latest 'wheeze' for raising funds for the persistently cash strapped club.

They had applied to the council for a licence to run regular Sunday markets on the large Deepdale Road car park adjacent to the West Stand. Chairman Alan Jones saw no reason why it couldn't go ahead. "No traffic hazards would be caused if the scheme goes ahead and there would be no inconvenience to residents in the area because the market would be opposite Moor Park."

The council deferred their decision, pending a meeting with North End officials.

Friday brought news of how Stiles and Kel were pulling all the loose ends together to get an idea of just what the team would be for the following day's FA Cup tie against Lincoln City.

The latest update from Hubbick's treatment room nerve centre was that Cross was out, Wilson more than likely out, Bruce good to go. Tunks had recovered sufficiently from his joust with a flu bug and would play.

As a precaution against Wilson failing a pre-match fitness test, the management duo added a now fit and raring to go John McMahon to the squad. McMahon, still the only player on the transfer list at his own request, had been notified during the week that North End had rejected a paltry offer for his services from Chesterfield, managed by former North End coach, Arthur Cox.

"The FA Cup is completely different from the League and we will have to raise our performance," Stiles warned.

"Like us, Lincoln will have learned something from last week, and both teams will have to start all over again. It's the same message from me – we will have to work hard, concentrate and keep our discipline."

Harry Wilson failed his morning fitness test, so John McMahon was recalled to the first team for his first game since September 24that right back, with Danny Cameron moving to the left back spot vacated by Wilson. Graham Cross, as expected, was still unfit so Stephen Doyle took his place once again the back four.

Tunks, McMahon, Cameron, Doyle, Baxter, Burns, Coleman, Haslegrave, Smith, Elwiss, Bruce. Substitute: Spavin.

Every home fan was hoping for a better outcome than the last time Deepdale had swung its doors open – the home defeat to Wrexham that was played out in a tempest. They wouldn't be disappointed!

North End began well enough, showing their attacking intent. A couple of offside decisions against Alex Bruce brought play back however before he was on the rampage again, testing Lincoln keeper Peter Grotier who palmed the ball away for a corner.

The corner led to a mad scramble in the away goalmouth, which ended with Mike Elwiss chipping the ball over the bar.

Lincoln began to come into the game and were generally holding North End back in midfield. Hubbard was proving a nuisance up front for the makeshift Doyle, and Alan Jones managed to wriggle through a couple of challenges before Tunks brought off a diving save to bring the defensive calamity to an end.

Peter Graham then thudded a header against the post with Tunks stranded following a cross from the right, but was pulled up for an earlier infringement.

To be fair to Lincoln, they had sounded the warning siren in advance and duly took the lead in the 23rd minute when Alan Harding put them ahead. The striker beat Tunks with a glancing header following a good cross by overlapping full back Denis Leigh.

An immediate equaliser almost came North End's way when Elwiss hit the post with a shot, the ball finding Bruce on the rebound. His first effort was blocked by Grotier; his second from a very acute angle, went wide of the post.

This was a nice little flurry from North End and Grotier was called into action again a minute later when called upon to tip a John Smith strike over the bar. From the corner, defender (and Worcestershire CCC opening bat) Phil Neale, rescued his team by clearing Smith's header off the goal line.

Another effort from the lively Smith was too high, and then to add insult to injury Lincoln went further ahead when Clive Wigginton converted a penalty following a foul by McMahon on Jones. The centre half's spot kick sent Tunks the wrong way, and Lincoln ran back to restart with back patting and clenched fists.

A fog of dejection descended over North End for the remainder of the half, despite trying to be roused by Tunks who had to run out of the area to boot the ball clear after his defensive cover failed to appear.

Quite simply, if whatever Nobby said to his charges at half time could have been bottled and marketed, he would have become an overnight millionaire. While the grumbling home fans sipped their cups of tea seeing this game as a 'gonner,' Stiles was busy putting the North End train back on the rails. Apparently, it was a calm talk in which the manager just asked for a 'bit more' from all of them.

It must have struck a universal chord with the team, as from the second half whistle onwards they were unrecognisable to the team that had walked off at half time. In fact, it's fair to say they were irrepressible as they totally dominated the remainder of the match.

After almost ten minutes of non-stop forward movement, Elwiss brought the game back to within reach. Sean Haslegrave found Francis Burns on the left side, he then pushed through a glorious through ball that found Elwiss tracking through the penalty area. The captain, socks around his ankles by now, proceeded to curl an exquisite low shot past the diving Grotier that looked too wide to begin with, but drew itself in perfectly to nestle in the far corner of the net.

It was a quality strike, and North End lifted by this, carried on driving forward.

Three times Mick Baxter headers were denied entry into the Lincoln net – twice due to the fact they hit Bruce en-route; the third gloriously tipped over the crossbar by the airborne Grotier.

At this point Lincoln's one and only second half attack took place, ending when Gordon Coleman headed away the ball for a corner from a centre by Glen Cockerill.

Back the Lilywhites came throwing everything forward. They thought they had equalised when Bruce headed in from an Elwiss centre, but the 'goal' was ruled out for offside.

A shot from Elwiss then went wide, as did a longer range effort from McMahon before Bruce brought North End back to par around 10 minutes from time.

Burns sent a right wing corner in and Bruce literally threw himself at the ball by the far post, forcing it beyond a defender and over the line.

There was much joy on the terraces as the fans, already hoarse after a largely silent first half, now urged their team on even louder. There was just over five minutes left when dynamic captain Elwiss took the game by the scruff of the neck and settled the tie once and for all.

The fightback!

Top: Mike Elwiss bends the ball perfectly around Grotier for the first goal

Middle: Alex Bruce hurls himself at the ball from a corner to equalise

Bottom: The Elwiss winner

PNE FC

He was roving around just outside of the box when a partial clearance by the Lincoln defence came his way. Taking a couple of touches to control and set himself up, he then swiveled and fired in a screaming 20 yard shot that had hit the back of the net with Grotier still in the early stages of flight.

What a goal!

Now the Deepdale fog of dejection engulfed the Lincoln team. Having eventually succumbed after withstanding tremendous pressure, they had nothing left after the Elwiss winner and couldn't wait to get off the pitch.

In contrast North End, cheered on throughout the second half for their phenomenal efforts, were gifted a long and loud ovation as they headed back down the tunnel.

Yes, we all like to see North End take other teams to the cleaners, but this was as an exciting a match at Deepdale as you could have wished to have seen.

Stiles was delighted with the result.

"The fight-back was magnificent. I didn't say much to the lads at half time, because I didn't think they had played that badly in the first half.

"We were unlucky to be two goals down, and all I wanted was for everyone to give a little bit more. They all responded and we might have scored five goals in the end.

"Mike Elwiss was terrific and Stephen Doyle played so well as Mick Baxter's partner in the middle of the back four that I may have a real problem deciding what to do when Graham Cross is fit again."

He added that the team spirit at Deepdale was tremendous and that Saturday's display had proved it.

Participants Burns, Doyle and Tunks paid tribute to the Preston fans afterwards, and Harry Wilson watching from the stand said there was more atmosphere at Deepdale than in the games he played at Brighton in front of crowds of over 20,000.

The draw for the FA Cup second round took place on Monday, November 28th. North End were drawn at home to Wrexham, the Division Three leaders who had capably dealt with North End at Deepdale just a couple of weeks earlier.

Nobby was quite looking forward to the challenge.

WEEKEND

Leisure and Football POST

Lancashire Evening Post

No. 28,212 SATURDAY NOVEMBER 26, 1977 8p

INSIDE

Refreshed & revitalised, STOKOE BOUNCES BACK ~ SEE PAGE 2

TURF TOPICS SEE PAGE TWO

PLUS

BOXES OF GAMES TO BE WON IN JUNIORPOST

Lincoln show amazing grit

GRAND SLAM EARNS PNE WIN

PRESTON staged a tremendous recovery at Deepdale today to beat Lincoln City 3-2 in the FA Cup First Round tie after being 2-0 down at the interval.

Alan Harding gave Lincoln the lead with a header and Clive Wigginton then scored with a penalty, but North End refused to give in and goals by Mike Elwiss, Alex Bruce levelled the score before Elwiss gave Preston a second round match with his ninth goal of the season.

Lincoln's Phil Hubbard and Elwiss were both booked in the second half in a fiercely

● Roy Tunks punches the ball clear under challenge from Lincoln forwards at Deepdale today.

Wanderers grab a late win

BLACKBURN Rovers proved their promotion potential when they held fellow challengers Brighton to a 2-2 draw at the Goldstone Ground this afternoon and Bolton snatched a sensational 1-0 win over Spurs.

Brighton's new £238,000 signing Teddy Maybank marked his debut with a goal after only seven minutes.

But Maybank's joy was shortlived for he was the player whose foul in the area led to Dave Wagstaff putting Rovers level from the penalty spot midway through the first half.

However, just on half time Brighton bounced back into the lead with a goal from Tony Towner. It took a goal from Jack Lewis in the 62nd minute to earn Rovers a point which they richly deserved.

In the other key promotion tussle between the top two BOLTON and Tottenham at Burnden, a late goal from Roy Greaves clinched a 1-0 win for Bolton.

Full reports — page 16.

Right Royle

JOE ROYLE, on loan to Bristol City, celebrated his arrival at Ashton Gate by putting City into the lead after just 11 minutes in the match against Middlesbrough.

Jubilant Joe went one better in the 22th minute by scoring a second.

SCOREBOARD

DIVISION ONE

Arsenal	1	Derby C	3
Aston V	P	N'wcastle	P
Bristol C	4	Midd'bro'	1
Everton	6	Coventry	0
Leicester	0	Liverpool	4
Man C	6	Chelsea	2
Norwich	1	B'm'gh'm	0
Nottm F	0	WBA	0
QPR	2	Man U	2
West Ham	0	Leeds U	1
Wolves	0	Ipswich	0

DIVISION TWO

Bolton	1	Tott'ham	0
Brighton	2	Blackburn	2
Burnley	0	Orient	0
Crystal P	2	Cardiff	0
Hull	0	Charlton	2
Mansfield	0	Oldham	2
Millwall	0	Notts C	0
Sheff U	1	Bristol R	1

FA CUP

(FIRST ROUND)

Leam'g't'n	6	Enderby	1
Arnold	0	Port Vale	0
Barnet	1	Peterboro	2
Barnsley	1	Hudd'f'ld	0
Bath	0	Plymouth	0
Blyth S.	1	B'scough	0
Boreham	0	Swindon	0
Bradf'd C	0	Crewe	1
Brentford	2	Folk'/Sh'p	0
Carlisle	2	Stafford R	0
Chester	4	Darl'gton	1
Chest'f'ld	1	Halifax	0
C'lchester	1	B'nem'th	1
Doncaster	0	Shrewsb'y	1
Enfield	3	Wimb'd'n	0
Gill'gham	1	Weym'th	1
L'therh'd	0	Swansea	0
Lowestoft	0	C'mb'ge	2
Minehead	2	Wycombe	0
Newport	1	Exeter	1
Nuneaton	2	Oxford U	0
Portsm'th	3	Bideford	1
Preston	3	Lincoln	2
Reading	3	Aldershot	1
Roth'ham	3	Mossley	0
Scarboro'	4	Rochdale	2
Sheff W	1	Bury	0
Southport	2	Runcorn	2
Spennym'r	3	Goole	1

RUGBY LEAGUE

JOHN PLAYER COMPETITION

(SEMI-FINAL)

W'field T 5 Warr'gton 15

SECOND DIVISION

W'haven 6 Keighley 11

RUGBY UNION

OTHER MATCHES

Otley 8pts Vale of Lune 13
Waterloo 8pts Fylde 7
Widnes 20pts Hoppers 7

LANCASHIRE COMBINATION

Bootle 0, Wren Rovers 1
Clitheroe 0, Skelmersdale 1

CHESHIRE LEAGUE

Hyde United 1 Chorley 0

NORTHERN PREMIER LEAGUE

Barrow 1 Gateshead 0
Morecambe 3 Frickley Ath 2
Macclesfield 4 Lancaster C 0
N'field 0 Northwich Vic 0

Chances missed

FROM the second minute, when Millwall's Richards kicked a shot by Beamish off the Notts County line, both sides wasted chances.

O'Brien took two free kicks, one of which went narrowly wide and Bradd, 10 minutes before the interval with Millwall goalkeeper Opedaro up the ground, shot wide of an open goal.

Half time: Millwall 0 Notts County 0.

Scarborough, from the Northern Premier League, ... Fourth Division

"It's the plum tie of this round, and it's always great to be at home.

"Despite the recent defeat at home, we have every chance of winning. The lads are delighted with the news and feel they have something to prove."

The month ended with news of added complications to the Wilson injury saga. It was reported that the full back, nursing a thigh injury was now resident in Preston Royal Infirmary following a car crash. This had resulted in a fractured rib, eye and facial injuries and undergoing an operation on his knee, ruling him out of football for 'several months.' In reality, he had already played his last game of the season.

North End had also signed a young hopeful, Jim Campbell from Portadown, NI. Aged 21, and standing at 6'2" tall, he was a striker with possibilities, but needing polish. 'Time will tell' is the old adage, and unfortunately Campbell never did reach the first team.

Meanwhile, this was cartoonist Ken Wignall's take on the proposed North End outdoor market idea...

Credit: Lancashire Post

"WELL YES, we do sell players - but only to other clubs!"

... and tickets for the first North End lottery were now available, and selling very well by all accounts.

Have Fun—Have a Flutter
Play the Instant Game
PRESTON'S VERY OWN LOTTERY
Tickets now on sale

£4,000 TO BE WON ON EVERY LOTTERY
THOUSANDS OF INSTANT PRIZES FROM 50p TO £500
TWO £1,000 JACKPOTS BEFORE CHRISTMAS
£1,000 JACKPOT PAID EVERY FORTNIGHT

Preston North End's new Lottery Tickets are now on sale. For just 25p you can have lots of fun and excitement playing 'The Instant Game'. In each lottery there's £4,000 to be won in prizes. What's more, you know whether you are a winner just an instant after you have bought our lottery tickets. There are Instant Prizes of 50p, £1, £5, £10, £100 and £500. Prizes up to £5 are paid out on the spot. Larger amounts you claim from the Lottery Office, P.N.E., Deepdale Road, Preston.

All Prize-winning Tickets are entered for the
£1,000 JACKPOT DRAW

TICKETS ON SALE FROM THE FOLLOWING VENDORS

ASHTON
Lane Ends Post Office
Wilson, 19 Tulketh Brow

AVENHAM
Whitehurst, 113 Avenham Lane

BAMBER BRIDGE
Green, 5 Station Road
Bamber Bridge Post Office
Dobson, 3 Poplar Avenue

BROOKFIELD
Brookfield Post Office

BROUGHTON
Dyson, Garstang Road

CHORLEY
Bus Station Kiosk
Rigby, 196 Eaves Lane
Morris, 68 Ash Grove

DEEPDALE
Rainford, 29 Lowthorpe Road
Deepdale Road Post Office
P.N.E. Lottery Office and Main Office

FRECKLETON
Eastwood, 2 Kirkham Road

FULWOOD
Nooklands Post Office
Garstang Road
Gore, 21 Beech Drive

GARSTANG
Leach, 'Carrs', High Street

GARSTANG ROAD
Kenmure Place Post Office

HOLME SLACK
Holme Slack Post Office

KIRKHAM
Pledger, 92 Poulton Street
Williams, 26 Poulton Street

LARCHES
Rawlinson, 6 Elswick Drive

LEA
Lea P.O., Blackpool Road

LEYLAND
Hindle, Chapel Brow
Plastow, 15 Hough Lane
Earnshaw Bridge Post Office

LONGTON
Wheeler, Newsagents & Post Office
Liverpool Road

LONGRIDGE
Hollingworth, Stone Bridge
Clayton, 71 Berry Lane

LOSTOCK HALL
Dobson, 47 Stanifield Lane, Farington
Kellett, Brownedge Road

NEW HALL LANE
New Hall Lane Post Office

PENWORTHAM
Hollingworth, Liverpool Road
Cop Lane Post Office
Pownall, 182 Leyland Road

PLUNGINGTON
McGuiness, 56 Plungington Road
Brookhouse P.O., Eldon Street

PRESTON RAILWAY STATION
Garlick, 2 Fishergate Hill
W. Jackson, Fishergate

PRESTON TOWN CENTRE
J. A. Atherton, Bus Station
J. A. Atherton, Orchard Street
J. A. Atherton, St George's
W. Jackson, Top Level, St George's
Lindley Travel, Lune Street
Friargate Post Office

RIBBLETON
Barlow, 76 Longridge Road P.O.
Grimshaw, Pope Lane
Rowe, 194 Ribbleton Avenue
Cragg, 234 Ribbleton Lane

SAVICK
Green, Birkdale Drive

STRAND ROAD
Littler, Strand Newsagency
Broadbent, 199 Marsh Lane

TARLETON
Tarleton Post Office

WALTON-LE-DALE
Laycock, 1 Severn Drive

WARTON
Gardner, 31 Clifton Avenue

The prospect of a £1000 lottery jackpot (equivalent value £6260 in 2019) every fortnight certainly seemed to appeal to the public of Preston. The very first winner in early December was Mrs. Alice Davies of Ribbleton.

Some of the shops where tickets were available to buy seem to have long since bitten the dust...

CHAPTER 6

DECEMBER

Portsmouth(home) – Shrewsbury Town (away) – Wrexham (FAC 2, home) – Bury (home) – Chesterfield (away) – Peterborough Utd (away)

Saturday, 3rd December saw North End entertain old adversaries Portsmouth. The two teams had played out many battles in the previous few decades, but a glance at the Division Three table showed our friends in 23rd position and in mortal danger of being dragged into any relegation dogfight.

North End's available headcount for the clash against Pompey had taken place the previous day – there would be no Graham Cross, (missing his fifth successive game) and obviously no Harry Wilson. Curiously, still no Steve Uzelac either, although Nobby was at great pains to explain why.

"Steve isn't still out of favour; the truth is that since I slotted Stephen Doyle into the back four to play alongside Mick Baxter, he's been so effective that I can't move him back to midfield just yet. He has played very well and gained valuable experience."

Mick Robinson was named as substitute, partially to enable Alan Spavin to get some game time with the reserves after warming the bench for the previous three games. The team was:-

Tunks, McMahon, Cameron, Doyle, Baxter, Burns, Coleman,

Haslegrave, Smith, Elwiss, Bruce. Substitute: Robinson.

North End proved far too strong for Portsmouth earning a comprehensive win in front of a very disappointing crowd of 5,936. Christmas around the corner, the bitterly cold weather and Division Two games at both Blackpool and Blackburn were all touted as possible excuses for such a paltry turnout.

However, considering we were tucked in behind the leaders in Division Three and fresh from a magnificent comeback in the FA Cup, the team surely deserved better support than this.

North End held the upper hand early on, with Alex Bruce, Gordon Coleman and Mike Elwiss all testing the away keeper. To partly redress the balance, Portsmouth midfielder Bobby Stokes, scorer of Southampton's winning goal in the 1976 FA Cup Final, then smacked a volley over the bar at the Town End that raised ironic cheers from the home fans.

This signaled a mini spell of pressure from the visitors who won two corners in succession. However, whilst Baxter and John McMahon cleared the immediate danger of the flag kicks, Pompey kept the pressure on and North End had to defend for a few more minutes.

Striker Mick Mellows then put a long shot in that failed to trouble Roy Tunks in the slightest, before David Kemp saw his drive safely caught by the North End keeper following good play on the right side of the penalty area.

North End broke quickly from the keeper's clearance, and within seconds Bruce was bearing down on Phil Figgins in the Portsmouth goal – the keeper doing well to stop a powerful shot.

It was no surprise when North End took the lead in the 24th minute with a goal by Bruce. It all started from a driving, pacey run down the North End right by Mike Elwiss. He had made acres of room for himself to cross the ball when he did, but still appeared to slightly mishit it.

Nevertheless, the ball bounced and 'boinged' its way straight across the penalty area towards the goalmouth where, much to Pompey's dismay, Bruce lay in wait.

Anchoring his feet as the ball reared past the last defender nearest to him, Bruce then thrust forward to meet the ball perfectly with his head, thudding it past Figgins from point blank range. No wonder Elwiss was elated out on the wing – his take on the 'bouncing bomb' had completely eluded the Portsmouth defence!

PNE FC

Right: Alex Bruce picks his spot to open the scoring for North End...

PNE FC

Left: ...and then runs forward to celebrate with the Kop

North End refused to sit back and carried on attacking. Francis Burns was the next to test the slightly nervous looking Figgins with a long range shot that demanded the keeper's best attention.

Just before the interval, a Bruce shot was palmed onto the bar by Figgins who could only thank his lucky stars that the rebound shot from Elwiss went wide as he lay prostrate on the floor.

Half time came and went, and things then carried on as before. Rare Pompey forays into the North End defensive zone, against the likelihood of another North End goal at any minute.

Bruce was all over the visiting defence like a rash. Roaming freely, firing in shots, winning headers. He was in great form. On 55 minutes he was unlucky with a dynamic, twisting header from a Danny Cameron centre, then his persistence in winning a further corner led to North End increasing their lead.

The corner by Burns was fisted out by Figgins straight to John Smith, whose immediate return shot was blocked. The ball then fell for Elwiss who drove it into the net with his left foot from a few yards out.

Bruce nearly grabbed his second of the afternoon shortly afterwards, when full back Norman Piper managed to scramble back in time to head the ball off the line after the North End striker had rounded Figgins and shot for goal.

PNE FC

John Smith heads home North End's third goal

The home fans didn't have to wait long for the next goal following more hard work by the tireless Bruce. Approaching the penalty area from the right, he fired in a low hard cross that Coleman successfully swung at, crashing the ball against the crossbar. Figgins, now reduced to spectator status, could only watch as the ball flew back into play where Smith, following up, headed the ball back firmly directing it very precisely into the corner of the net.

Steve Foster, who later in his career wouldn't go near a pitch without his headband, then came on as substitute for Portsmouth, replacing Stokes who had made little impact.

Things then improved for the visitors a little – they attacked a little more and when they did, they caused North End some difficulties.

Thankfully, Doyle cut out a dangerous centre by Matt Pollock when there was no North End cover beyond him, and Kemp should have done much better than shoot straight at Tunks following a goalmouth scramble.

North End were still the likelier lads though, and in a lengthy spell of pressure, shots from Elwiss (wide), Coleman (over) and a Sean Haslegrave centre that caused all sorts of mayhem in the goalmouth were all added to the 'near misses' list.

It was left to Kemp, the divisions leading scorer to sign off the game with a goal in the closing minutes. He claimed his 16th strike of the season after a defensive mix-up in the North End goalmouth following a Dave Pullar corner.

The match ended with cheers and applause for North End from the home supporters, now seemingly down to the core support.

When asked after the game, Nobby quashed all mention of promotion.

"None of the players are talking about promotion. But they are in good spirits and full of confidence. We have to play another team near the top this coming weekend at Shrewsbury. I will be taking a look at them on Tuesday night when they are at home to Gillingham.

"The players carried on from where they had left off against Lincoln in the FA Cup. They could quite easily have dropped off a bit in their standard of performance but they played just as well again. Mike Elwiss was tremendous at the front.

"It was also good to see John Smith back amongst the goals, getting his

WEEKEND
Leisure and
Football
POST
Lancashire Evening Post
No. 28,218 SATURDAY DECEMBER 3 1977 8p

INSIDE
LIFE AMONG
THE CLOGGERS
SEE
TOM FINNEY on PAGE 3
IN OFF 'THE POST'
—PAGE 4
PLUS
STONES
DOUBLE LPs
TO BE WON

GOAL HUNGRY PNE TOO HOT FOR POMPEY

PRESTON moved up the Third Division table with a 3-1 win over struggling Portsmouth in front of a crowd of 5,936 at Deepdale today.

Alex Bruce gave North End the lead in the first half and Mike Elwiss and John Smith added further goals after the interval.

David Kemp then scored a consolation goal just before the end which was his 18th of the season.

By
NORMAN SHAKESHAFT

• Alex Bruce and Portsmouth's Phil Roberts jump high for the ball in today's game at Deepdale

TV SOCCER

• BBC Match of the Day tonight — LEEDS v QPR and OXFORD v SHREWSBURY.

• GRANADA tomorrow — DERBY v MANCHESTER CITY.

Italians clinch it with 3—0

SCOREBOARD

DIVISION ONE

B'm'gh'm	0	Nottm F	2
Chelsea	0	Everton	1
Coventry	1	Bristol C	1
Derby C	2	Man C	1
Ipswich	2	Aston V	0
Leeds U	3	QPR	0
Liverpool	2	West Ham	0
Man U	3	Wolves	1
Midd'bro'	0	Arsenal	1
N'wcastle	2	Leicester	0
WBA	0	Norwich	0

DIVISION TWO

Blackburn	3	Crystal P	0
Blackpool	0	Brighton	1
Bristol R	1	Hull	1
Cardiff	1	Sheff U	6
Charlton	3	Sund'land	2
Fulham	2	Bolton	0
Luton	1	Burnley	2
Notts C	2	Stoke	0
Oldham	2	Millwall	2
Orient	4	Mansfield	2
Tott'ham	0	S'th'pton	0

DIVISION THREE

Bradf'd C	2	Lincoln	2
Carlisle	1	Port Vale	1
Chester	2	Chest'f'ld	1
Exeter	2	C'mb'ge	4
Gill'gham	3	Walsall	1
Hereford	1	Swindon	1
Oxford U	1	Shrewsb'y	1
Plymouth	0	Bury	1
Preston	3	Portsm'th	1

DIVISION FOUR

Aldershot	4	Scunth'pe	0
Barnsley	4	Reading	1
Darl'gton	1	Brentford	3
Doncaster	2	Crewe	0
Grimsby	0	B'nem'th	2
Hudd'f'ld	3	Southport	1
Newport	★	Hartlep'l	★
Rochdale	1	Southend	2
Stockport	2	Wimb'd'n	2

RUGBY UNION

INTER-REGIONAL COMPETITION MATCHES

Lond'n Sth	★	L'd'n Nth	★
N'th East	9	N'th West	16
S'th West	18	South	13
W M'dl'ds	12	E M'dl'ds	6

OTHER MATCHES

RUGBY LEAGUE

JOHN PLAYER COMPETITION

(SEMI-FINAL)

Widnes 14 B North'n 10

RUGBY LEAGUE

DIVISION ONE

Leeds 34 Wigan 10

F A CHALLENGE TROPHY

third of the season. The goal was a real beauty with Frannie Burns and Gordon Coleman sharing in the build-up, but we put together some other excellent moves.

"We have no new injuries, just the Cross and Wilson situations. I would really like to have Cross back in time for the Christmas programme where we have to play four league games in just seven days."

The other news of the weekend was that Jimmy Brown had come through his first game – in the reserves at Bury – suffering no apparent problems following his back operation earlier in the season.

The feeling of relative contentment at Deepdale with the way things were progressing was shattered on the following Tuesday morning when Ricky Thomson handed in a written transfer request.

The shock news was announced by manager Nobby Stiles.

"Ricky thinks he doesn't fit in at the club now and has put in a written transfer request for a move. I can understand the way he feels, but I think he is wrong and believe he can still play a big part in North End's future.

"We signed Jim Campbell because we felt that we needed an extra forward for our first team squad and because competition for places is a healthy thing we want at this club."

'Thommo' had become a regular in the Central League side in recent weeks after losing his first team spot to Mick Robinson in September. Robinson played only one first team game however, before John Smith then took over the number nine shirt.

The 21 year old had made his breakthrough into the first team towards the end of the previous season, and was undoubtedly a very skilful player much liked on the home terraces – all of which I'm sure Nobby realised. Everybody was hoping this matter could be quickly resolved.

The transfer request was to be discussed at the next board meeting.

News emerged that Leicester City manager Frank McLintock had been handed another wedge of cash to strengthen his team with. He was searching for another striker, and it was reported he had watched both Mike Elwiss and Alex Bruce amongst others in the recent past. McLintock had just added ex Derby County striker Roger Davis to the Foxes ranks at a cost of £170,000, bringing his total spend during the season so far to £370,000. If he decided to pursue either of the North End heroes, the feeling was North End wouldn't be able to resist.

What a depressing day this was becoming! Time for some good news...

The first winners in the new fortnightly North End £4,000 lottery were announced. Tickets sales had gone well, the level of prize money was good – everybody seemed happy!

While the lottery was being hailed as a big success, enthusiasm had cooled for the proposed Sunday market on the club car park opposite Moor Park. Town centre market traders had petitioned the council with their objections, basically arguing that there wasn't enough market trade to go around with the present arrangements without thinning it out even further at Deepdale.

Friday's team news was rather as expected. Graham Cross was slowly getting back to fitness, and would play in the Central League fixture against Sheffield Wednesday at Deepdale.

The first team, contesting an awkward fixture at Shrewsbury, were unchanged. The 'Shrews', like North End had been in the higher echelons of the section all season but had hit a poor patch of form in recent weeks, taking just one point from four games.

"I'm keeping faith with squad that beat Portsmouth last Saturday, with Alan Spavin returning as substitute in place of Mick Robinson," said Stiles.

"Alan had a game in the reserves last week to get some game time after three sub appearances in the first team and I think he is a better choice for an away fixture.

"Shrewsbury are a good team despite their recent form, and they will be

trying hard tomorrow after their midweek setback. The important thing for our players is that they shouldn't worry about having not won away from home so far. That is bound to come soon if they keep going along the same lines as they have been doing in recent weeks – namely keep working hard, apply themselves and make chances."

Although match day dawned fine and still, heavy rain throughout the week had made the Gay Meadow pitch leaden underfoot. There were no last minute hiccups, and North End fielded:-

Tunks, McMahon, Cameron, Doyle, Baxter, Burns, Coleman, Haslegrave, Smith, Elwiss, Bruce. Substitute: Spavin.

Play was laboured from the off, and slowly became bogged down in midfield. There was little for the spectators to get excited about, but after 15 minutes Paul Maguire produced the first decent shot of the game that demanded a diving save from Tunks at the foot of his left post.

Another Maguire shot that came to nothing finally prodded North End into action; Alex Bruce taking on and beating Colin Griffin before lashing in a shot at goal, forcing ex-Manchester City keeper Ken Mulhearn to make a good save.

Stephen Doyle was enjoying another good performance in the back four for North End and stopped a Shrewsbury move of potential danger dead in its tracks, emerging with the ball after a firm challenge on 'Shrews' centre forward, Brian Hornsby.

In the 28th minute Danny Cameron's long curling forward pass was collected by John Smith who quickly shot for goal. It was the right decision – he beat the mobile Mulhearn completely – but the ball struck the post and bounced to safety. It was to be the best chance of the match for North End.

Phil Bates tried to get things moving for Shrewsbury but was upended by Doyle, which led to the Northender being booked. Bates was again to the forefront a little later with his entry for the 'most embarrassing moment' of the match.

Having rounded Doyle deftly and starting to home in on Tunks from the left side, Bates slipped and fell in the mud – the ball rolling harmlessly out of play while the Preston keeper breathed a sigh of relief. In fact, several players were struggling to play football on surface that had fast become a quagmire and quite frankly, ruined the spectacle.

The first attack of the second half was direct from the kick off, and almost ended with Shrewsbury taking the lead after Bates wrapped his foot around an inside pass only to see his shot go inches too high.

The field of play was increasingly resembling a churned cattle paddock and the players could be excused for not being able to perform as it was impossible to race back to defend or break forward quickly enough to attack.

Credit: Shrewsbury Town FC

Roy Tunks collects the ball as it slows down in the Gay Meadow mud

One such case in point was when Sean Haslegrave punted a pass out of the mud in Shrewsbury's general direction for Bruce to chase. As Bruce 'progressed', two of the chasing defenders slithered to the ground, and for the umpteenth time Mulhearn had to bolt outside of his area and hoof the ball clear, back into the general direction of play.

Everything seemed to end up in midfield, but noble efforts from Mick Baxter who lost possession at the last hurdle in the Shrewsbury penalty area and a long range effort from Danny Cameron from a small patch of still-greenish playing surface out wide, were much appreciated by the travelling fans.

North End had to wait for 79 minutes to notch their first corner, which was instantly followed by a second. Nothing came of either. The final corner tally of Shrewsbury 2 Preston 2 was the only score the crowd were going to see that day, and as the players traipsed back to the dressing room at the conclusion, they looked very tired indeed.

Another away game, another without a win. Was it a point lost or a point gained? Frustrating yes, could you apportion blame on the North End team? No!

However, there was a growing feeling amongst some frustrated fans (and journalists) that North End's away form simply wasn't good enough for a club with promotion ambitions. Out of 10 away league fixtures, none had been won, seven had been drawn and three lost. Just four goals had been scored, and nine conceded.

Those bare facts made it look as though North End just boarded up their goal on awaydays, when in reality they created umpteen chances in every game – home *and* away – but just couldn't manage to convert them. The aim of the team seemed to be that they always tried to win.

When the subject of the away form was raised again after the game, a plain speaking Nobby said his piece.

"The conditions ruined the game, but our lads worked hard and the only chance in the whole match was when John Smith hit the post," started the North End manager.

"We don't play for just a point away from home, we go with the intention of winning – it's the opposing team or conditions that dictate the eventual result if we don't achieve success. The one thing you can't say about my lads is that they don't compete. Every one of them worked hard and competed. The attitude of the lads was right and they were sick that they didn't win.

WEEKEND

Leisure and Football POST

Lancashire Evening Post

No. 28,224 SATURDAY DECEMBER 10 1977 8p

INSIDE

THE JOKER

A TOUCH OF HUMOUR — JUST WHAT THE 'DOC' ORDERED — See Page 2

SOCCER ABROAD
SEE PAGE 4

PLUS

Christmas Present and food ideas

AND *TAPE GIFT SETS TO BE WON*

Rovers nosedive, but Blackpool win—page 10

PNE TAKE A POINT IN AWAY DEADLOCK

By NORMAN SHAKESHAFT

PRESTON gained a point from a gruelling goalless draw with Shrewsbury Town in front of a crowd of 3,764 at the Gay Meadow ground today.

John Smith was unlucky with a shot for Preston which hit a post in the first half and there were half chances at both ends.

But the teams gained only two corners each and the match was mainly a midfield battle.

Preston's Stephen Doyle and John McMahon were [illegible] along with Shrewsbury's Graham Turner and [illegible] Irvine, and neither side deserved to win.

Shrewsbury used their substitute Jon Nixon in place of Brian Hornsby in the last half hour but this made little difference.

The best thing from North End's point of view was that their defenders played well in keeping the team in touch with the contenders for promotion to Division Two.

SHREWSBURY: Mulhearn, King, Leonard, Turner, Griffin, Atkins, Irvine, Hornsby, Lindsay, Bates, McGuire. Sub: Nixon.

PNE: Tunks, McMahon, Cameron, Doyle, Baxter, Burns, Coleman, Haslegrave, Smith (J), Elwiss, Bruce. Sub: Brown.

Referee: Alan Seville (Bir-

Bruce beat Griffin cleverly in the 15th minute, but Mulhearn made a good save from his shot.

Doyle stopped Hornsby with a good tackle when Shrewsbury attacked again.

Mulhearn had to run out of his penalty area to stop Elwiss from collecting a Coleman pass a minute later and then Bates missed a chance for Shrewsbury by shooting wide after being put through by Irvine.

Smith was terribly unlucky for Preston in the 28th minute when he beat Mulhearn with a snap shot which hit the post and bounced to safety.

Shrewsbury retaliated and Bates was stopped by a tackle

MIKE ELWISS — worked hard in Preston's bid for their first away win.

TV SOCCER

Latchford hits the goal trail yet again

By JOHN LYON

SECOND in the table Everton were hoping to stretch their unbeaten run to 21 games against Middlesbrough at Goodison Park today. There was a party atmosphere before the kick-off when Manager of the Month Gordon Lee was presented with his award, a gallon bottle of whisky.

Everton. — Wood, Jones, Pejic, Lyons, Higgins, Buckley, King, Dobson, Latchford, Pearson, Thomas. Sub: Ross.

Middlesbrough. — Cuff, Craggs, Cooper, Souness, Boam, Ramage, Mahoney, Mills, Ashcroft, McAndrew, Armstrong. Sub: Hickton.

SCOREBOARD

DIVISION ONE

Arsenal	1	Leeds U	1
Aston V	3	WBA	0
Bristol C	2	Ipswich	0
Everton	3	Midd'bro'	0
Leicester	1	Derby C	1
Man C	3	B'm'gh'm	0
Norwich	2	Liverpool	1
Nottm F	2	Coventry	1
QPR	0	N'wcastle	1
West Ham	2	Man U	1
Wolves	1	Chelsea	3

DIVISION TWO

Bolton	6	Cardiff	3
Brighton	1	Oldham	1
Burnley	1	Charlton	0
Crystal P	2	Notts C	0
Hull	2	Orient	2
Mansfield	1	Blackpool	3
Millwall	0	Fulham	3
Sheff U	2	Blackburn	0
S'th'pton	0	Luton	1
Stoke	3	Bristol R	2
Sund'land	1	Tott'ham	2

DIVISION THREE

Bury	★	Oxford U	★
C'mb'ge	3	Sheff W	0
Chesr'f'ld	★	Tranmere	★
C'lchester	3	Exeter	1
Lincoln	0	Gill'gham	2
Peterboro	0	Chester	0
Portsm'th	3	Roth'ham	3
Port Vale	3	Plymouth	3
Shrewsb'y	0	Preston	0
Swindon	2	Carlisle	2

DIVISION FOUR

B'nem'th	1	Hudd'f'ld	0
Brentford	3	Grimsby	1
Crewe	1	Stockport	0
Halifax	3	Swansea	1
Hartlep'l	2	Aldershot	2
N'th'pt'n	1	York	1
Reading	3	Doncaster	0
Scunth'pe	★	Darl'gton	★
Southend	4	Newport	2

RUGBY LEAGUE

DIVISION ONE

St Helens	20	F'stone R	19
Hull KR	13	Salford	10

SECOND DIVISION

W'haven	9	Hudd'sf'ld	5

NORTHERN PREMIER LEAGUE

Altr'nch'm	★	Frickley	★
Boston U	0	Scarboro	0
Goole	★	N'wch V	★
Gt H'w'd	2	Wigan A	3
Lancaster	0	Buxton	1
Matlock	1	Bangor C	1
Mossley	★	Gorton'd	★
Netherf'ld	2	Gainsboro	0
Runcorn	★	Worksop	★
S Liverp'l	2	Barrow	4
Stafford R	★	M'clesf'ld	★
Work't'n	4	M'cambe	1

LANCASHIRE COMBINATION

Accrington S 3, [illegible] 3; Clitheroe 1, Kirkby T [illegible]; Leyland 2, [illegible] 1

"It was a dour affair, and you can't always play attractive football – in fact, we often lost similar matches in the past. Stephen Doyle, Mick Baxter and Gordon Coleman did particularly well on a pitch which became a bog afterwards."

On Monday, the manager issued an injury update. The Graham Cross news was positive.

"Both our teams came through Saturday without injuries, Graham Cross had no ill effects either from his game in the reserves and I was pleased that Ricky Thomson scored three goals even though he has put a transfer request in. Thomson, Steve Uzelac and Peter Morris all did well and will be in contention for the Wrexham cup tie."

The manager was waiting to hear from the authorities as to the amount of points that were to be added to Doyle's tally, following his fifth booking of the season at Shrewsbury. He had 16 points from four bookings so far and if he bagged another 'four-pointer' he would face an automatic two match ban.

"I thought the booking was a bit harsh, but I don't want to say anything else at the moment," said Stiles.

Doyle would still be available for the Wrexham game however, with any ban being confirmed at some point during the following week.

It was a busy week in terms of North End news.

In midweek, the big news was that Adrian Alston, the Preston-born Australian international had offered himself on loan to North End until April. That was when his American club, the Tampa Bay Rowdies would want him back for the new North American Soccer League season.

Back home for Christmas to see family, Alston said he would be delighted to join North End. "I think the club has a great chance of gaining promotion, and I would like to help. I could keep match fit with North End, providing the club agreed to insure me."

Stiles was pleased to hear of Alston's offer, but there were a few problems apparently. *"We have a big squad now following the arrival of Jim Campbell, and I have to be careful about signing players on loan. There is also the question of the money involved, as our wage bill is already high,"* he explained. Nevertheless, he had discussed the matter at length with his sidekick Alan Kelly, and was due to meet Alston later in the day.

By the following day, Alston was at Ewood Park, offering his services to Blackburn Rovers following Stiles' rejection of his approach to North End.

Rovers' manager Jim Smith, overjoyed upon hearing of North End's decision not proceed, had immediately contacted Alston and invited him over for talks. They had also been in contact with Tampa's manager Gordon Jago to register how serious their interest was.

"I'm a bit disappointed North End don't want me, but not that worried. I still hope Preston go up but my main obligation will always be to Tampa," said the striker.

Stiles meanwhile repeated the difficulties with the wage bill and North End's big squad as stumbling blocks but would really have liked more time to consider the approach.

"We are free of injuries to forwards, touch-wood, and it is up to the lads here already to do the job. We also have to remember that we may need loan players later in the season in the event of injuries and the league rule is that we can only have two at the most."

Alan Kelly added, "We both feel the players here deserve the chance to prove themselves. They have got the ability and it is up to them to achieve promotion. We already have a lot of players competing for places and this is a healthy situation to be in."

It was typical of the North End management to put their 'lads' first. It's obvious that a major factor in rejecting the approach was that Nobby and Kel didn't want to upset any of the players already on the staff and, in effect were backing them to succeed. Those players must surely have been given a huge boost to learn just how much confidence the management team had in them to achieve promotion.

Meanwhile Rovers went gung-ho into going about securing Alston's services, agreeing arrangements left, right and centre with all concerned. The whole thing collapsed around their ears a day later when the forthright Football League chairman of the time, Alan Hardaker, got involved and quashed the deal completely.

Alston's plans for a working holiday were shattered by Hardaker's intervention, his ruling being spelled out to Rovers in no uncertain terms.

"If a player wants to return here from the USA he must get a proper transfer for a full season. We are not allowing loan arrangements anymore because we have had a lot of trouble in the past."

Responding to the Blackburn manager's attempt to get around the rules and regulations with a £10 repayable fee for the period of the 'loan', Hardaker continued:-

"Nor can a Football League club pay a nominal fee and have it repaid by the Americans when the player is returned. This sort of thing just isn't on. There is a lot of trouble brewing with the USA. We started an arrangement that was helpful to the Americans but it didn't work out. Players can now only return if there are no strings attached and basically as far as we are concerned, any player that goes over there plays over there."

I wager that both Nobby and Kel were delighted with their decision to pass on Alston's offer after that dressing down!

We still hadn't quite heard the last of Alston however...

Meanwhile, Stiles named an unchanged squad for the FA Cup tie against Wrexham at Deepdale, although Graham Cross was now fully fit again.

"I have decided not to risk Graham, and also felt that bringing him back might upset the rhythm we have had in the three games the lads have been together since John McMahon returned," said the manager.

The last time Wrexham appeared at Deepdale just five weeks previously, the match had taken place in the remnants of a vicious storm. The conditions on December 17th were perfect for football – no wind and no rain.

Although North End put in a much better performance than in the recent league encounter, their interest in the FA Cup was ended by a Wrexham team who it seemed were just a little in advance of Preston in terms of development.

A crowd of 11,134 were inside Deepdale to witness the plum tie of the second round.

Wrexham got the game underway, kicking towards the Town End, but North End were the livelier in the opening exchanges. Bobby Shinton soon showed his quality, cutting in from the right wing and forcing Stephen Doyle to foul him before he could progress any further.

The free kick came to nothing but North End had been warned. Shinton popped up again a few minutes later, rifling in a 20 yard drive that went just wide, while Alex Bruce, intercepting a Dai Davies clearance was unlucky as the keeper managed to block his shot, thus avoiding further embarrassment.

Graham Whittle made room and shot over for Wrexham a few minutes after Dixie McNeil had fluffed a chance that required quick thought and action by Roy Tunks to recover the loose ball bouncing through his goalmouth.

A counter attack from North End concluded with John Smith striking a powerful drive that brought forth a magnificent diving save from Davies.

There was plenty to admire in this game. It was played at a faster pace than the usual Division Three fare and been an exciting half between two good teams, trading blow for blow.

Smith shot wide from another Preston attack, before Francis Burns had to have lengthy treatment from Harry Hubbick after being fouled by

McNeil. The Wrexham striker was booked for the challenge, while Burns received a lower leg full of ice cold water slopped from Hubbick's magic sponge.

PNE FC

Sean Haslegrave progresses through midfield

Burns recovered sufficiently and was called upon to take a corner which he floated dangerously under the Wrexham crossbar, but Davies clung on to the ball.

Wrexham then broke away signaling danger for North End. Mick Evans made a chance for McNeil with a good pass but the striker blasted over, then Les Cartwright tried a long delicate chip from the left wing which Tunks just managed to tip over the bar for a corner which was eventually cleared.

Just before the interval Bruce was involved in an almighty scramble in the Wrexham goalmouth but couldn't force the ball over the line after becoming quickly outnumbered.

The second half began with North End on the front foot as Burns swung in a free kick which Baxter rose to and met well, but Davies caught the ball well under pressure from Bruce.

As the half wore on, inevitable tiredness started to creep in for both teams after the first half exertions and the game took on a scrappier appearance.

It sprang to life again when Whittle, controlling the ball in the penalty area, turned quickly, beat Doyle and fired a shot past the helpless Tunks only to see the ball hit the base of the post and bounce to safety.

Sensing a refresh of midfield was needed, Stiles replaced Sean Haslegrave with Alan Spavin. North End attacked again and a powerful cross shot from Elwiss demanded the full attention of Davies in the Wrexham goal.

North End then won a corner, and Alan Dwyer made a desperate clearance off the line following a Smith shot from the goalmouth scramble that followed. Davies was called upon again to save dramatically from an Elwiss free kick that was despatched like a rocket homing in on its target.

As always seemed the case (and still does nowadays), just when you thought North End were going to break through, the visitors took the lead in the 79th minute.

Danny Cameron was pulled up for a foul on McNeil just outside the North End penalty box. Shinton side-footed the ball to skipper Gareth Davies who hammered a rising shot straight through the wall of Preston defenders. Tunks managed to get his hands to the ball but couldn't prevent it entering the net.

Still in a state of shock, the numbed home supporters then saw the tricky Mickey Thomas almost double Wrexham's lead less than a couple of minutes later with a shot that fizzed across the face of the vacant North End goal.

Try as they might, North End couldn't dent the Wrexham defence any further, and to add to the disappointment of imminent exit from the FA Cup, the visitors made it a racing certainty in injury time when McNeil tapped the ball home after Tunks failed to hold his initial header that followed a Whittle centre.

Wrexham, like their name implies, had that 'X' factor. They seemed to have a perfect blend of youth and experience about them, were slick and could give anybody a good game. They managed to progress to the quarter final stages of both the League Cup and the FA Cup, before being knocked out by Liverpool and Arsenal respectively.

There was no shame in this defeat for North End.

"There was nothing between the two teams this time and the free kick that led to Wrexham's first goal was the turning point," insisted Nobby.

"I thought the ref was wrong, and the decision should have gone our way because in actual fact it was Dixie McNeil who fouled Danny Cameron, but these are the things that happen in cup-ties.

In reply to a comment by Wrexham manager Arfon Griffths that Bobby Shinton decided to slip the free kick to Gareth Davis because he heard the North End players saying they thought he would chip the ball into the goalmouth, Stiles said he didn't know if that was true, but that was the way Wrexham often try to find Dixie McNeil – just as they did for the second goal.

"That second goal made no difference though, it was the first goal which won the game," added Stiles.

Reacting to Griffith's claim that North End were just intent on stifling his team, Stiles responded, *"That's just not true. In fact, it was the other way around. John Smith was unlucky for us when one of his shots was scrambled off the line but although we won a lot of corners, we didn't make many real scoring chances.*

"It was a typical cup-tie and you feel bad when you are beaten – but Sheffield Wednesday were knocked out by non-leaguers Wigan Athletic, so things could be far worse!"

Griffiths declared the match was much harder to win than the recent league encounter at Deepdale.

"Preston had certainly done their homework and tried very hard to stop us. I thought the team that scored first would win and that's how it turned out."

WEEKEND

Leisure and Football POST

Lancashire Evening Post

No. 28,230 SATURDAY DECEMBER 17 1977 8p

INSIDE

Preston's Progress

NORMAN SHAKESHAFT assesses North End's League form — See page 4

and on Monday TOM FINNEY recalls . . The best side I ever saw

PLUS

The many faces of Emery's Christmas

Plus Prizes in JUNIOR POST

Rovers on winning path, 'pool lose — p 10

WREXHAM END PNE HOPE IN LATE PUSH

● North End player Sean Haslegrave beats two Wrexham defenders during the game at Deepdale today.

By NORMAN SHAKESHAFT

PRESTON were knocked out of the FA Cup when they were beaten 2-0 by Wrexham in the second round at Deepdale today.

SCOREBOARD

FA CUP

SECOND ROUND

A.P. Leam	0	Southend	0
Blyth S.	2	Chest'f'ld	0
Carlisle	3	Chester	1
Crewe	0	Scarboro'	0
Gill'gham	1	Peterboro	1
Grimsby	2	Barnsley	0
Hartlep'l	4	Runcorn	2
Minehead	0	Exeter	3
N'th'pt'n	0	Enfield	2
Nuneaton	1	Tilbury	2
Plymouth	1	C'mb'ge	0
Portsm'th	2	Swansea	2
Preston	0	Wrexham	2
Roth'ham	6	Spennym'r	0
Shrewsb'y	1	Stockport	1
Swindon	2	Brentford	1
Walsall	1	Port Vale	1
Watford	2	C'lchester	0
Wealdst'e	2	Reading	1
Wigan A.	1	Sheff W	0

SCOTTISH F.A. CUP

FIRST ROUND

Brechin C	2	Falkirk	0
B'r'd S'y'd	1	Berwick	4
CSS	4	Selkirk	3
D'f'mline	0	Clyde	0
I'n'ss Caly	5	I'n'ss Th	0
Rosth	1	S'h'smuir	0

DIVISION ONE

B'm'gh'm	0	Everton	0
Chelsea	1	Norwich	1
Coventry	1	Arsenal	2
Derby C	1	Bristol C	0
Ipswich	1	Leicester	0
Leeds U	2	Man C	0
Liverpool	1	QPR	0
Man U	0	Nottm F	4
Midd'bro'	1	Aston V	0
N'wcastle	4	Wolves	0
WBA	1	West Ham	0

DIVISION TWO

Blackburn	2	Millwall	1
Blackpool	0	S'h'pton	1
Bristol R	3	Sund'land	2
Cardiff	0	Hull	0
Charlton	2	Bolton	1
Fulham	3	Stoke	0

RUGBY UNION

INTER-DIVISIONAL MATCH

Midlands ★ North

INTER-DIVISIONAL MATCH

London ★ S & SW

NORTHERN PREMIER LEAGUE

LANCASHIRE COMBINATION

Walsall let Newton go

The final, fun filled chapter of the Adrian Alston saga came to light on Tuesday, December 20th when it was revealed a whole new slanging match had blown up over the *'gissa job'* footballer between two clubs new to the saga... from the Preston Catholic Football Combination!

Apparently, the nonchalant Anglo-Australian had turned out for the Moorbrook Inn, helping them beat the Clover Inn 4-1 in a first division game on Moor Park.

Moorbrook manager Paddy Kelly was reported as saying Alston had signed a registration form for them on Saturday morning.

"I met him in a pub and he told me he wanted to keep match fit until his return to America. Adrian said that other American players turned out in local games while they were on holiday in England, so he didn't think there would be a problem. He scored twice, and could have got a few more but was very unselfish."

Some Clover players were aggravated, and the club were due to decide at their weekly meeting whether or not to formally complain about the appearance of a professional after raising the issue with the Combination powers that be.

The Combination officials were remaining tight-lipped until they knew what action Clover would be taking, although one did confirm a player called Alston was indeed registered with Moorbrook on the previous Saturday saying, "He played in a first division game – possibly thinking he wasn't good enough for the premier division!"

Clover decided not to officially complain after taking a vote, letting the result stand. Alston's response of, "There was no problem with Tampa. It was only an amateur game, I only scored twice as I was taking it easy. I wouldn't mind playing again – if selected," certainly cut no ice with Combination chairman and North End director, Howard McCann, who said there would be 'no chance' of Alston playing for Moorbrook again.

With the Alston diversion finally over, Thursday saw Stiles travelling down to London with Stephen Doyle to speak on his behalf to FA Disciplinary

Committee after the player had accumulated 20 penalty points via five bookings. The hope was that Stiles could articulate the players case, seeking leniency over the last of those bookings at Shrewsbury which he thought was harsh.

Convincing the panel would reduce the ban from three to two matches, and Nobby was delighted to confirm later that this was indeed the outcome. Doyle would now only miss the Monday Boxing Day fixture at Deepdale against Bury, and the match at Chesterfield just 24 hours later.

"It was a worthwhile trip; the committee gave us a fair hearing and a two-match suspension is better than a three-match ban. Some of the other players whose cases were being considered got three matches after reaching 20 points."

Christmas Eve brought news of the squad for the Boxing Day fixture against Bury. With Doyle now missing for the next two games, Stiles named the remaining 11 players from the Wrexham cup-tie team sheet, plus a fit again Graham Cross, along with Steve Uzelac and Ricky Thomson.

Thomson had been performing very well in the reserve team over the recent weeks, and four goals in the club's last two Central League fixtures had certainly boosted his confidence.

The board had still not met since he had submitted his written transfer request.

"I have to consider changes because we have not scored goals in our last couple of games, so I will leave it as long as I can until finalising the team." Stiles said.

"To the 14, I am adding reserve keeper Alex Smith, Ian Cochrane and Mick Robinson to make a pool of 17 players for the remaining games. They will be training on Christmas Day along with the other 14 chosen for the Bury match, and then available for the Tuesday game at Chesterfield.

"We have a busy programme and Christmas is a time when we have to

put in a lot of hard work. It is difficult, but it is our job."

I must admit the North End Boxing Day fixture is always the first I look up when the new list is announced in July. There is something just special to me about football on that day, especially if the Lilywhites win – although for whatever reason, history shows they don't often do! Therefore, when the rare opportunity of a Christmas win does rear its head, what better than to convert it into a 'mullering' and *really* enjoy the day!

And so it came to pass that, on Boxing Day 1977, Bury were 'mullered' amid glad Preston tidings of comfort and joy.

Nobby made a couple of changes to the team that lost to Wrexham in the FA Cup nine days previously.

With Stephen Doyle banned, Graham Cross returned to the back four and John Smith was rested in favour of Ricky Thomson. The team lined up thus:-

Tunks, McMahon, Cameron, Burns, Baxter, Cross, Coleman, Haslegrave, Thomson, Elwiss, Bruce. Substitute: Spavin.

A festive crowd of 10,297 – the second highest of the season to date – had assembled inside Deepdale to see this potential thriller, with the 'Shakers' just one point adrift of North End on the league ladder.

For what it was worth the teams sparred – or should I say 'shadow boxed' for a few minutes after Bury kicked off attacking the Town End. Somebody then threw the North End switch to 'on' and from that moment until the end of the game, Bury were totally outclassed.

Quick, fluid passing, movement off the ball, strong in defence and menacing in attack – the only surprise was that it took North End 20 minutes to blow down the Bury 'house of straw', after which the Shakers were never in a position to put their abode back together again.

The ball was passed sideways from the right just inside the Bury half along the North End chain of Sean Haslegrave to Francis Burns to Graham Cross. Whilst this was in motion, Alex Bruce moved into a position outside of the penalty area, unmarked.

Cross had spotted this, and perfectly guided the ball forward along the floor directly into the path of the North End marksman who took the ball in his stride, moved forward a few paces and then drilled a low hard shot past goalkeeper John Forrest, seeming to pick his spot in the process.

It was lovely football, and the perfect start.

Bury thought about attacking, but never really progressed once they inevitably met up with Mick Baxter and/or Graham Cross. Remarkably, there wasn't the slightest hint of any rustiness in their back-line combination following Cross's seven game absence due to injury. These two had a real dynamic going on between them; their partnership based on a sixth sense understanding of each other's position, movement and intentions.

All the football was from North End, who doubled their lead on 33 minutes.

This time the provider was Bruce, passing across the penalty area for skipper Mike Elwiss, socks down and meaning business, to fire in a shot with the velocity of a revolver past the hapless Forrest from almost the same position that Bruce had struck from earlier.

More Preston attacking, and Mick Baxter then went close after soaring high above all other contenders only to see his header cleared close to the Bury goal line by 'Shakers' desperate left back, Keith Kennedy.

Ricky Thomson had fitted in well on his comeback, his lively trickery keeping the Bury defence on its toes.

For all their excellent approach work it was something of a hopeful punt forward that led to North End's next goal, just before half time.

The high bouncing ball into the box caught the visitors defence completely off guard as Gordon Coleman and Mike Elwiss made their way quickly towards it, followed by goalkeeper Forrest. It was Coleman who got there first, twisting in the air as he headed the ball goalward. By now

Forrest had arrived and managed to take the pace off the header by pawing the ball downwards. He was in no position to control it however as he fell to the ground, leaving Coleman the simple task of pushing the ball over the line into a wide, open goal.

PNE FC

North End's first half salvo flattened Bury on Boxing Day.
<u>Top</u>: Alex Bruce fires home the first. <u>Middle</u>: Mike Elwiss puts North End two goals clear.
<u>Bottom</u>: Gordon Colman in the process of scoring the third goal.

Seasonal cheer was liberally exchanged amongst the home fans at half time – after all, Christmas had just got a whole lot better!

There was no let up in the second half for Bury either, apart from a spell right at the end of the game where they probably should have pulled one goal back following an Alan Suddick shot that curled just wide of the post.

The ex-Blackpool midfielder had joined up again with manager Bob Stokoe in a bid to bring their 'old Bloomfield Road magic' to Gigg Lane.

Suddick was always a thorn in North End's side during those early Seventies encounters with Blackpool, an excellent midfield talent and an early exponent of being able to curl a dead ball wickedly from wherever a free kick had to be taken. He certainly had my respect, but on this day he, like the rest of the Bury team, was sidelined.

North End effectively wrapped proceedings up in the 70th minute when Bury defender Tony Bailey fouled Elwiss in the penalty area, leaving Kendal referee Walter Johnson with the simplest of decisions to make.

Up strode Bruce, and with a familiar swing of his arms that often accompanied the launching of a thunderbolt from his right boot, North End's top scorer drove the ball east, while the unfortunate Forrest committed to west. Never the twain shall meet, and that made it 4-0.

North End's defence – apart from those last few minutes – was like a rock, the midfield all played well and Bruce and Elwiss were irresistible in attack.

After the match Stokoe – for once – had nothing withering to say about the North End team or the club – he saved that for his own players, locking them in the dressing room whilst he lectured them for over 30 minutes.

Happy Christmas to one and all.

Stiles fielded an unchanged team for the visit to Saltergate on the following day:-

Tunks, McMahon, Cameron, Burns, Baxter, Cross, Coleman, Haslegrave,

Thomson, Elwiss, Bruce. Substitute: Spavin.

The fans' opinion on North End's away form was split – this was obvious by just reading the LEP letters column. Gaining the first league away win of the season would be a fantastic way to back up the big win over Bury. Around 1,000 North End fans made the journey to Derbyshire, out of a total attendance of 6,484. With that level of support shouting them on throughout, the 'lads' let nobody down!

The first half, even in terms of possession, saw Chesterfield's Stuart Parker and Steve Cammack go close, as did the ex-Leicester City striker Rodney Fern, who was a handful for the Preston defence for the duration of the match.

North End attacked with enterprise, with both Alex Bruce and Ricky Thomson being very unfortunate not to score.

At half time the score was 0-0, but it was in the second half that the Lilywhites asserted control in their search for the elusive first away win.

Danny Cameron had been booked soon after the restart for a foul on Cammack, but North End soon recovered their composure and got on top to dominate their hosts.

A thunderbolt strike from Bruce was brilliantly saved by Gian Letheran, the Chesterfield keeper, who also managed to save a superb individual attempt by Thomson.

Roy Tunks was then called into action when Fern collected the ball just inside the North End penalty area and struck a low drive which Tunks deflected for a corner after a full length dive to the right.

There were just 16 minutes left when Bruce struck what turned out to be the winning goal.

It was the lively Thomson who displayed excellent vision when he launched a long range defence splitting pass down the right. Bruce brought the ball under control, then went around a defender. As Letheran advanced from the Chesterfield goal line to meet him, Bruce moved wider across him before smashing the ball into the empty net.

This was Bruce's 15th goal of the season, and it was a superb effort. Just 15 mins left to survive to make this a Christmas to remember!

North End went for the kill rather than trying to hold out, and twice came close to sealing the win through Mike Elwiss and Thomson. After more pressure, a neat move concluded when Baxter had a header saved.

With just five mins left, the 'Spireites' coach Arthur Cox hooked off ex-Northender Ricky Heppolette, replacing him with Glynn Chamberlain – signaling a 'charge of the light brigade' type last ditch effort to save the game.

They managed to pin North End back for a couple of attacking waves, but that was all. North End survived, had finally won away, and collected their second win in as many days.

The large contingent of North End fans, who had noisily backed their team throughout the game were ecstatic.

So this is Christmas, and what had we done...

Nobby was ecstatic too, declaring that it had been a wonderful festive period for North End.

"I'm over the moon! The lads have played superbly in their two holiday games. We've collected four points and I couldn't ask for better team performances. It's been marvelous.

"We got our reward at last for all the hard work we have been putting in. Everyone has played well and the team spirit has been tremendous. Beating Chesterfield was a particularly good result as they had won 2-1 at Rotherham on Monday."

The manager then revealed the bravery that Mick Baxter had displayed during the past 48 hours. The tall defender had sustained a fractured cheekbone early on in the match against Bury at Deepdale on Monday, but carried on to complete the game despite being in pain.

"He insisted on playing at Chesterfield, and this is typical of the lads we have at Deepdale at present – a wonderful bunch who are giving 100% in our battle for promotion.

"Mick is due to go into St. Joseph's Hospital on Mount Street tomorrow for an operation, and I'm keeping my fingers crossed that he will be ok to play in the New Year fixtures. He has made tremendous strides this season and is a vital member of the team."

The operation on Baxter's cheekbone was a success, and he was determined to keep his place in the team. On Friday, Stiles announced that for the clash with Peterborough United at London Road on New Year's Eve, the now available again Stephen Doyle would be added to the 12 that comprised the team at Chesterfield.

Besides the Baxter situation, Sean Haslegrave had picked up a niggling ankle injury on Boxing Day and aggravated it at Chesterfield, and Nobby was now hoping that he would be good-to-go too, come kick off time. The midfielder had hit a rich seam of form over the previous few games.

"I'm hoping both will be alright. Sean's injury has responded to treatment and he will play unless there is a reaction, while Mick says he will be fine. I am just delighted that both players are so keen to play."

The manager added that Doyle's availability now posed him with a selection problem.

"Steve was playing well in midfield before he dropped back to play in defence when Graham Cross was injured with a pulled muscle injury, and then played well there before Graham came back when he was suspended.

"Graham was superb though in the Christmas games, and the midfield men are playing well too – but competition for places is a great situation to have. It makes it harder for me, but that is the way I want it."

North End now sat in fifth position, with Peterborough right behind them in sixth. Both teams had 27 points from 22 fixtures played, goal difference being the separating factor.

Having traded some talent out of the club and raising cash to remodel Peterborough into more of an all-round fighting unit, Peterborough manager, John Barnwell had a warning for North End.

"Away from home, we are good enough to pick up some good points along the way, but at home I make it my business to make sure that everyone is mentally prepared.

"We are well aware of Preston's form. Both sides can suddenly visualise a place at the top.

"I know the style Nobby Stiles is trying to create. He has done a good job – mind you he inherited some good players in boys like Elwiss and Bruce but he has also brought several young players forward.

"It will take a damned good team to beat us at home. It will be interesting to see if Preston are good enough yet to take on the job. Naturally, I don't think they are."

After long deliberation, Stiles finally opted to keep the same starting 11 that had done so well at Chesterfield, the only change was on the bench where Doyle replaced Alan Spavin.

Tunks, McMahon, Cameron, Burns, Baxter, Cross, Coleman, Haslegrave, Thomson, Elwiss, Bruce. Substitute: Doyle.

This crucial battle was decided in the very last minute by a questionable refereeing decision on a surface akin to the Shrewsbury quagmire of just three weeks previously.

It certainly brought a halt to North End's holiday celebrations as the team and fans were left with the feeling that they had been the victims of a mugging.

Throughout this battle in the mud, it must be said that both teams battled gamely, both teams made and missed chances but neither team deserved to lose.

DIVISION I

	Profit or loss £	Previous figure £	Wage Bill £	Transfers £
Man. Utd. ...	+564,937	+301,348	631,853	+ 72,255
Leicester	+366,729	−192,827	313,403	−285,250
A Villa	+279,856	−135,014	463,737	− 27,748
QPR	+266,980	− 34,750	n/d	+ 21,278
Newcastle ...	+205,298	+ 19,003	379,695	− 4,000
Ipswich	+187,547	+ 87,770	105,015	—
West Ham	+174,454	− 22,021	399,715	− 46,696
Leeds	+140,135	− 74,187	432,231	− 35,001
Liverpool	+114,664	+105,132	575,939	−190,743
Middlesbro ...	+ 99,581	+140,281	253,722	− 51,000
Coventry	+ 95,825	+166,439	325,180	− 6,121
Man. City ...	+ 74,620	−127,354	331,011	− 62,476
Derby	+ 38,679	− 1,129	334,351	−173,732
West Brom ...	+ 37,987	−128,396	276,558	−184,166
Wolves	+ 11,007	+124,016	319,330	+ 26,824
Nottm. F. ...	− 20,476	− 13,513	220,928	−110,195
Bris. City ...	−113,039	− 5,900	303,529	−187,484
Everton	−114,026	− 48,529	513,969	−358,966
Birmingham ...	−121,124	+ 16,853	336,153	−120,000
Arsenal	−154,889	+ 23,146	520,104	−220,938
Chelsea	−194,184	− 57,579	n/d	n/d
Norwich	−250,037	+ 29,014	298,836	−261,708

DIVISION II

	Profit or loss £	Previous figure £	Wage Bill £	Transfers £
Stoke	+476,766	+ 87,873	369,952	+513,000
Southampton ...	+132,290	+ 1,454	216,818	− 2,635
Notts Co.	+ 59,676	+ 23,378	157,097	+ 45,000
Sheff. Utd. ...	+ 32,292	+ 761	232,826	+141,442
Bolton	+ 24,329	− 27,402	144,872	+ 60,263
Sunderland ...	+ 23,083	−229,272	n/d	+ 20,260
Millwall	+ 16,854	−155,877	180,601	+121,318
Oldham	+ 12,748	− 2,289	131,331	+ 9,550
Bristol Rov. ...	− 23,553	− 17,152	144,627	+ 212
Orient	− 25,288	−101,013	n/d	+ 13,000
Mansfield	− 44,221	− 12,283	92,590	− 14,520
Blackburn	− 45,674	− 60,781	175,531	+ 1,973
Luton	− 52,275	− 58,610	232,825	+120,000
Fulham	− 63,935	+ 99,655	228,063	+ 1,500
Charlton	− 75,468	+ 35,935	n/d	− 4,675
Brighton	− 85,839	−185,008	173,499	− 68,196
Blackpool	−102,687	− 4,921	n/d	− 64,755
C. Palace	−121,879	− 56,862	294,747	− 45,778
Hull	−133,591	+ 42,622	211,950	+ 35,633
Burnley	−146,871	+194,110	n/d	n/d
Cardiff	−203,767	+ 2,787	n/d	−119,798
Tottenham ...	−240,164	+ 98,419	324,540	−238,692

DIVISION III

	Profit or loss £	Previous figure £	Wage Bill £	Transfers £
Carlisle	+ 70,682	+ 7,325	134,302	+ 54,537
Oxford	+ 59,310	− 43,346	101,267	+ 66,458
Portsmouth ...	+ 48,516	−116,986	169,334	+ 22,724
Lincoln	+ 44,406	− 19,353	108,141	Nil
Preston	+ 36,616	+ 7,237	172,141	+105,000
Walsall	+ 18,110	− 14,925	60,510	− 60
Shrewsbury ...	+ 10,214	− 16,121	99,659	− 10,880
Swindon	+ 6.543	− 74,213	134,080	+ 35,000
Chesterfield ...	− 3,966	− 2,388	105,232	+ 9,375
Plymouth	− 6,418	− 501	250,121	− 3,125
Wrexham	− 7,167	+ 68,677	143,903	− 78,000
Peterborough ..	− 9,168	− 25,468	127,636	− 24,168
Gillingham ...	− 10,573	+ 33,665	89,488	− 6,189
Colchester ...	− 12,546	− 10,539	92,110	− 4,544
Rotherham ...	− 13,806	− 57,686	107,271	+ 9,750
Hereford	− 15,234	− 42,078	145,677	− 9,750
Port Vale	− 16,964	+ 17.831	72,874	− 6,293
Tranmere	− 18 203	+ 1,592	—— 95,892 ——	
Cambridge ...	− 18,456	− 28,665	83,214	− 2,166
Exeter	− 22,451	− 30,909	101,901	+ 13,500
Bradford C. ...	− 26,282	− 16,592	71,788	− 11,358
Chester	− 27,577	+ 48,008	101,396	− 31,000
Bury	− 30,339	+ 12,362	103,554	− 32,624
Sheff. Wed. ...	− 38,966	− 50.807	196,976	− 64,469

DIVISION IV

	Profit or loss £	Previous figure £	Wage Bill £	Transfers £
Southend	+26,297	+41,293	112,225	+65,200
Wimbledon	+20,657	−9,924	31,739	−200
York	+17,777	−7,130	118,769	+12,526
Reading	+8,921	−2,575	109,973	−2,963
Aldershot	+2,509	−580	82,641	−1.018
Brentford	−1,375	−11,409	71,632	−24,209
Swansea	−1,483	+15,741	76,246	−1,349
Halifax	−4,880	+3,628	61,212	+215
Northampton ...	−5,283	+44,365	97,613	+10,950
Barnsley	−5,630	−4,855	71,162	+4,250
Torquay	−7,895	−20,392	72,439	+13,141
Hartlepool	−8,384	−18,023	53,594	+800
Grimsby	−9,415	−45,107	62,047	−4,000
Stockport	−16,350	−40,870	61,365	+995
Darlington	−17,012	+319	63,521	Nil
Huddersfield ...	−19,400	−25,409	138,677	−54,130
Crewe	−22,780	−26,458	71,582	+8,705
Rochdale	−23,753	+6,607	55,959	+3,394
Southport	−26,017	−10,333	44,271	−1,000
Scunthorpe	−31,751	−16,704	72,375	−5,300
Newport	−32,591	+1,574	51,652	−9,000
Watford	−34,663	+8.543	129,443	−10,500
Doncaster	−42,967	+44,605	76,751	−8,500
Bournemouth ...	−88,588	−23,993	147,059	−3,500

N/d denotes no details.

HOW MUCH EACH CLUB IS IN THE RED

DIVISION I

	£
Chelsea	*2,155,599
Birmingham	† 541,600
Coventry	472,647
QPR	379,443
Everton	317,760
Bris. City	264,844
Norwich	243,748
West Brom.	216,638
Leicester	188,699
Middlesbro.	† 170,317
Nottm. For.	160,930
Derby	147,125
A Villa	120,693
Man. City	† 120,312
Ipswich	* 53,791
Wolves	23,962
Leeds	† 8,918
Man. Utd.	4,900
West Ham	† 4,200
Total	£5,596,126

Symbols show **1974 figures *1975 †1976

DIVISION II

	£
C. Palac e	†1,208,092
Sheff. Utd.	830,659
Brighton	* 412,522
Luton	† 406,847
Blackpool	391,707
Burnley	† 372,393
Fulham	* 349,509
Cardiff	** 344,295
Blackburn	299,935
Sunderland	† 180,515
Oldham	† 150,428
Charlton	** 150,051
Orient	† 138,435
Notts Co.	121,064
Hull	105,541
Mansfield	* 97,729
Millwall	† 96,885
Bolton	* 74,402
Bristol Rov.	† 68,480
Tottenham	* 34,495
Total	£5,833,984

**1974 figures *1975 †1976

DIVISION III

	£
Portsmouth	†588,527
Sheffield Wed	321,443
Plymouth	†240,449
Oxford	156,390
P.N.E.	132,254
Peterborough	129,447
Exeter	†108,130
Lincoln	†106,244
Walsall	*104.017
Cambridge	†92,978
Tranmere	†80,653
Port Vale	*79,170
Bradford City	**76,581
Chesterfield	†76,396
Colchester	*75,238
Swindon	†66,484
Hereford	†50,999
Wrexham	48,200
Bury	45,812
Rotherham	38,699
Gillingham	*26,906
Carlisle	†8,595
Chester	†8,164
Shrewsbury	1,769
	£2,663,545

DIVISION IV

	D
Bournemouth	† 286,424
Watford	† 184,644
Rochdale	** 172,060
Stockport	† 166,120
Barnsley	† 98,381
Southend	* 95,433
Northampton	† 88,264
Crewe	* 82,778
Scunthorpe	* 75,907
Swansea	† 73,622
Doncaster	* 67,593
Newport	** 62,006
Torquay	* 57,178
Southport	* 51,880
York	† 50,812
Reading	50,733
Hartlepool	* 47,143
Aldershot	† 38,925
Darlington	† 33,718
Brentford	† 32,903
Huddersfield	* 31,509
Halifax	* 31,469
Grimsby	† 18,678
Wimbledon	* 17,671
	£1,915,849

Over the holiday period a football magazine researched into the financial state of football in 1977, a spectator sport declining rapidly due to hooliganism. Many clubs refused to provide up to date figures for how much debt they were carrying. To grasp a very rough idea of how much those figures equate to today, multiply them by six.

The defenders were on top throughout, and although the home team did most of the pressing, there was little excitement to interest the spectators.

For Peterborough, strikers Billy McEwan and Barry Butlin each missed their opportunities to score, as did Alan Slough (three times), Jack Carmichael, Bob Doyle and Trevor Anderson, while North End created chances from Gordon Coleman (twice), Alex Bruce (four times), Sean Haslegrave, Mike Elwiss, Ricky Thomson and Danny Cameron.

The only really clear opportunity where the crowd had held its breath was towards the end of the second half, when Mick Baxter slipped in the mud, enabling Peterborough substitute Tommy Robson to race clear, bearing down on the North End goal. Tunks perceptively raced off his line, narrowed the angle to push Robson's effort wide of the post.

Robson had replaced Butlin shortly beforehand after the striker appeared to have somehow dislocated his shoulder following a tackle by Graham Cross.

The Peterborough goal arrived in the last minute from the penalty spot.

Essex referee Tony Cox had made the award after Peterborough skipper had gone down in the North End penalty area, and Slough, a recent acquisition from Fulham, gave Roy Tunks no chance to save with a powerful shot.

North End had vehemently disputed the 'gift' from the second Cox blew his whistle and pointed to the spot. Cross indicated that Turner merely fell over as he attempted to clear a loose ball.

After the game Cross stated that Turner was never going to gain possession and there was no danger for Preston at all – he just fell over.

"The penalty should never have been given," said Nobby afterwards, venting his grievance.

"These are the things that you cannot do anything about. The lads worked really hard out there to earn a point and are terribly disappointed to get

nothing from a tough game in tough conditions against a side that is unbeaten at home, and has the best defence in the division.

"We have to accept it, and get on with the preparation for the next game against Port Vale on Monday. These things even out over the season."

The North End officials insisted that the linesman flagged to the referee to say that no foul had been committed, and added that in the boardroom afterwards Peterborough manager John Barnwell, the Peterborough players and directors even admitted they were lucky to get a spot kick.

Words of consolation in a situation such as that are very easy to make.

Stiles mentions above that 'these things even out.' Perhaps whoever the 'great destiny decider in the sky' was judged that North End would just have to be patient – and wait until Peterborough's very last game of the season before matters were finally levelled out with them...

The end of the calendar year marked the halfway point of the league season. After 23 games, North End stood sixth with 27 points, just three points behind second placed Tranmere Rovers but with a game in hand. Wrexham were in pole position, with 32 points from 23 games.

Despite all the moans and groans about their away form, when put into context North End's points gained 'on the road' was only two less than leaders Wrexham's tally of 11. North End's strength was that they were resilient; a hard team to beat home or away – their tally of five defeats being the second best in the division.

As a result, they were considered serious contenders for promotion by both the local and national press.

Happy New Year!

CHAPTER 7

JANUARY

Port Vale(home) – Tranmere Rovers (away) – Plymouth Argyle (home)

After the disappointment of the Peterborough game, North End were straight back at it on Monday evening, following the New Year celebrations of the day before.

The big surprise on a wild, wet and windy evening was the size of the attendance – a hugely creditable 10,940 – Deepdale's best league crowd of the season to date, for the visit of Port Vale.

Nobby had done his best to pre-warn the home fans about the familiarity of the two clubs of late, and what this could mean in terms of getting the desired result.

"This will be our fifth meeting of the season, and the players know all about one another's abilities," he explained, adding, *"They will be a tough nut to crack."*

The team was exactly the same as the one that had gone down so controversially at Peterborough, save that Alan Spavin now replaced Stephen Doyle under the rug in the dugout:-

Tunks, McMahon, Cameron, Burns, Baxter, Cross, Coleman, Haslegrave, Thomson, Elwiss, Bruce. Substitute: Spavin.

The home fans were rewarded for braving the elements with a home win, the North End team overcoming appalling conditions and a very stubborn Vale game plan, based on giving 'nowt' away.

It was North End who applied the early pressure and the bright start brought forth close calls from Alex Bruce with a right footed shot into the side netting, and Mike Elwiss, who all but turned a Gordon Coleman centre from the right into the Vale net.

This shook the visitors into life, and following a Terry Bailey shot that went wide, Vale's free scoring former Blackburn Rovers striker Ken Beamish, saw his good effort clasped safely by North End keeper Roy Tunks.

Chances at both ends were traded, before Francis Burns tried his luck from long range – his shot drifting well wide.

One player on the pitch who was catching the eye at this point was former Northender Alan Lamb, one of the few who still looked totally in control with the ball at his feet.

The half got scrappier and scrappier, relative to the increasing strength of the wind – which was now causing the floodlight pylons to slightly sway. Control of the ball became very difficult and the arrival of driving rain only added to the difficulties.

By the start of the second half the conditions, if anything, were slightly worse. North End began well though, and Ricky Thomson – again prominent since his return to the side – was unlucky when Vale goalkeeper John Connaughton just managed to rob the young Scot in the goalmouth and in the process prevent North End from taking the lead.

A mix-up in the North End goalmouth then nearly saw the Valiants go ahead after left back Neil Griffiths had a shot blocked. The ball was picked up by Mick Cullerton who immediately crossed the ball back into the North End goalmouth from the left. Mick Baxter looked off-balance as he met the ball – his header banging against the North End crossbar before Danny Cameron hoofed the rebound away.

Following this close call, the Lilywhites retaliated and started to apply sustained pressure.

John McMahon blasted in one of his 25 yard specials that was blocked by Connaughton, an Elwiss free kick suffered the same fate and a Graham Cross shot was then turned around the post.

The crowd became livelier now despite the weather, urging the team on sensing that the Vale defences were about to be breached. A few moments after visiting captain Bill Bentley desperately intercepted a cross pass aimed for Bruce positioned just yards away from goal, the pressure finally paid off and Thomson struck gold in the 76th minute.

The goal was an absolute gem considering its construction and execution in such awful weather conditions.

Bruce started the move by neatly flicking the ball out to the right wing for Coleman to collect, move forward and swing in the most sumptuous of crosses towards the back post along the six yard line. The Vale defence hadn't had time to assume position and were chasing back as Thomson leapt forward to meet the falling ball with his outstretched right foot, skilfully steering the ball into the net.

Mobbed ferociously by his teammates, 'Thommo' was all smiles.

Lifted, North End resumed the onslaught and less than a minute later almost went two up when Bentley cleared a shot from Bruce off the Vale goal line.

The visitors couldn't resist much longer and in the 81st minute Bruce smacked in his 16th goal of the season to effectively end the contest. Thomson, having moved forward dangerously into the Vale penalty area, was tackled by midfielder Ken Beech – but the outcome couldn't have been worse for Vale as the ball spun away across the box. It was met with a powerful first time drive by Bruce which was beneath and beyond Connaughton's dive well before he hit the deck.

It was a very good win considering the prevailing conditions and Vale's record of 12 draws in their previous 16 games. It took the final holiday season tally to six points from a possible eight, and saw North End sat in fifth, just one point away from an automatic promotion place.

"It should have been seven points from eight," protested Stiles when asked about the run of four matches in a week.

"I suppose you could argue that Mick Baxter's header against our crossbar evened things up for the Peterborough penalty, but we fully deserved our win against Vale with the lads giving their all after we brought nothing back from London Road.

"Conditions were very poor, and Vale proved to be a tough side to beat, but our two goals were superb. Our lads have shown great spirit by training nearly every day in the holiday period and I am delighted with them."

North End's next game promised to be a tough encounter, away to fellow promotion contenders Tranmere Rovers, on Friday January 6th, kicking off at 7.30pm.

On the morning of the game, Stiles revealed some good news. Ricky Thomson had withdrawn his transfer request.

The 20 year old had asked for a move following the arrival of Jim Campbell from Portadown but he had won his first team place back on Boxing Day, had played well since his return to the first team and of course, scored that wonderful opening goal against Port Vale earlier in the week.

"I didn't want him to go in the first place, so I am delighted that he now wants to stay with us," said the manager. *"He played himself back into the first team by hard work and is doing well,"* he added.

Thomson's request was due to have been considered at the club's board meeting on Thursday evening and they were pleased when they learned of his change of mind.

This development left only John McMahon on the transfer list, who still hadn't signed a new contract. Stiles said he was working on this however, and couldn't fault McMahon's attitude and commitment to the North End cause.

On the Tranmere Rovers clash, assistant manager Alan Kelly said that chief scout Jimmie Scott had watched Tranmere beat Portsmouth recently, reporting back that the Birkenhead outfit were impressive.

"They are apparently playing very well, and challenging for promotion to Division Two, but then so are we.

"It is up to the lads to approach the match in the same way as they have approached others recently and to do the right things."

For the fifth consecutive time North End named the same starting eleven, the only change being on the bench where Stephen Doyle replaced Alan Spavin:-

Tunks, McMahon, Cameron, Burns, Baxter, Cross, Coleman, Haslegrave, Thomson, Elwiss, Bruce. Substitute: Doyle.

This was another of 'those games' when North End were palpably the better the team throughout but came away with nothing. The match was marred by a missile hitting a linesman after Tranmere had scored the only goal of the game, presumably from an aggrieved North End fan.

The North End domination started early at Prenton Park as efforts from Alex Bruce, Mike Elwiss and Gordon Coleman were all saved by the seemingly inspired Rovers goalkeeper Dick Johnson. He was throwing himself around like a man possessed, but tipping a John McMahon thunderbolt around the post was perhaps his greatest success in a busy opening half hour for the home defence.

Meanwhile, Roy Tunks had coped quite easily with the few shots that he had been required to save, before suddenly he was required to face a penalty.

McMahon was found guilty by referee George Flint after allegedly stopping a Clive Evans centre with his hand. Despite North End's furious protests, Flint was unmoved and booked Mick Baxter for arguing.

Russ Allen then stepped forward to take the spot kick. He wished he hadn't – for he placed it high and wide into the crowd to the jubilation of the North End players and fans.

The joy was short lived, for just a few minutes later Tranmere took the lead, once again amid controversy.

PNE FC

John McMahon's 25 yard shot is brilliantly parried away by the Tranmere 'keeper

It was striker Ronnie Moore who raced onto a through pass from midfielder Bobby Tynan to beat Tunks with a well placed shot for his 11th goal of the season.

The scenes that followed of North End protests for offside had an unsavoury ending when red flag linesman Don Bond suddenly collapsed in a heap after being struck by an object from the crowd and remained down. He was in no shape to continue, and there was then a five minute delay while a replacement was found to run the line.

The referee confirmed at half time that the incident would be reported to the FA.

The second half commenced and North End were once more enjoying the lion's share of possession. Mick Baxter soared above the home defence but headed over, Johnson pulled off yet another miracle save to deny a Ricky Thomson header and then ran off his line to block a Bruce shot.

As the game wore on and in search of the leveler North End threw men forward and thus were taking risks by leaving gaps at the back; Tunks, all alone having to charge off his line to hoof the ball upfield at one point as

WEEKEND

Leisure and Football POST

Lancashire Evening Post

No. 28,245 SATURDAY JANUARY 7 1978 8p

INSIDE

SPOT KICK KING !

Phil Neal reveals his recipe for success. PAGE 3

The goalkeeper who can't get in from the cold *See page 2*

PLUS

Travel Desk in Brussels AND PRIZES WITH JUNIOR POST

F.A. CUP SPECIAL Page 10

Rovers late win, Blackpool crash

United scrape draw, Liverpool out

SIMPLY NO LUCK FOR NORTH END

Last night's football

By NORMAN SHAKESHAFT

PRESTON were desperately unlucky when they were beaten 1-0 by Tranmere Rovers in a Third Division "four-pointer" at Preston Park last night.

The result was a big setback to North End's hopes of gaining promotion to Division Two, for Tranmere are now three points ahead of Preston, although North End still have a game in hand.

But Preston looked the better side throughout last night's match and their many fans in a crowd of 7,254, which was the best gate of the season at Preston Park, left feeling very aggrieved that they had not gained at least a point.

North End played as well as in any away game this season and seemed capable

before Tranmere were awarded a penalty when McMahon appeared to handle in stopping a left wing centre from Evans.

The North End supporters and players protested and there was a tremendous cheer when Russ Allen shot high and wide with his spot kick.

But Preston's joy was short-lived, for Tranmere got the goal they needed in the 37th minute.

Their leading scorer Ronnie Moore ran on to a through pass from

● *Sean Haslegrave beats the Tranmere goalkeeper but his shot was cleared off the line during last night's match at Preston Park. Pictures by ROY PAYNE.*

Francis starts Wigan downfall

SCOREBOARD

F.A. CUP — THIRD ROUND

B'm'gh'm	4	Wigan A.	0
Blackburn	2	Shrewsb'y	1
Blyth S	1	Enfield	0
Brighton	3	Scarboro'	0
Bristol C	4	Wrexham	4
Burnley	1	Fulham	0
Cardiff	0	Ipswich	2
Carlisle	1	Man U	1
Charlton	0	Notts C	2
Chelsea	4	Liverpool	2
Derby C	3	Southend	2
Everton	4	Aston V	1
Exeter	2	Wolves	2
Grimsby	0	S'th'pton	0
Hartlep'l	2	Crystal P	1
Hull	0	Leicester	1
Leeds U	★	Man C	★
Luton	1	Oldham	1
Mansfield	1	Plymouth	0
Midd'bro'	3	Coventry	0
Nottm F	4	Swindon	1
Orient	1	Norwich	1
Peterboro	1	N'castle	1
QPR	4	Wealdst'e	0
Roth'ham	1	Millwall	1
Sheff U	0	Arsenal	5
Stoke	4	Tilbury	0
Sund'land	0	Bristol R	1
Tott'ham	2	Bolton	2
Walsall	4	Swansea	1
WBA	4	Blackpool	1
West Ham	1	Watford	0

DIVISION THREE

Bradf'd C	1	C'lchester	2
Bury	L	C'mb'ge	L
Gill'gham	4	Hereford	0
Port Vale	2	Portsm'th	0
Tranmere	1	Preston	0

DIVISION FOUR

Barnsley	2	Darl'gton	1
Crewe	1	Scunth'pe	1
Doncaster	P	Swansea	P
Hudd'f'ld	3	Rochdale	1
Reading	0	B'nem'th	0
Southport	0	Torquay	0
Stockport	2	Aldershot	1
Wimb'd'n	1	Brentford	1
York	2	Newport	0

RUGBY LEAGUE

FIRST DIVISION

Wigan 18 B North'n 7

RUGBY UNION

REPRESENTATIVE MATCH

England ★ The Rest ★

LANCS JUNIOR CUP

Gt Harw'd v Bacup (Continued)

danger approached.

More bad luck tormented North End as a brutal shot from Elwiss crashed into the post before being kicked out of play for a corner.

Haslegrave then shaved the bar with a curling shot before a fantastic grandstand finish took place with goalmouth incidents at both ends. The game ended with arms and legs going in all directions in front of the Tranmere goal as Rovers fought desperately to keep North End at bay.

The equaliser never did come, but it wasn't for the want of trying or creating. North End were just unlucky, especially when details of why the team went berserk over Moore's goal emerged. The inside word was that they thought the striker was at least two yards offside.

The episode involving the linesman followed this incident, the projectile appearing to have been thrown from a part of the stadium occupied by Preston fans. A bottle, beer can and various other objects had been collected from the area around where the linesman fell and the referee left the ground describing the fans who were involved as 'animals'.

North End chairman Alan Jones was quick to issue a statement just after the game had concluded, stating that the club deplored incidents of this kind wherever they happened.

Nobby Stiles on the other hand said he was sick for the North End players and the fans about the defeat at Tranmere.

"But the team's attitude was right and the players couldn't have done more. Chances were missed, but I have to give my lads credit for creating so many and they will start to go in.

"It was a harsh decision when the Tranmere goal was not ruled offside, but we have to accept these things and we must bounce back. Luck has gone against us recently, but there is still a long way to go until the end of the season.

"Jack Charlton was in the stands watching, and he has told me we were much the better team."

Alan Kelly said, "Possibly the Tranmere goal should have been ruled offside, but we had enough chances to win. We were unlucky on some occasions, but didn't put some other good opportunities away as we should have done.

"Considering they were at home, Tranmere played with nine men back relying on breaks by their two forwards with passes supplied by Tynan. Their goalkeeper also played well, but I fancy us to finish above Tranmere at the end of the season.

"We have nothing to be ashamed of after attacking so much in an away game, and now it's up to the lads to pick themselves up."

On the eve of the home fixture against Plymouth Argyle, Stiles announced that Stephen Doyle, Alan Spavin, John Smith and Mick Robinson would be added to the 11 players who took the field at Tranmere, to form a 15 man squad. He also made a pledge to the fans.

"Despite the recent bad luck, the lads won't be feeling sorry for themselves when it's time to kick-off," said Stiles.

"We were terribly unfortunate at Peterborough and Tranmere after playing very well. I have nothing but praise for the way we have played recently, and if we carry it on the breaks will start to fall our way.

"The crowd can help us and I'm hoping that our fans will give us plenty of support tomorrow, because the players really respond to this."

As most of the fans expected, Nobby started with the same 11 for the sixth league game on the bounce, also retaining Doyle as substitute:-

Tunks, McMahon, Cameron, Burns, Baxter, Cross, Coleman, Haslegrave, Thomson, Elwiss, Bruce. Substitute: Doyle.

After the rotten luck at Tranmere, North End turned in the type of entertaining display that their loyal fans always secretly wished for after clanking through one of the old iron turnstiles that were dotted around the Deepdale ground.

Goals, good football, a North End win. Is there anything better? Even now, 43 years later, the hopes are just the same for succeeding generations gliding electronically into Deepdale.

A grey, grim, drizzly sky and a soft surface greeted the teams as they ran out of the tunnel for the five minute kick-in that proceeded games back then.

North End decided to kick towards the Kop, and early sparring saw both goalkeepers save easily, enabling them to get a feel of the ball.

After a couple of attacks and free kicks each, Plymouth went ahead in the ninth minute with a quickly executed but simple move that caught out North End completely.

Following a swift interchange of passes down North End's right that removed John McMahon from any defensive equation, Argyle left back John Uzzell raced clear and delivered a cross of pinpoint accuracy that was met square on by the visitors leaping centre half George Foster. Roy Tunks was left helpless as the ball flew into the roof of the net.

The back slapping and smiles amongst the Plymouth team trotting back for the restart were mirrored by the near silence and footwear observation of the North End faithful.

There was hope however, as North End retaliated immediately from the kick-off.

A flurry of close calls for Plymouth keeper, Paul Barron was crowned when the lively Gordon Coleman cut infield and slammed a humdinger of a shot against the base of the post – then, as always seemed the case for North End – the ball was desperately hooked clear.

The Lilywhites were not to be denied however, and by the 15th minute had achieved parity.

Following Barron's punch to clear a shot from Coleman, the ball travelled out towards the left edge of the penalty area into the path of the loitering Mick Baxter, avoiding the crowded goalmouth. The ball sat up perfectly for the centre half as his boot arced through it; the resultant low, rising drive comparable to a naval torpedo launch. It found the onion bag without any problem whatsoever, and North End, now level, had the impetus.

Back they came, kicking at the 'Pilgrims' door. A shot from Ricky Thomson was well saved by Barron before Alex Bruce threaded a cross into the goalmouth which caused real anxiety for the visiting defence before the scoring opportunity eventually passed. However, the breakthrough wasn't long in coming.

Mike Elwiss had been busy, tormenting both visiting full backs and once again skipped past Argyle right back Kevin Smart before launching a curling left footed cross into the Argyle goalmouth. Coleman was only too pleased to race in towards this perfectly placed ball and head past Barron from close range.

Now it was the home crowd who were cheering, with the Plymouth team looking at their feet as they slumped into place for the resumption. They had hardly been in the North End half since taking the early lead.

The home crowd were certainly driving their team on from the side lines, just as Stiles had requested before the game. The ball was still exclusively in the Plymouth half, and North End were working very hard.

As the clock ticked around to the half hour mark, North End increased their lead through Thomson.

An attempted one-two in the penalty area between Coleman and Bruce went awry but fortunately the ball broke to Thomson positioned in the inside left position. The young striker proceeded to coolly drive the ball into the back of the net for his second goal of the season.

The pattern of the half continued, and Bruce was unlucky when his powerful shot was blocked following a weaving run close to the left by-line.

The North End defence, basically redundant since the ninth minute, then

1

1 Mick Baxter equalises
2 Gordon Coleman heads home the second
3 Alex Bruce celebrates the fourth with the fans
4 Mike Elwiss smashes in the fifth

PNE FC

2

3

4

suffered a body blow as Graham Cross was visibly limping badly and making signals to home dug out. He was pulled off immediately; Stephen Doyle rushing on to partner Baxter in the middle of the home defence.

The murmurs in the crowd suggested that it looked as though his Cross's recently repaired calf muscle had gone again... this would be an awful blow for North End as they always looked safest with Cross and Baxter playing alongside each other.

The enforced change certainly affected North End's rhythm for the remaining seven minutes of the half, but with no further goals were added or conceded, the Lilywhites went in for a brew 3-1 in the lead.

North End continued to look a little 'clunky' in the early period of the second half, and Plymouth began to move downfield with a little more confidence. It was all pretty even until, with just 20 minutes to go, Doyle couldn't recover his position quickly enough and pulled back Argyle striker Brian Johnson's shirt as he made his way through the North End penalty area. The referee had no hesitation in pointing to the spot.

Johnson took the penalty himself, whacking in a well placed shot that gave Tunks no chance. Suddenly Plymouth had hope and the North End fans had jitters. In actual fact, the narrowing of North End's lead sparked the team into an all-out assault of the Plymouth goal – and very exciting it all was too!

Sean Haslegrave tracked the North End attack that followed the kick-off and hit a tremendous shot that thudded against the right post. Francis Burns then volleyed a great effort just over the bar before Bruce shot inches wide, all within a matter of a few minutes.

Bruce wasn't to be denied however...and his goal, 10 minutes after Plymouth's second, effectively clinched the win.

A centre from Danny Cameron was headed on in the box by Thomson into the path of Bruce. His first shot was blocked by Barron, he followed in and the desperately flailing Barron again got in the way of the ball. There was no third time lucky – for Barron that is – as Bruce advanced again to finally smash the ball into the bottom left corner of the Town End net to notch his 17th goal of the season.

The excitement had hardly died down when just two minutes later, Elwiss was on hand to net North End's fifth goal and his 12th of the season.

Attacking down the right Bruce centred, Thomson leapt to meet the ball and registered North End's third woodwork hit of the game as the ball struck the post before rebounding into the Argyle goalmouth. Elwiss was quickest off the mark, and drilled the ball low into the net before Barron or the defence could regain position.

The match ended to loud applause for an excellent win that consolidated North End's fifth place standing in the table with 31 points.

Nobby was a happy man.

"I'm delighted that we scored five and with the manner of the victory. Gordon Coleman played very well and I'm happy to see him getting into scoring positions – but everyone did well.

"People were saying after the Tranmere defeat that I would need to motivate the lads, but they don't need motivating. They have given everything for me in every game – I can't ask for anything more. They all worked hard throughout the match and never let up at any stage.

"They all went about their task in the right way, but the game is already history, we must forget about it and prepare for the next match at Hillsborough."

On the subject of the injury to Graham Cross, there was seemingly encouraging news.

"We took him off the pitch as soon as we saw him struggling to avoid making things worse. The problem is at the base of the calf that gave Graham the layoff recently, but isn't a recurrence of the same trouble.

"He will have treatment again at Leicester City during the week and I will assess the position with him on Thursday."

WEEKEND

Leisure and Football POST

Lancashire Evening Post

No. 28,251 SATURDAY JANUARY 14 1978 8p

INSIDE

Hurst of England stays ahead of the pack — SEE PAGE 2

COULD PRESTON COPE WITH BIG TIME SOCCER? See page 4

PLUS

BECOME A PINBALL WIZARD with JUNIOR POST

Blackpool's big win; Blackburn point—p10

• Mike Elwiss manages to keep control of the ball despite this sliding tackle from a Plymouth defender, at Deepdale today.

GOALS GALORE! PNE HAMMER PLYMOUTH

PRESTON thrashed Plymouth Argyle 5-2 in front of a crowd of 7,065 at Deepdale today to keep in touch with the Third Division leaders.

George Foster gave the visitors an early lead but Mick Baxter, Gordon Coleman and Ricky Thomson scored for Preston to make it 3-1 at half time.

Brian Johnson put Plymouth back in the game

By NORMAN SHAKESHAFT

SCOREBOARD

DIVISION ONE

Arsenal	3	Wolves	1
B'm'gh'm	2	Leeds U	3
Bristol C	0	Leicester	0
Coventry	5	Chelsea	1
Derby C	0	Nottm F	0
Everton	1	Aston V	0
Ipswich	1	Man U	2
Man C	3	West Ham	2
N'wcastle	2	Midd'bro'	4
QPR	2	Norwich	1
WBA	0	Liverpool	1

DIVISION TWO

Blackpool	5	Charlton	1
Burnley	1	Stoke	0
Cardiff	1	Blackburn	1
Fulham	1	Bristol R	1
Hull	1	Crystal P	0
Luton	0	Oldham	1
Mansfield	1	S'th'pton	2
Millwall	0	Brighton	1
Notts C	3	Tott'ham	3
Orient	2	Sund'land	2
Sheff U	1	Bolton	5

DIVISION THREE

C'mb'ge	4	Bradf'd C	1
Carlisle	2	Tranmere	2
C'lchester	1	Gill'gham	1
Chest'f'ld	★	Port Vale	★
Exeter	1	Walsall	1
Hereford	2	Chester	2
Lincoln	0	Bury	0
Portsm'th	2	Peterboro	2
Preston	5	Plymouth	2

DIVISION FOUR

Aldershot	1	York	1
B'nem'th	1	Crewe	0
Darl'gton	1	Grimsby	2
Halifax	1	Wimb'd'n	2
Newport	★	Doncaster	★
N'th'pt'n	2	Brentford	2
Rochdale	1	Barnsley	1
Scunth'pe	★	Southport	★
Southend	0	Reading	2
Swansea	1	Hudd'f'ld	0

SCOTTISH F.A. CUP (SECOND ROUND REPLAY)

C'd'nb'th	5	Peterhead	0

SCOTTISH PREMIER DIVISION

Aberdeen	2	Celtic	1
Clydeb'k	P	Dundee U	P
Moth'well	3	Ayr	0
Partick T	P	Hibernian	P
St Mirren	0	Rangers	2

SCOTTISH DIVISION ONE

Airdrie	P	D'barton	P
Dundee	6	Alloa	0
Hearts	1	Qu'n of S	0
Kilm'nock	1	Hamilton	1
Montrose	2	East Fife	0
Morton	2	Stirling A	0
St J'nst'ne	P	Arbroath	P

SCOTTISH DIVISION TWO

D'f'mline	P	Brechin C	P
E Stirling	1	Albion R	0
Falkirk	P	Stranraer	P
M'd'wb'k	2	S'h'smuir	3
Raith	7	Berwick	1

RUGBY LEAGUE FIRST DIVISION

Leeds	22	W'hingt'n	4
Castlef'd	21	Hull KR	21

L — Late-Kick-Off
★ — Result Delayed
P — Postponed

There was more good news for the North End fans on the following Tuesday.

It was reported that John McMahon had finally signed a contract with the club after asking for a transfer in the close season.

The player's change of heart followed long discussions with chairman Alan Jones and manager Nobby Stiles.

Gillingham and North American Soccer League club Portland Timbers had been willing to meet the board's initial asking price of £20,000 for the right back and former captain, but the player was disinclined to join either club. Chesterfield had then 'phoned in a bid that didn't come anywhere near the board's latterly reduced valuation of £10,000 – this for a player who was selected in the Division Three 'PFA Team of the Year' for the previous season!

Stiles said that McMahon had been tremendous since his return to the first team following fellow defender Harry Wilson's car accident, and had gone about everything with the right attitude considering his contract problem had not been settled.

"I'm delighted. John has put in some fine performances for us this season in the campaign for promotion to Division Two."

For his part, McMahon said he was happy to have finally signed, and that he was glad the dispute was finally over.

So were the fans!

Friday's team news for the trip to Hillsborough to take on Sheffield Wednesday – now managed by Jack Charlton – was encouraging.

Stiles was in a position to name Graham Cross in a squad of 14 following a full week of treatment at Leicester City. There was a rider to this however – Cross would only play if he came through a pre match fitness test with flying colours. Stephen Doyle, Alan Spavin and Steve Uzelac were added to the players who started against Plymouth.

"Jack has got them much more organised than when we beat them 2-1 at Deepdale on October 4th," said Stiles.

He added, *"They aren't playing as much attacking football but have key players such as Tommy Tynan and Roger Wylde who work very hard. We will have to play well against them and approach the match in the right way.*

"Their win the other night over Exeter City has raised them from rock bottom to sixth from bottom, which will have certainly lifted some of the pressure off them. But if we play as well as we can, we have every chance of winning."

As it happened, North End's fixture at Hillsborough was called off on Saturday morning, due to the presence of ice all over the pitch, so the fact that Cross had failed his fitness test wasn't actually an issue.

Although nobody realised it at the time, the nation was on the cusp of a long spell of wintry weather that would see hundreds of games wiped out over the coming weeks. In North End's case, the Plymouth game just played on January 14th would be their last league outing until February 4th, when they hosted Carlisle United.

In all, North End would endure three blank Saturdays over the next six weeks, their league programme finally back on track by the beginning of March. On this particular weekend, the Pools Panel was just one game away from being asked to fill in the coupon blanks, but they would have plenty of predictions to make over the following month.

Following the games that were played over the weekend in Division Three, North End remained in fifth spot but had fallen a little further behind leaders Tranmere and second placed Gillingham who both won their fixtures.

Although the *Football Post* of January 21st was without a North End match report to enjoy and then generally disagree with, the edition did carry an overview of North End's financial statement which was issued during the previous week.

Historically, these statements were depressing bulletins for the average North End fan, generally relating just how much deeper the club was sinking into the mire, lovingly embroidered with how a player or two would have to be sold to make ends meet. However, this year the report began with some positive news.

The club lottery launched in late November was apparently proving to be an inspired move. Previously, the club had a weekly bingo draw and the Golden Goal competition in place, which didn't raise a vast amount of income over the season. After the three lottery draws to date, a very useful total of £9,000 had been raised for the insatiable North End coffers – an equivalent total today of £55,000 or just over £18,000 for each event.

Then came the rest of the report. The club was sinking deeper in the mire and, surprise, surprise a player or two may have to be sold.

Even taking into account the transfers of Mark Lawrenson and Gary Williams to Brighton during the close season, the club had budgeted at the outset of the financial year for a loss of £40,000 – today's value £245,000 – based on a home attendance average of 7,000. This average had been achieved, but Sean Haslegrave had been signed from Nottingham Forest for £22,000 and Jim Campbell from Portadown for £4,000. Alan Spavin had also returned – for free – but all three were obviously drawing a wage.

This was estimated to increase the anticipated loss from £40,000 to £75,000 over the year.

Before any lottery dent could be made in those figures, even more deficit needed to be added. The Golden Goal and Bingo competitions – both dumped in favour of the new lottery – brought in a combined £10,000 per season in ticket sales, so the anticipated loss figure was actually £85,000 – an eye watering £519,000 in today's money.

If the rough level of £3,000 profit per lottery draw could be maintained this would take the club back to where they started the financial year –

WEEKEND

Leisure and Football POST

Lancashire Evening Post

No. 28,257 SATURDAY JANUARY 21 1978 8p

INSIDE

The Man behind Arsenal's climb back — See Page 2

P.N.E. FINANCIAL REPORT
By Norman Shakeshaft - see page 4

PLUS

THE FUN LOVING STAR OF WINGS

TRAVEL DESK IN UNSPOILT ITALY

No joy for Beaumont

BILL BEAUMONT — disappointment.

● Peter Morris shoots from the penalty spot to open the scoring for PNE Reserves against Blackburn Rovers Reserves at Deepdale today. Report — page 5

Match off is big blow to disappointed PNE boss

By NORMAN SHAKESHAFT

PRESTON manager Nobby Stiles said today that experienced defender Graham Cross would not have been able to play in the North End team if the Third Division match against Sheffield Wednesday at Hillsborough had gone ahead.

The 31 - year old Cross, who pulled a muscle in North End's 3-2 win over Plymouth Argyle at Deepdale last week, failed a fitness test and must be considered doubtful for Preston's next League match at home to Oxford United next Saturday.

Stephen Doyle who substituted for Cross in the Plymouth game would have played at

England fade in France

SCOREBOARD

DIVISION ONE

Aston V	P	Bristol C	P
Chelsea	5	Ipswich	3
Leeds U	2	Coventry	0
Leicester	0	QPR	0
Liverpool	2	B'm'gh'm	3
Man U	4	Derby C	0
Midd'bro'	1	WBA	0
Norwich	1	Man C	3
Nottm F	2	Arsenal	0
West Ham	1	N'wcastle	0
Wolves	3	Everton	1

DIVISION TWO

Blackburn	P	Fulham	P
Bolton	1	Hull C	0
Brighton	5	Mansfield	1
Bristol R	2	Blackpool	0
Charlton	0	Luton	0
Crystal P	1	Burnley	1
Oldham	2	Orient	1
S'th'pton	3	Notts C	1
Stoke	P	Millwall	P
Sund'land	5	Sheff U	1
Tott'ham	2	Cardiff	1

SCOTTISH PREMIER DIVISION

Aberdeen	P	Partick T	P
Celtic	P	Clydeb'k	P
Dundee U	P	Moth'well	P
Hibernian	P	St Mirren	P
Rangers	P	Ayr	P

SCOTTISH DIVISION ONE

D'barton	P	Montrose	P
East Fife	P	Alloa	P
Hamilton	P	Dundee	P
Kilm'nock	1	Airdrie	1
Qu'n of S	P	Arbroath	P
St J'nst'ne	P	Morton	P
Stirling A	P	Hearts	P

SCOTTISH DIVISION TWO

Albion R	P	Forfar	P
Brechin C	P	M'd'wb'k	P
C'd'nb'th	P	E Stirling	P
Falkirk	P	Clyde	P
Qu'n's Pk	P	Raith	P
S'h'smuir	P	Berwick	P
Stranraer	0	D'f'mline	2

L — Late Kick-Off
★ — Result Delayed
P — Postponed

DIVISION THREE

Bury	★	Exeter	★
Chester	2	C'chester	1
Gill'gham	3	C'mb'ge	1
Oxford U	3	Bradf'd C	1
Peterboro	P	Chest'f'ld	P
Plymouth	0	Carlisle	1
Portsm'th	1	Swindon	2
Sheff W	P	Preston	P
Shrewsb'y	0	Lincoln	1

DIVISION FOUR

Barnsley	P	Swansea	P
B'mem'th	1	Scunth'pe	1
Crewe	P	Southend	P
Darl'gton	P	Rochdale	P
Doncaster	P	Aldershot	P
Grimsby	0	Stockport	0
Hartlep'l	P	Southport	P
Hudd'f'ld	2	Newport	0
N'th'pt'n	P	Halifax	P
Reading	P	Brentford	P
Wimb'd'n	0	Torquay	1

NORTHERN PREMIER

GREENALL'S PREMIER CUP Third Round

Lancaster 0 Boston U 2

RUGBY UNION

INTERNATIONAL

Ireland 12 Scotland 9
at Dublin

JOHN PLAYER CUP
(FIRST ROUND)

Coventry ★ Wilmslow ★

RUGBY UNION

estimated to lose £40,000.

To further complicate matters, the club still hadn't collected all the money from Brighton for Lawrenson and Williams, and incredibly while this situation continued North End were paying interest on their outstanding debts!

This was an era of low football attendances, particularly outside Division One. There was a general disenchantment with the game from the public largely due to the crowd trouble and hooliganism that followed it around. An average home crowd in Division Three of 7,000 was therefore pretty good going.

The statement calculated that for every extra 1,000 through the turnstiles over a season, a further £15,000 would be generated to soothe the strain on the club's bank balance. If the average crowd was raised to 11,000 break-even point would be achieved, 'and no players would have to be sold.'

I wonder, like many others who followed the club back then and over the decades since, just what would have happened if the directors had been brave enough to take the other step available to them – namely keep the best players, increase the chances of promotion and consequently increase the crowd rather than continually sell the best players, lowering the standard of play and of course, the attendances. Just saying!

The other news of the weekend concerned Alan Kelly.

Whilst assistant manager to Nobby Stiles at Deepdale, Kelly was also assistant manager to Stiles' brother in law Johnny Giles who was in charge of the Republic of Ireland team.

Without any apparent warning, Giles had apparently walked away from the job over the weekend, and Kelly had no clue as to why.

"I haven't been able to get in touch with Johnny yet," explained Kelly. "Obviously I want to talk to him before deciding what I am going to do. I haven't signed a contract and have been appointed on a match to match basis."

Sources understood Giles had left his post over the Football Association of Ireland's (FAI) refusal to sanction his request to appoint Eamonn Dunphy and former North End player Ray Treacey as U-21 and youth coaches and, after finally locating and talking to Giles at length, Kelly lent his full support to the former Leeds United star.

"There has been a lot of trouble and Johnny has asked me not to get involved for the time being. I will see what happens, but I have always been fully behind Johnny and will continue to give him my support."

Kelly added that he was fully concentrating on his job at Deepdale until he was advised of the outcome.

He was busy preparing the reserve team for their daunting trip to Anfield later in the week. The Liverpool reserve squad was very strong and free scoring sitting level top of the Central League alongside Manchester City. That said, just a few weeks previously in the Deepdale fixture North End had lost by the odd goal in five; the winner from John Toshack only arriving in the last minute.

There was to be no close finish at Anfield, however!

The young North End team had done very well to limit the score to 2-0 in the 'Reds' favour at half time, and to 4-0 by the 80th minute.

It was then that the afterburners were turned on by a Liverpool reserve team containing amongst others, John Toshack, Jimmy Case, David Fairclough, Tommy Smith and Joey Jones, which resulted in four more home goals being banged in mercilessly during the last 10 minutes.

A final score of 8-0 was something to ponder indeed, but Kelly was phlegmatic about the situation. He was working with youngsters in the main, and certainly wasn't going to use this game as any kind of yardstick.

"It was like Dunkirk in the last ten minutes when Liverpool scored their four late goals, but losing to such a team was no disgrace. I was particularly pleased with the young apprentices, Andy McAteer and Alan

Byrom – it's important that the youngsters learn something from the match."

It should be noted too that Kelly and North End were severely handicapped by injuries to their two senior players Alan Spavin and Steve Uzelac, after having used their substitute earlier in the game.

On Friday, as North End's first team prepared for the home fixture against Oxford United at Deepdale, Nobby Stiles reported that Graham Cross was still considered doubtful despite another full week of treatment at Leicester City.

"I don't want to bring him back if he isn't fully fit, because we can't afford to be without him for a long time if he breaks down again.

"Steve Uzelac hasn't recovered from an injury he picked up at Anfield, and 'Spav' and John Smith are now carrying leg strains and I can't consider them either.

"We didn't want to miss the match at Hillsborough last week and have a long spell out of action, but if we play as well as we can, we must have a chance of beating Oxford."

Alas, another week of preparation was to be washed away by the weather.

Continuous heavy rain and sleet hammered down over Preston starting late on Friday afternoon and easing only by lunchtime on Saturday. By then, Kendal referee Keith Butcher had already called the game off, travelling down earlier in the morning at the request of the North End officials who didn't like what they saw following the biblical deluge.

Matches were called off coast-to-coast, and the Pools Panel were summoned to adjudicate once more.

The impact on North End's position in Division Three after the weekend games that did go ahead was that they remained in fifth position, but were now six points behind leaders Tranmere but with four games in hand, five points behind second placed Gillingham with two games in

WEEKEND

Leisure and Football POST

Lancashire Evening Post

No. 28,263 SATURDAY JANUARY 28 1978 8p

INSIDE

The Perfect Marriage

SEE PAGE TWO

DIRECTORS: Do they deserve bouquets or brickbats?—see page four

PLUS

Valentino

GREAT PRIZES AND THE SOUND OF '78?

F.A. CUP SPECIAL

Everton crash out as 'Boro hit form — p 10

Rovers sunk by Kitchen double

By PETER WRITE

BLACKBURN Rovers tumbled out of the FA Cup when Orient hit them with a late double salvo just when the teams seemed destined for Wednesday night replay date at Ewood Park.

With only four minutes left, leading scorer Peter Kitchen put Orient in front for the first time in the game and it was purely academic when Joe Mayo scored a third almost on time.

Orient: Jackson, Fisher, Roffey, Grealish, Hoadley, Roeder, Godfrey, Gray, Mayo, Kitchen, Bennett. Sub: Payne.

Blackburn Rovers: Butcher, Hird, Bailey, Metcalfe, Waddington, Fazackerley, Brotherston, Wood, Wagstaffe, Parkes, Taylor. Sub: Curtis.

Ref: J. Hunting (Leicester).

Hundreds of Rovers' fans had made the long trip south and once the turnstiles were open they poured into the ground and contributed to the cup-tie atmosphere.

Rovers welcomed back John Waddington and included Mick Wood in the place vacated by Keith Fear. John Curtis ... as substitute.

North End off again

PRESTON North End's Third Division match against Oxford United which was scheduled for Deepdale this afternoon, was postponed this morning after an inspection of the pitch by Kendal referee Keith Butcher (writes NORMAN SHAKESHAFT).

He declared the ground waterlogged and the Oxford squad were told of the decision when they stopped on the motorway to check about the match by telephone on their way north.

North End assistant secretary Derek Allan had arranged for Mr Butcher to travel down from Kendal earlier than originally planned after the heavy overnight and morning rain.

"We did not think there would be any danger of a postponement when we looked at the pitch yesterday, but the position changed overnight and we have had a tremendous amount of rain," said Allan.

North End have not played a first team game since beating Plymouth Argyle 5-2 at Deepdale on January 14 and have dropped further behind in their bid for promotion to Division Two as a result, with the leaders Tranmere Rovers gaining a point for a goalless draw at Colchester last night. Tranmere are six points clear of Preston, although North End have four games in hand.

Sleet, rain and Panel moves in again!

POOLS PANEL

			Pts
1	ARSENAL	WOLVES	1
2	BRIGHTON	NOTTS CO.	3
3	BRISTOL R	S'THAMPTON	1
4	CHELSEA	BURNLEY	1
5	DERBY	BIRMINGHAM	1

SCOREBOARD

F.A. CUP

FOURTH ROUND

Arsenal	2	Wolves	1
Bristol R	2	S'th'pton	0
Ipswich	4	Hartlep'l	1
Man U	1	WBA	1
Midd'bro'	3	Everton	2
N'wcastle	2	Wrexham	2
Orient	3	Blackburn	1
Walsall	1	Leicester	0
West Ham	1	QPR	1

POSTPONED

Bolton v Mansfield
Brighton v Notts Co.
Chelsea v Burnley
Derby v Birmingham
Millwall v Luton
Notts Forest v Man City
Stoke v Blyth Spartans

New FA Cup dates

NEW FA Cup dates

Tuesday

Bolton v Mansfield (7 30).
Brighton v Notts County (7 45).
Chelsea v Burnley (7 45).
Millwall v Luton (7 30).
Nottingham Forest v Manchester City (7 30).

Wednesday

Derby v Birmingham (7 30).
Stoke v Blyth Spartans (7 30).

DIVISION TWO

Cardiff	5	Sand'land	2

POSTPONED

Crystal Palace v Blackburn

DIVISION THREE

C'mb'ge	0	Chester	0
Chest'f'ld	★	Portsm'th	★
C'lchester	0	Tranmere	0
Exeter	1	Shrewsb'y	1
Hereford	1	Plymouth	3
Lincoln	3	Port Vale	0
Sheff W	3	Bury	2

POSTPONED

Bradford C v Gillingham
Carlisle v Rotherham
PNE v Oxford Utd

SCOTTISH F.A. CUP

THIRD ROUND

Arbroath	0	Moth'well	4
Berwick	2	Rangers	4
Hamilton	1	Dundee U	4
Hibernian	4	East Fife	0
M'd'wb'k	2	I'n'ss Caly	1
Qu n of S	2	Montrose	2

POSTPONED

SCOTTISH DIVISION TWO

D'f'mline	P	S'h'smuir	P
E Stirling	2	Raith	2
Falkirk	1	Clyde	0

SOUTHERN LEAGUE

Premier Division

Bath C	1	Nuneaton	1
Dartford	0	Hillingd'n	1
Granth'm	3	Bedford	2
Yeovil	1	Chelt'h'm	1

POSTPONED

L — Late Kick-Off
★ — Result Delayed
P — Postponed

hand, four points behind third placed Cambridge, with three games in hand and three points behind Wrexham in fourth place having played one match more than the Welshmen.

It was easy to see why Nobby wanted to avoid postponements. Their rivals were continuing to amass points and opening up clear water between themselves and North End. Having games in hand is one thing – winning them under pressure is entirely another.

Following the report in the Sunday People back in November, the prickly subject of other clubs rumoured to be about to bid for Mick Baxter's services had reared its ugly head again.

The updated article revealed that Wolverhampton Wanderers had now joined the previously outed Sheffield United in the 'interested' queue; North End chairman Alan Jones delivering an ambiguous knock-back when quizzed by the press.

"Mick is a very good defender and it may be that some clubs will be interested in him, but we have no desire to sell anyone," said Jones, delivering the stock answer the North End board always gave in situations such as this.

It wasn't in anyway a denial that Wolves or Sheffield United had contacted North End about Baxter, and 'having no desire to sell anyone' didn't mean they couldn't be swayed. The board had already hinted in their recent financial statement that if crowds didn't improve, a player would be sold.

This was the eternal issue the paying fans had with the club.

CHAPTER 8

FEBRUARY

Carlisle Utd(home) – Hereford United (away) – Oxford Utd (home) – Cambridge Utd (away) – Colchester United (home)

Friday, February 3rd brought the North End team news after a week of erratic, but less severe weather across Preston.

Nobby was hoping to field the same team who beat Plymouth Argyle so handsomely on January 14th – North End's previous league outing.

One 'positive' to come out of the recent postponements was that Graham Cross had enjoyed a three week recovery period without actually missing a game. He had been training with Leicester City and had contacted Stiles reporting that he was fit and ready.

"I will finally decide on the team after checking the conditions," said the manager.

There was more than a touch of caution present in the manager's words as he went on to speak about the contest itself. Nobby certainly didn't like breaks to the players routine!

His words also give away a sense of belief that his team could go all the way, and he didn't want anything to derail it.

"We need to remember why we played well three weeks ago and start all

over again. We won't let Carlisle worry us, but we hope our fans will help us if we find things difficult after having no match practice for so long.

"This is not the kind of situation anyone involved with the club is happy with.

"Players train hard all week and build up for Saturdays. They look forward to the excitement and tensions of a match, and to then to suddenly find themselves without a game isn't good for a professional.

"It's even more frustrating for us, as we had been getting our game together lately, especially since Christmas. We must work hard to make sure we don't lose what we have built up and concentrate on the good things that have been evident in our recent performances.

"We must be first to the ball, show aggression, want the ball and continue to work for each other."

Away from Deepdale, news also broke that Johnny Giles had withdrawn his resignation and been reinstated to the position of Republic of Ireland manager following long discussions with the FAI. This meant that Alan Kelly would be continuing as before as Giles' assistant.

The Deepdale pitch looked in surprisingly good condition as the spectators filtered into the ground on Saturday afternoon. There had been some overnight rain, but nothing like the deluges elsewhere in the country that had produced yet another swathe of postponements.

There were crowd disturbances between rival fans on the Town End before kick off and many police were parading up and down in front of the stand, monitoring the situation as the teams ran on to the pitch.

Stiles went with the same team that had started the previous six Division Three games:-

Tunks, McMahon, Cameron, Burns, Baxter, Cross, Coleman, Haslegrave, Thomson, Elwiss, Bruce. Substitute: Doyle.

North End kicked off towards the Town End, and from the very start Mike

Elwiss seemed determined to leave his mark on this game.

After firing in a powerful shot in the fifth minute that Carlisle United goalkeeper Trevor Swinburne did well to palm away for a corner, Elwiss never looked back. Driving forward down both wings with quick and incisive movement he repeatedly rampaged through the visitor's defence to the delight of the home crowd.

Credit: Lancashire Post

Carlisle 'keeper Swinburne denies Sean Haslegrave after a pass from Francis Burns

Surging down the right, forcing Mike McCartney into a high speed back-pedal that eventually saw the full back stumble and almost land on his back, he curled in a superb cross for Sean Haselgrave to meet and volley just wide.

A couple of minutes later saw him powering down the left flank, crossing the ball into the penalty area only to see Peter Carr clear desperately before it reached Alex Bruce.

It was all North End in the opening 15 minutes, and Elwiss once again caused panic in the Carlisle defence by weaving his way in from the left wing and launching a screaming shot which went inches wide of Swinburne's left post.

Swinburne was quickly off his line a few minutes later to collect the ball ahead from Haslegrave, chasing down a good through ball from Francis Burns.

All the action was at the Town End so to speak as more crowd disruption occurred with the police wading in and marching scores of fans out of the ground to, one presumed, waiting police vans.

On the half hour Carlisle finally registered an attack when Billy Rafferty put in a good effort, testing Roy Tunks for the very first time in the half with a shot from 20 yards.

There followed a short spell of Carlisle pressure, with McCartney's long shot being the only slight cause for concern, which hardly troubled the confident Tunks.

North End enjoyed one more salvo at the opposition end, but failed to take a lead into the interval when Danny Cameron shot over after the ball was spat out towards him on the edge of the box following a scramble in the Carlisle goalmouth.

More crowd trouble during half time meant more arrests, but as the second half got underway matters seemed to calm down.

Carlisle looked a different team after the break, and the game began to open up with incidents at both ends.

Elwiss drilled the ball wide following a neat through ball from Graham Cross, while at the other end, Tunks was quick to sprint out from goal and block a shot from Carlisle striker Mick Tait, following a neat pass from Phil Bonnyman.

Bruce was in the thick of the action over the next few minutes, firstly firing a 20 yard special just wide, then clearly obstructed on the edge of the visitor's penalty area, and finally appealing in vain for a penalty when he became the filling in a blatant Cumbrian sandwich.

Shortly afterwards, Carlisle won a corner which was fired low towards the penalty spot region by Jim Hamilton. Rafferty managed to swivel and get away a good low shot at the North End goal but this was blocked before it crossed the line. However, the ball then bobbled free towards Tait who prodded the ball home from close range to give the visitors a rather undeserved lead.

North End went immediately onto the offensive with captain Elwiss leading the way once again when he drove in a wonderful shot that thumped against the Carlisle post leaving goalkeeper Swinburne grasping at the cool Deepdale air.

Preston's forward thrust was leaving gaps at the back and they were nearly caught out when Rafferty burst clear; John McMahon saving North End's bacon with a great ball winning tackle.

Finally, North End made a breakthrough when they were awarded a penalty in the 67th minute, just 10 minutes after Carlisle's opener. Defender Ian McDonald made the decision easy for referee Bert Newsome when he blatantly handled to stop a centre from the magnificent Elwiss.

Up stepped Bruce, and with the minimum of fuss, the Scot drove the ball low and hard into the bottom left corner. Swinburne? He dived the other way and spent the next minute or two sweeping the mud off his front.

Level. North End now went in search of the lead.

It wasn't long in coming! Four minutes later Bruce, manoeuvring his way through the Carlisle box, was fouled by Carr as he strived to reach a centre from Gordon Coleman. Without hesitation the referee pointed to the spot, and after booking Ian McDonald for arguing, cleared the penalty area.

Up stepped Bruce (again), and with the minimum of fuss (again), he smashed the ball high into the top right corner of the net. Swinburne? He dived the other way and spent the next minute or two sweeping the mud off his front (again).

PNE FC

Left: Alex Bruce is blatantly felled inside the Carlisle box
Right: He celebrates after scoring the penalty, North End's second goal

Carlisle were unable to conjure up enough danger from their share of possession during the final 20 minutes or so, with the North End defence settling back into position after the lead had been secured. Despite a couple of long range attempts on their goal from John Lathan and Hamilton, North End were able to see out the game relatively comfortably and collect two more precious points.

Stiles said after the game that Elwiss had been *'tremendous'* against Carlisle.

"But all the lads worked very hard. Carlisle were a better team than when they beat us 3-1 in September.

"People will say we were lucky to get two penalties, but we deserved to win – and don't forget we were unlucky recently against Peterborough where the ref gave a far from clear cut penalty against us in the last minute, and at Tranmere where they beat us with what looked an offside goal."

In the lead up to the away fixture at Hereford, it was reported that John McMahon was a major doubt after straining his thigh during Tuesday's training stint.

There had been no overnight improvement, and none after completely resting the injury on Wednesday.

"We are setting off for Hereford early on Friday afternoon, so Mac has until Friday lunchtime to show some improvement.

WEEKEND

Leisure and Football POST

Lancashire Evening Post

No. 28,269 SATURDAY FEBRUARY 4 1978 8p

INSIDE

FINNEY'S FAREWELL

READ TOM'S OWN STORY IN MONDAY'S 'POST'

KELLY ON THE CUP ~ PAGE FOUR

PLUS

WIN TICKETS FOR GILBERT O'SULLIVAN IN LEISUREPOST

Four goals for 'Pool striker—see page 10

SPOT ON ALEX GIVES PNE BOTH POINTS

Pools panel meets again

By NORMAN SHAKESHAFT

TWO penalties by Alex Bruce, which brought his total of goals for the season to 19, gave Preston a 2-1 win over Carlisle United in front of 9,095 spectators at Deepdale today.

The defeat was only Carlisle's fourth in their last 19 matches and they took the lead when Mick Tait scored his ninth goal of the season after 57 minutes.

Preston deserved their success, however, and both teams played good attacking football on a pitch which cut up and became very muddy in the second half.

North End's victory has enabled the club to keep in touch with the Third division leaders and it also gave

● The ball falls behind Preston's Gordon Coleman during a Carlisle attack at Deepdale, today.

POOLS PANEL

			Pts
1	ARSENAL	ASTON VILLA	1½
2	BIRMINGHAM	MIDDLESBRO	1½
3	BRISTOL C.	NORWICH	1
4	COVENTRY	LIVERPOOL	1

SCOREBOARD

DIVISION ONE

Arsenal	0	Aston V	1
B'm'gh'm	1	Midd'bro'	2
Bristol C	3	Norwich	0
Coventry	1	Liverpool	0
Everton	2	Leicester	0
Ipswich	0	Leeds	1
Nottm F	2	Wolves	0

DIVISION TWO

Blackpool	5	Blackburn	2
Burnley	3	S'th'pton	3
Fulham	1	Tott'ham	1
Hull	1	Brighton	1
Orient	0	Charlton	0

DIVISION THREE

Chester	3	Bradf'd C	2
Oxford U	1	Gill'gham	1
Peterboro	0	Lincoln	1
Plymouth	1	C'lchester	1
Portsm'th	0	Wrexham	1
Preston	2	Carlisle	1
Tranmere	0	C'mb'ge	1

DIVISION FOUR

B'nem'th	3	Brentford	2
Darl'gton	2	Newport	1
Doncaster	1	Stockport	0
Grimsby	3	York	2
N'th'pt'n	1	Southport	0
Southend	2	Scunth'pe	0

SCOTTISH PREMIER DIVISION

Ayr	0	Dundee U	1
Moth'well	0	Aberdeen	0
Rangers	1	Clydeb'k	0
St Mirren	1	Partick T	1

SCOTTISH DIVISION ONE

Arbroath	1	East Fife	0
D'barton	2	St J'ns'ne	1
Hearts	1	Hamilton	0

SCOTTISH DIVISION TWO

Berwick	3	Albion	3
M'd'wb'k	1	Clyde	1
S'h'smuir	1	C'd'n'h	4
Stranraer	1	Brechin	1

L — Late Kick-Off
R — Result Delayed
P — Postponed

LANCASHIRE COMBINATION

"If he isn't fit enough to be included, Stephen Doyle is the obvious man to come into the team. I have three alternatives – Steve could play in Mac's place at right back as he reads the game well and has good positional sense. I could even put Gordon Coleman at right back and play Steve in Gordon's midfield spot or move Frannie Burns to left back, switch Danny Cameron to right back and let Steve have Frannie's midfield position."

In the event, McMahon travelled down with the squad on Friday after having shown some improvement, but Stiles wasn't happy enough with the crucial Saturday morning fitness test and he was left out of the 12.

Nobby went for option two in his list of 'Doyle scenarios' – moving Coleman to full back, and plugging the subsequent midfield gap with the Welshman.

There was some doubt during the morning as to whether the game would actually go ahead, with Stiles voicing his concerns about the hardness of the icy pitch. It was agreed that the best thing to do was wait a few hours and see if the bright sunshine softened the surface sufficiently to allow the match to start. A 1pm final inspection was approved by all parties.

"At 10 am when we arrived at Edgar Street, I would have said play was impossible. However, by 1pm the pitch had thawed out somewhat to the extent it was taking a short stud. It was agreed by all that the match should go ahead," said Stiles.

What Nobby didn't bargain for was a sudden and significant temperature drop after half time which started to revert the pitch back to an icy solid surface. The game was completed however, and considering everything a point gained from an outing such as this was fair enough.

Mick Robinson was drafted in to replace Doyle on the bench. The North End team lined up:-

Tunks, Coleman, Cameron, Burns, Baxter, Cross, Doyle, Haslegrave, Thomson, Elwiss, Bruce. Substitute: Robinson.

North End, resplendent in an alternative strip of yellow shirts, white shorts and yellow socks were forced back during the early exchanges.

Steve Crompton looked lively for the home team as they strove to make an early impression, heading wide from a left wing cross. The midfielder then popped up again shortly afterwards seeing his first time shot blocked by Mick Baxter following good approach work by Peter Spiring.

North End's first real sortie forward resulted in a fruitless flag kick following good work by Alex Bruce and Mike Elwiss, but the game soon settled into a cautious mode, with neither team displaying any real ascendency.

It quickly snapped back into life a few minutes later however when Roy Tunks was called upon to make two saves in quick succession, the first a header by John Layton and then a Spiring shot two minutes later after a good run by winger Kenny Stephens.

North End gradually saw more of the ball, with Francis Burns notably displaying an excellent touch in midfield on such a difficult surface. Indeed, it was a superbly weighted pass from Burns that sent Sean Haslegrave into space but his shot went wide.

A couple of North End centres from wide were caught cleanly by Hereford keeper, Peter Mellor before Spiring was once again moved forward, manufacturing time and space for himself before slinging over a cross for Crompton that Tunks cut out with ease and authority.

Bruce then made an eager run forward, beating one defender with ease before slamming a shot in towards goal that cannoned off Layton to safety.

Hereford's big new stand was now casting a shadow that covered well over half the pitch, and looked to be causing some concern for the players.

North End returned for the second half with a spring in their step and looked the likelier of the two teams.

Elwiss thundered up the right then cut infield but disappointingly saw his centre hit the side netting as he lost his footing at the vital moment. Burns stepped forward and drilled a low shot wide of the post before Ricky Thomson breezed past a defender on the left and fired in a great shot which Mellor saved well, low to his left.

There was nearly an embarrassing incident in the North End penalty area when Danny Cameron appeared to overhit a back pass to Tunks, but the keeper brilliantly recovered the situation with a diving save.

The North End goal mouth was now completely shaded and fingers were crossed that this wouldn't hinder Tunks in any way. A right wing free kick was awarded to Hereford and the Preston 'keeper managed to pull off a good save from the Stuart Cornes header that followed.

Spiring moved forward, bearing down on the North End penalty area once again. He almost found a way through, beaten only by the number of North End players hurtling back to assist in relieving him of the ball.

The referee then booked Elwiss at the other end of the pitch for what appeared to be obstructing the goalkeeper. The Preston skipper, already on 16 penalty points for the season would now face a nervous wait to see if he would be facing a two or three match ban if his points total went above 20.

Stephen Doyle then went down injured following a collision; the cold water treatment from trainer Harry Hubbick soon seeing him back on his feet.

As the game drew to a close it was 'the Bulls' who were producing the half chances.

There was a real scare for North End when Baxter shanked the ball over his own bar via a rather carefree swing of his boot while attempting to break up a late Hereford attack. The resulting corner was swung in menacingly but Tunks rose commandingly to fist the ball far away from the North End goalmouth.

WEEKEND

Leisure and Football POST

Lancashire Evening Post

No. 28,275 SATURDAY FEBRUARY 11 1978 8p

INSIDE

CAN PNE HOLD ON TO THEIR STARS?

Read Norman Shakesfaft and Nobby Stiles PAGE FOUR

PLUS

STAR WARS MUSIC TO BE WON

and The lovely songs of Chris de Burgh

MICK WALSH — on target for Blackpool at White Hart Lane.

Blackpool grab point, Rovers win—p 10

● Milija Aleksic the Luton goalkeeper, punches clear a centre from Taylor in the match at Ewood this afternoon

PNE HOLD HEREFORD TO DESERVED DRAW

PRESTON North End and Hereford United finally settled for the safety of a goalless draw on a rock hard pitch at the Edgar Street ground today.

By NORMAN SHAKESHAFT

Preston — Tunks, Coleman, Cameron, Burns, Baxter, Elwiss, Doyle, Haslegrave, Thomson, Elwiss, Bruce, Robinson.

Ref: M. R. Baker (Wolverhampton).

POOLS PANEL

			Pts
1	ASTON VILLA	NOTT'M F	1½
2	CHELSEA	MAN. UTD	3
3	LEEDS	DERBY	1
4	LEICESTER	ARSENAL	3
5	LIVERPOOL	IPSWICH	1

SCOREBOARD

DIVISION ONE

Chelsea	2	Man U	2
Leicester	1	Arsenal	1
Man C	2	QPR	1
West Ham	1	Bristol C	2

POSTPONED

DIVISION TWO

Blackburn	2	Luton	0
Brighton	2	Burnley	1
Bristol R	2	Orient	1
Charlton	2	Oldham	2
Crystal P	1	Sheff Utd	0
Mansfield	2	Cardiff	2
S'th'pton	2	Millwall	3
Tott'ham	2	Blackpool	2

POSTPONED

DIVISION THREE

C'mb'ge	3	Plymouth	0
Exeter	1	Peterboro	0
Hereford	0	Preston	0
Lincoln	1	Portsm'th	0
Oxford U	0	Carlisle	0
Sheff W	3	Port Vale	1
Walsall	3	Shrewsb'y	0
Wrexham	1	Chest'f'ld	1

POSTPONED

DIVISION FOUR

Newport	★	Rochdale	★
Watford	0	Barnsley	0
Wimb'd'n	0	Scunth'pe	0

POSTPONED

RUGBY LEAGUE CUP

(FIRST ROUND)

Leeds 25 Halifax 5

POSTPONED

LANCASHIRE COMBINATION

POSTPONED

RUGBY UNION

POSTPONED

NORTHERN PREMIER LEAGUE

POSTPONED

CENTRAL LEAGUE

Everton 1 Preston 1

Incredibly, there was still time for a similar event – this time in the Hereford penalty area. Kevin Sheedy sliced a loose ball 10 yards away from the goal line that looked bound for the back of the net until Mellor flung himself across the face of his goal to pull off an excellent save.

Obviously, the surface was now starting to play tricks and it was a relief for all the players when the final whistle was blown.

A goalless draw but there was a clear winner – the pitch.

After the match, Stiles revealed that he was pleased to come away with a point.

"The conditions made it very difficult to play football, but Francis Burns and Sean Haslegrave did well for us.

"Everyone worked hard and it was great to get such a good result in the circumstances. These kind of away games are much harder than some of the more glamorous matches."

On the subject of a potential ban for skipper Mike Elwiss, the manager added, *"I thought the booking was harsh, and if Mike is banned it will be a big blow to us. I protested to (referee) Mr Baker at the end of the match but he insisted the booking was justified."*

Elwiss claimed that he stood a yard in front of Hereford keeper Peter Mellor when Mellor was about to clear the ball and that Mellor moved towards him.

The big question was just how many points would be recommended in Mr Baker's report to the FA Disciplinary Committee. Anything under four points and Elwiss was free to continue playing, four points or above meant an automatic ban of two or three games, largely dependent on how frequent a visitor Elwiss was to visit the gentleman of the committee. Fingers – everything – were crossed over the next few days.

The crystal clear cold weather that had made the Hereford pitch so difficult to play on now settled over the country for well over a week. Yes, it was more preferable than the constant heavy rain, sleet and snow of the previous few weeks, but just as big a blow if you happened to be a football fan. As a consequence, the nights were bringing repeated severe frosts, and the ground was getting harder and harder everywhere.

Thursday brought the much hoped for good news about Mike Elwiss.

A copy of the referee's report of the Hereford contest had been pushed through the Deepdale letterbox and it transpired that a conciliatory Mr Baker had only recommended a two point tariff for the North End captain's obstruction offence.

It was obvious that all of the North End staff had been sweating over the decision, as assistant secretary Derek Allan who, seemingly clicking his heels in the air at the news, gushed out the first statement from the club. "Everyone is over the moon that he has not got four more points and that he has been given another chance."

Elwiss himself was reported to be delighted, and so was Nobby – who also brought a touch of reality to the situation.

"I didn't think he should have been booked, but if the caution had to stand it was only right that it warranted being a two-pointer.

"I am very glad for Mike and North End's sake because the loss of such a good forward and captain would have been a big blow to our promotion hopes.

"Now Mike is going to have to keep his head in order to avoid another booking which would definitely mean an automatic suspension. The truth is he has been doing just that in the last few weeks and was terribly unlucky to be booked at Hereford."

John McMahon's thigh strain still hadn't recovered fully, and now the defender was now at home suffering from a stomach upset. Stiles was to make a decision on Friday about McMahon's fitness, and the naming of the squad for the forthcoming game against Colchester United at Deepdale.

It was a decision he never had to make.

With the Deepdale pitch resembling a miniature version of the Canadian tundra on Friday morning, and with Colchester's long journey in mind, assistant secretary Derek Allan arranged for local referee Norman Glover of Adlington to make an inspection.

Mr Glover soon pronounced the rock-hard surface 'dangerous' and Colchester were told to unload their coach and stay in Essex. The immediate weather forecast of more clear, cold weather gave no hope of a reprieve at mother nature's attempt to cover the nation with permafrost, so the rearranged home fixture with Oxford United on the following Tuesday was now becoming a doubt.

The weekend's football programme was decimated, with reports claiming it was the worst wave of postponements for 15 years.

Any hopes of a Saturday off for the North End players quickly evaporated as Nobby arranged an extra training session at Deepdale to keep the players fresh for when the thaw eventually came.

"Naturally we are all disappointed that we haven't been able to play this week, but it wouldn't have been fair to either the players or spectators.

"Last Saturday at Hereford we played on a rock hard pitch and the lads adapted well. They were all brave and they all worked hard, but games in those conditions are a lottery and it's difficult to play good football. Good teams are at a distinct disadvantage because the surface evens things out and gives inferior teams a chance of winning.

"We don't let horses race in those conditions, and we shouldn't expect footballers to turn out either."

The weather turned again on Monday, when finally the arctic conditions were moved away by an approaching warmer wet front, which duly deposited varying amounts of snow over the country as it met the departing cold air.

While Deepdale thankfully had only a thin blanket of snow covering the pitch, Bournemouth's Dean Court ground had suffered something akin to

WEEKEND

Leisure and Football POST

Lancashire Evening Post

No. 28,281 SATURDAY FEBRUARY 18 1978 8p

INSIDE

Is it worth trying to play on ICY PITCHES?

READ TOM FINNEY - P 3 ALAN KELLY - P 4

PLUS

the comeback GIRLS

AND PRIZES WITH JUNIOR POST

- Most postponements for 15 years
- Extra training session for North End

LAST GASP GOAL ROBS SPARTANS

MIGHTY minnows Blyth Spartans won a second bite of the cherry with a 1-1 draw against Third Division Wrexham at the Racecourse Ground today.

AN 11th minute goal by Kerry Johnson gave Blyth the lead against the fancied Welsh outfit. But an own goal gave Wrexham another chance.

The jubilation of the non-Leaguers was scarred by a double sending off in the 68th minute when Wrexham substitute John Lyons and Blyth's Steve Carney were both given their marching orders.

A last minute goal by Martin O'Neil gave Nottingham Forest a 1-1 draw against QPR to keep their treble hopes alive.

Thirty people were injured [illegible]

Bolton drop vital point

PETER REID — gave Bolton the lead at Oldham.

BOLTON took the lead at Oldham when a right wing centre from full back John Ritson skidded through the Oldham defence and Peter Reid lashed in a fierce shot from the edge of the penalty area.

SCOREBOARD

FA CUP

(FIFTH ROUND)

Arsenal	4	Walsall	1
Bristol R	2	Ipswich	2
Millwall	2	Notts C	1
Orient	0	Chelsea	0
QPR	1	Nottm F	1
Wrexham	1	Blyth S	1

POSTPONED

Middlesbrough v Bolton
Derby v WBA

DIVISION TWO

Fulham	P	Cardiff	P
Oldham	2	Bolton	2

POSTPONED

Burnley v Mansfield
Crystal Palace v Blackpool
Hull v Southampton
Luton v Tottenham
Sheffield Utd v Brighton
Sunderland v Stoke

RUGBY UNION

INTERNATIONAL MATCH

Wales	22	Scotland	14

(At Cardiff)

R — Result Delayed
P — Postponed
V — Void

DIVISION ONE

Bristol C	2	Man C	2
Everton	2	West Ham	1

POSTPONED

Coventry v Newcastle
Man Utd v Leeds Utd
Wolves v Aston Villa

DIVISION THREE

Plymouth	0	Bradf'd C	1

Abandoned after 61 minutes. Snow

POSTPONED

[illegible]

DIVISION FOUR

Barnsley	0	Stockport	1
Reading	2	Hartlep'l	3
Southend	5	Halifax	0
Swansea	4	Newport	0

POSTPONED

[illegible]

SCOTTISH F.A. CUP

(FOURTH ROUND)

D'barton	1	Hearts	1
Hibernian	V	Partick	V
Morton	3	M'd'wb'k	0
Rangers	1	Stirling A	0

POSTPONED

Aberdeen v St Johnstone
Celtic v Kilmarnock
Dundee Utd v Queen of Sth
Motherwell v Queens Park

SCOTTISH DIVISION ONE

POSTPONED

Alloa v Montrose
Hamilton v Dundee

SCOTTISH DIVISION TWO

POSTPONED

[illegible]

SOUTHERN LEAGUE

Premier Division

Gravesend	1	Nuneaton	1
Kettering	1	Hill'gdon	0
M'dstone	1	Yeovil	1
Wealdst'e	2	Redditch	1
Weym'th	4	Barnet	0

POSTPONED

[illegible]

NORTHERN PREMIER LEAGUE

Altrinch'm	4	Goole	0

POOLS PANEL

			Pts
1	ARSENAL	WALSALL	1
2	BRISTOL R	IPSWICH	2
3	DERBY	WEST BROM	3
4	MIDDLESBRO	BOLTON	1
5	MILLWALL	NOTTS CO.	1

Everton's bid hits icy patch

By JOHN LYON

WITH league leaders Nottingham Forest playing in the FA Cup and most other matches cancelled, Everton saw a great chance to narrow the gap at the top of Division I when they met West Ham at Goodison Park today.

Duncan McKenzie put them on the right track with a goal in the 24th minute but West Ham hit back and [illegible] put them level before half-time.

Everton should have put the skids under West Ham when they were awarded a penalty for hands in the 37th minute — but Trevor Ross shot wide.

Everton took a deserved lead in the 24th minute. The move was started by Mike Lyons and Andy King sent over a great ball from the right wing which was lashed into the back of the net by McKENZIE.

There were loud appeals for a penalty in the 27th minute when Andy King was brought down but the referee waved play on.

King looked certain to score in the 31st minute when he worked his way past a West Ham defender only for Ferguson to smother the ball.

West Ham showed signs of recovery and began to press Everton on the half hour. Wood was called into action but seemed well in control.

In the 34th minute West Ham got the goal for which they had been pressing. [illegible]

[illegible] scorer, who had a pelvic strain.

Everton pressed hard for another goal and Thomas and then McKenzie both had shots which were blocked.

In the [illegible] minute Everton should have gone into the lead when they were awarded a penalty after Frank Lampard had handled when there was no apparent danger.

[illegible] took the spot kick but pushed it three yards wide of goal — and hung his head in his hands in despair.

Everton were not downhearted and once the ball came back into play they produced tremendous pressure with McKenzie creating all sorts of problems to the [illegible] back line.

There was a heavy sprinkling of sand on the pitch and the fact that there was a game at all was a great tribute to the ground staff. The players made a memorable occasion, because the conditions were terrible. The ball was not bouncing through and at times the players had difficulty keeping their feet.

Everton took the lead in the 65th minute with a beautiful goal by DAVE THOMAS.

a blizzard. Only the top three feet of the goalposts were visible at one end of the ground, and the snow had drifted up to the 20th row of seats in one of the stands.

On Tuesday, the day of the rearranged Oxford United game, the referee arrived at Deepdale early in the morning to inspect the pitch. Despite a litany of reservations about how things may change later in the day, he deemed that as the top surface was taking a stud the pitch was playable, and decided on balance that the game could go ahead.

Unfortunately, John McMahon was still not fit enough to take part so Stiles went with the same line-up as at Hereford:-

Tunks, Coleman, Cameron, Burns, Baxter, Cross, Doyle, Haslegrave, Thomson, Elwiss, Bruce. Substitute: Robinson.

With the top inch or so of the pitch now softened and hidden under a blanket of snow, it seemed that the referee's decision to give the game the green light earlier in the day was the correct one. Technically it was, but with the ground under the soft crust still like rock, the fans were treated to a surreal event of what appeared to be learner ice skaters on Blackpool Pleasure Beach ice rink trying to play football.

It took a matter of minutes for the top of the pitch to become runny mud, but to their credit both teams battled spiritedly and, astonishingly, play some structured football in a game that could have easily gone either way.

Understandably there was a lot of 'sounding out' of the pitch early on by both teams, and play was generally cautious as the players made their way around with their first priority being to stay upright.

The first of the five goals was North End's, and considering the vigilant speed of the game so far was executed at brutal speed.

Finding clear space, Alex Bruce suddenly fired in a low cross from the right. The ball pinged off defender Brian Drysdale and rapidly towards the Oxford net whereupon goalkeeper Roy Burton brilliantly saved, desperately palming the ball forward – but only as far as a ruck of watching players. Ricky Thomson was quickest to react and he flicked the ball back into the net just inside the right hand post.

Two minutes later North End were two goals clear following a sensational strike from Alex Bruce.

PNE FC

Left: Ricky Thomson (extreme left) opens the scoring
Right: Alex Bruce brilliantly smashes home North End's second

This was the striker at his very best, controlling a chipped pass from Mike Elwiss with his left foot and before it came down blasting the volley high into the roof of the net with his right. Over and done with in just a couple of seconds, it was an incredibly spectacular goal and considering the surface it was scored on, the work of a rare talent indeed.

Oxford rallied, and having noted North End's 'mode d'emploi' drilled a few low balls of their own across Roy Tunks' goalmouth, with David Fogg and then Les Taylor going very close.

It was the much travelled stalwart centre forward, Hugh Curran who set up the visitor's opening goal when Colin Duncan raced forward to hit Curran's flicked pass hard, low and under the diving Tunks.

The second half was only a minute or two old when Oxford drew level, after utter chaos ensued in the home penalty area with the North End defence slipping and sliding in every direction.

Tunks made two failed attempts to gather the ball in safely and Graham Cross completely mishit an attempted clearance as the ball flashed about the North End penalty area as though it had been fired in by a pinball machine. The carnage came to an end when Curran, served perfectly with the ball rolling slowly towards him, crashed home a 15 yard drive into the top corner.

Players of both teams slowly got reacquainted with the vagaries of the pitch as the half wore on, and it became apparent that any ball driven low in either penalty area could create the lucky bounce that would potentially secure the points.

In the 73rd minute, the flying fickle finger of fate decreed that it would be North End who should take that vital lead.

Francis Burns moved the ball forward into the path of Stephen Doyle. He played in the required forceful forward pass into the box, where the ball took a deflection and fell directly into the path of Thomson who made no mistake from around seven yards out.

PNE FC

Ricky Thomson lashes home the winner in the 73rd minute

The last 15 minutes were very tense for the home crowd, and there was great relief at the final whistle.

North End had thus consolidated their fifth position in the league table but had also opened a handy five point gap between themselves and sixth placed Colchester United. Looking upwards, North End were three points behind leaders Gillingham, with a game in hand.

It was reported that a raft of representatives from Division One clubs watched the contest. With Newcastle United reported to be yet another club interested in Mike Elwiss – Magpies manager Bill McGarry had watched the recent match between North End and Carlisle United – the North End fans were on pins every time the LEP dropped on to their doormats.

Stiles eased any immediate need to reach for the tranquilisers saying that he had not received any offers for North End players before or after the game.

On the match itself, the North End manager was a relieved man.

"Our lads did well to win in those conditions. I give all credit to our groundsman for his work on the pitch which enabled us to get a game under our belt.

"Although it took a stud, it became very sloppy on top and was always hard underneath. It got more and more difficult but the game was very entertaining.

"We played well in the first half and we could have scored more than two goals, then Oxford improved after half time to prove what a good team they are.

"The conditions didn't suit the big men, but the lads kept going and didn't let their heads drop after Oxford equalised.

"I was going to pull Ricky Thomson off just before he hit the third goal, as I thought they were just getting on top and that our substitute Mick Robinson might be able to bring about a change, but Ricky popped up to score and ran after everything afterwards.

"I'm very pleased with him and I'm sure he will become a very good forward."

The build up for North End's next match away at high flying Cambridge began with a prediction from the club's new manager John Docherty, recently promoted from his role as coach following Ron Atkinson's departure for West Bromwich Albion in January.

"Preston are doomed to another season in Division Three. They won't go up because they can't win away from home.

"This game is virtually worth four points to the winners – it's got to be us. We've got just the right blend of youth and experience to go up and make an impact in Division Two."

This impetuous outburst brought a swift reaction from North End manager, Nobby Stiles.

"That kind of talk is water of a duck's back to me, but I'm not getting involved in a slanging match. I have every confidence in my players and it is the players who do the talking on the field. I believe that our lads are good enough to go up whether they win or lose tomorrow.

"We will treat them with respect, but will be going all out to win."

Full back John McMahon remained a doubt but was named in the squad that travelled down on Friday afternoon. Meanwhile, Cambridge's preparations had suffered a blow earlier in the day when 'Big Ron' had returned to sign their full back Brendan Batson for £30,000.

Nobby stuck with the same 12 that had played against Carlisle United and Oxford United:-

Tunks, Coleman, Cameron, Burns, Baxter, Cross, Doyle, Haslegrave, Thomson, Elwiss, Bruce. Substitute: Robinson.

This was to prove a real test for North End, who nevertheless picked up another vital point in second placed Cambridge's own backyard. It wasn't the away win that many desperately craved – another late and questionable penalty award to the home side saw to that.

The pitch was wet as the game got underway, and it was the home side who held the early upper hand.

In fact, with the game just a few minutes old, Danny Cameron was alert enough to clear off the North End line in a goalmouth scramble following a corner.

It was all Cambridge as they desperately tried to overwhelm the

Lilywhites, and despite a breakaway that led to Alex Bruce having a shot blocked, Roy Tunks was for a long time a very busy man.

Bruce thought he had scored on the half hour when he headed home a Mike Elwiss cross, but the referee was quick to rule out the effort for pushing by the North End striker. North End kept going and following a powerful run, Elwiss fired in a tremendous shot that seemed to skim the crossbar as it went out of play.

Back came the 'U's' to win a whole series of corners as North End just couldn't seem to clear their lines for a few minutes. Tunks finally plucked the ball out of the air and set North End off again.

Shots from Stephen Doyle and Ricky Thomson were saved by Malcolm Webster, the Cambridge keeper before Tom Finney (no, still not the original), tested Tunks with a header.

The half concluded with honours just about even, although Cambridge had certainly tested the resolve of North End's defence.

Sammy Morgan, a transfer target for North End during the close season almost put the home team ahead just after the restart, but his well timed header flashed just wide of the post.

North End's midfield consisted of Doyle on the right, Francis Burns in the middle and Sean Haslegrave on the left but was somehow not reliably producing the openings despite their endeavours.

After 15 minutes of the second half, North End had settled sufficiently however, and a mazy run saw Elwiss eventually win a corner.

Burns slung the corner over into the danger area, but the ball was only half cleared. Mick Baxter then failed to get a foot onto the loose ball, but Thomson managed to put in a low drive that took a glance off defender Dave Stringer taking it past Webster and into the net. The goal, despite the aid of the slight deflection was credited to the in-form Thomson.

Cambridge certainly didn't lie down and die, and North End's defence was subjected to considerable scrutiny over the next 15 minutes or so. They remained calm under this pressure and on 80 minutes, Cambridge sent on big defender Floyde Streete to replace midfielder Graham Watson.

Streete was planted up front with obvious instructions to 'get involved', and this he did when three minutes later the referee decided that Cameron's tackle in the box on the substitute was worthy of a penalty award.

Long and vociferous protests from the North End team were waved away by the referee and Alan Biley duly stepped up and drove the ball past the helpless Tunks for the equaliser.

With one point secured, both teams seemed content to play out the remaining few minutes by taking no big risks.

North End were understandably frustrated by yet another late goal ruining their away day party, but to actually not lose at Cambridge, whose home record was comparable to North End's, was no failure whatsoever.

"Once again a harsh penalty decision robbed us of another away win," lamented Nobby after the game.

"However, it was given and we just had to get on with the game. With just seven minutes to go there is always a danger that you could lose your composure completely, but the lads didn't and all credit to their professionalism.

"The manner in which we played was very pleasing and once again it was a very good all-round team performance – a feature of our play all season in my opinion."

If the North End performance did one thing, it forced a complete climbdown by Cambridge manager John Docherty, concerning his belligerent pre-match predictions about North End's promotion hopes.

Far from repeating his comments on Preston, he appeared to have undergone a rapid conversion to the North End faith.

"They were a credit to Nobby Stiles. Certainly, they were the best side

WEEKEND

Leisure and Football POST

Lancashire Evening Post

No. 28,287 SATURDAY FEBRUARY 25 1978 8p

INSIDE

THE MUNICH REPORT

Tom Finney and Nobby Stiles pass Judgement on England

- SEE PAGES THREE & FOUR

PLUS

I'm too 'omely' to be a STAR

Says Pam

plus

TWO GREAT PRIZE CONTESTS

New boy Radford scores in great Rovers victory — p 10

• Noel Brotherston beats two Oldham defenders in a Rovers attack at Ewood Park today.

Kidd's goal gives City victory

A GOAL by Brian Kidd, just ten minutes from time, gave Manchester City victory in the vital top-of-the-table battle against Everton at Maine Road today.

PNE TAKE WELL EARNED POINT

PRESTON collected a valuable point from a 1-1 draw with Cambridge United in front of 5,766 at the Abbey Stadium today.

By NORMAN SHAKESHAFT

SCOREBOARD

DIVISION ONE			
B'm'gh'm	1	Aston V	0
Leeds	2	Chelsea	0
Leicester	1	Wolves	0
Liverpool	3	Man Utd	1
Man C	1	Everton	0
Midd'bro'	3	Derby C	1
N'wcastle	0	Ipswich	1
Norwich	3	Nottm F	3
QPR	2	Bristol C	2
WBA	3	Coventry	3
West Ham	2	Arsenal	2

DIVISION TWO			
B'ckb'n R	4	Oldham	2
Brighton	2	Sund'land	1
Bristol R	2	Charlton	2
Cardiff	2	Blackpool	1
Fulham	1	Crystal P	1
Mansfield	1	Hull	0
Millwall	1	Burnley	1
Notts C	2	Luton	0
S'th'pton	2	Sheff Utd	1
Stoke	0	Bolton	0
Tott'ham	1	Orient	1

DIVISION THREE			
Brad'f'd C	3	Roth'ham	0
Bury	★	Port Vale	★
C'mb'ge	1	Preston	1
Chester	0	Tranmere	0
C'lchester	2	Carlisle	2
Exeter	P	Chest'f'ld	P
Gill'gham	1	Plymouth	1

DIVISION FOUR			
Aldershot	2	Swansea	2
Doncaster	4	Hudd'f'ld	3
Grimsby	1	Newport	0
Halifax	1	Brentford	1
Hartlep'l	1	Crewe	1
N'th'pt'n	1	Scunth'pe	2

SCOTTISH DIVISION ONE			
Arbroath	2	Morton	2
D'barton	1	Hamilton	1
Dundee	2	East Fife	0
Hearts	3	Airdrie	0
Kilm'nock	4	Alloa	0
Qu'n of S	2	St J'nst'ne	2
Stirling A	4	Montrose	2

SCOTTISH DIVISION TWO			
Albion R	4	C'd'b'th	3
Brechin C	3	E Stirling	2
D'f'mline	1	Clyde	1
Falkirk	0	Qu'n's Pk	3
Raith	4	M'd'bank	0
Stranraer	0	Berwick R	1

SCOTTISH PREMIER DIVISION			
Aberdeen	3	Hibernian	0
Ayr	0	Clydeb'k	0
Celtic	1	St Mirren	2
Moth'well	3	Rangers	5
Partick T	0	Dundee U	2

LATE NEWS

BURY 3 PORT VALE 0

I've seen at Cambridge this season. They denied us space and passed the ball better than we did. I thought they were a little unlucky to see us keep going to get that late equaliser."

There was hardly time to catch breath as North End were in action again just a few a few days later. The very last day of February saw them quickly squeezing in the rearranged fixture with Colchester United that had been called off at Deepdale just 10 days previously.

Colchester had waned a little over the previous few weeks but were still on North End's tail, and a win for them would push them back to within 3 points of the Lilywhites.

Nobby warned of a *'stern test ahead'* before the game, and with John McMahon still not fit enough to take part, the manager stuck with the same team for the fourth consecutive game.

Tunks, Coleman, Cameron, Burns, Baxter, Cross, Doyle, Haslegrave, Thomson, Elwiss, Bruce. Substitute: Robinson.

This game will long be remembered by the North End faithful of that era – and Alex Bruce! The size of the North End win doesn't really do Colchester justice; for an hour they manfully kept the scoresheet blank.

The last 30 minutes however brought forth Bruce at his best, bringing his very own brand of carnage to the match to delight the home fans.

The Deepdale pitch looked more like its usual self, and held out hope for a good game rather than those spoiled over recent weeks by the rain, sleet, frost and ice.

In the first half, the visitors looked very solid in defence, and with a quick counter attacking style they could well have been the first to score.

Eddie Rowles, the visitor's centre forward missed two golden opportunities to put his team ahead, first failing to get a shot away from a centre with North End keeper Roy Tunks stranded, and then heading the ball straight at Tunks following a flick on from winger Steve Foley.

Rowles then had a good shot saved with Ian Allinson, who would eventually play for Arsenal, regularly supplying dangerous crosses that demanded the undivided attention of the North End back line.

The Lilywhites kept plugging away however, with Bruce firing in three notable first half shots, Mike Elwiss two more, while individual efforts from Francis Burns and Gordon Coleman also registered the crowd's approval.

Colchester weren't shy when it came to stopping any North End menace dead in its tracks, with both full back Steve Wignall and Foley having to spell their names out for referee Peter Willis to enter into his book.

The interval arrived and so far, Nobby's prediction of a 'stern test' was bang on the money.

Preston were 'shooting on sight' more in the second half and Ricky Thomson was unlucky when he fired in a good shot that went just over the bar. Coleman then tried his luck, as did both Elwiss and Bruce, all placing their shots wide.

Colchester weren't as prominent in attack, but didn't look under any desperate threat either until the referee spotted that defender Steve Dowman had handled in his haste to prevent Bruce getting past full back Micky Cook and himself in the box.

Bruce strode forward, placed the ball on the penalty spot and slammed the ball into the back of the net, sending Walker the wrong way in the process.

Colchester's defence was now creaking, and they were largely penned in their own half.A Thomson pass to Elwiss around 15 minutes later began the process for North End's second goal. The Preston captain set off down the left wing and fired in a curling cross that was met by the onrushing Bruce perfectly, the ball powering into the roof of the net with Walker and his defence left stranded by the sheer speed at which the goal had been fashioned and taken.

Credit: Lancashire Post

<u>Top left</u>: Alex Bruce puts North End ahead with a penalty and <u>(top right)</u> celebrates the goal. <u>Left</u>: Bruce meets a cross from Mike Elwiss perfectly to make it 2-0 with a header.

PNE FC

<u>Above</u>: Bruce canes home North End's second penalty of the game and <u>(left)</u> celebrates his hat-trick in front of the Town End. <u>Below left</u>: Bruce connects with another Elwiss centre and volleys the ball into the roof of the Colchester net.

ALEX BRUCE'S FOUR GOAL DEMOLITION OF COLCHESTER UNITED

Three minutes later with the crowd still buzzing, Wignall fouled Thomson in the penalty area and once again the referee had no hesitation in pointing to the penalty spot, reigniting the crowd's excitement and indeed anticipation of a very rapid 18 minute hat-trick for Bruce.

The penalty was despatched like a bullet into the bottom right corner with Walker choosing the wrong way once again.

This brought the house down, as the North End fans went into delirium with Bruce saluting them behind the Town End goal.

Surely, that was it... a fantastically rapid hat trick by Bruce wraps up the points for North End!

Not a bit of it!!

With just five minutes left on the clock, another Elwiss ball swung in from the left evaded Thomson's forward lunge, but not the boot of Bruce who caught the ball on the volley crashing it into the roof of the net like he was shelling peas. Unbelievable!

Needless to say, the fans wandered home in a happy mood that night after such a sensational performance from the North End favourite.

After the game there was a lot of talk about whisky. In the hope of encouraging attacking football, a local company had promised a case of whisky for every hat-trick scored during the season and Bruce would be receiving a case to share with the 12 man squad.

There was talk too of manager Nobby Stiles being a candidate for a gallon of the hard stuff in the Bell's Manager of the Month competition, as North End had remained unbeaten in February.

Nobby was a contented man, not particularly about the whisky – but about 'his lads'.

"Bruce was magnificent, but Mike Elwiss and Ricky Thomson also played well in attack and I wasn't worried who found the net.

"Colchester made things difficult for us by playing very defensively with five men across midfield and just one up front. We kept working hard and put pressure on them after the interval.

"The first penalty was a debatable decision, but it made up for the one given against us at Cambridge last Saturday. We now have to forget all

about this win and concentrate fully on Saturday's home game against Bradford City."

DIVISION THREE

	P	W	D	L	F	A	W	D	L	F	A	Pts
Gillingham	31	9	6	1	30	14	4	8	3	24	23	40
Cambridge	32	12	3	1	37	9	4	5	7	19	31	40
Wrexham	28	9	6	0	29	14	6	3	4	16	14	39
Preston	31	13	2	1	38	15	1	9	5	6	12	39
Tranmere	32	11	2	3	30	13	3	8	5	14	14	38
Bury	30	7	8	1	27	13	4	4	6	16	22	34
Walsall	30	8	5	3	24	12	2	8	4	14	20	33
Swindon	28	9	4	1	31	12	2	6	6	17	26	32
Colchester	31	6	8	1	24	11	4	4	8	16	23	32
Peterboro	29	7	6	1	15	8	4	4	7	8	14	32
Shrewsbury	32	7	5	5	30	18	3	6	6	15	23	31
Chester	30	8	6	0	23	13	0	9	7	10	26	31
Chesterfield	28	9	3	2	21	6	3	3	8	13	21	30
Carlisle	30	6	6	2	22	16	3	6	7	17	22	30
Exeter	31	7	4	4	20	15	3	5	8	14	28	29
Oxford	32	8	6	2	25	14	1	4	11	19	34	28
Lincoln	31	5	6	5	19	18	4	4	7	14	22	28
Sheffield Wed	31	8	5	3	19	11	0	5	10	12	27	26
Port Vale	31	5	8	2	23	15	1	5	10	11	33	25
Plymouth	30	3	5	6	16	17	3	6	7	19	29	23
Rotherham	27	5	4	4	14	12	2	4	8	18	31	22
Portsmouth	32	3	9	4	23	23	1	5	10	7	29	22
Bradford	29	6	4	4	25	19	1	3	11	10	32	21
Hereford	30	5	7	3	17	15	0	4	11	4	26	21

North End now moved up into fourth spot on the back of this huge win, one point behind the joint leaders Gillingham and Cambridge United and one point clear of Tranmere, in fifth.

CHAPTER 9

MARCH

Bradford City (home) – Swindon Town (away) – Gillingham (away) – Exeter City (home) – Chester (away) – Chesterfield (home) – Bury (away)

If promotion was to be won, the improved form of February would have to be carried on throughout March. At this crucial stage of the season, the manner in which games were won didn't matter a jot to me, nor did the 'issue' of North End's away form.

It's always nice to be all-conquering and powerful both home and away, but the old reality of generally win at home and draw away has always largely produced a 'good enough' points tally to achieve advancement.

North End were standing in third position thanks to an adverse result for Wrexham that crucially affected their goal difference. In fact, they had a reasonable chance to be Division Three leaders if results went their way on Saturday, March 4th.

North End were entertaining Bradford City, while the top two, Cambridge United and Gillingham, had difficult away fixtures at Carlisle United and Rotherham United.

It always gives the fan a 'kick' when they see their team at the top of the pile, but quite rightly all that meant nothing at all to Nobby. He wouldn't be drawn into such chatter, and didn't want his players put under pressure.

"We will not talk about promotion or look too far ahead; we will just carry on fully concentrating on each game as it comes up."

There was a big decision to make in terms of selection for the management team as John McMahon was now fully fit again. Alan Kelly had given the right back a run out in the reserve team fixture at Sheffield United during the week, and after checking with him at half time that all was well, told him to get showered and changed to avoid taking any further injury risks.

The only other news was that Wrexham manager Arfon Griffiths had ultimately been named Division Three Manager of the Month. Wrexham, just behind North End in the league on goal difference, had enjoyed a strong month that had also seen them reach the FA Cup quarter finals.

Stiles eventually decided that McMahon was to return to his right back berth, moving Gordon Coleman back into midfield and Stephen Doyle to the bench.

The team was:-

Tunks, McMahon, Cameron, Burns, Baxter, Cross, Coleman, Haslegrave, Thomson, Elwiss, Bruce. Substitute: Doyle.

There were a couple of issues before kick-off. One was the matter of crowd trouble with rival fans clashing on the Town End, the other concerned the very strong wind that was blowing diagonally across the ground, from the corner of the Spion Kop and West Stand.

The Black Knights sky diving team were due to land en-masse near the centre circle as part of the pre-match entertainment, but the wind was so strong only two actually made it onto the pitch – the others drifted way past the corner of the Town End on the Lowthorpe Road side and were last seen heading in the direction of the Skeffington Road rail crossing!

On top of that it was a clear cold day and the gale was freezing. I was on the West Paddock, just to the Town End side of halfway, a place where it was easy to strike up relaxed, friendly conversations about football matters, as with no mobile phones to gaze into silently for hours on end, people used to speak to one another.

It was then that I picked up by chance a piece of knowledge (as I often did) from a random North End fan who was obviously winding up another – who I think may have been his son. There were a few other people listening in too; the comical discussion centring around the younger lad's rapidly plunging body temperature.

The older man then lapsed into a tale from days of yore about a raging gale that, legend had it, always blew before a North End player was about to pass away.

His audience of about 10 people, captivated but smiling disbelievingly, watched on as he asked the younger fan if he knew what this mysterious, freezing cold, deadly draught had come to be known as.

Before he could answer a bloke behind him shouted, "The Deadly Deepdale!" The older bloke turned and shook his head. Another said, "The Deepdale Doctor?" (which I thought very clever as there is actually a breeze called the 'Freemantle Doctor' in Western Australia). "No, no, no" said the bloke, "it's called (*pause*) 'That Bastard Wind'... and it's coming for somebody out there playing today."

By now people were in hysterics and speculating who the hell the victim could be. "Do Bradford players count?" asked one bloke. "Those sky divers looked like they may have copped it," reasoned another with a straight face nodding in the direction of where they were last spotted.

The man telling the tale then revealed that we would probably all find out tomorrow who it was, because apparently, once That Bastard Wind blows... it blows till it gets the bastard.

Duly educated, I turned away to concentrate on forthcoming matters on the pitch.

The match began with North End kicking towards the Town End. North End started the more dominant, a lovely defence splitting pass from Mike Elwiss for Gordon Coleman almost paid early dividends, but the midfielder couldn't keep the ball under control; City defender Mick Wood taking control and clearing the danger.

City hit back and Don Hutchins was unlucky with a powerful wind assisted strike that screamed just over the North End crossbar.

The 'Bantams' had settled the better of the two teams, and Hutchins was proving a handful. Another rocket shot all but put the visitors into the lead on 16 minutes, but Roy Tunks made a magnificent save, leaping high to tip the ball over the bar.

Tunks was bright and alert once again a few minutes later, running from his line to safely gather a menacing through pass by Terry Dolan with Hutchins rapidly approaching.

North End's goal attempts were sporadic at best, a Francis Burns shot was saved by City keeper Peter Downsborough, who was right behind another long range attempt by North End a few minutes later from John McMahon.

Back Bradford came, and there was a huge sigh of relief as a David McNiven shot was cleared off the North End line following a low cross from the left. Graham Cross seemed to appear from nowhere to block the ball with his chest and clear.

The visitors wouldn't relent and Tunks had to block a McNiven shot from point blank range to keep matters all square. From the corner, McNiven rose and headed the ball against the bar. The ball dropped vertically, fortunately for North End finding the head of Burns underneath who managed to clear.

City, who had won their last two games, were certainly a confident outfit and nobody could have argued if, by this stage, they had been two goals up. They had tormented North End who had looked listless in comparison.

The events of the five minutes or so that remained of the half surely had most of the Bradford team considering retirement during the interval, for after being dominated for almost all of the first half, North End would unbelievably wander in for their brews with two goal lead.

On the 40th minute, North End won a corner on the right. Coleman floated the ball in and City keeper Peter Downsborough rose well to firmly punch the ball well clear. 'Well clear' I am estimating to be 25 yards or so, as that is where it was about to drop before it met a full swing of the airborne McMahon's right boot.

The volley screamed into the roof of the net, as time seemed to stand still. It certainly did for Downsborough! He was still glued to the ground as the net almost flew off its hooks behind him and into the Town End crowd. The flawless, exquisite rising drive was simply unstoppable.

I have witnessed a few 'Mac' specials at Deepdale in my time watching North End. They were certainly an event, but this was an incredible strike, something else!

If having to watch that unfold wasn't bad enough, the Bradford players were forced to watch Downsborough picking the ball out of the net again just a minute later.

Mike Elwiss slides in North End's second goal just before the interval.

PNE FC

Ricky Thomson, in space on the left of the penalty area, drilled in a low angled shot towards goal which Downsborough could only turn aside. The ball bobbled into the six yard box, whereupon the sliding Elwiss forced the ball over the line despite the attentions of a couple of defenders.

Preston, behind on merit for 90% of the first half, left the field at half time to cheers, while Bradford, having dominated and been full of enterprise, trooped off with heads hung low totally and utterly deflated.

A quick half time scan of the pitch didn't reveal any deceased North Enders, but 'That Bastard Wind' was still blowing...

The visitors were certainly more subdued in the second half, no doubt following a 'meaning of life' discussion in the changing room at half time.

After the interval North End were in control without really displaying any real killer touch. It was left to Elwiss to provide most of the threat, with Alex Bruce strangely quiet.

There was a huge shout all around Deepdale midway through the second half when Coleman was brusquely bundled off the ball by Wood in the penalty area but referee Tony Morrisey perhaps thought by then that Bradford had suffered enough.

In the 80th minute however, new life was breathed into the Bantams' cause when substitute Joe Cooke reduced the arrears.

Right back Cec Podd's centre from deep floated into the area and Cooke, gifted acres of room, headed past the helpless Tunks.

PNE FC

Elwiss smashes the ball underneath Downsborough to put the game beyond doubt

With renewed vitality, the visitors threw everything forward in an attempt to grab a point out of the game. This was short cut by the temper of centre half John Middleton, who decided to retaliate after a Coleman tackle. His marching orders and North End's late third goal sealed a vital win for the Lilywhites.

WEEKEND

Leisure and Football POST

Lancashire Evening Post

No. 28,293 SATURDAY MARCH 4 1978 8p

INSIDE

Meet the toast of LONDON

SEE PAGE TWO

John Morrell NORTHERN PREMIER LEAGUE PAGE 3

Don Jones NORTH WEST FOCUS PAGE 3

PLUS

Keeping in trim AND PRIZES WITH JUNIOR POST

Butcher is Blackburn point saver —See P10

Alex Bruce storms into the Bradford City goal area, putting Bradford City goalkeeper Peter Downsborough under pressure at Deepdale this afternoon

PNE COURAGE EARNS FINE WIN

PRESTON North End kept up their strong challenge for promotion to Division Two when they beat struggling Bradford City 3-1 at Deepdale today.

By NORMAN SHAKESHAFT

It was Preston's eighth home League win in succession and they have scored 26 goals in these games and conceded only seven.

But victory did not come easily and Bradford were very unlucky after looking the better side for most of the first half.

John McMahon and Mike Elwiss got Preston's goals just before the interval and Joe Cooke scored for Bradford after substituting for Bernie ...

Mick Wood before sending off Bradford's John Middleton just before the end.

Preston North End: Tunks, McMahon, Cameron, Burns, Baxter, Cross, Coleman, Haslegrave, Thomson, Elwiss, Bruce. Sub: Doyle.

... injury which made him miss the previous four North End games.

Gordon Coleman, who deputised for McMahon, switched back to his normal midfield position, with Stephen Doyle relegated to substitute. Mick Robinson, who was the sub on Tuesday night, was left out.

Bradford manager John Napier kept an unchanged team after two successive victories so there was still no room for former Preston defender Alex Spark, who watched from the stand after ...

SCOREBOARD

DIVISION ONE

Arsenal	3	Man C	0
Aston V	0	Leicester	0
Chelsea	3	Liverpool	1
Coventry	4	B'm'gh'm	0
Derby C	1	N'wcastle	1
Everton	3	QPR	3
Ipswich	2	WBA	2
Leeds	0	Bristol C	2
Man Utd	0	Midd'bro'	0
Nottm F	2	West Ham	0
Wolves	3	Norwich	3

DIVISION TWO

Blackpool	P	Fulham	P
(POSTPONED)			
Bolton	1	Brighton	1
Bristol R	2	Burnley	2
Charlton	2	B'ckb'n R	2
Crystal P	0	Stoke	1
Hull	3	Millwall	2
Luton	3	Cardiff	1
Oldham	1	Tott'ham	1
Orient	0	Notts C	0
Sheff Utd	2	Mansfield	0
Sund'land	0	S'th'pton	0

DIVISION THREE

Carlisle	1	C'mb'ge	1
Chest'f'ld	★	Sheff W	★
Hereford	1	C'lchester	0
Peterboro	2	Bury	1
Plymouth	2	Chester	2
Portsm'th	1	Walsall	2
Port Vale	1	Shrewsb'y	2
Preston	3	Bradf'd C	1

SCOTTISH F.A. CUP

(FOURTH ROUND)

Hibernian	★	Partick T	★

SCOTTISH PREMIER DIVISION

Ayr	P	Partick T	P
(POSTPONED)			
Clydeb'k	2	St Mirren	2
Dundee U	0	Celtic	1
Moth'well	P	Hibernian	P
(POSTPONED)			
Rangers	0	Aberdeen	3

NORTHERN PREMIER LEAGUE

Northwich Vic 1, Netherfield 1

Frickley Ath 2, Morecambe 2

Cheshire Lgue Cup

Formby 0, Chorley 0

RUGBY UNION

CLUB MATCHES

Hoppers Spk. Derby 9

LANCASHIRE COMBINATION

Leyland Motors 3, Clitheroe 0

RUGBY LEAGUE

FIRST DIVISION

Leeds	P	Warr'gt'n	P
(POSTPONED)			
Salford	27	Hull	18
(PLAYED LAST NIGHT)			

TV Soccer

BBC MATCH OF THE DAY

Arsenal v Manchester City

With just seconds left, the predatory Elwiss ran clear, rounded a defender and smashed home a low drive past Downsborough.

The best home crowd of the season to date of 11,920 had witnessed a strange game, not North End's best performance, but enough to see them go top of the league as other results went their way.

If 'That Bastard Wind' did claim a victim, I never heard about it.

After the game Stiles said, *"It was a hard game with Bradford playing very well – a game that could have gone either way.*

"The lads kept plugging away and earned their reward. Any points gained from now on are very precious."

North End's next two games looked difficult. Away fixtures, starting at seventh placed Swindon on Tuesday evening, and then fourth placed Gillingham on Saturday were not going to be easy.

"The matches from now on will all be just like cup-ties," declared the manager, indicating his feeling that the season had just turned into the home straight.

With hardly time to prepare for the contest at Swindon, Nobby was pleased that that all the first team squad reported in on Monday fit and well.

This made life easy for him, and he pinned his instincts on the same squad of 12 that had beaten Bradford City at the weekend – hoping no doubt, to win the game in a more convincing style! The unchanged team was:-

Tunks, McMahon, Cameron, Burns, Baxter, Cross, Coleman, Haslegrave, Thomson, Elwiss, Bruce. Substitute: Doyle.

Before the match started, long serving Swindon Town veteran full back John Trollope was awarded with a special memento to commemorate his 832nd appearance for the club, breaking the record held by Jimmy Dickinson of Portsmouth. An excellent crowd of 10,211 applauded this magnificent achievement before settling down to enjoy the game.

There wasn't much enjoyment to be had for the vast majority of those present however, as North End turned in a superb display which prompted Swindon Town manager Danny Williams to hail North End as the best side to visit the County Ground all season.

Preston dominated from the off with both Mike Elwiss and Alex Bruce in top form. After early attacks that ended with a wide shot from Elwiss and a stinging shot from Bruce that was tipped over the crossbar, the visitors took the lead in the 19th minute through Mick Baxter.

Latching onto a through ball down the left from midfield, Sean Haslegrave made progress forward. Meanwhile Baxter, seeing the opportunity unfold, joined the attack – arriving in the goalmouth as Haslegrave swung the ball into the penalty area.

Baxter met the ball perfectly and Jim Allen, the Swindon goalkeeper, was unable to prevent the inevitable.

There was no question of North End sitting back, and they played some superb football thereafter.

Credit: Swindon Town FC

Graham Cross shields the ball back to goalkeeper Roy Tunks

Bruce was desperately unlucky when he thrashed in a shot that beat Allan, but bounced to safety after hitting the inside of the post. He then grazed the outside of the post with another superb effort.

John McMahon romped down the right and fired in lethal looking cross that flashed across the face of the Swindon goal, without any North End attacker able to reach it in time. Ricky Thomson then fired a shot wide, Francis Burns curled a shot too high, but it looked absolutely certain that North End would post their second goal as Bruce waltzed past two defenders, but his shot was blocked desperately by Allan and he had to settle for a corner.

The only sign of Swindon life in the North End box during the first half was a good shot from Kenny Stroud that whistled just wide and a hacked clearance away by McMahon, when keeper Roy Tunks couldn't hold onto a David Moss drive.

Swindon were obviously given a talking-to at half time by their manager and as a result, the game became a little more even upon the resumption.

The earliest goal worthy attempts of the half were manufactured by North End. Thomson drove a shot fractionally wide from 15 yards and Bruce forced Allan into a brilliant save with powerful, low skimming drive.

Swindon rallied and eventually put North End under pressure. Roy Carter missed a golden chance to bring the home side level when he shot wide from 12 yards when clean through, then a Chris Guthrie header then flew over the bar following a corner before Tunks made an excellent save to deny David Moss.

North End were always dangerous though, with the movement of Elwiss, Bruce and Thomson always elevating the Swindon defence into a state of panic whenever they were in possession.

As the game drew to a close, Elwiss and Bruce connected yet again to put North End two up in a manner that the typical North End aficionado had become so used to over the past couple of seasons.

Elwiss made a driving run down the right wing, centring a curling cross towards the Swindon goalmouth where Bruce made no mistake by swiftly and efficiently burying the ball into the back of the net via his right boot.

The Robins' unbeaten run of 12 league matches was over. They had been put to the sword by a terrific performance from the Lilywhites, and Elwiss and Bruce in particular. This was a point that didn't go unnoticed by

Swindon manager Danny Williams, the first of the managers to be interviewed after the game.

"Preston are certain to be promoted," began Williams. "They were the best team to play here this season. We had been unbeaten in our previous 12 league games, but there was no disgrace in going down to such a good team and I am a good loser in those circumstances.

"They were better than us in every department. They tackled better, passed the ball more accurately, defended better, and were more incisive in attack. I have got to hold my hands up to them.

"Alex Bruce is very dangerous and very sharp and I also cannot understand why no big club has made a massive offer for Mike Elwiss. Mike may not get as many goals as Alex, but he is a real handful for any defence.

"We have some good players here but we could never match those two."

Williams waited for 30 minutes after the game to speak to Stiles so that he could offer his personal congratulations, and also to pass on his good wishes to all the Preston players.

That's what you call 'professional'.

Nobby and the players were delighted with the result but the manager was already looking forward to Saturday's showdown at Gillingham.

"We will have to try and play just as well on Saturday, as it will be a tough game.

"I'm very pleased with the way all the lads stuck to their task and worked hard throughout the match. This was a victory they fully deserved and it was gained a very good side.

"We showed we are too good for Division Three and we are worth a higher grade of football. We played it simply, just like Manchester United did when I used to play for them."

There were no concerns on the injury front either. Substitute Stephen Doyle had not been used during the game but it was reported that he, Alan Spavin, Mick Robinson, John Smith and Harry Wilson who all travelled as part of the overall squad were all as delighted with the display as the players on the field.

This was a minor point, but also a vital point. When those players who for whatever reason were omitted are just as pleased as the on-field participants with a success, a massive but invisible weapon has been wheeled into the armoury. Team spirit means success.

Nobby and Kel had obviously moulded a team that had it in spades.

Thursday, March 9th was transfer deadline day for the 1977/78 season. If truth be told, I'm not sure any of the North End fans with everything crossed in the hope of promotion were expecting or even hoping for any arrivals. They just didn't want any departures.

Reassurance came in the form of a statement from North End chairman Alan Jones that headlined the back page of the LEP.

"It doesn't matter how much any club might offer. There is not enough time for any bids to be considered or for proper negotiations to take place, and the directors as responsible people could not be expected to rush through a deal.

Angered by rumours that Blackpool were about to table an offer of just £100,000 for Mike Elwiss, Jones continued, "They have not made an offer and even if they did what player would wish to leave North End to go to Blackpool at the present time?

"They have had all sorts of problems, and the comments regarding Elwiss that have come out are irresponsible. In any case, a figure of £100,000 is an insult to us and to Mike. If they think that their centre forward Mick Walsh is worth £350,000, our strikers must be valued in the same bracket.

"I don't think any Preston player would want to leave Deepdale at the moment and, with regard to speculation about Elwiss and Alex Bruce interesting Portsmouth and Plymouth Argyle, they would certainly not want to go to another club in Division Three."

With all that sorted, there was nothing but the forthcoming clash at Gillingham to concentrate the minds of Nobby Stiles and Alan Kelly.

Gillingham had been leaders of Division Three for some time, but had recently relaxed their grip and had already drifted down to fourth spot. In fact, the Swindon manager Danny Williams, when asked about the Division Three promotion race after the clash with North End earlier in the week had said, "Gillingham have gone; Preston should be able to win there."

Sensibly, Nobby was more cautious, speaking as the team were about to board the coach for Kent on Friday afternoon.

"Gillingham may have lost their heads a bit lately but they have shown they can play good football. They are sure to be determined to put things right against us, a fellow promotion challenger.

"We beat them 2-0 at Deepdale in October, but that result is history and it will be very hard for us tomorrow. We played well at Swindon and that result is behind us too, so we now have to apply ourselves all over again."

Unsurprisingly, Stiles named an unchanged team:-

Tunks, McMahon, Cameron, Burns, Baxter, Cross, Coleman, Haslegrave, Thomson, Elwiss, Bruce. Substitute: Doyle.

Unfortunately, North End went down by 2-1, succumbing to a late Gillingham winner with just 10 minutes to go. The good news was that they weren't trounced or even disappointing, and deserved at least a draw.

The game commenced in excellent conditions, perfect for football.

The first incident of note after early raids were repelled by both defences, was when North End played their way towards the home penalty area. It looked certain that Ricky Thomson had been impeded on the edge of the box, but despite vociferous North End appeals, the referee waved to play on.

A minute or two later, following a failed handball appeal by the Lilywhites, referee John Homewood of Sunbury on Thames ran across to the North End dugout to lecture manager Nobby Stiles and issue a 'calm down' order.

Ken Price then took full advantage rubbing more salt into the North End wounds by firing Gillingham into the lead in the 11th minute.

Following a North End goal kick, Charlie Young found Danny Westwood with a long through ball down the middle. Arms were raised immediately for offside by the North End defence, but the move wasn't brought to a stop by the referee or linesman.

Westwood duly progressed and lost control when he tried to round North End keeper Roy Tunks, but centre forward Ken Price had followed up behind and crashed the ball into the open North End goal before any defenders could return to defend it.

Despite surrounding the referee and protesting vehemently, Mr Homewood pointed to the centre circle for a goal, then booked Gordon Coleman for arguing. He also chastised Graham Cross but didn't take his name.

North End then built their way back into the game gaining control of midfield, consequently attacking with increasing frequency.

Mike Elwiss was prominent and won several corners for the Lilywhites by attacking down both flanks. Danny Cameron shot wide, Francis Burns was too high with an effort from 20 yards and a centre by Thomson was cleared at the expense of a corner.

After Thomson had shot into the side netting from a promising position, Elwiss received the ball and drove forward releasing it into the path of Coleman who slotted the ball past Gillingham keeper Ron Hillyard to level the scores.

Whereas Alex Bruce had been well marshalled and kept very quiet as a result, there seemed to be no such shackles for Elwiss, who was enjoying yet another superb storming performance. In fact, the captain nearly put North End ahead on half time when he launched a terrific shot that shaved the bar as it flew into the crowd.

The second half saw play drift from end to end, as both teams sought what became an ever more elusive winner.

Westwood was Gillingham's striker most likely to score. Mick Baxter and John McMahon had to double up to take the ball off him early in the second half as he chased down a defence splitting pass from Damien Richardson.

Elwiss won another corner for North End after he attacked down the right, but Baxter headed wide.

The Preston captain was then unceremoniously hacked down with a vicious 'no-frills' tackle by Young; the referee obviously in some form of trance to assess such an appalling tackle as a mere foul.

Elwiss and North End bit their lips and carried on.

Credit: Gillingham FC

Roy Tunks cannot prevent Gillingham's Danny Westwood from scoring a brilliant winner

Richardson was proving a handful, and working well in tandem with Westwood. He successfully split the defence again with a good ball for his partner, but Tunks was out quickly to block the shot and then saw Westwood blast the rebound over the crossbar.

North End retaliated and an Elwiss shot was deflected for a corner, from which a Ricky Thomson shot was saved well by Hillyard.

North End hopes were the well and truly dashed however when Westwood restored Gillingham's lead with his 18th goal of the season after bringing a pass from Graham Knight under control in the penalty area. He then flicked the ball over the head of Cross and beat Tunks with a superb delicate chip, having run around the defender in the process.

It had taken a piece of brilliance to breach the North End barrier, and Preston couldn't really get back into their stride with just under 10 minutes left on the clock. Gillingham were buoyed however, and Price was unlucky for the home team on two further occasions before the final whistle.

First it needed Sean Haselgrave to pop up from nowhere to head off the line following a corner, and then Price was denied brilliantly by Tunks who deflected his powerful shot against the crossbar and over.

A win for 'the Gills' then, but no need for despondency from the North End camp. North End were still third, and still well set.

Nobby was still confident about North End's promotion prospects after the match, and said he didn't want to place any pressure upon the players.

"Losing was a setback to our hopes, but we have to show we can recover from such a reverse. We have to approach our fixtures in the same way whether the opponents are from the top or the bottom of the table.

"We were unlucky – all the lads worked hard and deserved a reward. Their first goal was definitely offside and decisions continued to go against us throughout the match. But, hands-up, the winning goal was a real cracker and all credit to Danny Westwood for scoring it.

"It was a goal fit to win such a hard fought game, but now we have to put this result behind us and concentrate on the next match."

No injuries or knocks were reported by the North End players after the game, but cover defender Steve Uzelac had sustained a hairline fracture of the skull at Deepdale in the Central League fixture against Aston Villa. This had followed a clash of heads, and would rule him out of any action for between two and four weeks.

Meanwhile, arrangements regarding the testimonial match for David Sadler, the former North End defender, were well underway.

The game was to be against FA Cup holders Manchester United on April 11th at Deepdale.

WEEKEND

Leisure and Football POST

Lancashire Evening Post

No. 28,299 SATURDAY MARCH 11 1978 8p

INSIDE

PROMOTION

Can North End go up?

see NORMAN SHAKESHAFT and NOBBY STILES ON PAGE 4

PLUS

The return of our Rambling Series and Colouring Sets to be won

Stunner by Sunderland

BOTH Supermacs passed late fitness tests, 28 goal Dixie McNeil taking his place in the Wrexham side and Malcolm Macdonald in the Arsenal line up. Arsenal were clear favourites for the Cup before the game with the bookmakers, but they faced a tough task. The Welshmen had only been beaten once on their own ground in the past 17 years in a cup match.

Regis rocket hits Forest's treble bid

TREBLE chasing Nottingham Forest were at full strength for their sixth round FA Cup clash against West Bromwich Albion at The Hawthorns this afternoon. The experienced John O'Hare was named as substitute with Albion leaving out England Under 21 winger Laurie Cunningham. He took the number 12 shirt.

LATE SHOCK SENDS PNE TO DEFEAT

By NORMAN SHAKESHAFT

PRESTON'S attempt to regain the Third Division lead was unsuccessful at the Prestfield Stadium today when they lost 2-1 against Gillingham in front of a crowd of 9,568.

Gillingham who are still strong promotion contenders, took the lead in the 11th minute with a disputed goal by Ken Price, and Preston equalised in the 40th minute with a goal by Gordon Coleman.

SCOREBOARD

F.A. CUP (SIXTH ROUND)

Midd'bro'	0	Orient	0
Millwall	★	Ipswich	★
WBA	2	Nottm F	0
Wrexham	2	Arsenal	3

DIVISION ONE

Bristol C	0	Everton	1
Coventry	1	Leicester	0
Derby C	1	Chelsea	1
Liverpool	1	Leeds	0
N'wcastle	2	Man Utd	2
Norwich	2	Aston V	1
West Ham	1	Wolves	2

DIVISION TWO

B'ckb'n R	0	Bristol R	1
Blackpool	3	Hull	0
Brighton	2	Stoke	1
Burnley	4	Sheff Utd	1
Fulham	1	Luton	0
Mansfield	0	Bolton	1
Notts C	3	Oldham	2
S'th'pton	2	Crystal P	0
Tott'ham	2	Charlton	1

DIVISION THREE

Bradf'd C	2	Carlisle	2
Bury	★	Portsm'th	★
C'mb'ge	2	Hereford	0
Chester	2	Roth'ham	1
Exeter	3	Lincoln	0
Gill'gham	2	Preston	1
Oxford U	3	C'chester	0
Port Vale	1	Swindon	0

DIVISION FOUR

Doncaster	1	Rochdale	1
Grimsby	1	Barnsley	0
Hartlep'l	1	Southend	0
Hudd'f'ld	2	Darl'gton	1
N'th'pt'n	0	Crewe	0
Reading	1	Scunth'pe	0
Southport	1	Brentford	3
Stockport	2	Newport	0
Torquay	L	Halifax	L
Watford	1	Aldershot	0
Wimb'd'n	3	B'nem'th	1
York	2	Swansea	1

SCOTTISH F.A. CUP

Aberdeen	2	Morton	2
Dundee U	2	Qu'n's Pk	0
Partick T	2	D'barton	1
Rangers	4	Kilm'nock	1

SCOTTISH PREMIER DIVISION

Celtic	3	Ayr	0
Clydeb'k	0	Moth'well	2
Hibernian	5	St Mirren	1

RUGBY UNION

JOHN PLAYER CUP (QUARTER FINALS)

H'quins	18	Liverpool	6

RUGBY LEAGUE (FIRST DIVISION)

Bramley	10	Hull KR	18

RUGBY LEAGUE CUP (SECOND ROUND)

Wigan	10	Bradf'd N	22

The North End manager, Sadler's teammate at both clubs said, *"David was very unfortunate to have to finish his playing career at the end of last season because of persistent knee trouble. He is only 31, was a superb player and also did a lot to help the development of young players like Mark Lawrenson and Mick Baxter while at Deepdale."*

As the weekend approached and attention turned to the home game against Exeter City on March 18th. The Grecians player-manager Bobby Saxton, was interviewed about the forthcoming contest.

Saxton would, over the following decade, becoming something of a legend within the game.

Wherever he plied his trade players would adore him, and John McGrath immediately recruited him for the latter half of the 1986/87 promotion season as his assessor of opposition teams after Blackburn Rovers had sacked the Yorkshireman as their manager.

His evaluations about teams and players were said to have been spot on, so to read now what impression the North End of 1977/78 had made on him well before his assessor days is quite interesting.

"I went to watch Preston at Swindon last week. I was very impressed with the performance and their three front runners Bruce, Elwiss and Thomson are terrific.

"They are the best I have seen in the division this season, and I'm not surprised they have scored a lot of goals. I also think that Gordon Coleman is a very good player too.

"It should be a good game on Saturday as we have been playing well lately too."

At Deepdale, Nobby was telling his lads not to forget the manner of their 2-0 defeat at the hands of Exeter back in October.

"We learned a harsh lesson in that match. Our attitude was not right and we gave our worst display of the season. We have got to remember what happened and it must be in our minds on Saturday. We mustn't think we are the better side and therefore able to win. We have to prove we are the better side by working hard on the field."

Stiles added that he could not ask any more of North End's regular fans.

"They have got right behind us and have appreciated what we have been trying to do. They lifted us tremendously in our last home game when we were struggling against Bradford City and helped us win the match."

Stiles was expected to name an unchanged team for the fourth successive time, albeit without Stephen Doyle, who had missed some training during the week because of a heavy cold.

It was Alan Spavin who got the nod to warm the bench on a cool, bright day and North End lined up with:-

Tunks, McMahon, Cameron, Burns, Baxter, Cross, Coleman, Haslegrave, Thomson, Elwiss, Bruce. Substitute: Spavin.

It was another case of 'unlucky North End' as the game ended goalless. Many chances were created – some were missed and some were well saved by the Exeter goalkeeper Richard Key, who had a tremendous game.

North End kicked off towards the Kop, which generally meant Mike Elwiss had won the toss.

After a couple of early Exeter incursions into the North End half were repelled, Alex Bruce made a break for Preston down the left and centred into the penalty area. Ricky Thomson then went down under challenge as he tried to control the ball, prompting shouts for a penalty from both the home crowd and players but the referee waved play on.

Exeter's attacks seemed to lack bite and more than one ended with Graham Cross taking command of the situation and calmly rolling the ball back to Roy Tunks, the North End keeper.

After more excellent work from Cross that had earned the crowd's applause, he passed forward and set Sean Haslegrave away down the left, which led to a North End corner. Francis Burns swung the flag kick in, but Thomson shot too high and the chance was missed.

Thomson needed to lower the crosshairs somewhat, as after Gordon Coleman played him in following a quick throw-in from Mike Elwiss, his shot from a good position was once again way too high to worry Key in the Exeter goal.

A Burns shot was then deflected for a corner which produced a massive goalmouth scramble before the ball was eventually cleared.

Striker Keith Bowker then managed to get on the end of two swift Exeter attacks, but both headers were collected safely by Tunks.

Each team appeared to lack a cutting edge, and only in the last few minutes before half time did North End manage to really up the tempo but were still unable to take the lead before the referee decided he was in need of a cup of tea.

The second half began and it was plain to see that North End had been told to play at a higher tempo. This was more like it, and within a minute of the restart the charging Elwiss was abruptly stopped, winning a free kick.

PNE FC

Sean Haslegrave fires in a shot that was saved by the Exeter goalkeeper

This was eventually cleared but North End came straight back with Coleman firing in a good shot that was blocked by Key, and the defence cleared.

More good approach work from North End saw Elwiss gamble with a long shot, but it was too high to seriously worry the Exeter keeper.

This was much better from the Lilywhites, and following a left wing break by Harry Holman for the visitors that ended with a cross being intercepted by Tunks, they moved forward again.

One again it was Elwiss leading the way, this time flying down the left flank before whipping in a brilliant cross that Bruce embellished with a first time volley that flew just wide of the post, with Key still in the process of falling to earth.

The crowd were now well behind the team too – surely North End would soon break through...

Two North End free kicks came to nothing before Tunks was called upon to make a decisive save as Holman cut in dangerously from the left wing. A corner soon followed for the visitors but was dealt with easily by Tunks.

A corner from Burns at the other end concluded with the ball being propelled goalward via a Bruce overhead kick that was on target – but well saved by Key.

Burns played Haslegrave in soon afterwards, but once again Key got in the way of the shot and managed to get the ball away to safety.

It was all North End now, and Bruce was desperately unlucky to see his header hit the post after another cross had been whipped in by Elwiss.

Thomson then shot wide from a corner and yet another Preston attack saw Haslegrave have a good shot deflected by Key with the Exeter defence in disarray. From the resulting cross, Mick Baxter headed just wide. An Exeter attack followed, but North End were soon back pounding at the visitor's door.

Coleman drove in a good shot that Key blocked from yet another corner as the pressure became relentless.

Stiles then sent on Spavin for Thomson with around 10 minutes left.

Soon afterwards Elwiss found himself in space inside the box and fired in a rocket shot, but once again Key tipped it around the post.

Time was rapidly running out now, as another North End surge forward once again brought the best out of Key. Bruce collected a pass in the box from Danny Cameron, beat a defender and lashed in a fine shot that was palmed wide of the post by the outstanding Exeter goalkeeper.

Three successive North End corners and the accompanying goalmouth scrambles were survived in the last couple of minutes of the game, but North End could not find a way through and had to settle for a point.

The Lilywhites had been brilliant in the second half – as was Key in the Exeter goal – but for all that, this felt as frustrating as a defeat. Despite the various 'expert' post mortems that North End would undoubtedly receive as to where they had failed, there was patently little wrong with the team or the football they had produced.

Stiles said after the game that he was disappointed with the result and Preston had not played as well as in some games during the first half.

"Exeter defended well and made it very difficult for us, but we made a lot of chances in the second half and were unlucky not to score.

"I still regard it as a point gained rather than one lost, and would only really start to worry if we were not creating opportunities. Their goalkeeper made four fantastic saves and we hit the post with another effort.

"The game is now gone and behind us, and it was unlikely we would win every home match after an eight game winning run. We are certain to have setbacks, and some of our promotion rivals have also started to drop points or lose games as the tension increases. The lads worked hard and our character has got to show through in the weeks ahead.

"I sent on Alan Spavin for Ricky Thomson near the end to try and get more of the ball in midfield and to push Gordon Coleman forward, but we still didn't get the breakthrough."

The following day, the North End fans were alarmed to read in a Sunday newspaper that manager Nobby Stiles 'might be moving to Blackburn Rovers' in the wake Jim Smith's decision to walk out of Ewood Park and straight into the manager's seat at Birmingham City during the previous week.

The rumour was repeatedly quashed on all Radio Blackburn sports desk bulletins during Monday by Rovers chairman William Bancroft.

WEEKEND

Leisure and Football POST

Lancashire Evening Post

No. 28,305 SATURDAY MARCH 18 1978 8p

INSIDE

THE F.A. CUP

BOBBY ROBSON why this could be Ipswich's year - SEE PAGE 2

TOM FINNEY & ALAN KELLY Page 3 Page 4 GIVE THEIR CUP PREDICTIONS

PLUS

WIN with The Rescuers and YOUR EASTER ENTERTAINMENT GUIDE

● Alex Bruce powers his way forward against Exeter at Deepdale today

Wembley salute for hero Woods

INEXPERIENCED goalkeeper Chris Woods was the Nottingham Forest hero as this afternoon's League Cup final went into extra time. Despite incessant Liverpool pressure, Woods kept his cool and pulled off some great saves to keep the scoresheet blank at the end of normal time.

Conditions were perfect for today's 18th League Cup final between League champions Liverpool and their most obvious successors Nottingham Forest.

A capacity crowd were paying a League Cup record £371,100 to watch an unchanged Liverpool take on a depleted Forest side, who were missing their three cup-tied stars Shilton, Gemmill and Needham, and Colin Barrett whose injury earned Frank Clark a lucky last-minute place in the final.

Liverpool — Clemence, Neal, Smith, Thompson, Kennedy, Hughes, Dalglish, Case, Heighway, McDermott, Callaghan. Sub: Fairclough.

Nottingham Forest — Woods, Anderson, Clark, McGovern, Lloyd, Burns, O'Neill, Bowyer, Withe, Woodcock, Robertson. Sub: O'Hare.

Referee: Pat Partridge (Durham).

Kenny Dalglish, Liverpool's £440,000 striker, missed a glorious scoring opportunity after only 20 seconds.

Kenny Burns completely missed his header as he went for a through ball from Liverpool captain Emlyn Hughes and left Dalglish on his own. But the Scotland star hesitated with only 18-year-old Chris Woods to beat, and then shot tamely into the side netting.

Forest recovered from this early shock and built up a neat movement on the right wing, which ended with a tantalising right-foot shot from O'Neill that flashed across the Liverpool goal-

PRESTON SETTLE FOR A POINT

By NORMAN SHAKESHAFT

PRESTON dropped a point when they were held to a goalless draw by Exeter City in front of 9,189 at Deepdale today.

North End had several chances to score but some were wasted and Exeter goalkeeper Richard Key also thwarted the home team with brilliant saves and deflections.

There was plenty of excitement in the second half after a poor first half but Preston's patience was not rewarded.

They had no luck at all in the Exeter penalty area and

Grand Slam for Wales;

SCOREBOARD

LEAGUE CUP (FINAL)

Liverpool	0	Nottm F	0

(AT WEMBLEY) Extra time being played

DIVISION ONE

Arsenal	4	Bristol C	1
Aston V	4	West Ham	1
Chelsea	2	N'wcastle	2
Derby C	1	B'm'gh'm	3
Ipswich	1	Coventry	1
Leeds	5	Midd'bro'	0
Leicester	2	Norwich	2
Man Utd	1	WBA	1
Wolves	1	Man C	1

DIVISION TWO

Bolton	0	S'th'pton	0
Bristol R	2	Tott'ham	3
Charlton	0	Notts C	0
Crystal P	0	Brighton	0
Hull	1	Burnley	3
Luton	4	Blackpool	0
Oldham	1	Cardiff	1
Orient	1	Fulham	1
Sheff Utd	5	Millwall	2
Stoke	4	B'ckb'n R	2
Sund'land	1	Mansfield	0

DIVISION THREE

Carlisle	1	Gill'gham	0
Chest'f'ld	★	Bury	★
C'lchester	2	C'mb'ge	1
Hereford	2	Bradf'd C	1
Lincoln	3	Sheff W	1

DIVISION FOUR

Aldershot	4	Grimsby	2
Barnsley	1	Hudd'f'ld	1
B'nem'th	1	N'th'pt'n	1
Brentford	2	Hartlep'l	0
Crewe	1	Reading	1
Darl'gton	1	Doncaster	1
Halifax	2	Southport	1
Newport	2	Watford	2

RUGBY UNION

INTERNATIONAL MATCHES

England	15	Ireland	9
Wales	16	France	7

NORTHERN PREMIER LEAGUE

Gatesh'd	3	Barrow	0
Scarboro'	0	Bangor C	2
Staff'd R	★	Frickley	★

CENTRAL LEAGUE

Blackburn	3	Sheff W	5

L — Late Kick-Off
★ — Result Delayed
P — Postponed

LANCS JUNIOR CUP (SEMI-FINAL)

RUGBY LEAGUE

The LEP carried the story too, quoting Bancroft as saying, "The Stiles rumours are utter rubbish," adding that he had even telephoned his North End counterpart Alan Jones to reassure him that was indeed the case.

"The press speculation is embarrassing and Blackburn Rovers have no intention of causing problems for Preston North End."

Stiles' take on all of this was very composed, saying that he had not received any approach from Blackburn and that, even if he did, there would be no question of him leaving Deepdale.

"I have an important job to do here and I am only interested in Preston North End and the bid for promotion to Division Two.

"I am very happy at Preston where everyone is working hard and pulling together. Nothing would make me happier than if we go up at the end of the season, but there is a tough Easter programme to get through yet.

"I am pleased though that some people believe Alan Kelly and I are doing a good job at Deepdale."

On an entirely different note, news of another event over the past weekend broke too. Over the recent weeks, a few managers from competing Division Three teams had not been shy in coming forward to laud some of the Preston players who they had watched or their teams had played against.

Whilst management could obviously see the quality of Nobby's 'lads', it appeared that their on-field opponents could not – as not a single North End player was named in the PFA Division Three team of the year.

What an utter farce! Clearly they still needed to do more to prove their ability to some opposing players...

As Easter approached, and North End having games on Good Friday, Easter Saturday AND Easter Monday, Stiles was keen to have as many of his players as 'good to go' as possible should any injuries arise to disrupt the first team squad.

Whilst it was hoped that Harry Wilson may just about be ready to return after his trauma earlier in the season, Stephen Doyle, although back in full time training again, was still a few days off full fitness.

Jimmy Brown, after eventually recovering from back trouble after an operation on a ruptured disc had now pulled a leg muscle, and the season now looked over for him in terms of the first team squad. Steve Uzelac could and would not be considered for football until the hairline fracture of his skull had mended.

The good news was that Alan Spavin, Ian Cochrane, John Smith and Mick Robinson were all fit and likely to be called up to the first team squad in such an unparalleled period of fixture congestion.

Many clubs' immediate future paths would be decided by the results they brought home over the long Easter weekend, and with North End facing Chester (away), Chesterfield (home) and Bury (away) it wasn't going to be easy for the Lilywhites either.

Six critical and season defining points up for grabs in just four days – that's real physical and mental pressure. The Good Friday match at Sealand Road, pitted Stiles up against his old Manchester City adversary and friend, Chester player-manager, Alan Oakes.

Chester had put up a decent show at Deepdale earlier in the season, losing 2-1. Oakes had played a major part in his team's performance on that day and they had improved their league position considerably since then. Just one league defeat in the last 13 games had moved them up to ninth place, and Oakes had not given up on promotion just yet.

"North End are seven points ahead, but whilst we still have a mathematical chance of going up, we will continue to battle on," Oakes said, adding "we haven't lost at home all season and the club is hoping for a bumper crowd."

Stiles was fully expected to name an unchanged team for the contest. Doyle had now been declared fully fit for the Easter schedule of matches, which the LEP had repeatedly described as 'make or break' also expressing the opinion that the team 'must aim for at least a four point haul from these three games'.

Nobby would not be drawn into agreeing with those sentiments when interviewed, as he strictly wanted no extra pressure putting on his team. He merely said,

"We beat them 2-1 at Deepdale back in October but they have improved since then, so it is vital that the lads go into the game with the right attitude.

Alan Kelly and I refuse to look beyond the next game and we never look ahead until the match is over."

On a bright, sunny spring day North End were, as expected, unchanged. The only swap was the substitute, with Doyle returning to the bench in place of Spavin:-

Tunks, McMahon, Cameron, Burns, Baxter, Cross, Coleman, Haslegrave, Thomson, Elwiss, Bruce. Substitute: Doyle.

North End certainly delivered the goods in the first of their three Easter outings, turning around an early deficit to win in some style in front of a crowd of 7,864 – more than double Chester's average home gate. It was North End's first win at Chester in six visits.

The Sealand Road pitch, much shorter and narrower than Deepdale was used to good advantage by the home team early in the first half – as was the decision at the toss to have the blinding sun behind them, beaming straight into the North End defender's eyes.

They got the ball forward quickly and peppered the North End defence with a series of centres – difficult enough for the North End back four, but doubly so when the sun was searing out their eyeballs at the same time.

Less than two minutes after the match commenced, North End were restarting a goal down.

All of the defenders appeared to lose sight of the ball, except ex-Northender Paul Crossley who promptly rammed the ball into the net to give Chester a massive early advantage.

The bombardment of the North End penalty area continued apace, Roy Tunks having to make two excellent, goal denying saves and Graham

Cross quickly heading a centre over his own crossbar as a 'safety first' measure.

Ron Philips, then had a 'goal' ruled offside, before another major scare for North End occurred when Tunks lost the ball completely has he leapt to catch a centre.

Gradually, things settled down and North End started to move forward with a menace of their own. Gordon Coleman and Ricky Thomson put in decent shots that tested Chester goalkeeper Brian Lloyd, as did the formidable Alex Bruce, looking increasingly dangerous as the half wore on. Three times the Scot was denied – along with the huge North End following who were frustratingly kept on the edge of massive celebration.

The flow of the match by now had been completely turned on its head; it was all about North End.

Thomson mishit after being presented with another opportunity, a Mick Baxter header flew just over the bar, Bruce shot wide on two occasions, then had another well saved. Sean Haslegrave ventured forward and his shot was deflected for a corner.

All the way through the first half Francis Burns had stood out for North End in the middle of the pitch, distributing the ball to his colleagues with class and calm authority.

Tunks was then called upon to snuff out an increasingly rare Chester attempt on the North End goal, and this eventually led to the fully deserved North End equaliser in the 40th minute.

Mike Elwiss flew down the left wing, and centred. Coleman met the ball and knocked it on to Bruce who beat Lloyd with a well placed shot to notch his 26th goal of the season – equalling his previous best total. This was a cue for the North End disciples on the terraces to finally erupt!

Cross managed to get himself booked for a foul on Ian Howat on the stroke of half time, but that aside, North End had 'winners' written all over them as they exited the arena at half time to the noisy chants of their confident fans.

Now it was Chester's turn to undergo the 'eyesight challenge' as there was still enough of the sun to cause problems. North End put them under pressure from the off, with Thomson heading just wide and Danny Cameron having a good shot saved by Lloyd.

The crucial moment of the match – North End's winner – was looking increasingly imminent and duly arrived in the 50th minute, courtesy of Elwiss's boot when he blasted a shot past Lloyd from around 10 yards after an attempt by Burns had been deflected into his path. It was the captains 15th goal of the season, and once again the North End faithful on the terraces made the most it!

Chester came back and thought they had scored but the referee had already blown for a foul on Tunks.

Preston continued to control proceedings – Bruce fired in a shot that was too high, and was then ruled to be narrowly offside with the goal at his mercy shortly afterwards. Another attempt from him was saved as were further efforts from Burns, Coleman and Elwiss which also went close.

Chester, who had started the match in the perfect manner, ended it well beaten. They were confined to infrequent breakaways throughout the second half by a very confident North End team who looked the 'real deal'.

Oakes thought so anyway. The Chester boss joined the growing list of Division Three managers ready to heap praise on Nobby's team.

"Preston were the better team," he began. "We got off to a good start with our early goal and then Tunks made a good save to stop us scoring again, but we were always second best after the first few minutes.

"Preston were superior all round and looked a very good team."

Stiles was beaming with delight through his large spectacles and said it was a great North End performance.

"The heads of the lads never went down after Chester's fast start and we created plenty of chances. We gained control by working at the game, keeping our composure and playing good football. "If I have a complaint, it is only that we should have won by three or four goals."

With less than 24 hours to garner everything together, assess the fitness of the players and prepare them for another vital game, Nobby Stiles made his way home a happy man.

Once the team had confirmed that there were no niggles or strains still evident on Saturday morning following the clash at Sealand Road, Stiles decided to name an unchanged team for the sixth successive time for the Deepdale encounter with Chesterfield:-

Tunks, McMahon, Cameron, Burns, Baxter, Cross, Coleman, Haslegrave, Thomson, Elwiss, Bruce. Substitute: Doyle.

'The Spireites' were stuck bang in the middle of the table but were another team in good form, arriving at Deepdale on the back of only losing one game in their past 11 outings – so this would be no pushover for North End.

And so it proved. In a contest very similar to the Exeter City game, North End were held by the visitors to a goalless draw. It was still another point to add to the tally however, and North End still retained their second place status in the league table, albeit on a goal difference advantage over Cambridge United of just two goals.

Unlike the bright, fine day at Chester, heavy rain and a stiffening breeze greeted the players as they ran down the Deepdale tunnel just before kick off. It kind of summed up what this particular game was about to throw up – frustration and a touch of gloom. Frustration after a crowd of 10,922 turned up and failed to see North End repeat the winning form of the day before, and a touch of gloom in that 80% dominance of the match doesn't necessarily guarantee even a goal, never mind a win for your team.

North End kicked off towards the Town End, and attacked from the start.

Gordon Coleman was first to chance his arm, shooting over from at least 20 yards after Alex Bruce had rolled the ball into his path from inside the penalty area. It was Bruce who next had the crowd on their toes as he moved forward in the area menacingly but lost possession after the ball refused to come out of the mud at the same pace as the striker.

Chesterfield eventually got a forward movement together and saw what the Kop looked like close up. Steve Cammack moved in from the right wing and fired in a shot at goal that North End goalkeeper Roy Tunks patted down with nonchalance.

Danny Cameron earned applause for a good effort when he ran past two defenders only to see his shot hit the side netting.

Glen Letheren, the Chesterfield goalkeeper was being kept busy having to block a free kick, cut out a dangerous John McMahon centre and then beat Bruce to a through ball by running off his line, all in the space of a few minutes. He was then called upon to make another good interception from a Francis Burns centre before enjoying some respite as Andy Kowalski moved into the Preston half and tried his luck with a long shot.

North End came back again. Sean Haslegrave leant back too far and shot over from a Bruce pass and then Ricky Thomson was extremely unlucky to see his skilfully flighted chip shot from the left bounce on top of the bar and go over for a goal kick.

While the visitors were existing off dour defence and sporadic long pass breakaways, the proper football was being played by North End.

Burns was still in the rich seam of form he had enjoyed at Chester the day before, and he was at the hub of everything North End were doing. He curled a beautiful pass defence splitting pass down the right for McMahon to run onto but the full back's shot was too high.

Coleman, Cameron and Elwiss all had good efforts on goal before the teams retired to the dressing rooms at half time, leaving the North End fans plenty to consider. This game had the feel of 'we are going to win... aren't we?' about it, as in reality the Lilywhites should have been at least three up.

The first move of the second half after Chesterfield restarted the contest was a shot by Cammack from all of 20 yards that flew high into the Town End. The visitors were obviously going to dish up more of the same tactics as in the first half, which meant that North End might have a struggle on their hands.

North End got stuck in despite their forwards being heavily shackled and Thomson headed wide from 10 yards out from a free kick after he had been brought down on the left.

The pitch was sodden and ploughing up into mud in the areas of highest activity, such as the Chesterfield penalty area. Twice the ball became stuck under North End's feet, terminating very promising prospects of opening the score.

Bruce then lashed in a shot/centre from the left and Letheren did extremely well to bend backwards in mid air to grasp the ball tightly. The keeper then intercepted a good centre from Elwiss as North End kept on pressing forward relentlessly.

PNE FC

Outstanding Chesterfield 'keeper Glen Letheren was the main reason why North End didn't score – here he saves a point blank piledriver from Alex Bruce

A Coleman header was then saved after Cameron had overlapped down the left, before Burns drilled in a waist high shot that flew fractionally wide.

Time was running out when Letheren dashed forward from his line to pull off the crucial save of the match. Coleman passed the ball inside the box to Bruce, who with his back to goal, swivelled to immediately launch a shot goalward. The young keeper's excellent anticipation saw to it that the attempt was blocked, and North End remained scoreless.

Another Chesterfield punt forward, another long shot for Tunks to deal with, another period of heavy North End pressure – this was the cycle of play throughout the game.

Two North End corners in quick succession produced two almighty goalmouth scrambles... but still no goal.

Both Graham Cross and Mick Baxter were now playing well forward too, as Stiles gambled for the elusive win. Indeed, it was a Baxter header that flew inches too high following a Cameron centre into the penalty area, and his shot that Letheren fingertipped around the post as the game entered the final few minutes.

Two more North End corners were repelled before the referee drew a veil over proceedings. It has to be said the main reason that North End didn't win was Letheren.

Preston North End 75 attempts, Chesterfield 3. Result 0-0.

The onus, however – as the football pundits keep telling us – is always on the home team, and Chesterfield, racked with injuries, stuck to their pre-planned task manfully.

"Our defensive plan was forced on us rather than advocated," explained their coach, Arthur Cox.

"I rate North End very highly, and we were pushed back by them throughout the match, but my team stuck to their task. We may not have deserved a point if you look at the game territorially, but we did for the effort and work we put in.

"Elwiss and Bruce are the equals of Shinton and McNeil at Wrexham. I told the lads that we must blot them out and we restricted Alex to just one real chance, while Mike wasn't really able to get in a decent shot.

"There was no way we were going to take risks to allow Alex and Mike any room – and it will be more difficult for Preston when they are playing at home from now on than it will be in their away games."

Stiles was still positive however after the match.

"Chesterfield made it difficult for us as they had a sweeper behind their back four and used the rest of their players in midfield most of the time.

"Three points out of four isn't the end of the world. We have got to keep

WEEKEND

Leisure and Football POST

Lancashire Evening Post

No. 28,310 SATURDAY MARCH 25 1978 8p

INSIDE

INSIDE ANDY HOYLE'S EASTER MONDAY RACING PREVIEW P2

SPOTLIGHT ON PETER BARNES P2

GOOD FRIDAY MATCH REPORTS P6

PLUS

Delights of The BLACK FOREST

DOLLS TO BE WON!

Cambridge take Boat Race dive!

OXFORD won a drama packed 124th Boat Race when Cambridge sank just after Barnes Bridge today. The Dark Blues, the favourites, were leading at the time and they went on to complete the course in 18 minutes 58 seconds.

The water was very rough and Cambridge shipped so much that they gradually sank, and were rescued by the following launches. This was the fifth time there had been a sinking in the race, but the first since 1951 when Oxford went down.

Oxford had won the toss and chose the Surrey station. There was an unusual mix up at the start. Oxford went off before the Light Blues were ready, and had to be recalled.

On the second occasion the umpire's flag was still raised as both crews started. He allowed them to continue and Oxford quickly went into the lead.

Cambridge came back and were nearly level at the mile post but the Dark Blues forged ahead and were just over a length in front at Hammersmith Bridge, as rain and wind made the water very choppy.

Later Oxford caught a "crab", but recovered well and were over two lengths in front passing under Barnes Bridge.

Shortly afterwards the Cambridge crew disappeared into the water, and the Dark Blues went on to score their third successive victory.

Sent off

● A Mike Elwiss free kick slams against the Chesterfield wall, during the game at Deepdale, today.

LUCKLESS PNE LET POINT SLIP

PRESTON dropped a point in their campaign for promotion to Division Two when they were held to a goalless draw by Chesterfield in front of 10,922 at Deepdale today.

By NORMAN SHAKESHAFT

Chesterfield, who were beaten 1—0 by North End at Saltergate in December, gave a fine defensive performance and Preston were frustrated despite having most of the possession.

SCOREBOARD

DIVISION ONE

Arsenal	4	WBA	0
Aston V	0	Derby C	0
Bristol C	0	B'm'gh'm	1
Everton	2	Leeds U	0
Leicester	2	Man Utd	3
Man C	2	Midd'bro'	2
Norwich	1	Coventry	2
Nottm F	2	N'wcastle	0
QPR	3	Ipswich	3
West Ham	3	Chelsea	1
Wolves	1	Liverpool	3

DIVISION TWO

Bolton	2	Blackpool	1
Brighton	2	Fulham	0
Burnley	4	Oldham	1
Crystal P	1	Bristol R	0
Hull	1	Notts C	1
Mansfield	3	Tott'ham	3
Millwall	1	Cardiff	1
Sheff Utd	4	Luton	1
S'th'pton	4	Charlton	1
Stoke	★	Orient	★
Sund'land	0	B'ckb'n R	1

DIVISION THREE

C'mb'ge	1	Portsm'th	0
C'lchester	1	Bury	0
Gill'gham	0	Peterboro	0
Hereford	4	Exeter	0
Oxford U	1	Port Vale	1
Plymouth	0	Swindon	2
Preston	0	Chest'f'ld	0

DIVISION FOUR

Aldershot	3	Southend	0
Barnsley	2	Southport	1
Darl'gton	1	Hartlep'l	2
Doncaster	0	Wimb'd'n	2
Grimsby	0	N'th'pt'n	1
Hudd'f'ld	3	Crewe	0
Newport	★	Brentford	★

CENTRAL LEAGUE

Blackpool 1 Everton 1

L — Late Kick-Off

★ — Result Delayed

P — Postponed

NORTHERN PREMIER LEAGUE

CHESHIRE LEAGUE

LANCASHIRE COMBINATION

RUGBY UNION

LATE NEWS

NEWPORT 1 BRENTFORD 2

STOKE 5 ORIENT 0

plugging away. I have no grumbles and was pleased with the way my lads worked today."

There were a few injury concerns for Nobby to ponder on Easter Sunday, a day of well earned rest for the team before their final holiday encounter at Bury the following day. Mick Baxter had hobbled off the pitch in the final minute against Chesterfield with a knee injury and Francis Burns was also carrying a limp at the final whistle. To complicate matters further, Graham Cross telephoned Stiles from his Leicester home complaining of a painful thigh strain.

Of the three only Burns made it onto the Gigg Lane pitch. It meant a major reshuffle for North End as both the big centre backs were now missing. With reserve centre half Steve Uzelac still unavailable, Stiles put his trust in the versatility of Stephen Doyle and Gordon Coleman to occupy the centre of the North End defence, while Alan Spavin took over Coleman's midfield spot. Winger Ian Cochrane was the substitute, for the re-shuffled team:-

Tunks, McMahon, Cameron, Burns, Doyle, Coleman, Spavin, Haslegrave, Thomson, Elwiss, Bruce. Substitute: Cochrane.

The weather was grey, fine and still as the teams trotted out, in front of a large crowd which seemed to have more North End fans within it than locals.

Stiles, shorn of his two defensive pillars, opted for a different *modus operandi* for this game. With no recognised centre half, North End would attack from the start.

It almost worked, but North End conceded yet another late goal and had to settle for a share of the spoils. This meant that they had taken four points from a possible six over the three match/four day slog; an excellent overall performance.

Alex Bruce, Mike Elwiss and Ricky Thomson all created good scoring attempts as the first half rolled on, but Bury had their moments too, with headers from Andy Rowland and Jimmy McIlwraith being safely snaffled by Roy Tunks.

North End eventually struck gold however, when a Danny Cameron free kick was helped onto Mike Elwiss by Sean Haslegrave. Down the left flank Elwiss flew, before slinging a centre in to the penalty area which Thomson rose to meet unchallenged. The young Scot appeared to pick his spot as the ball flew beyond John Forrest and into the net.

PNE FC

Ricky Thomson heads home the North End goal at Gigg Lane

The home side had a dejected look about them as they trooped off at half time – they hadn't won a game since February 25th.

The second half began and North End were not holding back. Bruce managed to force Forrest into three good saves before Bury rallied a little and put in a couple of decent shots of their own from Brian Stanton and McIlwraith.

Collective Preston breaths were held a few moments later when a Rowland back header bounced across an empty Preston goalmouth, but the ball was safely cleared.

The golden opportunity for North End to seal this game arrived in the 65th minute when the referee pointed to the penalty spot after Bury's Danny Wilson handled a centre by Sean Haslegrave.

The delighted expressions of the Preston players were soon wiped off their faces as Bruce shot wide of Forrest's right post. He seemed to have mishit the ball somehow, and now with head in hands, 'Brucie' looked a forlorn figure – for just a little while anyway.

PNE FC

Alex Bruce miscues his penalty kick

He was soon back at the coalface soon afterwards however, firing in a couple of shots while both Doyle and John McMahon had attempts tipped over the crossbar.

Bury stuck to their task and took full advantage when awarded a free kick in the last minute. With McIlwraith still lying injured on the spot where he fell following the foul, the free kick was taken a full 10 yards further up the field which incensed Stiles in the dugout.

The free kick was floated in, Tunks struggled to get to the ball cleanly after moving well off his line, and Thomson, in attempting to play the ball out of the danger area, lost possession to Peter Farrell. Playing his first league game of the season following two cartilage operations, the striker seized the opportunity to beat Tunks with a neat lob.

That certainly took the edge of things for the travelling North End fans who had loudly supported their team all afternoon.

Stiles appeared to be in an animated discussion with the referee after the game.

The real fun and games started well after the match, not for anything plainly apparent but just because Bob Stokoe seemed to simply love criticising Preston North End.

He couldn't hold back in 1972 when Blackpool came to Deepdale and won 4-1. Neither could he in 1973, when North End defeated his Sunderland FA Cup winning team 1-0 at Deepdale. After that particular game he issued the nearest thing to a witch's curse I've ever heard...

"Don't get carried away with Preston's recent successes. You have had it bad for a long time at Deepdale, so enjoy things now while you have the chance."

This time his advice was for Nobby Stiles.

"Preston will have big problems when they are promoted to Division Two. Alex Bruce and Mike Elwiss will not find it easy to score goals even though they are very good forwards in Division Three. The trouble with Preston is that, if you took those two players out of the side, they would be nothing."

There then followed criticism of his own players, before he summed up with, "Although Preston were the better of two very ordinary sides, they still couldn't beat us. I know that Bruce missed a penalty, but Preston were lucky to get that in any case and it was a very harsh decision."

The LEP reported that Stiles answered Stokoe by saying that North End's problems were nice ones to have – and then walked away, past the Bury manager, back to the dressing room. The Preston manager was described as 'far from pleased' with Stokoe's theories that North End were a two-man team with big problems ahead should they achieve promotion.

"I was asked to comment after the game about the Bury side, but said it wasn't my job to talk about another team, and that I was only interested in Preston.

"It seems that managers of other clubs want to talk about North End. They are welcome to do so, and some have praised us. Others have criticised us, but we just keep proving them wrong.

"Our success in getting into second place in the table this season has come about because of team performances and people should remember that. When 11 players play well as a team, individuals are also able to play well.

"We dominated the game and were unlucky not to win. I'm sick that we didn't get both points.

"My complaints on the touchline at the end of the game were made because the free kick which led to Bury's equaliser had been taken well ahead of where the incident happened. Taking the free kick in a much better spot made a big difference, as it enabled Bury to get the ball right into our penalty area.

"We worked hard and did really well when you consider that Steve Uzelac's injury meant three centre halves were ruled out. Alan Spavin played very well too to complete his first full game of the season, as did Gordon Coleman and Stephen Doyle who both demonstrated their versatility."

A huge clash lay ahead for the Lilywhites at Deepdale at the weekend against fellow promotion challengers Peterborough, who were in sixth position but with two games in hand over North End. They also had the meanest defence in the league.

Attention turned to Graham Cross and Mick Baxter in their battle to beat the odds against injury and resume their tenure in the North End backline.

The North End management team had tried Harry Wilson, himself feeling his way back after a major injury, at centre half in the Central League fixture against Newcastle United to see how he fared in that position just in case Cross and/or Baxter failed to make it. Wilson performed well, and it gave Stiles and Kelly the comfort of a back-up plan should the worst happen.

On Thursday, the message from Stiles was *'fingers crossed'* regarding both defenders; by Friday after Baxter had trained at Deepdale and Cross had telephoned Stiles saying he was 'optimistic' after a run out with Leicester City, there was a tangibly more positive feel all round Deepdale about the 'crisis'. As so often during this action packed season, Stiles would leave selection to the last possible minute, but now there was every chance that the team could be back to full strength.

"Peterborough beat us 1-0 with a disputed last minute penalty at the end of December, and they have improved even more since then," said Nobby.

"We will treat them with respect, but my lads are also playing well and they will go into the game with the right attitude."

Peterborough manager, John Barnwell was expecting that North End would be out for revenge after their previous encounter.

"It's always a tough game up there at Deepdale, and our record there doesn't exactly set anything alight. Preston are nobody's mugs, but I think the pressure will be on them to deliver."

All was set for the big match, which if North End could win would leave them in a very strong position for promotion.

The kick off was scheduled for 3:00pm on Grand National day, April 1st. The BBC tv cameras would be at Aintree of course, but also at Deepdale to cover the clash for Match of the Day.

CHAPTER 10

APRIL

Peterborough Utd (home) – Walsall (home) – Wrexham (away) – Lincoln City (home) – Sheffield Wed (away) – Portsmouth (away) – Rotherham Utd (away) – Shrewsbury Town (home)

The good news on a still, grey April Fool's day was that Mick Baxter and Graham Cross both passed morning fitness tests and were immediately returned to their back four berths by North End manager, Nobby Stiles.

The North End team that took the field at Deepdale therefore had a familiar ring to once again:-

Tunks, McMahon, Cameron, Burns, Baxter, Cross, Coleman, Haslegrave, Thomson, Elwiss, Bruce. Substitute: Doyle.

Everything was set up; the Lilywhites were at full strength again and a win would widen the moat between themselves – bedded in second place – and the chasers... such as Peterborough United. The match highlights were due to be replayed on Match of the Day too, so that we could all relive North End's latest triumph. What could possibly go wrong?

A well arranged, tactically aware team that grew in confidence called Peterborough United – that's what went wrong!

To be fair North End were very unlucky not to at least halve the points, but once 'the Posh' went in front after 16 minutes the division's best defence were never going to willingly surrender.

North End kicked off towards the Town End, and in a bright opening salvo, saw Peterborough keeper Keith Waugh deflect Alex Bruce's shot for a corner after he had collected a delicate through ball from Francis Burns. There was more encouragement too when Gordon Coleman shot narrowly wide following the corner, but it wasn't long before the parsimonious visiting defence settled down and got their house in order.

The visitors were operating with just two men up front and packing midfield and defence with as many players as the immediate threat from North End demanded.

A good save by Waugh from a shot/centre by John McMahon was followed by a similar effort from Mike Elwiss on the left, before the crowd suddenly fell silent as Peterborough went ahead through Tommy Robson.

Robson, who would become akin to Peterborough over the years just as butter is to bread, finished off a swift, no frills attack when he drilled a shot past Roy Tunks in the North End goal from the left of the penalty area after Barry Butlin had headed on a centre.

PNE FC

Alex Bruce is surrounded by the Peterborough defence during the second half

North End regrouped and attacked bravely without seriously denting the visitor's defensive barrier over the next 30 minutes.

After playing the advantage when Elwiss was fouled but retained possession, the referee then decided to blow for the offence as the Preston captain was hurtling down the left wing and in the clear.

This brought forth a huge roar of disapproval from the home crowd, along with some other friendly suggestions as to where the ref should put his whistle.

In fact, North End won two more free kicks immediately after this, both on the edge of the Peterborough penalty area, and both dealt with efficiently and with the minimum amount of fuss.

Next the Lilywhites won a corner but this was eventually cleared too, frustratingly so when no North End players were close enough to take advantage after Waugh had completely mistimed his leap.

Shots by Ricky Thomson and Bruce were safely gathered in by Waugh, as was a long range effort by Burns before Coleman headed over a few minutes later.

Certainly, North End were working hard, but the visitors had an ever increasing confidence about their play, passing and moving well when North End allowed them possession.

Bruce and Elwiss placed efforts too high just before the interval, but it had become obvious that North End were going to have a real battle on their hands if they were going to retrieve even just a point from this affair during the second half.

North End restarted all guns blazing, and a swift move came to an end when Thomson's header was well saved by Waugh.

What was it about Deepdale that inspired visiting goalkeepers? Waugh was the latest to be added to the list of 'keepers going far beyond the call of duty,

After Bruce had crashed in a shot on the turn that was too wide, Peterborough calmly moved forward, and after being teed up just outside the North End penalty area, Alan Slough was just a few inches away from doubling Posh's lead following a full blooded drive.

Stiles sent on Stephen Doyle to replace Thomson on the hour in an attempt to wrestle the initiative in midfield, where Peterborough had dominated through sheer weight of numbers.

WEEKEND

Leisure and Football POST

Lancashire Evening Post

No. 28,316 SATURDAY APRIL 1 1978 8p

INSIDE

WE'RE GOING TO WEMBLEY! - says Albion boss — page 2

WE'RE GOING UP - says PNE President Tom Finney — page 3

PLUS

WIN WITH THE JUNGLE BOOK

A PRINCELY PORTRAIT

Alex Bruce battles it out for possession during today's game at Deepdale.

National thriller as brave Lucius clinches victory

By ANDREW HOYLE

BOB DAVIES, three times Champion Jockey, enjoyed a large slice of Liverpool luck today when he came in for the "chance ride" on Lucius and took full advantage of the heaven-sent opportunity to win his first Grand National.

In one of the most exciting Nationals of all time, Lucius battled on gamely up the Liverpool run-in to beat Sebastian V by half a length with Drumroan only a neck away in third place.

Coolishall was fourth, followed home by The Pilgarlick, Mickley Seabright and Lord Browndodd, after all the first seven finishers had been in the race with a winning chance in the home straight.

Ridley Lamb must have thought that he was going to win the first ever Grand National for Scotland as he stormed over the last two fences to the lead on Sebastian V.

But Bob Davies was only biding his time on Lucius who came to forge passed the pacemaker on the run in and held on tenaciously.

Irish challenger, Drumroan, partnered by Gerry Newman was also putting in a strong late effort but he was narrowly denied the runner-up position.

Cruel

The National outcome was a cruel result for David Goulding, stable jockey to Lucius's Penrith - based trainer,

UNLUCKY PNE GO DOWN FIGHTING

PRESTON'S hopes of gaining promotion to Division Two suffered a setback at Deepdale today when they were beaten 1-0 by Peterborough United.

It was Preston's second League defeat of the ... and their first at Deepdale since

SCOREBOARD

DIVISION ONE

Arsenal	3	Man Utd	1
Aston V	0	Liverpool	3
Bristol C	3	N'wcastle	1
Everton	2	Derby C	1
Leicester	0	WBA	1
Man C	2	Ipswich	1
Norwich	3	Leeds U	0
Nott'm F	3	Chelsea	1
QPR	1	Midd'bro'	0
West Ham	2	Coventry	1
Wolves	0	B'm'gh'm	1

DIVISION TWO

Bolton	2	Orient	0
Brighton	3	Notts C	1
Burnley	2	Tott'ham	1
Crystal P	0	Oldham	0
Hull	1	Luton	1
Mansfield	0	Charlton	3
Millwall	1	Bristol R	3
Sheff Utd	0	Blackpool	0
S'th'pton	5	B'ckb'n R	0
Stoke	2	Cardiff	0
Sund'land	2	Fulham	2

DIVISION THREE

Bradf'd C	1	Portsm'th	0
C'mb'ge	2	Walsall	1
Carlisle	0	Bury	3
Chester	2	Exeter	1
C'lchester	1	Shrewsb'y	2
Gill'gham	0	Wrexham	0
Hereford	0	Sheff W	1
Oxford U	1	Chest'f'ld	1
Preston	0	Peterboro	1

DIVISION FOUR

Aldershot	2	N'th'pt'n	1
Barnsley	3	B'nem'th	0
Darl'gton	2	Crewe	0
Doncaster	1	Torquay	0
Grimsby	2	Southend	0
Hudd'f'ld	1	Brentford	3
Newport	*	Reading	*
Rochdale	2	Southport	1
Stockport	1	Scunth'pe	1

LANCASHIRE COMBINATION

CHESHIRE LEAGUE

NORTHERN PREMIER LEAGUE

RUGBY UNION

JOHN PLAYER CUP

M'lequins	*	Glouc'ter	*
Leicester	25	Coventry	16

OTHER MATCHES

RUGBY LEAGUE

Salford	12	Widnes	20

BBC cameras at Deepdale

PRESTON'S match against Peterborough will be featured on BBC's Match of the Day tonight. The other game will be Arsenal v Manchester United.

● GRANADA tomorrow BURNLEY v TOTTENHAM.

LATE NEWS

NEWPORT 0 READING 0

Coleman went down in the Peterborough penalty area claiming he was pushed, but the referee wasn't interested. A few moments later North End came as close as they possibly could to drawing level when the diminutive midfielder tried his luck with a long shot on the turn that hit the post but bounced to safety.

North End were driving forward at every opportunity, but the well drilled Peterborough defence repelled all the Lilywhites efforts and even managed to carve an opening or two for themselves.

So totally absorbing had this contest been, that hardly anybody had left the ground when the gates had opened 15 minutes or so from time. This time marker was thus lost, and with North End still attacking gamely, many people were surprised to hear the whistle blow for full time just after a magnificent Bruce header had been brilliantly saved by Waugh.

However, it was met with great delight by the Peterborough manager and indeed his team, but with sheer frustration by their hosts.

All that attacking and nothing to show for it! This was the third home match on the bounce where North End had failed to score against teams who had decided to play with defensive tactics that swamped their midfield and defence.

Nobby wasn't depressed after the game – well at least he didn't show it even if he was.

"Peterborough defended very efficiently and their goalkeeper made a great save from Alex Bruce early on, and Alex was very unfortunate with his header near the end.

"I have no complaints about the lads because they all worked hard, did things right and didn't lose patience. We know we have to keep plugging away and battling, and we know that the breaks will finally come.

Peterborough manager, John Barnwell was obviously delighted with his team's league double over North End.

"Preston put us under immense pressure and there was nothing else we could do other than to defend all the time. I'm delighted to have won however, but I would have settled for a point before the match.

"We didn't give them many clear cut opportunities, but Preston are a still a good team. Elwiss and Bruce I rate very highly, and my players were told to concentrate on blotting those two out."

Match of the Day was extended that evening to include a full re-run of the Grand National. For the record, it was won by Lucius. North End v Peterborough was the main feature game, was almost scanned through, it passed so quickly. The 'supporting' feature, Arsenal v Manchester United, lasted almost three times as long. Norman Shakeshaft noted in the LEP that Jimmy Hill was 'almost apologising' when he introduced North End's game to the nation.

Despite now racking up 270 blank minutes since recording their last goal, (Mike Elwiss against Bradford City in injury time on March 4th), North End had another opportunity to 'get back on the horse' quickly, as on Tuesday evening Walsall were due to visit Deepdale.

Keith Waugh (Peterborough United), Glen Letheren (Chesterfield) and Richard Key (Exeter City) were the last three goalkeepers to visit Deepdale, and without exception had enjoyed the game of their lives. Now we had Mick Kearns of Walsall to contend with again, who was the 'star turn' when the Saddlers had knocked North End out of the League Cup at Deepdale back in September. In fact, in the three contests between the teams to date, North End hadn't yet put the ball past Kearns.

North End had no injury concerns following the defeat by Peterborough, bar Danny Cameron complaining of a leg strain.

Stiles was still positive despite the previous weekend's setback.

"People have said to me that if we had won our last two games, promotion would be a forgone conclusion, but we have never had it easy and will have to work harder than ever over the next few weeks.

"Even after the setback we are still in a good position. We can't change our style now with just seven games left, so will continue to play as we have done all season, passing well and playing good constructive football.

"I think the battle will go on right until the end of the season."

Never have more prophetic words been spoken!

Match of the Day was extended that evening to include a full re-run of the Grand National. For the record, it was won by Lucius. North End v Peterborough was the main feature game, which was almost scanned through, it passed so quickly. The 'supporting' feature, Arsenal v Manchester United, lasted almost three times as long.

In the event, Cameron was fit to take part against Walsall, but there was a change in the North End line-up, as Stiles replaced Ricky Thomson with Mick Robinson.

Tunks, McMahon, Cameron, Burns, Baxter, Cross, Coleman, Haslegrave, Robinson, Elwiss, Bruce. Substitute: Doyle.

North End managed to finally get back on the winning trail by the narrowest of margins, but it wasn't without some huffing and puffing. As feared, Kearns had an excellent game in goal for Walsall, and certainly made life difficult once again for the North End attackers.

Preston began well, with Gordon Coleman unlucky with a shot after Francis Burns had played him in with a through ball, and Robinson having a header saved.

The Walsall supporters thought they had something to shout about following a rapid break from inside their own half after 15 minutes. New signing Terry Austin drilled the ball home past Roy Tunks; his obvious glee muted as he turned around and see the referee pulling play back for offside.

Alex Bruce then shot wide, and had another attempt saved by the leaping Kearns shortly after.

Austin had a shot blocked by Tunks when it seemed certain he would score; the North End 'keeper seeming to loudly remind his defence about their responsibilities!

It finally came together for North End in the 42nd minute, when a powerful Robinson shot hit 17 year old Walsall debutant Ian Paul on his planted left leg. The ball then ricocheted beyond the stranded Kearns and into the net to bring a much happier feel to Deepdale.

In the second half North End dominated proceedings, although Walsall

did have their moments. PNE FC

Mick Robinson fires in the shot that led to North End's vital goal

The aforementioned Paul tried to make amends with a John McMahon style drive for goal from some distance but it went just over the crossbar.

Alan Buckley, lower division striker supreme, had a shot on the turn well snaffled by Tunks who pulled off further fine saves to deny both Austin and Alan Birch.

Despite this, it was always North End who seemed likeliest to score with Bruce (two shots), Robinson, Danny Cameron and Mike Elwiss all bringing the best out of Republic of Ireland international Kearns.

The match ended Walsall's faint hopes of tagging onto the promotion chase of 77/78.

It was a decent performance from North End, who never stopped trying – nobly refusing to compromise their attacking style of football following the frustrations of the recent home games.

"It was a very hard game and Walsall proved they are a good side," said Nobby after the match.

"They made things difficult for us, but we showed a lot of character and grafted for 90 minutes. The lads' heads never went down after the Peterborough game."

Stiles was then asked about the results from the other games played on the same evening that affected the top of the table standings.

"I'm not worried about the other teams. All I know is that we have a good chance of going up and we will have to continue to work very hard. We must not lose our heads but we must keep our feet on the ground, because as I said after the Peterborough game, I don't think the promotion battle will be over until the very last match."

Next up with only six games remaining in the season, was a jaunt out to Wexham, where North End would take on the Division Three leaders, now surging towards the title.

Thursday brought news that both Dixie McNeil, Wrexham's leading scorer and central defender John Roberts were almost certain to miss the clash with North End at the Racecourse Ground on Saturday.

McNeil was reported to have been sidelined with a mystery injury over the past few weeks and was still receiving treatment from a physiotherapist, while Roberts was suffering from a hip injury.

Wrexham manager Arfon Griffiths, waiting as long as he could for more clarification on the injury siutuation before finally naming his team, was looking forward to the crunch game. He had nothing but respect for the Lilywhites.

"I rate Preston very highly, and think they will be promoted come the end of the season," he began.

"We have beaten them both in the FA Cup and League at Deepdale this season, but we had to give our best two performances of the year to achieve those successes.

"They played very well, and are a good side who are not easy to beat. We are looking forward to the game on Saturday and we all think that Preston will go up with us, and that Cambridge will probably be the other team.

"Elwiss and Bruce are two very good players who complement each other, but Preston have other good players too and we will have to play well against them all. They may have suffered from a bit of tension lately, but we will not be taking any chances."

Rather unusually Stiles declared his team on Friday, naming the same team that eventually pushed Walsall over earlier in the week.

"I know that tomorrow's game is completely different and that our win over Walsall is also behind us, but our victory has put the pep back in us and we know what we have to do at Wrexham. I don't know why we shouldn't be confident.

"Our two defeats against Wrexham have gone and I am sure it will be no harder for us to play at the Racecourse Ground than it was at Deepdale. We will need to work harder than ever before, but it won't be any good playing at 100 miles per hour. We must play to our strengths, pass the ball about accurately and be patient.

"They are a very good team and deserve to be Division Three leaders, but we are a very good side too and we fully deserve our third placing."

Nobby then had a few words for the North End fans, describing them as 'understanding' and 'terrific'.

"They have been terrific this season and understood the situation when we have been playing against packed defences in our recent home games. Even though we lost at home last Saturday against Peterborough, they continued to give us their help on Tuesday night and we are very grateful.

"They were tremendous in our last away games at Chester and Bury, helping us to give two very good performances, so we know they will be behind us again tomorrow and we hope we don't let them down."

The big day dawned fine and dry, with over 19,000 fans packing themselves into the Racecourse Ground, including a large North End contingent.

There had been no late dramas concerning player fitness, and the North End team was:-

Tunks, McMahon, Cameron, Burns, Baxter, Cross, Coleman, Haslegrave, Robinson, Elwiss, Bruce. Substitute: Doyle.

North End acquitted themselves very well, and took the honours in this tense, goalless epic. Yes, it is possible to witness a goalless epic! There are certain games that are played amid a sea of tension surrounding the possible outcomes for either participant that somehow produce wonderfully absorbing football – and no goals!

This encounter reminded me of another crucial April 'run-in' game in the previous North End promotion campaign of 1970/71, when a Deepdale crowd of well over 22,000 witnessed a superb goalless football match in a must-not-lose encounter against promotion rivals Aston Villa.

At Wrexham, North End were never overawed and fully deserved their point.

As it happened, Wrexham centre half Roberts was risked, and player/manager Griffiths rejigged the midfield and attack of the home side, making the unexpected move of turning out himself.

The game commenced to the accompaniment of a loud cheer, and Wrexham launched their first attack. This was cleared and in the first few minutes neither team could assert themselves.

Preston's passing, particularly through midfield was brisk and neat and they certainly looked the more confident of the two teams.

Griffiths' reshuffle seemed to be aimed at pumping long balls into the North End penalty area at times, in the hope that Mickey Thomas could run around the North End defence and capitalise. It wasn't working though, as Mick Baxter and Graham Cross were in outstanding form.

North End progressed down the pitch and Gordon Coleman, always ready to shoot at goal, did just that but the ball flew over the Wrexham crossbar. Bruce then took possession of the ball and entering the home penalty area, fell to the ground to loud shouts of 'penalty!' from the North End faithful. The ref was having none of it and waved play on.

Mick Robinson then drove a shot at goal and won a corner after it was deflected by a defender. The corner came to nothing, but North End were still looking the better team.

In the latter stages of the half, Wrexham tried to increase the tempo and it looked as though Thomas had been put through the North End back line but the referee blew for offside before he could get near the North End goal.

Roy Tunks then appeared to fumble a centre from the right from Mel Sutton, enabling Bobby Shinton to eventually drive the ball home, but the celebrations were immediately muted as the home fans saw the referee indicating that Graham Whittle had pushed the Preston keeper.

The football had been enthralling during the first half which seemed to have passed very quickly.

The second half commenced, and Thomas went past Danny Cameron before centring from the left. It never troubled Cross however, his clearing header travelling downfield to be picked up Sean Haslegrave.

PNE FC

A Wrexham welcoming committee assemble to deal with this shot from Alex Bruce

North End broke and appeared to have scored, but the 'goal' was disallowed after Robinson bundled the ball into the Wrexham net. John McMahon had whipped in a cross and both Robinson and Bruce had challenged goalkeeper Dai Davies as he leapt to catch the ball. There was no evidence of foul play in the eyes of the North End followers however, and they certainly let the referee know about it!

Once again, North End were looking the tastier of the two teams and on the hour launched the play of the match, a slick move that required a superb piece of goalkeeping craft from Davies to prevent North End taking the lead.

Mike Elwiss found Sean Haslegrave on the left wing with a superb pass. The midfielder progressed forward and then inward for a few yards before curling a low cross into the path of Bruce whose shot was blocked by the Wrexham goalkeeper who had moved forward off his line early in anticipation of such a situation.

A goalmouth scramble in North End's penalty area was finally cleared via a punt from Cameron, and Tunks came to the rescue a few minutes later when he dealt with a snap shot from Whittle.

Robinson then played Bruce in but his shot flew wide. Griffiths took himself off with just over 20 minutes left and this forced another reshuffle of the home attack; Thomas now fell back into midfield leaving Shinton, Whittle and substitute Lyons in attack.

Time wore on, attempts at both ends were made and beaten back. A Wrexham penalty appeal was rightly refused when Shinton seemed to lower himself to the ground in instalments, however the 'Miracle of the Racecourse' occurred a few seconds later as the striker sprung to his feet as a shooting opportunity arose!

The game ended in a draw; an excellent performance by the Lilywhites whose fans set off back home in good spirits.

Wrexham boss Griffiths said after the game, "It was very tense, and maybe we were over cautious. We didn't want to lose the game and didn't go forward as much as we should have done.

"Our fans were as edgy as we were and were very good considering we didn't create a single chance. We were always conscious of the game's importance, I was uptight so I hoped that John Lyons would cause problems when he replaced me, but he didn't and Alex Bruce's chance was the only one in the game.

"Unfortunately, Mickey Thomas couldn't get around the back of the Preston defence at all. The only player who could get away from his man was Preston's Mike Elwiss who was the best player in the game and would be an even better one if he got into the penalty area more often. Preston played very well and marked us really tightly."

Nobby was delighted.

"Everybody worked very hard and I am chuffed with our display. The

WEEKEND

Leisure and Football POST

Lancashire Evening Post

No. 28,322 SATURDAY APRIL 8 1978 8p

INSIDE

ANDREW HOYLE'S GOLD CUP PREVIEW CHELTENHAM PAGE TWO

NORMAN SHAKESHAFT ON £SD AT PNE PAGE FOUR

THE TEAM THAT'S ALREADY WON PROMOTION PAGE TWO

PLUS

WINNERS GALORE!

AND MORE PRIZES IN JUNIOR POST

● Blackburn Rovers forward Jack Lewis gets the ball past Brighton's Clark during today's Division Two match at Ewood. Report page 10

Arsenal gun down brave Orient to reach Final

By MICHAEL MORRIS

FAVOURITES Arsenal gunned down gallant Orient at Stamford Bridge today to reach the FA Cup Final.

Two goals in the first half from Malcolm Macdonald and another from Graham Rix after the interval reflected the Gunners' overall semi-final superiority.

ARSENAL: Jennings, Rice, Nelson, Price, O'Leary, Young, Brady, Hudson, Macdonald, Stapleton, Rix. Sub: Walford.

ORIENT: Jackson, Fisher, Roffey, Grealish, Hoadley, Bowder, Clarke, Gray, Mayo, Kitchen, Bennett. Sub: Banjo.

Referee: P. Partridge (Stockton).

The big guns of Arsenal were quick to open up and Orient caved in under the pressure of some sustained attacking.

First only a desperate lunge by Jackson and clearance by Gray kept out a shot by Price. Then with Hudson commanding the operation, the ball was channelled to Young at the far post and the big defender's header hit the crossbar.

In the 16th minute MACDONALD scored the first of two almost identical goals.

After some direct play by Hudson and Stapleton the ball was crossed to Macdonald and the striker, who has scored in every round of the Cup, found the goal when his shot was deflected off the unfortunate Roffey.

Four minutes later MACDONALD, looking at his sharpest, trapped the ball on the edge of the Orient area, turned and volleyed. Once more there was a deflection and the ball hit the back of the Orient net.

The Orient defence looked no match for the Arsenal attack that was switching wings with fluency and Hudson was

BRAVE PNE GAIN PRECIOUS POINT

By NORMAN SHAKESHAFT

PRESTON took the honours in a goalless draw with Third Division leaders Wrexham at the Racecourse ground today and maintained their strong hopes of gaining promotion.

North End, who are in third place in the table, were never overawed by the talented players in the Wrexham side and always did their fair share of attacking.

The defenders were efficient with Mick Baxter and Graham Cross outstanding, the midfield men worked

Wrexham: Dai Davies, Evans, Dwyer, Gareth Davis, Roberts, Thomas, Shinton, Sutton, Griffiths, Whittle, Cartwright. Sub: Lyons.

Preston: Tunks, McMahon, Burns, Baxter

SCOREBOARD

FA CUP

(Semi-Finals)

Ipswich	★	WBA	★
(at Arsenal FC)			
Orient	0	Arsenal	3
(at Chelsea FC)			

DIVISION ONE

B'm'gh'm	2	Norwich	1
Coventry	3	Everton	2
Derby C	3	Wolves	1
Leeds U	1	West Ham	2
Liverpool	3	Leicester	2
Man Utd	3	QPR	1
Midd'bro	2	Bristol C	0
N'wcastle	1	Aston V	1

DIVISION TWO

B'ckb'n R	0	Brighton	1
Blackpool	1	Stoke	1
Bristol R	4	Sheff Utd	1
Cardiff	2	Crystal P	2
Charlton	0	Hull C	1
Fulham	1	S'th'pton	1
Luton	1	Sund'land	2
Notts C	1	Millwall	1
Oldham	0	Mansfield	1
Tott'ham	1	Bolton	0

DIVISION THREE

Bury	★	Bradf'd C	★
Chest'f'ld	★	Plymouth	★
Exeter	2	Gill'gham	1
Lincoln	4	C'mb'ge	1
Peterboro	1	Roth'ham	0
Portsm'th	3	Carlisle	3

DIVISION FOUR

B'nem'th	1	Rochdale	0
Brentford	2	Barnsley	0
Crewe	2	Swansea	1
Halifax	3	Newport	1
Hartlep'l	2	Stockport	0
N'th'pt'n	0	Doncaster	0
Reading	0	Grimsby	0
Scunth'pe	★	Watford	★
Southend	2	Darl'gton	0

RUGBY LEAGUE

Hull KR	7	Bradf'd N	15
Leeds	16	Widnes	13

RUGBY UNION

CHESHIRE LEAGUE

RUGBY LEAGUE CUP

St Helens	12	Warr'gt'n	8

Doc offers £250,000

pressure was on for both sides, but we still played three men at the front and created the best chance of the game.

"We deserved a goal and our attitude was great. The lads were disciplined and passed the ball about well.

"We were well beaten first time out against Wrexham this season, it was touch and go in the second and we really believed in ourselves this time. Wrexham are a brilliant team and yet we looked the better side, especially in the first half. I'm happy with a point because you can't be greedy, but I couldn't fault the lads on their display and I think it was terrific."

The league scene now went on the back burner at Deepdale for a couple of days as Tuesday evening, April 11th saw the David Sadler testimonial match take place at Deepdale against Manchester United, who had sent a strong squad up the M61.

United were managed by Dave Sexton at that time, and stuck in the middle of Division One. He was quoted as hoping that this tribute to Sadler would also be a good workout for his team. Stiles was looking upon the game in a similar light, and said that United's agreement to play was a "great gesture." Unfortunately, Graham Cross and Sean Haslegrave had reported troublesome knocks after the Wrexham game and wouldn't therefore be taking part whilst work on them continued in preparation for the home clash with Lincoln City at the weekend.

Coincidentally, North End reserves had beaten Manchester United reserves in the Central League at Deepdale by 2-0, while the first team were busy earning a precious point at Wrexham. Inspired by the presence of veteran Alan Spavin who totally commanded midfield, the North End youngsters outplayed a United team that included five players with Division One experience.

Ricky Thomson had fired North End into the lead, breaking through the visitor's defence after 20 minutes; the win sealed by Ian Cochrane's shot with around 10 minutes remaining.

An excellent crowd of 10,380 braved the very cold and windy weather to pay homage to a player who was a European Cup and Division One title winner whilst at Old Trafford, as well as becoming a full England international.

Sadler was the consummate professional footballer at both his league clubs, and I can still remember the general opinion amongst North End fans when he first arrived that he would be a superb signing for the club.

Indeed he was. A skilful central defender, he proved a calm but imposing influence in the North End defence during his time at Deepdale, and I think it is fair to say that Mark Lawrenson and Mick Baxter must have benefitted greatly by playing alongside him in the North End back four in their formative years.

PNE FC

David Sadler is applauded onto the pitch by both teams before kick-off

A player with a temperament a manager could only wish for, he never let his teammates or his employers down at Old Trafford or Deepdale. David Sadler was class.

When it was confirmed that after just three and a half years at Deepdale he was having to retire following a knee injury, Sadler neither sought nor expected anything from North End. It was the Preston directors who granted him a testimonial as a gesture of thanks, for being, in the words of chairman Alan Jones "an excellent asset to the club."

The contest itself was won rather surprisingly by North End to the tune of 3-0, with most of the interest in the first half when United's first team, fresh from their 3-1 win over Queens Park Rangers four days previously, went up against North End's first team.

The three goals were all scored in that first half... and all scored by the rampant Mike Elwiss.

Of course, it wasn't a full blown league or cup contest, but United certainly didn't give the impression they had turned up to be whitewashed. North End didn't give the impression that they were going to be overawed either.

Elwiss started the ball rolling as early as the fourth minute when he cut in from the left wing in his time honoured fashion, accelerated past United captain and Scottish international Martin Buchan along the way before drilling the ball a right footed shot past Alex Stepney's dive into the corner of the net.

Play then went back and forth, with United's all-star internationals putting the North End defenders under pressure at times. Roy Tunks commanded his area well, and North End contributed to the spectacle by moving the ball about quickly and accurately.

The hat-trick goal from Mike Elwiss

On the half hour Elwiss found himself in the clear, with only Stepney to beat. The North End skipper was never going to miss this opportunity, and duly crashed the ball past the helpless United keeper from around 15 yards.

United's defence couldn't quite get the hang of dealing with the roving game of Elwiss and after collecting a pass from Mick Baxter he galloped forward – once again leaving Buchan trailing in his wake. With only Stepney standing between him and a hat-trick, Elwiss smacked in a low, hard and unforgiving left foot shot into the corner of the net.

Friendly or not, this was one hell of a show from Elwiss, who almost added a fourth when his rapier-like shot slammed against Stepney's crossbar, sending it into a 'wobble spasm'.

Obviously, the pressure of the promotion campaign had been switched to 'off', and the North End team really looked as though they were enjoying things.

The second half was a little more subdued as each manager made a raft of personnel changes at half time. It was a slight disappointment for the crowd, but in North End's case at least, the reality was that there was a promotion crusade to resume concentrating on in just a few day's time.

For North End, on came reserve keeper John Kilner plus teammate Peter Morris, and from the first team squad Harry Wilson, Ricky Thomson, Steve Uzelac, Alan Spavin and John Smith, leaving just Stephen Doyle, Gordon Coleman, Ian Cochrane and Mick Robinson of the starting XI.

With United similarly changed, the game became competitive but even with the retention of centre forward Joe Jordan and winger Steve Coppell, the visitors couldn't find the net before time was finally called on an entertaining game... and Sadler's fine career.

Following the game, the teams and guests headed to a reception held at the Trafalgar Hotel, Samlesbury. After thanking the United and North End players and officials, Sadler expressed his gratitude to the North End supporters in particular, almost breaking down as he said he would never forget their kindness.

Sadler was due to start work at the Chester branch of the Town and Country Building Society the following week. How football has changed!

With no injuries reported by the players following the testimonial, and Graham Cross and Sean Haslegrave both making full recoveries from knocks sustained at Wrexham, Stiles had the luxury of naming an unchanged team for the third time in succession for the contest against Lincoln City at Deepdale.

"We must have the right attitude and keep working hard against Lincoln and realise that all our remaining games are going to be difficult," said the manager. *"Our supporters can really help us now.*

"They have been terrific all season, but we need all the support and cheering we can get. If we are ever going to be a really successful club again, the players and the fans will have to work hand in hand.

"I know the fans can get frustrated at times, especially in home games when opposing teams concentrate on defending. The recent defeat against Peterborough was very disappointing for our fans but they came back in numbers for the Walsall game and that was terrific.

"It lifted us and enabled us to win."

Since replacing George Kerr with ex-Birmingham City manager Wille Bell, Lincoln City had only lost five games in 21 outings transforming their plight from a dogged relegation struggle to the comfort of mid-table security.

With North End's deep well of league goals running dry of late, a comment by David Sadler after the midweek testimonial game that, 'North End could well benefit from the hat-trick feat of Mike Elwiss by becoming a little more relaxed and confident in front of goal against Lincoln,' proved to be bang on the money.

Granada Television were recording the match for their Sunday afternoon highlights programme, 'Kick Off', this causing some apprehension apparently amongst the North End team, as they couldn't remember North End ever getting a good result in front of the cameras!

The North End team for this television feast was:-

Tunks, McMahon, Cameron, Burns, Baxter, Cross, Coleman, Haslegrave, Robinson, Elwiss, Bruce. Substitute: Doyle.

On a cool, sunny spring day Lincoln kicked off towards the Town End. After the opening jousts, Francis Burns sent Danny Cameron haring down the left, who then prodded the ball on to Alex Bruce; the move coming to halt when Lincoln City centre half Clive Wiggington conceded a corner.

Sean Haselgrave curled in the corner which was eventually cleared to John McMahon deep on the right touchline. A twist to the left saw him create a enough room to cross the ball back into the goalmouth where Wigginton, aerially challenged by Mike Elwiss, could only help the ball on across the face of goal where it was met by the leaping Mick Robinson who headed firmly past the helpless Lincoln keeper, Peter Grotier.

One up after just three minutes, and on television. It must be a dream! It certainly felt like one when North End went two up after 15 minutes.

PNE FC

<u>Top left</u>: 1-0 Mick Robinson heads home <u>Top right</u>: 2-0 Mick Baxter smashes the ball in
<u>Middle</u>: 3-0 Alex Bruce lashes the ball into the net
<u>Bottom</u> : 4-0 Gordon Coleman clips the ball over the Lincoln 'keeper

A pacey run down the left wing by Elwiss produced a corner following a headed clearance by Phil Neale, the Imps full back and Worcestershire CCC opening bat.

Haslegrave's corner was glanced on by Robinson, which led to a goalmouth scramble whereupon Elwiss had two point-blank shots blocked. Following the second attempt the ball rolled out of the melee to the watching Mick Baxter who proceeded to 'welly' the ball high into the roof of the net from around seven yards.

Giving the happy home fans 10 minutes or so to settle down again, North End went three clear in the 25th minute.

After a clearance had been hooked forward by Cameron, Robinson's looping header from the edge of the visitors box fell between the Lincoln keeper and defenders. Elwiss dashed forward and his challenge on goalkeeper Grotier saw the ball eventually bounce away to Alex Bruce, six yards out and just a defender on the goal line. Bruce needed no second invitation. The ball was leathered home mercilessly, to the loud cheers of the home crowd.

The match then settled down into a slower tempo, but North End remained comfortably in control.

After 55 minutes the match was very much all over for Lincoln City as the Lilywhites added a fourth goal to their tally.

A throw-in from Haslegrave to Elwiss on the left was how it all began. From there, Lincoln defender Terry Cooper was turned inside out in an instant before the North End captain punched in a superb left footed centre that was met by Robinson about seven yards out.

Grotier, having to palm the ball away from the bottom corner with a sprawling dive, watched prostrate as Gordon Coleman, who had followed up on the right side of the goalmouth, fired the ball back over him into the net.

Lincoln had a couple of attempts at getting a consolation goal, but couldn't quite get the ball over the line with their best effort, a leaping header from Phil Hubbard which was cleared off the North End goal line by the ever alert Graham Cross.

However, additional North End efforts from Robinson, Bruce, Cameron and Coleman threatened to increase the North End score still further, all ably assisted by Elwiss who seemed to have far too much power for the Lincoln defence.

WEEKEND
Leisure and Football POST
Lancashire Evening Post
No. 28,328 SATURDAY APRIL 15 1978 8p

INSIDE
CURRIE comes in from the cold — see page 2
IN OFF THE POST PAGE FOUR

PLUS
TRAVEL DESK IN CYPRUS
DISNEY THEATRES TO BE WON

'Pool go down at Millwall, Rovers draw at lowly Mansfield

PNE HIT FOUR IN PROMOTION DRIVE

By NORMAN SHAKESHAFT

PRESTON maintained their strong challenge for promotion to Division Two when they beat Lincoln City 4-0 at Deepdale today in front of a crowd of 11,208.

1978

Sparks fly in Guild Hall finale!

By DON JONES

THE sparks were flying at Preston Guild Hall today, both on and off the court!

Shortly after Nora Perry and Anne Statt had picked up the women's doubles title in their European Badminton Championships final against another English pair, Barbara Sutton and Jane Webster, the BBC lights fused in a shower of tiny fire balls.

The Championships were held up as technicians feverishly worked to mend the damage.

Mrs Perry and Mrs Statt were clear 15-7 15-7 victors over Mrs Sutton and Miss Webster who received her second loser's medal within the space of a couple of hours.

SCOREBOARD

DIVISION ONE

Arsenal	2	N'wcastle	1
Aston V	2	Chelsea	0
Bristol C	1	Liverpool	1
Everton	1	Ipswich	0
Leicester	1	B'm'gh'm	4
Man C	1	WBA	3
Norwich	1	Man Utd	3
Nottm F	1	Leeds U	1
QPR	2	Coventry	1
West Ham	3	Derby C	0
Wolves	0	Midd'bro'	0

DIVISION TWO

Bolton	3	Bristol R	0
Brighton	★	Tott'ham	★
Burnley	4	Cardiff	2
Crystal P	1	Orient	0
Hull C	0	Fulham	1
Mansfield	2	B'ckb'n R	2
Millwall	2	Blackpool	0
Sheff Utd	1	Charlton	0
S'th'pton	2	Oldham	2
Stoke	0	Luton	0
Sund'land	3	Notts C	1

DIVISION THREE

Bradf'd C	1	Exeter	2
C'mb'ge	2	Chest'f'ld	0
Carlisle	1	Shrewsb'y	0
Chester	1	Bury	0
C'lchester	1	Wrexham	1
Gill'gham	2	Sheff W	1
Hereford	0	Portsm'th	2
Oxford U	3	Walsall	1
Plymouth	1	Peterboro	0
Preston	4	Lincoln	0
Roth'ham	1	Swindon	[illegible]

DIVISION FOUR

Aldershot	0	Halifax	0
Barnsley	2	N'th'pt'n	3
Darl'gton	1	B'nem'th	0
Doncaster	3	Hartlep'l	0
Grimsby	2	Crewe	2
Hudd'f'ld	0	Reading	2
Newport	★	Southport	★
Rochdale	1	Scunth'pe	1
Stockport	3	Torquay	0
Swansea	2	Brentford	1
Watford	1	Southend	1

RUGBY UNION
Hoppers 12, Wakefield 28
Fylde 13 N. Brighton 12

RUGBY LEAGUE

Castlef'd	34	Wigan	10
F'stone R	★	Warr'g'n	★
Leeds	34	Salford	7

NORTHERN PREMIER LEAGUE
Stafford R. 2, Netherfield 0
Macclesfield 1 Morecambe 2

CHESHIRE LEAGUE
Leek 0, Chorley 0

LATE NEWS
FOOTBALL FINAL SCORES
BRIGTON 3 SPURS 1
NEWPORT 1 STHPORT 1

A 4-0 trouncing of the opposition, and on television too. It certainly made up for the Peterborough defeat in front of the cameras a fortnight earlier!

Nobby of course was thrilled

"All the lads played well and we got the reward we have deserved for some time.

"Mick Robinson and Mike Elwiss also played great at the front, Robinson having worked very hard on improving his heading ability, and Elwiss having improved tremendously since he arrived at Deepdale.

"His crossing of the ball was terrific and we could have had a few more goals with a bit of luck.

"I was glad that we played so well in front of the television cameras too, and I told the lads beforehand that things had to change some time. But it's behind us now, and we will need to carry on applying ourselves against Sheffield Wednesday on Tuesday, and then the three remaining games."

The Sheffield Wednesday encounter at Hillsborough had fallen foul of the weather when it was originally scheduled to take place in January.

Wednesday were in deep relegation trouble at the turn of the year, but the 'Jackie Charlton effect' had taken hold since then, and they were now comfortably placed away from any relegation worries.

"Jack Charlton has done a good job since taking over as manager and the tactics have changed," said Stiles.

"The team plays to more of a pattern, and the defence is better organised. They are difficult to beat on their own ground and Jack always does his homework on opposing teams."

The LEP's North End correspondent Norman Shakeshaft, reckoned that North End still needed five or six more points from their final four games to be sure of promotion. This presumed that all the other clubs in contention for promotion would be taking maximum points.

There were no injury complaints following the Lincoln victory, so Stiles named an unchanged team for the fourth successive game:-

Tunks, McMahon, Cameron, Burns, Baxter, Cross, Coleman, Haslegrave, Robinson, Elwiss, Bruce. Substitute: Doyle.

On a cold, cloudy evening North End turned in a performance that was entirely the opposite of what was needed or expected. Complacency may have been involved, but both Stiles and Kelly had stressed to the players beforehand that there had to be none. The North End attack was clunky too and looked meagre in comparison to the ruthless forward line that had destroyed Lincoln City just a few days previously.

Despite a crowd of 12,426, the massive Hillsborough stadium still seemed rather empty and this added a hollow echo-like feel for the spectator.

It was as if North End had pre-determined that they would be happy to settle for a point, against an organised but negatively drilled team. If a just point had been brought home this probably would have been seen as good enough, but this North End team should have done much better than even that.

The knock back to goalkeeper Roy Tunks was the most common pass in a dreary first half, where one-dimensional Wednesday were not good – or unwilling – enough to ask any real questions of the visitor's defence, while North End were seemingly content not to do what had come naturally to them all season – attack!

Just once in the first half did North End sally forth with some intent, when Francis Burns pushed an exquisite through ball for Alex Bruce to chase, but he shot wide under challenge from defender Hugh Dowd.

The rest of the half was occupied with safety-first football.

Having laid out their tactics for all see, it would only need Wednesday to score first to massively disrupt North End's masterplan – and on the hour the worst happened.

A shot from Brian Hornsby, recently acquired from Shrewsbury Town, was saved by Tunks but he couldn't hold the ball. In the ensuing goalmouth fracas, Tommy Tynan managed to prod the ball into the net despite a bold effort by Graham Cross to hook it away.

With their original game plan now in shreds, North End suddenly had to take risks but with just 30 minutes left, it was all rather panic stricken. As they scrambled to put moves together, the wheels very nearly came off completely when Wednesday midfielder Ian Porterfield fired in a snap shot that rattled the North End crossbar before bouncing to safety.

Mick Baxter was unlucky to have an appeal for a penalty turned down when he appeared to be blatantly pushed from behind in the Owls penalty area, but the referee evened up matters by reprieving Tunks when he seemed to have impeded Tynan.

Efforts from Robinson, Bruce and skipper Mike Elwiss were valiant, but in vain.

Tempers flared and both Mick Robinson and Tynan were booked in separate incidents. Stephen Doyle was then sent on as a final measure to help the North End flow forward, but this was tempered by Charlton substituting Rodger Wylde for Denis Lehman 10 minutes from time – a move which basically closed the game out completely.

Wednesday had now taken their points tally to 13 from their last eight games. A superb run, but it must have been difficult to watch!

The North End manager admitted that his team didn't play well, and told the fans not to feel sorry for the team.

"Obviously the result was a big setback to our hopes of gaining promotion to Division Two, we are all very disappointed and sick, but we may now have to show our character. We mustn't feel sorry for ourselves and we must just get on with the job of working hard and applying ourselves.

"We felt the pressure, and Wednesday made things difficult for us. Some of our passing was not up to our usual standard and on the whole the game was poor.

"Whatever the press or pundits say, promotion will not be decided until the last game has been played. We have never had things easy this season, certainly not in this game and certainly not in our last three fixtures to come.

"I know Peterborough have closed the gap at the top but the outcome of our bid is still in our own hands and it is up to us to show the right attitude."

Thursday 20th April arrived and the participating players at Hillsborough hadn't reported any injuries so they joined the remaining squad members of Harry Wilson, John Smith and Alan Spavin on the Friday afternoon coach down to Portsmouth. The south coast outfit were doomed to relegation.

"We gave the ball away far too much at Hillsborough," said assistant manager Alan Kelly. "We have played much better in nearly all our other games and we can play much better, so we hope that Tuesday night's display was a one-off thing.

"Obviously we need to get two points from a win."

Nobby was trying to calm matters down however before the coach set off.

"It won't do any good to start flapping at this stage of the season," he began. *"Losing the other night was a setback and we didn't play well, although we only went down to a scrambled goal.*

"We have got to believe in ourselves, and make things happen on the field. The lads got back on the rails after the Peterborough defeat and I have every confidence that they can do again.

"Obviously we are feeling the pressure, Preston and Portsmouth have great traditions and I would rather have the pressure that is on us than that which is on Portsmouth."

Stiles kept the same team for the fifth game in succession:-

Tunks, McMahon, Cameron, Burns, Baxter, Cross, Coleman, Haslegrave, Robinson, Elwiss, Bruce. Substitute: Doyle.

North End certainly kept their fans biting their nails in this match, waiting until the last 10 minutes before finally sealing the win. It was just the tonic needed after the defeat at Hillsborough during the week.

North End playing in yellow shirts, blue shorts and yellow socks certainly looked the part, and the game started brightly, with Mick Robinson going nearest when his header from a John McMahon cross went just wide.

Mike Elwiss and Alex Bruce both put shots in for no reward, but then quite out of the blue, Portsmouth centre half Steve Foster had a header cleared off the North End line by Graham Cross following a free kick.

North End keeper Roy Tunks was then called upon to save a long shot from Pompey full back Keith Viney before Bruce had a shot scrambled away, and Elwiss then shot over from a free kick.

A powerful Francis Burns shot from all of 30 yards tested Steve Middleton, the ball seeming to hit the Portsmouth goalkeeper, rather than be saved by him.

A late home flurry before half time gave the travelling North End fans the collywobbles, with Tunks thankfully on hand to save a David Pullar shot, diving full length to clutch the ball.

Colin Garwood then shot over, and another shot was well saved by Tunks at the expense of a corner. This was half cleared by North End, but the ball was drilled back into the Preston net by Foster from near the penalty spot; his leaps of joy ended by the linesman ruling offside.

Although there had been close calls for North End in the first half, they had made chances too, and it was infinitely more preferable to the frustrating performance at Hillsborough a few days before.

North End definitely upped the ante when play recommenced. The problem was they couldn't finish off a string of promising and positive moves as they piled forward in search of a goal.

On top of a 'goal' disallowed for offside from Gordon Coleman, attempts by Bruce, Elwiss, Burns, Mick Baxter and Sean Haslegrave all went begging.

North End HAD to score! They couldn't afford to leave Fratton Park without taking home the points from already relegated Portsmouth. Anything less would be a massive blow, and would undoubtedly terminate all hopes of promotion.

It took until the 81st minute for the vital goal to arrive. And then, like a corporation bus, another arrived soon after.

John McMahon started the move, passing the ball forward down the right for Elwiss. His centre found a completely unmarked Bruce who headed the ball over and beyond Middleton to put the Lilywhites ahead. Cue fist pumping and celebration from the delighted visitors.

After Pullar had seen his shot saved by Tunks following the restart, North End went straight down the pitch and doubled their lead. Robinson squared the ball across the Portsmouth box into the path of Elwiss on the left, who hammered in a low left footed shot from around 15 yards which flew past the diving Middleton.

With victory sealed, North End saw the remaining minutes out confidently.

North End left it late before hitting Portsmouth with 'the old one-two' as the game drew to a close.

<u>Top</u>: Alex Bruce connects with a Mike Elwiss cross to put North End ahead

<u>Bottom</u>: Elwiss secures the win when he slams the ball home following a pass from Mick Robinson

PNE FC

Dreamland! North End had done it, and were still well positioned in the promotion race. There was relief all round for the management, players and of course the fans, both at Fratton Park and back home, listening on BBC Radio Blackburn.

Stiles was delighted with the vital win.

"It was fully deserved for displaying patience and character... but I was anxious until we increased the pressure in the second half.

"John McMahon played superbly in the defence and Mick Robinson did a tremendous job at the front, but we had to work very hard. We got the breaks in the end, and I was relieved when the ref disallowed their 'goal' for offside just before the interval, because that kind of decision has gone against us in some of our games."

Nobby ended with a big thankyou to North End fans who had made their way down to the game.

"I want the fans who watch us away from home to know that we and the players really appreciate them. They were well behaved at Fratton Park and didn't retaliate despite being incited by a group of Portsmouth fans who forced them onto the pitch. I spoke to them and they returned to the terraces quietly and were only interested in our players getting the result they deserved. They gave us a great reception outside the ground after the match."

After the jubilation of the win at Fratton Park, North End had only to face relegation threatened Rotherham United away at Millmoor on the following Tuesday, and mid-table Shrewsbury Town at Deepdale on the last day of the season. Surely, it wasn't unfair for their devoted followers to assume that the team could hold things together for just another week and collect the four points that would cement them as runners-up to Wrexham – already promoted after trouncing Rotherham at the weekend.

Little did they know it, but the North End squad were about to enter what would surely be the most nerve-wracking six days of their entire careers. The race for the two remaining promotion places would seemingly change hands on a daily basis. Fans, and no doubt the players too, would go over all the possible permutations time and time again.

WEEKEND

Leisure and Football POST

Lancashire Evening Post

No. 28,334 SATURDAY APRIL 22 1978 8p

INSIDE

JIM SMITH & HIS NEW JOB — Page 2

Do North End deserve better support?

Read Norman Shakeshaft and Letters — Page 4

PLUS

What Now for the Hollies?

And

SELF SUFFICIENCY

LOTS OF PRIZES

Bruce and Elwiss boost promotion bid

NORTH END GRAB POINTS WITH A LATE GOAL BURST!

ROY TUNKS

PRESTON improved their chances of gaining promotion to Division Two at the end of the season when they collected two points from a 2-0 win over Portsmouth in front of a crowd of 6,866 at Fratton Park today.

Portsmouth, who are doomed to relegation to Division Four had little to offer but North End did not break the deadlock until leading scorer Alex Bruce headed in a centre from Mike Elwiss nine minutes from the end.

TV Soccer

● BBC Match of the Day: Coventry v Nottingham Forest, Middlesbrough v Everton.

● GRANADA tomorrow: Manchester United v West Ham United.

SCOREBOARD

DIVISION ONE

B'm'gh'm	1	Man C	4
Chelsea	1	Wolves	1
Coventry	0	Nottm F	0
Derby C	4	Leicester	1
Ipswich	1	Bristol C	0
Leeds U	1	Arsenal	3
Liverpool	3	Norwich	0
Man Utd	3	West Ham	0
Midd'bro'	0	Everton	0
N'wcastle	0	QPR	3
WBA	0	Aston V	3

DIVISION TWO

B'ckb'n R	1	Sheff Utd	1
Blackpool	1	Mansfield	2
Bristol R	4	Stoke	1
Cardiff	1	Bolton	0
Charlton	3	Burnley	2
Fulham	0	Millwall	1
Luton	1	S'th'pton	2
Notts C	2	Crystal P	0
Oldham	1	Brighton	1
Orient	2	Hull C	1
Tott'ham	2	Sund'land	3

DIVISION THREE

Bury	★	Plymouth	★
Chest'f'ld	★	Chester	★
Exeter	0	C'lchester	0
Lincoln	3	Bradf'd C	2
Peterboro	1	Tranmere	0
Portsm'th	0	Preston	2
Port Vale	0	Carlisle	1
Sheff W	0	C'mb'ge	0
Shrewsb'y	1	Oxford U	0
	1	Hereford	0

DIVISION FOUR

B'nem'th	1	Grimsby	0
Brentford	2	Darl'gton	0
Crewe	2	Doncaster	0
Halifax	1	Watford	1
Hartlep'l	1	Newport	1
N'th'pt'n	3	Swansea	1
Reading	0	Barnsley	0
Scunth'pe	★	Aldershot	★
Southend	3	Rochdale	1
Southport	1	Hudd'f'ld	1

RUGBY LEAGUE

Division One

Leeds	23	Worr'gt'n	15
St Helens	33	Hull KR	13
Worr'gt'n	41	N Hunslet	8

RUGBY UNION INTER-SERVICES TOURNAMENT

Army 16 R.A.F. 6

Early boost

With a rallying cry from Nobby urging the fans to get behind the team on their final road trip of the season, the North End team set off for Millmoor.

There were no changes to the team, which made its sixth consecutive outing:-

Tunks, McMahon, Cameron, Burns, Baxter, Cross, Coleman, Haslegrave, Robinson, Elwiss, Bruce. Substitute: Doyle.

The North End fans travelled across the Pennines in their numbers to cheer on the team, as Nobby had hoped. Rotherham, still applying the ointment after a 7-1 caning at Wrexham just three days ago were surely no match for the Lilywhites.

Everything was in place.

Just 90 minutes later, those travelling North End devotees were walking back to their cars and coaches looking at the floor, shaking their heads in disbelief and hardly speaking. Was this the reward for their undying support?

No matter which way you looked at it, North End had put in a great display – yes, despite losing 2-1. That went a long way to explaining the head shaking – well that, and an incomprehensible error from the usually brilliant Graham Cross that led to Rotherham's opener.

The will to earn their living in Division Three in 1978/79 undoubtedly played a massive part in Rotherham United's positive response to their humiliation at Wrexham. They needed a win just as badly as North End did. Whilst North End were actually the best team on view, it was Rotherham who got the breaks. That's what this match boiled down to.

It all started so well. Two corners in the first minute of the game showed North End's intent, a pointer to the sustained attacking performance that was to follow.

A word at this point about North End skipper, Mike Elwiss. Nobody played better or gave more for the Preston cause than he. Leading by example he ran miles, contested every ball within range, and was desperately unlucky not to score on several occasions.

As half time approached, Tom McAllister the Rotherham goalkeeper had been kept busy with three attempts from Elwiss, two from Mick Robinson, another couple each from Alex Bruce and Gordon Coleman.

Then, in the 39th minute, disaster. Cross failed to execute a straightforward clearance from a long through ball from David Gwyther, leaving Trevor Phillips one on one with Roy Tunks. As the former Rotherham keeper advanced from his line, Phillips kept his head and slid the ball past him into the net.

North End emerged after half time not with heads lowered, but more determined than ever to claw the game back.

Intense pressure from the Lilywhites saw several corners won, and Elwiss almost equalised when he turned on a sixpence and sent a screaming shot goalward which was somehow scrambled away.

Bruce and McMahon were both booked in separate incidents as a degree of frustration at not being able to get the ball over the Rotherham goal line began to shine through.

Rotherham were working hard too, and created several openings as North End pushed men forward. Phillips was a player Preston were having to constantly watch and he went very close to adding to his first half goal on two further occasions.

Coleman and Sean Haslegrave both tried their luck with excellent shots, but McAllister deflected them away. The North End goal attempts tally must have been approaching a hundred when Cross conceded a foul on Phillips at the other end.

Jim Goodfellow swung the ball into the North End box, whereupon Paul Stancliffe headed the ball past Tunks to put Rotherham 2-0 up. Despite all the North End effort, it was as quick, simple and clinical as that.

Cross was pulled off by Stiles and Stephen Doyle ran on in his place. The censored instructions Nobby barked out from the bench must have been on the lines of, "Tally-ho boys, let's go for it!" as North End threw everything they had forward.

Elwiss and Robinson both went close, the latter having a header saved and shooting narrowly, but excruciatingly, wide. Another Elwiss shot was then rifled in before finally, with just eight minutes left, the long overdue but fully deserved goal arrived – courtesy of Bruce.

Collecting a Coleman pass in the area, he flicked the ball out to Robinson on the right, charged forward taking Robinson's return pass as he slid in, crashing home his 29th goal of the season.

Try as they did, another goal wasn't forthcoming for North End.

PNE FC

Alex Bruce slides in to notch his 29th goal of the season

It was indeed a spirited win for Rotherham, but North End deserved so much more than to lose.

The match was best summed up with the images of the Rotherham fans invading the pitch to mob their heroes, while the North End players were cutting lonely figures as they walked through the crowd, heads bowed, back to the dressing room. In their heads it must have seemed like a whole season's graft was about to disappear, no matter how hard they tried on the pitch.

Nobby needed to find the right words after the game for both the disconsolate players and fans.

He did just fine. A mixture of defiance, continued belief in his 'lads' and hope was his message to the faithful via the press.

"Naturally the players are dejected at the moment, and nobody can expect anything else. But they will only feel sorry for themselves for a day or so and won't need lifting for the Shrewsbury game because they are good professionals and good players.

"I won't criticise any of my players. They all worked very hard, their heads never went down until the final whistle, and I could not ask any more of them. I can only praise their efforts.

"Graham Cross has been criticised by some for making a mistake which led to Rotherham's first goal, but the game is all about mistakes – and he hasn't made many. He has been magnificent this season and has been one of the reasons why we are still near the top of the table.

"We needed a break and didn't get it, but you have to credit Rotherham for playing very well too. They needed a result very badly as well – but also got the break.

"We got the goal, but were unlucky not to get one or two more. Mike Elwiss was terrific and he was particularly unfortunate not to score.

"I thought our fans were tremendous. It was great to see a lot of them still giving us their support on the way back home. I can assure them that the players really appreciate their backing and hope to see them all again on Saturday.

"We will go all out to win our match on Saturday to make it hard for Peterborough and Cambridge and we are still in with a chance. You have to be optimistic in football and fight all the way to make things as difficult as possible for your rivals."

The lingering after effects of this game in the players' minds – doubt, failure and rising tension, were to rear up again in the final match of the season.

As a consequence of the defeat at Rotherham, the top of Division Three was re-drawn again.

Whilst North End were losing at Millmoor, Cambridge United had beaten champions Wrexham 1-0 and moved above the Lilywhites into second place. Cambridge weren't the real threat to North End however; that honour belonged to Peterborough United, one position below the Liliywhites in fourth.

Peterborough remained one point behind, but now had two games in hand! If there was a faint ray of hope for North End, it was that all three

DIVISION 3

	P	W	D	L	F	A	Pts	Goal diff
Wrexham	43	23	13	7	76	42	59	+ 34
Cambridge	45	22	12	11	70	50	56	+ 20
Preston	45	20	15	10	61	36	55	+ 25
Peterboro	43	20	14	9	41	26	54	+ 15

of Peterborough's remaining games were away – at Oxford United, Chester and... Wrexham, on Britain's first ever May Day Bank Holiday.

On Thursday morning, it was reported that there was a slightly brighter atmosphere at Deepdale amongst the players, as Peterborough United's Wednesday evening away match at Oxford United had ended in a 3-3 draw. This left North End still clinging on to third place – but now just by the virtue of their positive goal difference of 25.

The margin of difference over Peterborough was 10 in North End's favour, and would be worth a notional 'extra point' if the season was to end with both teams tied.

On Friday the LEP sports page ran the headline, "BOSS ASKS FOR FINAL PUSH" as the nerve-wracking promotion race hurtled towards its dramatic climax.

Nobby addressed the fans first, thanking them yet again for their fabulous support over the season.

"The supporters who have watched us this season have been great, I am

delighted with them all. I also know that if they pay to watch us, they are entitled to criticise – but in fact, they have been right behind us.

"We have had gates of over 11,000 in some games at Deepdale and a few thousand have also watched us away from home, which is terrific. Even on such long distances the same faces have been there cheering the lads on and I hope they realise how much the players really appreciate their support.

"A lot of them saw the team give everything at Rotherham on Tuesday night, and although they were disappointed, they knew we had battled right to the end, and cheered us after the game. This was great for the lads and I can't ask any more of the fans except that I hope they give us the same kind of support tomorrow."

Stiles then hinted that it was unlikely there would be any changes to the team.

"There is always a danger of making a panic decision. It would be silly to change the things we have believed to be right all season. We have got to do the correct things again tomorrow and have got to go out and win.

"It won't be easy and the lads are upset that our setback at Rotherham means that whether or not we get promotion is not completely in their own hands.

"They are a tremendous group of lads who don't stay down-hearted for long and have bounced back several times already after bad results. We must not treat tomorrow's game as a foregone conclusion because Shrewsbury will make things difficult for us."

Nobby was certainly right about his last comment – Shrewsbury manager, Richie Barker was apparently very determined to make life difficult for North End.

"We want to end a disappointing season with a flourish, and Preston will soon know that they really have a game on their hands.

"You somehow get a sadistic pleasure out of making life tough for a team in Preston's situation.

"Perhaps you can put it down to envy because we have missed the promotion boat ourselves, but whatever the reason, we can guarantee Preston this will be their toughest match of the season."

The match was the most mentally draining and exhausting affair that a devoted fan could ever be asked to witness. The story didn't end with the final whistle either!

It soon became apparent that North End's promotion hopes were still dangling by a thread and would only be resolved for certain at the conclusion of the Wrexham v Peterborough United contest on Monday afternoon.

Saturday, April 29th provided a mild, fine spring afternoon – the perfect conditions for football – as the same North End team ran out for the seventh time in succession... and for the final time in the 1977/78 season:-

Tunks, McMahon, Cameron, Burns, Baxter, Cross, Coleman, Haslegrave, Robinson, Elwiss, Bruce. Substitute: Doyle.

Deepdale was absolutely buzzing. A season-high crowd of 16,078 eventually pushed their way through the turnstiles as peripheral North End fans joined the diehards in response to Nobby's battle cry for loud support.

Indeed, there was a huge cheer to welcome the Lilywhites onto the pitch, and another a few minutes later as they kicked off towards the Town End. Within 60 seconds, Deepdale then fell suddenly and eerily silent as Shrewsbury took the lead. In fact, the silence was deafening.

A free kick was conceded on the Shrewsbury right wing, whereupon full back John King stepped forward to float the ball straight in to North End goalmouth where striker Ian Atkins leapt high, burying the ball into the back of the net. Frustratingly the defence had been caught napping as Atkins was totally unmarked.

Looking slightly bewildered as they kicked off for the second time in as many minutes, North End managed to get their focus together again and launched a series of raids on the Shrewsbury goal.

A spell which produced four corners was survived by the visitors, who finally re-emerged from their trenches to purposefully set up an opportunity for Steve Biggins, but he placed his shot wide.

Alex Bruce was holding his breath along with the crowd a few minutes later, when he beat Ken Mulhearn the Shrewsbury goalkeeper, with a neat lob. Left back Carleton Leonard tracked back behind his goalkeeper and managed to clear the danger; even so this brought loud appreciation from the North End crowd who were trying hard to lift their team.

Bruce then collected a long through ball and ran into the Shrewsbury box but Mulhearn managed to save as the North End striker was quickly outnumbered.

While Atkins lay prostrate in the centre circle following a tackle from Mick Baxter, fighting broke out in the Town End between rival supporters which resulted in many being frogmarched away by the police.

The game resumed with Atkins and his leg still joined together and goalkeeper Tunks was forced to dive toward the very same limb a few minutes later to end the striker's progress towards the North End goal.

Gordon Coleman was then unlucky with a good shot that veered over the visitor's crossbar, before Mick Robinson won a corner on the right for North End. Although this produced a goalmouth scramble and lots of noise from the crowd, Shrewsbury managed to belt the ball away – a case of anywhere will do.

There was a growing sense that soon the 'Shrews' were going to finally cave in, and in the 38th minute their defence was finally breached.

A free kick was awarded to North End just outside the penalty area, to the right. Mike Elwiss strode forward and proceeded to lash in a tremendous drive that found its way past the wall, ending in the back of the net via the post.

Hallelujah! The crowd were ecstatic. Level at last with around 51 minutes still left to get the win.

Just four of those minutes passed before the next seismic wound was inflicted on this anxious North End run-in.

PNE FC

Captain Mike Elwiss leathers in a free kick to draw North End level

That was when Francis Burns inexplicably dwelt too long over a simple back pass to Roy Tunks in the North End penalty area. Although the distance the ball had to travel back to Tunks didn't seem great, a hesitation seemed to set in between the pair. The mutual confusion lasted long enough for John Keay to nip in between them and prod the ball into the unguarded net.

A catastrophic misunderstanding between Roy Tunks and Francis Burns allows Shrewsbury's John Keay to poke the ball into the empty North End net

PNE FC

It's fair to say that both Tunks and Burns were mortified. As commentator Martin Tyler once said during a match, "He had an eternity to play that ball... but he took too long over it!"

The half time whistle blew to the usual shouts of advice ringing out loud from the frustrated crowd, but unfortunately that wasn't going to help. North End had just 45 minutes in which to score at least two goals and concede none.

The half time scores from the games involving Cambridge and Peterborough were slotted in to positions B and D on the scoreboards. Cambridge versus Exeter remained goalless, while Chester versus Peterborough stood at 1-1.

Although it was completely meaningless after just 45 minutes, at this moment North End were now in fourth position in the table, and out of the promotion places.

Obviously revived by a half time pep talk from manager Stiles, North End flew out of the traps in the second half.

Baxter headed wide after joining the attack for a corner, and Bruce then shot wide after collecting a pass from Elwiss. He then headed past the post from a right wing cross.

Another corner was cleared by the visitors, who despite North End's busy start were not moved to panic.

A shot from Sean Haslegrave was well askew, and a stinging drive from Robinson was blocked before the visitors almost picked North End's pockets again when a header from Biggins went just wide of the post.

Stiles replaced Robinson with Stephen Doyle with around 25 minutes left; Doyle operating from midfield while Coleman was thrust forward into the attack.

It was a good decision as almost immediately Coleman was in the thick of things, heading an Elwiss cross just the wrong side of the post. He then won a free kick after being fouled by Leonard, but the centre from John McMahon which followed was cut out by keeper Mulhearn.

With just 10 minutes left, a foul by Keay on Elwiss down the left resulted in a free kick. The ball found its way to Coleman who immediately launched an unforgiving drive from the right side of the penalty area. Mulhearn was left hanging in the air as the ball crashed against the bar before frustratingly bouncing over for a goal kick.

Desperation on the pitch and on the terraces was becoming evident but just two minutes later, North End equalised for the second time – just reward for their unrelenting attacking performance.

A centre from the right wing was headed on across the goalmouth by Baxter towards Bruce who found the net from close range near the back post to notch his 30th goal of the season.

Credit: Lancashire Post

The formidable Alex Bruce scores the equaliser that crucially secured an extra point. North End's entire season rested on that goal going in just eight minutes from time.

Despite an all-out assault on the Shrewsbury goal, with Coleman, Baxter, Elwiss and Bruce all going so very close, North End had to be content with honours ending even.

A crowd invasion of the Deepdale pitch then occurred, but while that fantastic comeback felt like a late win, it was only a draw. In fact, Cambridge had beaten Exeter 2-1 and were promoted as runners-up, while Chester had quite remarkably beaten Peterborough by 4-3! I'm sure Nobby would have telephoned his old friend and Chester player-manager Alan Oakes to thank him for his efforts!

The point 'gained' by North End thus maintained them in third position, now one point clear of Peterborough, who now had to go to Wrexham and win to pip North End to promotion. For one weekend only, Preston became the 'shredded nerve centre' of the world.

The North End squad must have been wondering when it was exactly that they had inadvertently climbed aboard this 'will they-won't they' promotion rollercoaster ride. What had looked a smooth drive home at the end of March had morphed into journey fraught with danger.

WEEKEND

Leisure and Football POST

Lancashire Evening Post

No. 28,340 SATURDAY APRIL 29 1978 8p

INSIDE

F.A. CUP FINAL VERDICT

PAGES 3 AND 4

PLUS

GREAT STAR WARS CONTEST

3-DAY TELEVISION GUIDE

Blunders, but rally gains 2-2 draw

NOW PRESTON WILL HAVE TO WAIT AND HOPE!

PRESTON North End must wait until Monday before knowing whether or not they will be promoted to the Second Division.

Although they gained a point from a 2-2 draw with Shrewsbury Town at Deepdale today, and Peterborough lost 4-3 at Chester, the issue is still in doubt.

By NORMAN SHAKESHAFT

The Posh play at Wrexham on Monday afternoon and a victory there would ensure them promotion and doom North End to another season of Division Three.

However, should Peterborough drop a point at Wrexham then North End would be promoted. It's a real cliff-hanger!

Cambridge clinched promotion with a home win against Exeter.

There was an invasion of the pitch at the end of the game at Deepdale.

Preston's performance had been a nervous one but they had shown great character in equalising twice.

Shrewsbury took the lead in the first minute with a ... lowing a bad mistake by Francis Burns did not depress North End and leading scorer Alex Bruce eventually got the point with a goal eight minutes from the end.

Preston had sent on Stephen Doyle as the sub for Mick Robinson and Shrewsbury's Carleton Leonard was booked before the final ...

● Preston forward Gordon Coleman beats two Shrewsbury defenders to cross the ball, during the game at Deepdale today.

● Three Shrewsbury defenders police Preston striker Mike ...

SCOREBOARD

DIVISION ONE

Arsenal	1	Midd'bro'	0
Aston V	6	Ipswich	1
Bristol C	1	Coventry	1
Everton	6	Chelsea	0
Leicester	3	N'wcastle	0
Man C	1	Derby C	1
Norwich	1	WBA	1
Nottm F	0	B'm'gh'm	0
QPR	0	Leeds U	0
West Ham	0	Liverpool	2
Wolves	2	Man Utd	1

DIVISION TWO

Bolton	0	Fulham	0
Brighton	2	Blackpool	1
Burnley	2	Luton	1
Crystal P	5	B'ckb'n R	0
Hull C	0	Bristol R	1
Mansfield	1	Orient	1
Millwall	2	Oldham	0
Sheff Utd	0	Cardiff	1
S'th'pton	0	Tott'ham	0
Stoke	1	Notts C	1
Sund'land	3	Charlton	0

DIVISION THREE

Bradf'd C	2	Walsall	3
C'mb'ge	2	Exeter	1
Carlisle	2	Swindon	2
Chester	4	Peterboro	3
C'lchester	1	Sheff W	1
Gill'gham	0	Lincoln	0
Hereford	1	Wrexham	1
Oxford U	0	Bury	0
Plymouth	3	Port Vale	2
Preston	2	Shrewsb'y	2
Roth'ham	0	Portsm'th	1

DIVISION FOUR

Aldershot	3	Hartlep'l	0
Barnsley	3	Wmb'd'n	2
Darl'gton	1	Scunth'pe	1
Doncaster	2	Reading	2
Grimsby	2	Brentford	1
Hudd'f'ld	2	B'nem'th	0
Newport	★	Southend	★
Rochdale	1	Torquay	3
Stockport	1	Crewe	2
Swansea	2	Halifax	0
Watford	3	Southport	2

(PLAYED LAST NIGHT)

F.A. TROPHY

FINAL

Alt'cham 3 L'th'head 1

RUGBY UNION

WELSH CUP

FINAL

Newport ★ Swansea ★

RUGBY LEAGUE

PREMIERSHIP

FIRST ROUND

Widnes 33 Warr'gton 0

L — Late Kick-Off
★ — Result Delayed
P — Postponed

LANCASHIRE COMBINATION

LATE NEWS

FOOTBALL FINAL SCORES

NEWPORT 1 SOUTHEND 2

RUGBY WELSH CUP

NEWPORT 9 SWANSEA 13

Now there was nothing more they could do. The whole season depended upon already promoted Wrexham being bothered enough to deny highly motivated Peterborough United a win. If the match was drawn – happy days! North End's superior goal difference would push them over the line and the hex would be finally banished.

Credit: Lancashire Post

Deepdale is invaded after the Shrewsbury Town game, fuelled mainly by the 70's equivalent of 'fake news' that suggested North End had done enough to be promoted.

CHAPTER 11

MAY

Wrexham v Peterborough Utd, and the celebrations

As luck would have it at the same time Wrexham kicked off against Peterborough on bank holiday Monday, North End reserves were already entertaining West Bromwich Albion reserves at Deepdale in their penultimate game of the season.

Assistant manager Alan Kelly and chief scout Jimmie Scott had departed Preston for North Wales earlier in the day, to meet up with Nobby Stiles, Francis Burns and John McMahon at the Racecourse Ground while a few members of the North End board had also travelled down to Wrexham separately.

A veritable army of North End fans had also arrived at the ground, this time to cheer on the Welshmen, which paradoxically speaking, was a quite magnificent gesture to the North End team.

The rest of the North End playing staff assembled in the Guild Club to watch the reserves and wait for any news of the Wrexham game to be relayed back.

They were joined by an above average crowd for a reserve game, those deep-rooted North End devotees taking in a final fix of Deepdale for that season; wanting to be there, hoping to hear good news.

The reserves won their fixture against West Bromwich Albion by 2-0, with

Ricky Thomson and Jimmy Brown scoring the goals and everyone's attention was then switched to what was left of the game at Wrexham.

Wrexham, under strength due to injuries, eventually emerged unscathed despite some very close-calls. The match ended in a 0-0 draw, and North End were duly promoted by virtue of their superior goal difference.

The celebrations began for the players, and lasted long into the night. The partying also began for the fans, as the grey cloud of apprehension that had hung over Deepdale ever since the Rotherham defeat a week earlier now instantly dispersed.

It was certainly a day of redemption for North End stalwart Francis Burns who had been involved in that unfathomable mix-up with Roy Tunks that had led Shrewsbury's second goal on Saturday.

He said that he had suffered the "worst weekend" of his career, but was overwhelmed by the sight of the hundreds of North End fans in the crowd – as indeed were the North End directors.

Nobby was of course overjoyed, but that was far from the case at half time, according to legend. Trying desperately to hold still his rattling teacup in a saucer he is reported to have said, *"I don't need a spoon to stir this tea, do I?"* After the game, a relieved Stiles said,

"Wrexham were tremendous considering their injury problems, with goalkeeper Dai Davies playing particularly well.

"I suppose the game could have gone the other way, but luck was on our side – for once – and I always said it would even out over the season.

"Gaining promotion is even more of a thrill for me than my other achievements as a player, including being a member of the 1966 World Cup winning team. I'm also delighted for all the Preston players and for all the members of the staff, as well as for all our supporters who have been terrific this year.

"Now we have to believe that we are good enough, not just to stay in Division Two, but to do well in that division."

Team captain Mike Elwiss summed things up perfectly by saying he was tremendously relieved and now needed a few days to let everything sink in!

Nobby and Kel managed to enjoy the achievement for a day or two before they were asked by the board to submit their retained list. This had to be done immediately as the board needed the information before a civic reception, planned for later in the week. *"I am having the economics of the situation spelled out for me,"* lamented Stiles.

Civic reception for promoted PNE

TOAST OF THE TOWN!

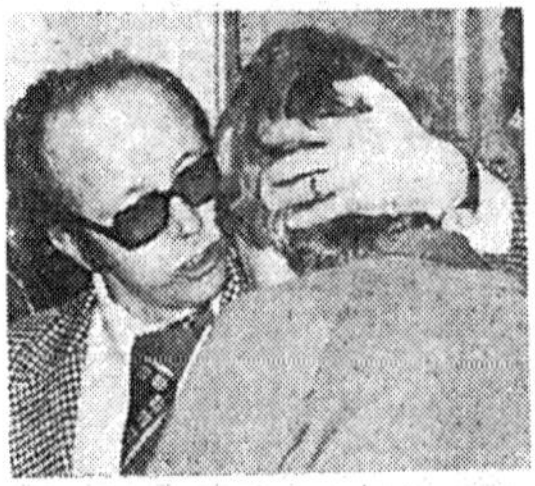

Stiles consoles keeper Roy Tunks after Saturday's draw.

And this is the moment that put Preston back in the big time

By NORMAN SHAKESHAFT

JUBILANT Preston is to make its soccer heroes the toast of the town.

As a wave of euphoria swept the town today at the news of North End's promotion to Division Two plans were announced for a massive civic reception.

And a plea has gone out for the public to give the players and officials an end-of-season tribute in a planned town centre "thank you".

Preston's Mayor, Coun Joe Hood, a life-long Preston fan has arranged the reception for Friday and the players and officials will appear on the balcony of the Harris Art Gallery in front of the flag market.

Young fans last night began celebrating North End's success and today manager Nobby Stiles said that for him gaining promotion was "even better than being in the England team which won the World Cup in 1966."

He said: "I would like to thank all our supporters who have been terrific this year."

Coun Hood said that the club's achievement was the "icing on the cake" for him as far as his year in office was concerned.

He hopes that the public will respond by giving an end-of-season salute and said the reception would start at 5 pm.

BREATHER

Club chairman Mr Alan Jones said today that he was very grateful and that everyone at the club could now take a short breather after all the hard work put in in the last few seasons.

The Mayor will also make the presentation to North End's "player of the year" on Friday after the votes of supporters have all been counted and will also present tankards to all the players who have turned out in the first team this season.

Like many other Preston fans, the Mayor had a nerve - wracking weekend, after North End's 2—2 draw with Shrewsbury in their last game of the season on Saturday.

But Peterborough, who could only share a goalless draw at Wrexham yesterday in their last game, finished in fourth place in the Third Division table, and Preston are promoted in third place after four seasons in the division.

● Read Norman Shakeshaft's full story on the back page, as well as more reaction from PNE manager Nobby Stiles.

Wrexham 0, Peterborough 0 — Young North End players go wild as the radio gives the result that meant promotion.

The LEP captured the moment when North End were promoted without even playing!

The Scout: 30—1 TREBLE

DAILY EXPRESS THE VOICE OF BRITAIN

No. 24,208 Tuesday May 2 1978 8p.

NOBBY DAZZLER!

A great day as manager Stiles leads Proud Preston to promotion

By Bill Elliott

SOCCER great Nobby Stiles led Preston North End back into the Second Division the hard way yesterday.

The former Manchester United and England player did it while sitting in the stands at Wrexham.

For the Welsh club's 0—0 draw against Peterborough means that the East Anglia team stay in Division Three while Nobby and Preston move up because of a superior goal difference.

[illegible]

DRAINED

[illegible]

End of the agony: See Back Page

[illegible]

Nobby Stiles celebrating at home with his greatest fans, sons John, 14, Peter, 12, and Robert, 9

Credit: Express Newspapers

The management team and their wives pictured at the club's celebration evening at The Orchard on May 2nd.

From left: Alan Kelly, Mrs Kay Stiles, Mrs Mary Kelly and Nobby Stiles.

Thousands pay tribute to PNE's success

ALL HAIL TO THE HEROES!

Mike Elwiss and Nobby Stiles on the balcony.

Report by DON JONES
Pictures: JOHN GRONOW

THE ancient flagstones on the square nearly cracked under the stamping feet of thousands of delirious fans as Preston's heroes came out to take a bow.

North End are up — "and now you had better believe us" chanted the supporters as they saluted the team that has won promotion to Division 2.

As the players and officials emerged on the steps of the Harris Museum and Art Gallery a cheer went up that was nearly sufficient to shake the leaves from the trees.

The carnival atmosphere affected everyone. Even mayor Coun Joe Hood was seen to toss back a toilet roll that had somehow managed to find its way on to the balcony.

Scarves were waved and banners were hoisted aloft. Champagne bottles popped and the fizzy contents were sprayed into the air as the faithful followers celebrated their new found football wealth.

Singing

Speeches had to be made but only manager Nobby Stiles could calm the throng. He silenced the huge crowd for a while to thank them for their support during the season — and the mayor, a lifelong PNE follower, just managed to pay a personal tribute before the singing started again.

The players and Deepdale staff all received tankards to mark the occasion and were cheered individually for their efforts.

None more so than skipper Mike Elwiss who was presented with a silver cup as "player of the year". He was the choice of the fans and they made it plainly obvious.

Elwiss said later: "The reception was something that will remain in my memory for ever. It was a very special moment for myself and everyone involved with the club. I would like to thank everybody who turned out."

One banner which stated: "Look out Europe, here comes Preston" might have seemed pie in the sky but the flavour of the occasion was certainly one of optimism for the future.

The Civic reception took place on Friday, May 5th. Thousands turned up to see their heroes take a bow on the Harris Museum and Art Gallery balcony.

Speeches were made, including one from Nobby thanking the fans for their terrific support throughout the season. The players and staff all received tankards to mark the occasion and were cheered individually for their efforts. Team captain Mike Elwiss was awarded the 'player of the year' trophy, holding it aloft as the fans chanted his name.

On May 8th it was announced that Alex Bruce was to be awarded with an Adidas 'Golden Shoe' for his feat in finishing the football season as leading scorer in Division Three.

He was to be presented with the trophy at a special ceremony in London at Painter's Hall.

The prolific 'Brucie' had scored 30 goals during the season, with 27 of them being notched in the league.

For the record, the recipients of the divisional awards were:

Division One – Bob Latchford (Everton) 30 goals

Division Two – Bob Hatton (Blackpool) 22 goals

Division Three – Alex Bruce (Preston North End) 27 goals

Division Four – Alan Curtis (Swansea)/Steve Phillips (Brentford) 32 goals

Meanwhile, there was surprise still in certain quarters at the fact that the managers retained list hadn't found room for a couple of the more promising youngsters in the Central League team.

"I sincerely hope that I am proved wrong about the young players we have decide to release," said Nobby.

"The retained list presented me with some very difficult decisions. I would have liked to have left the list until after the promotion celebrations last Friday, but I was informed that the board wanted the players told before Saturday.

"I felt I had to keep faith with the members of the first team squad who did so well for most of the season.

"The directors told me what we needed to do for economic reasons and ask me to reduce the staff to a set number of players, and this is what I did."

CHAPTER 12

THE MANAGEMENT TEAM

The passionate, humble **NOBBY STILES**

Preston North End are the only football club to employ two of the England World Cup 1966 team as their manager.

Indeed, we have to thank the first of those, Sir Bobby Charlton for bringing the second, Nobby Stiles, to the club in 1973. Nobby was ostensibly brought in to bolster the North End midfield, but Charlton knew there would be other benefits to having Nobby around when it finally came time for the little fella to finally hang up his boots as a player.

Charlton and Stiles had many things in common as members of the highly successful Manchester United and England teams of the Sixties. Throughout their careers they had been taught everything they knew about the game by Sir Matt Busby and Sir Alf Ramsey.

It was a precious gift.

Manchester United had put their name against the League Championship and FA Cup in the Sixties, topping that by becoming the first English team to lift the European Cup in 1968. England of course, were World Cup winners in 1966.

As often happens for superstars of the game, the task of managing a team rather than playing in it is a bridge too far, and unfortunately Charlton didn't manage to cross it.

Nobby however, was to be a different kettle of fish.

He nobly refused to step into close friend Bobby's still warm managerial seat in 1975 when North End offered him the position after Charlton resigned over the John Bird transfer saga. That was very understandable but when Nobby decided to resign too, alarm bells were sounded.

This was a potential talent North End could not afford to see walk away, and when new manager Harry Catterick was unveiled as Charlton's successor, part of his brief was to get Nobby back to Deepdale.

This was done, and Nobby was re-appointed – this time as chief coach, while former North End goalkeeper and club legend Alan Kelly Snr, would work alongside him as his assistant.

After a couple of indifferent seasons marking time in Division Three, Catterick was sidelined and the board offered Nobby the job as manager once again in July 1977.

This time, there was no hesitation and with Kelly promoted to the role of assistant manager, the duo set to work in a bid to change Preston North End's fortunes.

Nobby told the press he was only able to promise one thing – that the players would be working harder than ever before on the North End fans behalf. That, he insisted, was the only thing that would bring back any success.

Nobby's North End teams always worked hard. Yes, they sometimes got things wrong and they lost games, but they still worked hard. The team, like both their tutors was honest.

The football style was attack based, and very pleasing on the eye. With Alex Bruce and Mike Elwiss up front, North End were a team that was always going to score goals.

A long first season at the helm was brought to a nerve-wracking conclusion when the team suddenly acquired a touch of hesitancy on the final straight. They started to tread water when points were desperately needed.

The whole town was on a knife edge on the new May Day Bank Holiday, as a now helpless North End team – some at the Racecourse Ground watching, many back at Deepdale waiting – were hauled over the promotion line by virtue of their superior goal difference when Peterborough United failed to win at Wrexham.

Promotion in his first season as manager – but then what else would you expect from Nobby? The man was a winner. The whole task of turning North End around had taken just 254 days.

He had watched and learned how Busby and Ramsey had man managed their players and certainly implemented some of their nuances in his very own Deepdale domain.

He lost his inspirational captain Mike Elwiss to Crystal Palace during the summer break, which would prove a massive void to fill. Elwiss had a dynamic, unique style crucially scoring and supplying goals on a very regular basis.

As a result, the new season of 1978/79 refused to take off no matter how hard the team tried, and on October 7th the LEP front page headline read **'Stiles – North End's Fallen Hero'**.

The article by Norman Shakeshaft must have been a sickening blow to Nobby. The personalisation of the headline made it appear that all North End's woes were down to him – when in actual fact they weren't.

All this in just eight footballing weeks since the team had been promoted. It beggared belief. No team has ever been promoted or relegated in the first week of October!

Failing to sign any new players before the start of the season despite having the green light from the board was apparently Nobby's big sin. That allegation was factually true; but it certainly hadn't been for the want of trying.

In fact, Nobby had been pursuing utility player Mick Martin of West Bromwich Albion throughout the summer. Eric Potts then arrived in late August but Martin finally knocked back North End's offer around the same time. So too did Coventry City midfielder John Beck at the end of September.

Possible signings were not just rushed in; Nobby had a process. While monitoring a player he ideally liked to see the transfer target have an average game too, and see how they reacted next time out. And because it was always in short supply, he also wanted to spend the money wisely.

Don O'Riordan, a central defender, had arrived at the beginning of October and full back Brian Taylor was in negotiations to join North End when the article went to press. He would officially sign on October 11th.

While Stiles 'accepted the responsibility' for the team's slump, the article continued, a lot of 'damage' had been done.

It didn't really help matters either when the board had apparently asked Nobby if he needed any help from the chairman's good friend Jimmy Armfield. That offer was politely declined.

Shakeshaft must have thought the season was already unrecoverable, but Nobby had spectacular will and fight within him, harbouring no such

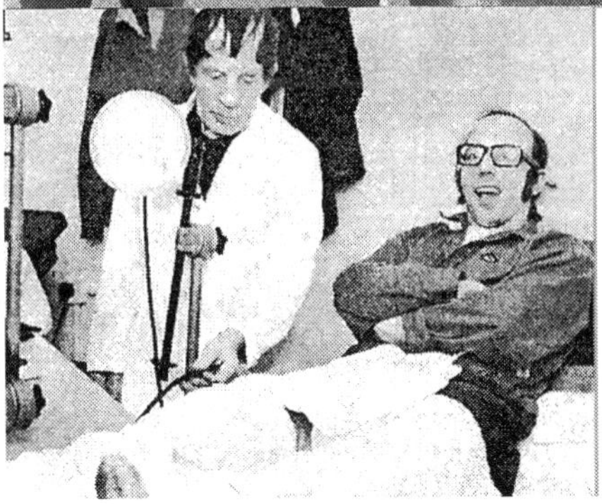

Top left: Bobby Charlton welcomes Nobby to Deepdale

Top right: In North End colours during 1974/75

Left: Receiving 'the short wave treatment' to a leg injury in Harry Hubbick's lair

PNE FC

thoughts. He knew that once the players he had signed had bedded into the system matters would improve.

After being defeated 3-1 at Upton Park by West Ham United on November 4th 1978 – a match remembered for a very special goal from Ricky Thomson – North End sat in 21st position with just six points from 13 matches played.

The match was screened by London Weekend Television on their Sunday afternoon highlights programme, 'The Big Match'. Following the defeat, Nobby was interviewed by the host, Brian Moore.

Moore was a brilliant interviewer and he managed to bring out all of Nobby's traits for the viewers – the best being Nobby's passionate defence of his lads, and how certain he was that despite being at the foot of the division, the season would certainly not end in disaster.

Moore told Nobby, "I think it would be hard for any team to drop its head when they have you urging them on," an observation which, as they say these days, was 'bang on'.

From that day on until the end of the season, the upswing in North End's form was quite remarkable.

They lost just four matches out of the remaining 29, and rallied to such an extent that they finished seventh – their highest position in the Football League since the glorious season of 1963/64 when the team reached the FA Cup Final at Wembley and finished third in Division Two.

It certainly made the early season speculation that surrounded Nobby's capabilities look quite ridiculous.

The following season of 1979/80 produced another encouraging performance, with North End finishing 10th in an even stronger division that now included Chelsea and Queens Park Rangers.

Although the club had sold Mick Robinson at the back end of the 1978/79 season for £756,000, frustratingly very little of that fortune was ringfenced for the transfer kitty at a time when it was perfect to strengthen the team further ...and make an assault on the summit of Division Two.

The lack of attention by the board in regards to stadium maintenance over the decades was now looming like the grim reaper, and would swallow up every penny of the Robinson transaction and much more besides.

Strict enforcement of the *Safety of Sports Grounds Act 1975* began. Alas, there wasn't much to show for all this infrastructure investment – just new crush barriers and fencing. Something had to give however, and inevitably it was the team.

The management team were informed that for 1980/81 there would be harsh cutbacks throughout the club; the board advising Stiles and Kelly exactly what they would be managing with in terms of staff. All playing positions were covered in the board's opinion and they duly announced that only rudimentary funding would be made available for any incoming players. Only striker Peter Sayer was added to the squad, but made just five appearances all season.

Predictably, North End – a club now in massive reverse on all fronts, were relegated – albeit on goal difference and despite the false hope of a final day away win at Derby County.

It was to be the end of Nobby's association with Preston North End. It was also perhaps the most reckless decision ever made at board level, heralding the start of the worst period in the club's long and distinguished history.

Nobby's replacement lasted only 165 days, having to listen to the Deepdale crowd chanting 'We want Stiles' from the terraces as his time ran out. It was a classic and harsh lesson for the directors of 'you don't know what you have got 'til it's gone.'

The plain fact is, the merits of Nobby Stiles became so very conspicuous when he was absent.

The settled and harmonious feel that he and Kel had brought to the club over their three year tenure was instantly replaced with player turmoil and latterly, a high-speed, panic driven managers revolving chair.

Just five years after sacking Nobby the club had crumbled to such an extent they were forced to humiliatingly seek re-election to the Football League. They had also ploughed their way through five managers and two caretakers during this most inglorious period of the club's history.

Alan Ball, Nobby's England teammate once said of him, "He is a true professional. He goes out to do a job to the best of his ability, no matter what that job is."

Nobby as manager at North End? He was absolutely brilliant!

His 'lads' loved him. He proved to be an excellent communicator and teacher. He also created a most magnificent team spirit that enveloped the club. The players loved going in to work.

For the North End fan he was perfect. He provided pragmatism, a robust determination to succeed and very real hope.

He was in his element at Deepdale.

To perfectly sum up the man, here is what the late Sean Haslegrave had to say about his boss:-

"Nobby Stiles was a super manager to play for and a lovely man. I thought the world of Nobby, and the rest of the lads did too – there was no edge about him.

"He was a very humane individual who was passionate about his football and loved his players."

I think you will agree that says it all.

PNE FC

The brilliant, dedicated **ALAN KELLY**

It was great being a North End fan as kid back in the Sixties. Street football was rife everywhere in Preston, and on those wonderful pitches of make believe the two keepers were always Alan Kelly and Gordon Banks – and Banks was rarely the first choice…

That's the esteem my generation held Alan in.

We often used to pedal our bikes down to Willow Farm in the school holidays to watch North End train, lying on the grass right behind Kelly's goal to watch the practice matches.

I have many memories of those days, one being then manager Jimmy Milne being a bit grumpy about us being there, but we did retrieve the ball for the players to help justify our presence and made sure we were always polite.

Another was when we were led down behind Kelly's goal on a very warm day, and a North End youngster from Scotland called Ian Marshall completely mishit a shot from around the penalty spot. The ball, arriving at our hero's feet at slower than walking pace, was accompanied by another type of volley – one of the four letter type from the anguished Scot.

The three of us immediately burst out laughing. After throwing the ball out quickly Kelly shouted, "Ian, Ian." Marshall trotted back and Alan said something to him, before turning around and pointing in our direction. Marshall then sort of nodded and meekly waved at us before dashing back into the hub of things.

We had an idea what message had been about, and it made us laugh even more. Just a brilliant, random unforgettable moment!

I was in the crowd at Deepdale when Alan made his unscheduled, final appearance for North End. And, like every other North End fan, I thought he would be back in a few weeks or so. It was Kelly; he always came back from injury.

Not this time though.

Up to that point, 15th September 1973, I had never known another first team 'keeper at Deepdale. I had first started watching sometime in 1965 and had seen other goalkeepers trot out for North End now and again such as John Barton, Gerry Stewart and John Brown – good 'keepers all – but this was only when Kelly was injured.

It had seemed a typical Kelly save to all intents and purposes – diving to save a shot from Bristol City midfielder Gerry Gow. His right shoulder had borne the brunt of an awkward landing however, and it soon became evident there was a big problem when trainer Harry Hubbick summoned the St. John Ambulance team to the scene. A suited bloke then ran onto the pitch, presumably the club doctor.

There was real concern in the crowd as poor Alan was slowly stretchered off, apparently receiving oxygen. He appeared to be in agony.

The shoulder was dislocated, but was reseated again quickly at Mount Street hospital. So far, so good, but complications set in during the healing process and Alan could no longer move the fingers properly in his right hand when he had left hospital. That situation never improved and consequently he learned to write with his left hand.

Retirement suddenly loomed on the horizon.

Thankfully, he was already a qualified coach and joined the coaching staff at Deepdale. In April 1974 he was also appointed as the Republic of Ireland's assistant manager under Johnny Giles.

After around 16 loyal years at Deepdale the least North End could do was to award this goalkeeping giant a testimonial match, and this took place in November 1974.

At the time, he had appeared for North End 513 times – a record still standing today – and had been capped 47 times for the Republic of Ireland, record that stood for some time after his enforced departure. His international career spanned 17 years.

By the time Harry Catterick took over from Bobby Charlton at Deepdale, Alan was involved largely with the reserve team.

Ex-Everton manager Harry Catterick was from a completely different era. He had won both the League title and the FA Cup while at Goodison in the 1960's and had an excellent CV.

<u>Top left</u>: 'Train heavy, play light'
<u>Top right</u> : Looking remarkably like Alan Jnr, 'Kel' keeping goal for the Republic of Ireland against Scotland in 1963
<u>Left:</u> Pulling off a brilliant save at Villa Park and helping North End to a vital win in 1968

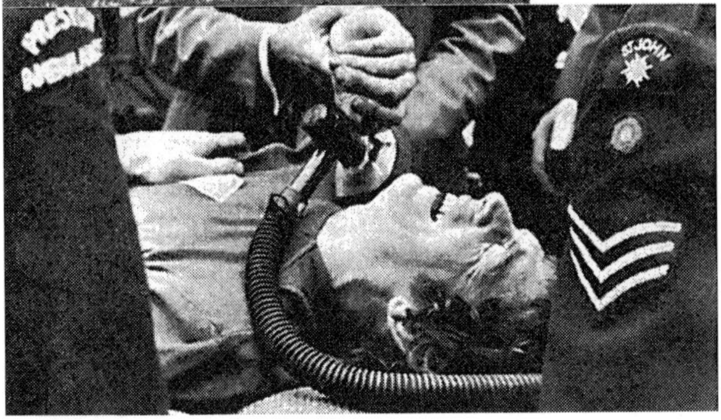

Kel's final match, September 15th 1973 against Bristol City at Deepdale. Here he is stretchered off the pitch in agony with a dislocated shoulder.

PNE FC

The North End players saw very little of him from week to week, perhaps a glimpse or two of him in his camel – hair coat briefly watching from the sidelines at Willow Farm.

He made a big but sometimes comical impression on the coaches but as the pair would find out, there was a hard, tough professional underneath that exterior.

The story goes that at their first meeting Catterick asked them to submit in writing a full pre-season training programme, including morning and afternoon sessions and have it on his desk the next day.

The boys got to work and Nobby included everything he had picked up from Busby and Ramsey, and England trainers Harold Shepherdson and Les Cocker. Nobby then left the plans with Catterick's secretary.

A couple of days later, when the boys returned to their office at Deepdale there was a nice handwritten note from Catterick, along with two bottles of beer. He thanked them both for their efforts and told them to enjoy the beer, it was well deserved.

However, after drawing them both in with compliments on that particular Friday, Catterick blew them out on the following Monday morning when he delivered an almighty rollicking to the stunned coaches in his office. He picked holes in their plan and pointed out clearly to them both that they were very much on trial. Afterwards, the pair both agreed that the best policy was to keep their heads down and just get on with their work!

They learned that it was the way Catterick worked – underlings had to be kept on their toes!

Catterick eventually left and Alan was promoted to assistant manager when Nobby landed the top job.

This was brilliant timing by the board. It was also very imaginative.

Nobby was 35 years old, Alan 41. Both young and ambitious, both internationals, both stuffed to the gunnels with the finest football knowledge. In many ways, a dream team.

Promotion at the first attempt was the perfect reward for them.

Being ultimately responsible for the team's performance on the field was unchartered waters for them both when they were suddenly appointed just before the season began. It was a big leap in responsibility but they had the players 'on board' from the off, and both management and staff worked hard for each other.

In Alan's case, a promotion season at Deepdale as a player was a rarity but the 1977/78 season must have been extra special for him. Winning promotion as a North End player is surely a great feeling, but to play a big part guiding the team to a higher level must take some beating.

Kel carried on covering the reserve team after becoming assistant manager. In this respect he was continuing his success in developing a very youthful pool of talent, and rescuing the odd career that seemed doomed to hit the rocks.

"Catterick said I was finished – and it was Alan Kelly who spoke up for me and kept me at the club. He came back with me in the afternoons for extra training and also worked me on my days off. He would hit hundreds of balls in the air for me to challenge Mick Baxter for the ball, crosses and passes to make me shoot with my weaker foot, as well as getting me to knock the ball off in tight situations. He 'bullied' me at times but I have to thank him for everything."

So said the late Mick Robinson, who for a time was North End's record export when he was sold to Manchester City in 1979 for £756,000.

The management pairing went on to deliver Division Two placings of seventh and 10th immediately following promotion, achieving in a way what the equally young and ambitious Alex Neil has done at Deepdale in the here and now, 40 years later – developing and attempting to drive forward a club that is perceived by the rest of the football world as unfashionable.

Relegation arrived in 1980/81, but that had little to do with Stiles and Kelly. A professional football team needs constant renewing, but with the Deepdale stadium repairs demanding all of the finances, the board gambled that the team would get by.

The management team were sacked from their positions, and replaced... we know the catastrophic rest.

Every North End fan who saw him play will have a memory of Alan. I have a few in the memory bank, but one save I will never forget was against Manchester United at Deepdale in the FA Cup 4th round in February 1972. It wasn't especially spectacular; it was just superb goalkeeping from a craftsman doing his job and keeping his team in the cup-tie. Kelly had shone all afternoon, performing with sure handling and a coolness that inspired confidence to team and fans alike.

North End matched United for 80 minutes in all departments, until the visitors ramped up the pressure towards the end against the tiring home team.

With North End's defence in shreds, the ball fell to Bobby Charlton around 10 yards out. In the milliseconds it had taken Charlton to take a touch before deploying his missile shot, the North End keeper had launched himself forward valiantly from the goal line in an attempt to get something – anything – on the ball to block it.

Against the odds, he did. Spreading himself in the air, the ball thudded into his legs as he met the ball five yards out before it bounced away to safety to keep North End level and their hopes intact.

But then bravery came as second nature to Kel. In September 1971 in the Division Two match at Deepdale against Oxford United, he was forced to leave the pitch after damaging ligaments in his left arm following a collision with the visitors centre forward, Derek Clarke.

With the substitute already used, North End were down to 10 men for the last half hour as centre forward Hugh McIlmoyle took over the gloves.

While 'Mac' performed heroically between the sticks fisting away everything he could get near, Kelly did his bit too – returning to rapturous applause from the astonished crowd with 15 minutes still left – not as goalkeeper; as a winger with his left arm now in a sling.

Staggeringly, one of Kelly's first touches of the ball almost led to a goal for North End as his long through pass was picked up by Bobby Ham, whose shot went just wide of the post.

Thanks to Kelly's courageous effort to ensure Preston had their full complement on the pitch, the match was won on a day of valiant deeds far and beyond what any paying crowd could have expected.

Alan's affection for North End ran very deep. After being relieved of his duties with Nobby Stiles in the summer of 1981, he actually saved North End the cost of compensation by being reassigned to the coaching staff.

It proved a handy move, as Kelly was the man to whom the board turned to handle the first team affairs in the short term after they sacked the management team that had replaced Nobby Stiles and himself!

Alan finally got his chance to manage North End in December 1983. By then, the job had become something of a poisoned chalice, with negligible investment in the team and the club's spiral of decline tightening.

Kel deserved better than this for the nigh on 30 years of loyalty he had given to the club. He couldn't make it work, and took the decision to resign in February 1985.

Alan had finally left North End it seemed, but this wasn't the last we had heard of the great man.

Everton employed him as a specialist goalkeeping coach where he worked with the outstanding Neville Southall during the 'Blues' highly successful time in the mid Eighties.

He had of course coached the goalkeepers at Deepdale in his time there, and Roy Tunks for one absolutely loved and appreciated the sessions he had with Kel. The sessions were physically punishing and exhausting but Roy insists they improved him greatly and extended his career.

Kelly moved to Washington, DC later in 1985 with a desire to train young goalkeepers. He opened one of the first indoor playing facilities in the region and, in 1993, founded the 'Alan Kelly Soccer Programs' to offer year-round training options for players of all levels.

A five year spell with DC United as goalkeeping coach was clearly very productive, as he developed a string of goalkeepers that went on to play in six trophy winning teams between 1997 and 1999.

Following the DC United assignment, Kelly returned to coaching youth soccer and continued to assist with United's Academy programming.

Indeed, two of his three sons became goalkeepers in the English professional game; Gary who enjoyed notable spells at Newcastle United, Oldham Athletic and Bury and Alan Jnr, who followed in his father's footsteps at Deepdale, then moved on to play for both Sheffield United and Blackburn Rovers. Both played for the Republic of Ireland – Alan Jnr earning 34 full caps, while Gary turned out at four junior and intermediate levels.

Alan Snr eventually retired, and sadly passed away in the US in 2009 at the age of 72. He will always be fondly remembered at Deepdale as the greatest goalkeeper in the club's history, and fully deserving of the accolade.

He was still so admired in Preston that when it became the turn of the old Town End to be demolished in 2001 and rebuilt as part of the ongoing re-development of Deepdale, it was renamed the Alan Kelly Town End Stand.

His portrait, like those of other legends Sir Tom Finney and Bill Shankly in the stands beside him, has been cleverly mapped into the seating.

It's a constant reminder for the North End faithful that Alan is back at Deepdale – this time permanently, where he belongs.

PNE FC

"He was just a great mate since the time I came down to Preston in 1958. We were very close on the field and off the field. He was great, just a nice fella to know" – the late George Ross talking about his friend, Alan Kelly.

Dad **ALAN KELLY Jnr.**

My dad had an incredible work ethic on the training pitch, first as a player and then as a coach, assistant manager and manager.

He worked his players hard but fair.

Dad had a saying, "train heavy, play light." The goalkeepers would train wearing a weighted sweat shirt and be put through gruelling drills that pushed them to the limits of their physical capacity... and I know, because I was on the end of a few of those sessions!!!

Dad would have worked with Roy Tunks using the same ethos and work rate that made him the goalkeeper he was, and I remember dad telling me that it was Arthur Cox who saw this trait when he was a coach at Preston North End.

They fed off each other in that respect.

'Tunksy', quite rightly, said my dad would have been one of the first specialist goalkeeper coaches in world football at that time and it went a long way into forming Roy as a goalkeeper at the time, and as a goalkeeping coach in the future.

Dad spent four years working alongside Nobby and winning promotion in 1978 was another fantastic achievement in his Preston North End career.

I was nine or 10 at the time, and dad brought me to every home game.

I was permitted to be in the changing rooms and also helped the kit men, and sat on the bench of the dugout during the game! I was also allowed in the manager's office after the game for a lemonade.

I remember being in the Guild Club on the top floor of the old Pavilion Stand when news came through that promotion for Preston North End had been confirmed and someone handed me a bottle of champagne to open.

I shook the bottle because I didn't know what else to do and the cork shot out like a cannonball!

Nobby was fantastic with my brothers and I, and the fact his sons were also at every home game meant we all played together before the match, watched it together and then recommenced playing after the game! It was all very family orientated.

We were very lucky to be so involved with everything about Preston North End at the time, being behind the scenes on match days, helping out on training days when we were off school or, on Sundays, when we would roam the stands of Deepdale, exploring every nook and cranny of the ground.

They are wonderful memories.

PNE FC

Alan Kelly Snr saves the ball on the Lowthorpe Road training ground in the late 60's. Great surface!

CHAPTER 13

NORTH END MEMORIES

ROY TUNKS

MIKE ELWISS

JOHN SMITH

ALEX BRUCE

RICKY THOMSON

Credit: Lancashire Post

Sure handed, educator **ROY TUNKS**

Speaking to Roy Tunks about football is an absolute joy.

He's seen the game change immeasurably in his long association with the sport, which began at Rotherham United in 1968 and ended at Manchester City in 2016.

During that time, he became a Preston North End veteran of well over 300 games and played almost as many for Wigan Athletic after leaving Deepdale in 1981. In all, Roy played for seven different clubs, and upon retirement developed a new and highly successful career as a goalkeeping coach.

His first game on Deepdale's hallowed turf was for Rotherham United on that unforgettable night of May 4th 1971, when North End beat the Millers 3-0 to clinch the Division Three title.

It was a good night to be inside the ground, and it made a big impression on the young goalkeeper.

"I remember looking at the Kop from my position at the Town End and it was packed to the rafters. There was over 28,000 on that night, and the place was absolutely bouncing. With the history of the club behind all that too, who wouldn't have been impressed?

"We lost 3-0, but shared in the celebrations when Alan Ball Snr came into our dressing room with six bottles of champagne, and then told chairman Tom Nicholson to bring another six in when he we were running low."

Ironically almost 30 years to the day, Roy would again be drinking champagne in that very same away dressing room, but this time as the goalkeeping coach of Blackburn Rovers. Their 0-1 victory sealed their promotion as runners-up, while North End ended up falling at the last hurdle in the play-off final against Bolton Wanderers.

At the end of the 1972/73 season, Roy's contract at Rotherham had run out, and now a 'free agent' – although the club still held his registration – he was put out on loan first to Ipswich Town where he played under Bobby Robson, and then to Newcastle United under Joe Harvey. He played a few months at both clubs.

Both managers wanted to sign him, but Rotherham's asking price was around the same as the world record fee that Stoke City had paid Leicester City for Gordon Banks - £50,000. Ipswich did offer £30,000 but Rotherham turned them down.

Upon his return to Millmoor, Roy was told that Liverpool would like to take him on loan as cover for Ray Clemence as the European Cup squad, but feeling annoyed and disheartened with matters his response was, "If they want me, tell them to come and buy me."

Liverpool then went out and signed Peter McDonnell from Bury, who over the next four years never made a single appearance for Liverpool.

Maybe Roy's reluctance to go out on loan again was a blessing in disguise. As the atmosphere soured further at Millmoor between player and club, Roy approached the PFA and his case went to an independent tribunal.

Terry Venables represented Roy and a fee of £30,000 was finally set by the tribunal, with the stipulation that for every month that Roy remained at the club his transfer fee would halve. If that wasn't an incentive for Rotherham to stop dragging their heels, nothing was.

At £15,000 there was a lot of interest, but at £7,500 North End manager Bobby Charlton appeared on the Millmoor doorstep keen to sign Roy.

"I just wanted to get away by then, and Preston North End were a bigger club so I signed.

"Bobby was player-manager and would stop training to demonstrate a point now and then. He would say 'don't play that ball when you can pass it over there to him out wide,' and calmly smear a 30 yard pass to show how it was done before adjusting his quiff of hair once again. The rest of us used to look at each other and say, 'yeah, of course, just like that...!'.

"There were two World Cup winners at Deepdale then, Bobby and Nobby, and two other players who had played at a very high level in Francis Burns and David Sadler.

"After training we would sit in the big communal bath and they would regale us with tales about their careers and events until the water went cold. They loved telling us the stories and we enjoyed listening."

Charlton would eventually resign his position over the John Bird transfer.

"I don't think the issue was about Alex Bruce coming back in Bobby's eyes, it was that the keystone of the defence was being taken away from the team. Losing John was going to expose the team a lot more.

"I remember when Preston won promotion in 1970/71 I used to look at the paper and see clean sheet after clean sheet with 'Budgie' and Graham Hawkins as the centre backs and Alan Kelly in goal. John was a very important player.

"Always ask a goalkeeper how good a centre back is – and I can tell you John Bird was a very good centre back to play behind."

With that in mind, I then took the opportunity to ask Roy to briefly assess the North End team and staff of 1977/78 through his goalkeeper eyes.

John McMahon?

"Stavros lookalike from Kojak, the old television show. Good going forward, great right foot. He used to play back passes blind – I used to go beserk at him. Lovely fella, a good player. I played with him at Wigan too – quite a few ex North End players ended up there."

Harry Wilson?

"That should be Harry 'the dog' Wilson, as he had the same name as a notorious Millwall fan back then, and thus acquired his nickname. I recall a fixture against Wrexham I think, where he caught my fingers clearing the ball. We had let's say, a disagreement. It was soon forgotten though. Harry was a very good defender, good on the posts and had plenty of guile."

Francis Burns?

"A great player and a good bloke to have around. He was a marvellous passer of the ball, had a very good left foot, great communicator and had great coaching ability within the game itself. Well respected. I can remember a match at home against Stoke City and there had been massive traffic issues in and around Preston. We were about to take the field with just nine men, then Francis steamed in ripping his clothes off as he ran through the dressing room door while wearing a crash helmet. Absolutely hilarious! He had been delayed on the M61 and had hitched a lift on a motorcycle. Then as we were taking the field Mick Baxter raced in taking his clothes off and putting his kit on as we were trotting out.

After that Nobby arranged that we always met at the Crest hotel next to the bus station at 11:30am on home match days so that we were all together."

Mick Baxter?

"Excellent defender, classy player. He was the better player of the two brothers, but Stuart has gone a long way in the coaching side of the game. In today's game Mick would be great playing out from the back. He learned a lot from David Sadler and Graham Cross."

Graham Cross?

"A super player, don't know how he managed to travel up from Leicester every day, also played cricket for Leicestershire. Good to have around the place, very good in dressing room. By the time he arrived at Deepdale he had lost some of his pace, but had a brilliant ability to read the game, clear danger away early and make it look easy at the same time."

Gordon Coleman?

'Coley' was perfect for the team, utility player, brave as a lion, gave his all every time. An educated man too, often referred to as 'Lord Snooty' by Mike Elwiss and I. He would more often than not take a book along with him to read or study on a long coach journey to an away fixture. So, we used to rip out the last few pages when he wasn't looking. The team needed him for balance – he was nothing flash, but nothing fazed him. Still as laid back now as he was then."

Sean Haslegrave?

"He brought great experience to the side. Was a Division One class player who decided to drop down, he didn't resent that or 'lord it' over anybody else. He came in and gave 100%. Would put his foot in and used to work his socks off. I had a great understanding with him, as soon as I collected the ball he would go haring off down the left and we set off many attacks like that, catching the opposition on the break. He and Coley balanced the team perfectly."

Stephen Doyle?

"Made my debut for North End with him at Tranmere, Stevie was just 16. He gave us some steel in midfield when we needed it and could turn his hand to covering other positions. Had a couple of good moves after he left Preston."

Mike Elwiss?

"'Marvin' is a good mate. We teamed up and played a few pranks just to keep the place buzzing and the team spirit going. 'Marvin' because that was the name of Frank Spencer's dummy – 'Marvin the Magician', and it just stuck. He calls me 'Ron' – still does – which all started at an away fixture when the announcer, unfortunately for him, asked if we could help him by telling him the first names of the North End team. So, at the kick in when the teams were being announced it was 'Ron' Tunks, 'Ernie' Potts, 'Marvin' Elwiss and so on. The lads were in hysterics. Seriously though, Mike was a very good player who always gave 100%. He was quick, strong and direct. Mike would do all the spade work, win the ball, bomb down the wing, cross it and Brucie would tap it in. I used to choose my moment afterwards and drop into the conversation, "I see Brucie scored another tap-in today…" Mike used to run his socks off on heavy pitches but he had the legs to do it. Mustn't forget he could score goals too. A quality player."

Alex Bruce?

"Absolutely lethal. Alex was simply a great goalscorer with either foot, but mainly the right. He could look after himself when required despite the nice face. Another 100% player, perfect foil for Marvin."

Ricky Thomson?

"'Thommo' was a very, very talented player. Would have loved to have seen another two or three seasons from him to see what sort of player we would have got. He was the one who could do something special, like the Brian Mooney's of this world. He had something a little bit different, never a physical player but very aware and could skip out of the way of things or see things coming and use it to his advantage."

John Smith?

"'Smudger' was another who always gave 100% whenever he came in. That was one of the secrets of the team – everyone gave their maximum, we never carried anybody. Steady player, he was one of the fringe players between the reserves and the first team but scored a few goals when he was in the team."

Alan Spavin?

"Very technically gifted, bright, astute, great vision – Tony Currie but sadly without his pace. He came back from the States and helped Alan Kelly with the reserves and coaching the kids. He and Kel were good mates, very close."

Harry Hubbick?

"Always something going on with Harry. One night at Hillsborough, Mick Baxter went down injured and Harry ran on with the bladder full of cold water and a sponge. It was the usual repair, wet the sponge and rub it on Mick's sore leg. Shortly afterwards, I collided with one of their forwards, took a knock to the face and broke my nose. I was led on the floor when Harry arrived and started the cold water treatment all over my face. I then got cotton wool stuffed up my nose, a quick eye test – how many fingers can you see? – and off Harry ran. He had been gone less than a minute when suddenly my eyes started watering and my face was stinging all over like mad. Harry had only gone and rubbed the winter green off Mick's leg into my eyes and face. Fortunately, I had nothing to do in terms of goalkeeping for the five minutes it took me to recover, otherwise they could have walked past me."

Nobby Stiles?

"I really liked Nobby. He was a good choice as manager because he had done it all as a player but he had been a coach for a few years too. He had a good knowledge about things, and had the respect of everybody. When you played with Nobby it was brilliant. He was great at just filling holes, he sort of just drifted into the right position then all of a sudden would just do something – a bit of magic. You would think, 'wow, did I just see that? I didn't expect that off him!' He would pop up in just the right place at just the right time to mop up. He could play."

Alan Kelly?

"Kel was assistant to Nobby but he was also not frightened to say what he thought. He was a very good coach. He was part time I think after his injury when I arrived and I asked him if we could get together a couple of times during the week so he could put me through my paces. There were no goalkeeping coaches then as there are now. He worked me to death, up down, up down, up down to the point of me feeling sick sometimes –

but I reckon those sessions put another two or three years on my career. It was great that I had someone to speak to about goalkeeping too. Kel would see things I wasn't doing quite right and it was sorted before it became a problem.

Nobby and Kel worked very much in tandem. Both could bark a bit when necessary – there was a game at Ninian Park where Nobby chewed me up at half time and I even had a go back at him. I played like an octopus in the second half, saving everything. When we got back in, he came straight over to me smiling and shouted, "yeahhh" then turned to the rest of the players, "that's how you respond to a bollocking!"

Nobby was a great coach but he needed Kel. Together they were perfect, and they had the utmost respect of the players."

When Roy speaks he is very engaging, his ability to explain is excellent. It is very easy to see why Roy succeeded so well at teaching hopeful coaches and indeed, some of the game's best exponents the art of goalkeeping upon retiring from playing.

He was a very real trailblazer for the modern 'goalkeeping coach'.

Does he enjoy the modern game as a spectacle?

"Yes, I do. Before I retired from work completely, my last five years was coaching at Manchester City. That is a different world. It is a different type of football altogether these days. It's brilliant. When you see it close up – bang, bang – the pace that they move the ball at – stunning.

"I'm not one of those types who say, well, you know in our day it was this, that and the other. No, things have changed, you get 15 and 16 year old's who are as strong as we were. They're built better than we were at that age and there are specialists involved in every facet of their development you can think of. It's unbelievable really."

Back in 1989, Roy's path crossed with John McGrath's, a manager who did so much to revitalise the ailing Preston North End of the early Eighties. It was after Roy had left Wigan Athletic to help John Bird out, who was then manager at Hartlepool. 'Budgie' then moved on to become manager of York City, and Roy was paid up and despatched by the new Hartlepool manager Bobby Moncur.

"I was back in Preston, so I thought I would ring John up and ask if I could come in and do a bit of training. John said, "You can come in and play!" After a few reserve games John put me in the first team and I played 20 games or so but I was around 40 by now and found that I was having more and more collisions with opposition players.

"Reactions slow over time, and I was just a click of the fingers too late sometimes – milliseconds – and didn't really fancy any breakages at my time of life, so thought it was time to retire.

"John was a very good coach, he operated a sweeper system and his teams played football – unlike when he was a player when he just kicked everything that moved!

"There are some great stories about John, like the time he got the sack at Preston. He walked out of the entrance onto Lowthorpe Road to be met by the press, one of whom shouted out, 'What does it feel like to getting the sack,' to which John brilliantly replied, 'I feel exactly like I did the first day I walked through these doors...fired with enthusiasm.' Everyone burst out laughing, but it was typical of John."

Following the hanging up of his boots in 1990, Roy's journey into the coaching side of the game is one that is littered with achievement at every turn.

He began by taking his 'A' Licence outfield coaching certificate at Lilleshall. Peter Reid and Les Chapman were in the same group.

"I passed that and joined the FA as a staff coach for the Lancashire region, and also did goalkeeping work with 16-20 year olds within the England youth team set-up, for three years. I did the World Cup and European Championship with them. The European Championship was held in Luxembourg and France and we came third. France won it with a front three of David Trezeguet, Thierry Henri and Nicolas Anelka!

"Mind you, we had Michael Owen, Emile Heskey, Frank Lampard – and David Lucas from North End was part of the squad too.

"I really enjoyed all that, and then I received a telephone call from Roy Hodgson who had just taken over at Blackburn Rovers who asked me if I would like to become goalkeeping coach there. I said yes, and the FA were brilliant about it all.

"I did around eight years there with Roy, Brian Kidd and Graeme Souness.

I worked initially with Tim Flowers and then around five years with Brad Friedel.

"I left Rovers in 2004, joining Graeme when he was appointed at Newcastle United. Up there, I worked with Shay Given and Steve Harper. Tim Krul hadn't been there long when Graeme was sacked.

"All Graeme's staff all had to go at the same time, but they couldn't really sack me because Shay had just been picked by his fellow professionals as goalkeeper of the year in the PFA team. I eventually reached an agreement with them and left.

"I then went for a couple of years to the States to help run Brad Friedel's soccer academy in Cleveland, Ohio, and when I came back I eventually received a telephone call from Scott Sellars, the ex- Rovers player who was by now in charge of the Manchester City academy coaches.

"He asked me if I would like to be the head of goalkeeping for the 23 year olds and younger? Lovely! I had just turned 60 years old and had five or six coaches working for me.

"Although Roberto Mancini and Manuel Pellegrini had their football styles, the youth teams all played the Barcelona way.

"Before I got to retirement age, I gave them fair warning that I was going to finish. I had done just about 50 years in football and it was time to stop. City asked if I would consider being a part-time goalkeeping-specific scout for them. The job description sounded glorious, but I didn't fancy making such a big commitment at 65 years old."

Roy finally – and modestly – reveals something that he is so very rightly proud of.

"There is a goalkeepers conference held at St. Georges Park, Burton where 250 goalkeeping coaches from all over the world assemble every year for the weekend. I was invited along in 2016 although I had just retired. It ends with a dinner, and I was sat at a table with my wife and all the FA people.

"Ray Stubbs was on the podium and started talking down the microphone about somebody, and it became obvious that he was talking about me! It ended with him asking me to go up and receive an award from him for an 'outstanding contribution to goalkeeping'.

"Of course, I was really pleased and after the presentation I sat down at the table again, and told everyone how thrilled I was. Somebody replied saying that I was now in very exalted company, as that particular award had only ever been awarded on four previous occasions – to Gordon Banks, Pat Jennings, Ray Clemence and Peter Shilton."

Credit: Lancashire Post

Roy takes command and punches the ball clear for North End against Stoke City at the Victoria Ground in February 1979

Roy found it easy to transition the gap that lies between playing and coaching that many others just can't. With over 850 games under his belt he knew the on-field art inside out, but felt just as relaxed imparting his knowledge directly to a goalkeeper or as a coach educator.

"I always found coaching comfortable somehow, it wasn't difficult for me to get things over. My philosophy was that trying to improve a goalkeeper's natural style was more important than imposing a similar robotic style on everyone. In a match situation a goalkeeper will revert to his natural style, so I would ask the coaches to just assess what was natural for the goalkeeper and work on that."

Roy rates the Nobby Stiles/Alan Kelly seasons as the best of his Deepdale days. During that promotion season of 1977/78 he was an ever-present, kept 20 clean sheets out of 46 games, and conceded just 38 goals in the league all season – an outstanding performance. That rich seam of form continued and he was named as Preston North End player of the year for the 1979/80 season.

There is no doubt that Roy was an excellent goalkeeper, but to be in constant demand as a goalkeeping coach too at the top level is far from being just good fortune. As his success demonstrated, having Roy Tunks involved with the goalkeepers at your club was a prestige appointment indeed.

PNE FC

A disconsolate Roy after the last game of the 1980/81 season. Although North End had pulled off an excellent away win at Derby County it wasn't enough to prevent the club's relegation back to Division Three.

This match was to be the last in part one of Roy's North End career as he was inexplicably never selected by manager Tommy Docherty, who replaced Nobby Stiles in the summer of 1981.

The rampaging, marauding **MIKE ELWISS**

I wish I could transport the younger fans of today back in time and show them Mike Elwiss in action for Preston North End.

He had just about everything you could hope for in a forward.

He was brilliant. A unique, dynamic, plundering player who roved the opposition half with real power and intent. If it was today's 'modern era' that he was playing in, his computer readout would show his 'assist' rate as 'off the scale'.

However, Mike was no one trick pony. He could score goals too – plenty of them!

That isn't just me or the thousands of others who saw him play for Preston North End becoming overdosed on romantic nostalgia. Terry Venables, the bright, young go-ahead coach of the 1980's who was later to become England manager, obviously thought so too.

In fact, Mike's connection to Preston North End goes back to May 1964, when his dad took him to Wembley to watch the FA Cup final against West Ham United.

He was a typical, football mad 10 year old back then. He never dreamt that one day one of the superstars of the game whose face looked down on him from a Ty-Phoo tea poster on his bedroom wall would actually ask him to come and play for his club.

Bobby Charlton signed Mike from Doncaster Rovers in February 1974 a month after Alex Bruce's departure to Newcastle United. A two-goal debut at Carlisle United went a long way towards soothing the feelings of the North End fans who were still seething at Bruce's departure.

He never really looked back after my debut. He kept his place, and at the end of the season had scored five goals in 11 appearances.

"We were relegated, and Bobby decided to play again the following season but we still missed out on promotion back to Division Two."

Charlton then resigned at the start of the following season, over the issue which saw John Bird leave for, and Alex Bruce return from, Newcastle.

"Bobby was a naturally gifted footballer, a brilliant player. We would watch him hit 40 yard passes to either side of the pitch and land them on a sixpence. He was a lovely bloke, and at the end of the day, it was he who bought me for Preston North End. I really appreciate that fact.

"Harry Catterick then came in just after the start of the 1975/76 season and he brought Nobby Stiles back to the club a few weeks later – he had resigned soon after Bobby had left. Nobby was appointed chief coach, but in all honesty, we never really saw Catterick around – just at the weekends usually. I don't think his heart was really in what he was doing.

"His plan for the way I was to play just didn't work. After five or six games I was useless! So, I thought I would revert to my usual way of playing and ditched it. 'Brucie' and I clicked immediately, and the partnership really began."

By the end of the season the pair had netted 31 goals between them and a further 48 more goals were credited to the partnership's tally by the end of the 1976/77 season. They would smash home a further 47 in 1977/78.

The board had suddenly replaced Catterick with Nobby Stiles and new assistant manager Alan Kelly on the eve of that 1977/78 campaign.

"Nobby was brilliant. He was an excellent coach and a lovely bloke. When he wanted us to work, we worked hard for him, but he was one of the lads too. He always allowed you to play your natural game and was honest, humble with absolutely no ego. If you ask the other lads, I'm sure they will all say the same.

"That was part of the secret, the atmosphere and team spirit were great at that time. I used to look forward to going in to work.

"He never complicated things, just kept everything simple. I suppose you could say we played a 4-4-2 or a 4-3-3 system depending on the opposition, but there was a lot of freedom for the players within those structures. It wasn't rigid."

Stiles appointed Mike as captain, but the team's form was patchy at the start of the season. However, from around October they began to gel after the arrival of Sean Haslegrave and were considered 'promotion contenders' by the national press.

“Captaining the team was quite easy actually. I knew that everyone was going to give 100% on the pitch, and Nobby selected such a good backbone for the team.

“I knew that behind me Roy Tunks (experience), Graham Cross (experience), and Frannie Burns (experience), would be constantly pulling players in at the right time. The team just ‘worked.’ I could concentrate on working with Alex setting up and scoring the goals.

“Alex will tell you the same – we never really practiced at what became quite a partnership. If we had, we might have been dangerous!

“Brucie wasn’t that big, but he was very strong and hard to knock off the ball. It was one of those occasions when it all just came together for us. It was simple really – we just played what we saw. There was no need to complicate matters.”

I ask Mike, as leader of the North End pack, for a quick run-down of the rest of the promotion team, and he obliges – tongue in cheek, of course!

“Ron Turps was a very good goalkeeper, safe and reliable. Did a lot to keep the team spirit going.

“John McMahon liked a moan, always pointing, but seriously, he was great bloke, a very good full-back, very good on the ball and at going forward. We were once training on the pitch on Lowthorpe Road, John hoofed the ball out of the ground, and through a house window. He was sent around to get the ball and when he got back, he said, “they were having a coffee morning…”

“Danny Cameron I had known from my early days at Doncaster, as he played for Sheffield Wednesday intermediates. Very solid, never gave up.

“Francis Burns was a very good player. Would constantly pick up the bits and pieces in the middle of the pitch. When Frannie and David Sadler came to Preston from the great Manchester United they used to say, ‘we love it here.’ Actually, that’s what everybody said about being at North End. When we played away and were stopping overnight, sometimes Tunksie and I would torment them both after having stocked up at the joke shop.

“Mick Baxter was a very good player, just a very sad, tragic story.

"Graham Cross played in Division One for a long time, and had a wealth of experience. Kept players in check, and good for Mick Baxter's football education.

"Gordon Coleman was very adept, not flashy but an essential part of the mixture. You could wind 'Coley' up and he would run all day for you. Would break up opposition moves and win the ball back. Very bright lad, always reading.

"Sean Haslegrave was quality. Very skilful player with Division One experience.

"John Smith always gave his best for the team. Once said that if you passed the ball to Brucie, you knew you were never going to get it back!"

All good things come to an end, and in the close season following that memorable campaign Mike joined Crystal Palace.

"I knew that I had been watched over the season by Aston Villa, Norwich City and Leeds United, and It seemed that I could be on my way to Villa, but their manager, Ron Saunders had to go into hospital for an eye op, so it never progressed."

Mike joining forces with Tony Morley again as Villa won both the League Championship and European Cup in the early Eighties would have been absolutely fantastic to witness for the North End fan.

Villa certainly played a style of football Mike would have revelled in, but Terry Venables pipped everyone to the post when he flew out to Spain to sign Mike while he was on holiday.

"I was ambitious as a player, and never wanted to look back on my career and have regrets. It was sadly the time to leave North End, a club I still love dearly.

"The Palace set-up was fantastic, and Terry was very astute and forward-thinking about the game. I liked him and we got along well. There was a great feel about the club too; the team was full of talent and on top of that they had won the FA Youth Cup for the previous two seasons."

It started so well for Mike. He was in a similar role as to that at Deepdale, and his powerful non-stop display in Palace's 'derby' win against Brighton at Selhurst Park was outstanding. A crowd of over 34,000 crammed themselves into the ground, with highlights of the clash recorded by

London Weekend Television for The Big Match. It makes for good viewing, especially the when Mike 'turns' his ex-North End teammate, Mark Lawrenson!

Just a couple of weeks later, he scored what he describes as a 'fortunate' late winner upon his return to Deepdale in Palace colours.

<u>Left</u>: Mike in the process of curling the ball into the net against Lincoln City at Deepdale in the FA Cup, November 1977 (see page 133 for an alternative angle)

<u>Left</u>: Mike pounds down the left wing in typical fashion against Halifax Town at Deepdale in February 1976

Credit: Lancashire Post

Mike was an ever-present in the Palace team until what turned out to be a fateful game for him against Burnley at Turf Moor on November 4th 1978.

He came off worst in a tackle that was to effectively end his career. He gamely soldiered on upon his return to the Palace first team a fortnight later, somehow still managing to score goals in his regular career ratio of around one goal in every three games.

"I wasn't happy though; I just knew deep inside that it was serious. I was just hanging around up front really, not getting involved. That just wasn't me.

"The knee kept giving way and would blow up like a balloon. Then they would have to drain the fluid off it."

The attempts by Palace to rehabilitate Mike included a loan spell back at Deepdale for the last 10 games of the 1978/79 season in which he scored three goals. The knee wasn't getting any better though and after five operations in three years had failed to correct Mike's knee, he unsurprisingly lost faith in the surgeons.

"Each would tell a different tale to the other, and after three years of repeated hope and frustration, the whole thing was just getting on top of me."

It was all over for Mike at the age of 27. It was such a gut-wrenching way to pull the curtain down on a career that was on the verge of such great things, for himself and his many fans. Paradoxically, in his entire time at Deepdale, out of a possible 195 appearances he could have made for the club he missed just three, such a fit specimen was he.

Released from Palace, and now back in the locale, he made a last ditch effort to come back in the North End reserves in 1982, but it was to be a non-starter.

Mike then forged a successful living outside of the game, starting out with a milk round before involving himself in property renovation. He then helped run a pasteurising plant, which he did until his retirement.

There is a more than positive note to report about Mike's knee, however.

After years of increasing discomfort, Mike found a surgeon in London with the knowledge and know-how to repair the damage in his knee. The result is that Mike walks very freely now.

"Treatment of injuries like mine has moved forward and improved vastly since I was playing and I'm really pleased with the outcome."

Because of the way it all ended for Mike I am even more grateful for his time at Deepdale and witnessing him destroy defences along the way with Alex Bruce.

I was young when I saw Alex Dawson and Brian Godfrey play and nobody respects their work at Deepdale more than myself, but in Mike and Alex I surely witnessed North End's greatest strike force ever.

Speaking to Mike at a very leisurely pace about football past and present in the sunshine while under the watchful eye of Alfie, the family black Labrador, was just a fantastic experience.

You can still sense the happiness in Mike's voice as he recalls his Deepdale days and the notorious exploits both on – and off the pitch. He is a real gentleman too, and made me feel very welcome even though, ahem, I turned up at completely the wrong time for the interview!

Here's a 'good times' tale from the 'Ron and Marvin' back catalogue to end on. It highlights perfectly the team spirit that Nobby and Kel had fashioned at Deepdale.

"If you worked hard for Nobby and Kel there was always time for a laugh and a joke. Once, we were in a hotel on a Friday night before an away match. Rooms were shared – two players to a room. Roy and I were wandering down a corridor when we noticed a fuse box. We slipped the cover off and saw that each fuse was identified with a room number. Bingo! So, we sought out Nobby's room number – he shared a room with trainer Harry Hubbick. They liked to watch television in the evening, and we could hear from outside that they were busy watching a cowboy programme. We crept back to the fuse box and switched their power off. We could hear Nobby saying "You must have touched it," and Harry protesting his innocence. After a couple of minutes, we switched it on again. "Leave the bloody thing alone now," Nobby told Harry. A few minutes elapsed before we plunged their power off again. The air was blue inside Nobby's room. "I told you to leave the ******* thing alone," Nobby was shouting while Harry was saying "I never touched the ******* thing! It was hilarious! We left them to it and wandered away. A short while later, we could see some hotel staff about to swap Nobby's television for another, so switched the power back on again. All was well for a while – until we turned their power off once more and Harry was getting it in the neck from Nobby again. We switched it back on, then telephoned Nobby from our room. "Thought we'd stay in our room tonight Nobby, can you tell us what's on telly? There was a very slight pause, then – "You! It's you isn't it?! You pair of **************!!!!"

As the song goes, 'Those were the days, my friend...'

The industrious, supportive **JOHN SMITH**

John arrived on trial at Deepdale in 1972, one of the many Jimmie Scott recruits for North End from north of the border.

"Alan Ball was manager then, a real character and life was never dull. My lasting memory of him is the five-a-side games on Monday mornings. We would play on the training ground on Lowthorpe Road, and everyone would jump in and set to it. Then Bally would tun up in a suit and dark glasses and just join in! I think he must have still been feeling the effects of, let's say, a heavy weekend...

"He was the one who signed me, so I will always be thankful to him for that.

"I was staying at their youth hostel on Moor Park Avenue. I remember Tony Morley was there at the same time. He was a brilliant even then. A few of us were having a kick about on Moor Park one afternoon and he was doing tricks with the ball I had never seen before. He was always with a football, so focused on the game.

"I had managed to get injured on my first turnout for the second string just before the first team squad were off to Scotland on a pre-season tour.

"The coach pulled up outside the hostel and Bally came in and said to me, 'right, pack your bags and get on the bus.' That's all he said to me, so straight away I thought this is it; he's getting rid of me and dropping me off at home.

"The bus went past Glasgow and I'm thinking where the hell is he taking me? We eventually arrived at Dundee where the first team squad were due to play. Bally then rang my mum and dad up and signed me on there and then! It was just a fantastic feeling after what had been going around in my head.

"Bobby Charlton took over, and he was a gentleman but not really cut out to be a manager. When you look at what he and Nobby Stiles achieved in football to what they were like as people in the way they treated and spoke to others, they were such genuinely nice guys.

"Nobby wasn't appreciated for the footballer he was. People were fed the impression of a little, no-teeth footballer kicking lumps out of

Eusebio, but he could actually play. You don't play in the England world cup winning team if you can't play football. He had a great touch.

"Harry Catterick then came in and we wouldn't really see him from one week to the next, but he would often select me for the first team, but I was happiest as a player under Nobby.

"When he became manager, he was the pro-active involved on the training pitch type, as was 'Kel' who fancied himself as a closet centre forward. There was no such thing as specialist goalkeeping coaches back then, Kell was Nobby's assistant. He gave Nobby strong support and they were good together.

"Charlton was 'boss', Catterick was certainly 'boss', but Nobby was always happy to be called 'Nobby'.

"I was a worker, decent in the air too, but I was never a flair player. Nobby would encourage me by telling me that if I kept working hard, things would happen for me.

"I did work very hard but when you have players like Ricky Thomson coming along fast, and Brucie knocking the goals in, there's only so many players a manager can play. You have to be realistic about things. My chances were therefore limited.

"Tactics were not heavily used like they are today. You were told where you were playing and what your role within the team was. That was the basic structure and you had the freedom to express yourself but to be aware that if for instance, Ricky was banging forward I would need to fill in behind. It was common sense teamwork without restrictions.

"I've watched games with the other players over the years at North End, and straight away you can pick out players who have been told not to stray in to certain areas. It's totally different today, but in our time there was certainly no diagrams with arrows and all the stuff that went with it.

"As far as Nobby was concerned as long as you were doing your job, you were fine."

As a spectator on the terraces that season, I used to hear John get some stick from the crowd. Nobby wasn't listening though. *"People just don't or won't see the graft John puts in,"* he told the North End AGM in October 1977. *"He gets a lot of criticism, but I don't care who scores our goals and I will defend any of my players."*

"Nobby told me on occasions to ignore the critics as did John McMahon and Alex Bruce in a newspaper article, but when I was on the pitch I was occupied and I didn't give it too much thought. I was only bothered by it when I wasn't playing."

John often played behind the fantastic partnership of Mike Elwiss and Alex Bruce in the 1977/78 promotion winning team, and I ask him what was it like to watch them at work.

"Brucie was the greediest so and so you'll ever meet – and the laziest – but I'll tell you what, you would always have him in your team!

What a striker! If the ball came anywhere near him there was no messing. It was either a goal or a corner. He would never pass inside the box, he would hardly involve himself in play outside of the box – but what a finisher. Brilliant!

"I once got a pass off him in a charity match. I needed smelling salts.

"Mike in contrast worked very hard outside of the box, scored quite a few goals himself but provided loads of opportunities for Brucie. He was a very strong lad. A dynamic player.

"I would say it's probably the best attacking partnership North End have ever had."

After that, John runs down some other members of the team.

"John McMahon was a nice bloke. He had a transfer issue in the past with North End that took him a long time to get over. Good player.

"Frannie Burns' knees were both troublesome but he could still pass a ball very well. Very knowledgeable about the game and a very good player. He emigrated a long time ago to Australia and I looked him up when I was over in Perth. He was involved in the white goods business.

"Alan Spavin was a brilliant player in his time, but in 1977/78 had just returned from the States. He was mainly helping with the kids and the reserves but played the odd first team game. Was also the club bookie. When any big event was on, he would be there collecting the bets.

"Stephen 'Taffy' Doyle has been in Port Talbot for a while now. He was a decent player with two good feet and liked a tackle.

"Sean Haslegrave was a very good player in midfield, and very fit.

"Gordon Coleman was very underrated, a real team player. He was one of those players that was essential because of his contribution to the team.

"Graham Cross was a cracking player, he helped turn Mick Baxter into a

<u>Left</u>: John (with ball) at a PNE youth team session
<u>Below left</u>: John and Mick Baxter lodged with kitman George Warr and wife Betty
<u>Below</u>: Firing in a shot at Deepdale in 1976

<u>Above, middle left</u>: John in his Los Angeles Skyhawks strip
<u>Above, middle right</u>: John determinedly chasing down the ball
<u>Bottom left</u>: Relaxing by the pool after a training session in Los Angeles
<u>Bottom right</u>: John crashes in a shot on the turn at Deepdale

classy performer.

"Danny Cameron is in South Africa now. He went back to Scotland after North End let him go. Had he habit of pinging the ball into you from just a few yards away. I think in 1977/78 he covered both full back spots.

"Roy Tunks was a great goalkeeper but typical of the breed – he's not quite right. Actually, Roy is great and very funny too; he and Mike Elwiss were the club clowns."

Talk of Roy Tunks brings back memories of the last game of the season against Shrewsbury Town at Deepdale, when a misunderstanding between Tunks and Francis Burns resulted in a goal for the visitors.

"I can actually remember more about the following Monday when Wrexham played Peterborough.

"Frannie Burns and John McMahon had gone to the game with Nobby. There was a reserve game on at Deepdale and we were sitting there just waiting until the score was confirmed. When the result was confirmed, had a lot to drink in the club then made our way to the Withy Trees to have a lot more...

"It's maybe the same now, but back in my time the players loved playing for the club and a lot of them ended up settling down in the area when their playing days were over. We certainly all got on and have remained good mates."

'Smudger' left North End at the end of the 1978/79 season. Lying immediately ahead was a mini adventure in the North American Soccer League – in Los Angeles too!

Before John left North End, Nobby put him in touch with his friend Shay Brennan, the ex-Manchester United right back who was a conduit for Waterford FC in Ireland and Los Angeles Skyhawks in the United States. He also told John that he was always welcome to come back and train at Deepdale to keep his fitness levels up, should the need arise.

After a short spell at Waterford, John made it across the pond and played the best part of a season for the Skyhawks. He had just married Alison and both remember it as a great experience, although John recalls pranging his car soon after arrival!

"We really enjoyed it there, it was a very good lifestyle," continues Alison. "We lived in the Canoga Park district of Los Angeles. It was always warm and sunny. It was very much a beach life and sitting around the pool.

"I wasn't bothered about the football! While John was doing that, I was either in the sun or visiting places like Disneyworld or Universal Studios!

"Football over there was so different to what I was over here. It was very family orientated, a real day out."

John scored six goals in around 20 appearances for the Skyhawks, playing behind the strikers.

"Players had no rights over there, unlike in England, so if a club didn't want you anymore, it was thanks very much and goodbye. The clubs held all the aces," explains John.

"The reason I and the others had to leave is that the Skyhawks franchise was sold on and the new owners wanted to choose their own staff."

That meant moving back to England and, after popping into Deepdale to see Nobby, John took up his old boss on the offer of the chance to come in and train to keep himself fit. Typical of the man, Nobby also rang around a few clubs on John's behalf.

His next stop was Halifax Town where the highlight of his stay was being part of the team that dumped Malcolm Allison's Manchester City out of the FA Cup in the third round in 1980.

City were awash with big money signings – Michael Robinson and Steve Daley to name but two. Robbo's presence on the pitch along with Smudger and Halifax's ex-North End goalkeeper John Kilner, certainly added a special interest to proceedings for the curious Lilywhite fan.

On a quagmire pitch – the kind of which the modern footballer would take one look at and then return to his sports car – Halifax worked their socks off, none more so than the ex-North End pair. Both played blinders, and still goalless with around 15 minutes to go, Halifax drove forward once more.

John received a wide ball which, with a deft first touch, turned the ball through for striker John Hendrie to run onto and slam home from close range. Halifax held on, and the superstars had to help themselves to large slices of humble pie.

After his spell at the Shay, John moved across to Workington AFC and then Lancaster City FC, before pursuing an occupation outside of the world of football.

Smudger is honest enough to tell you he wasn't a lynchpin in that promotion team of 1977/78. However, the simple fact is any successful team needs players like him; the essential reliable performers who repeatedly bring their 100% to the table.

I found John to be great company, very helpful, very witty and articulate. He looks fit too, and is still running around the pitch wearing a Hoole United shirt on the very rare occasion. Alas, he says he aches all over the day after!

He is very proud of his time at Deepdale. As a fan who saw him play and now fortunate enough to meet and talk to him about North End, it was an absolute pleasure to listen to his football experiences.

Even after all his considerable footballing adventures, he's still very much a Lilywhite.

Preston North End youth team squad 1974/75

Proof – if any were ever needed – that North End's ability to produce good players through their youth system has been going on for time immemorial. Five of those above would appear in the first team during 1977/78, while another had already moved onto to bigger things. A few more made it to reserve team level.

<u>1977/78 first teamers</u> – Stephen Doyle (back row, second left), Mick Baxter (back row, extreme right), Michael Robinson (front row, third left), Ricky Thomson (front centre) and John Smith (front row, second right).
<u>Reserves</u> – Gary Hudson (goalkeeper back row), Mark Fielding (back row, second right) and Royston Taylor (front row, third right).
Mark Lawrenson (back row, fourth left), left for Brighton in June 1977.

The lethal goal machine **ALEX BRUCE**

There was only one period in all my years following North End that I had a 'joint favourite player'. I'm sure Alex won't mind that he shared the mantle with Mike Elwiss however, because as he readily admits, Mike was pretty kind to him on the pitch.

I first noticed Alex in the late Sixties when he started to play regularly for the reserve team in the Central League – yes, my loyalty to North End is that deep I'm afraid!

He stood out not only for the fact he had a magnificent red barnet, but also for the way he was – even at such a tender age– quite fearless in front of goal.

Quite often the Central League gave the young aspirants of the region an opportunity to play and test their skills against established pro's of the top division who would be regaining form, or fitness after injury. Goalkeepers were often first team understudies and already a 'name' in their own right.

Their reputations meant nothing to the North End upstart who would smash the ball past them at every opportunity. The paltry crowds at those reserve games at Deepdale were however the fortunate few who witnessed the genesis of a bright new star.

"I arrived at Deepdale in 1968. Bobby Seith was in charge then; he was a good coach. He was great with us young lads, always very encouraging with his words.

"Alan Ball came in and he was a character! He gave me the chance to get into the team and built my confidence up. Growing up, as far as my football was concerned, I wasn't physical. I just wanted to put the ball in the net. It was like a tunnel-vision.

"As a professional though, managers want other things from you, but 'Bally' told me he wasn't bothered if I couldn't outjump a 6'4" defender or didn't win a tackle. He just wanted me in the box and told me to play the way I wanted to.

"The only other manager to give me that kind of freedom was Nobby Stiles when he was appointed in 1977.

"Bally and the coach Arthur Cox used to take us up to Willow Farm and take me aside to improve my instincts around the goalmouth and sense where the goal is. So, with my back to goal Arthur would say 'look at the goal, now don't look at the goal' as he fed a random ball into me and I hopefully found the net without looking.

"They told me that my senses and speed of thought would sharpen and improve because it was essential in the first team.

"When I finally broke into the first team, Hugh McIlmoyle was a great help and I learned a lot from him. I loved playing with 'Spav' too. It was brilliant when you received a pass from him, it was in just the perfect spot for you. He was a great player.

"Bobby Charlton was a nice bloke, a great player but I think found the transition to coach a little difficult.

"I think that was because he had been a high level player who had spent his playing career amongst other high level players. Frannie Burns told me that at Manchester United they just used to keep the players fit, and on Saturday the players would just run out and do their stuff. At Preston though, I think we needed a little bit of direction too – the lower the standard, the more direction is needed."

Out of the blue, Alex found himself being despatched from North End to Newcastle United in January 1974, before just as surprisingly, being retrieved in August 1975.

"The day I was sold, our left back at the time Jimmy McNab, needed a lift in as his car was being repaired. He jumped in and the first thing he said was, "They're selling you today."

"I was shocked – I knew nothing about it, so when we got to the ground, I made straight for Bobby and asked him what was going on. He said Preston were indeed selling me, to Newcastle United.

"He told me that that I might not be able to keep my place at Deepdale and that this was a good opportunity for me. I explained that I really didn't want to go, and needed at least a little time to think about it, but he said Newcastle manager Joe Harvey was already on his way with his assistant Len Richley.

"I was just 21 and stunned by all this. What was I going to do? I met them, and had no option really but to sign."

I remind Alex that in the previous season, Bobby was quoted as saying after a match that, "I have no intention to sell him. Alex is a vital player in our plans..."

"He must have changed his mind then!" laughs Brucie.

"When I got to Newcastle the front two were Malcolm McDonald and John Tudor. They were brilliant, and I knew I was never going to displace them.

"To be fair, Malcolm was absolutely superb with me. I learned a lot from him, so seeing him in action close-up was a real education. I was on the subs bench most times, so I got that chance to see how he worked.

"He used to miss some from close in, but then would be in the thick of it near the goal line again a few minutes later. He used to tell me to just keep going in. It doesn't matter if you miss. You are going to miss chances, but you are going to put some away too.

"After that, missing a chance didn't bother me at all.

"Besides knowing how difficult my task on the field was going to be, the actual move itself turned into a nightmare."

It did indeed, and you feel a bit nonplussed as to what Alex had to endure when he relates just how difficult it was to even get started with his new club.

"When I had signed, I was told there was a club house available and after a couple of days I drove up to St. James Park with my wife to see the house that they had mentioned. I went in and spoke to Joe Harvey and he said, there actually was no club house available as somebody else was in it."

There then followed more wasted journeys back and forth after further promises of finding Alex and his family accommodation never materialised. This culminated with yet another arranged visit up to St. James Park only to find the club locked up and, according to the cleaner, all the players apparently in Buxton for the week, training! It was pure pantomime!

Alex got back to Preston and stood fast.

Eventually North End director Cyril Pilkington made contact and told Alex he had to go, despite the players' deep reservations. Pilkington told him that the Newcastle team bus would pick him up at Buxton station and take him on to the hotel.

Nine days after Alex had signed for Newcastle United, he boarded a train and headed for Derbyshire to finally meet up with his new teammates.

"I told the management that I couldn't keep running backwards and forwards from Preston to Newcastle as I had a wife and son to think about, so they put us up at the Airport Hotel in Newcastle.

"In this football era even a very young player is managed in situations like the kind I found myself in. The saga would never have got as far as it did if it had happened today.

"By the start of the 1975/76 season, the Newcastle manager was now Gordon Lee and he told me that North End were interested in me returning, and would I drive down and talk to them.

"I met Alan Jones, Tom Gore and Bob Bolton at a place on Garstang Road and having seen everything in the press about Bobby being prepared to resign if John Bird left in the opposite direction, I told them I wasn't coming back if Bobby resigned as soon as I returned.

"They told me that Bobby was leaving anyway whether 'Budgie' (John Bird) or I didn't leave or arrive and that Harry Catterick was lined up to take over. So, I went back to Newcastle, thought about it and decided to return.

"I never really settled in Newcastle. I decided I would rather enjoy life and my football than struggle to make a name for myself in Division One. North End told me that they had spoken to Catterick who had no problem with me returning.

"Catterick was a figurehead really, not a track suit manager. Managing a club like North End after a club like Everton was never going to be the same. He did bring Nobby Stiles back to the club though after he had resigned when Bobby left.

PNE FC

Top left: Young Alex in the reserves, on the cusp of a first team call up
Bottom left: A decidedly un-elated Alex on the day he signed for Newcastle United
Top right Smashing home an early career goal against Brighton in 1972
Middle right: Scoring against Portsmouth in 1973
Bottom right Alex's second goal of the game against Bristol Rovers in 1979

"Nobby was great. A lovely man, couldn't be nicer. He encouraged both me and Mick Elwiss, and it was a dream come true when he told us just to play up front where we wanted to.

"He was a tracksuit manager, always involved. A good coach and a good manager. I actually played against him when he was at Middlesbrough.

"He was short-sighted too. He once rolled up late at Deepdale after racing through traffic dressed in a pin stripe suit. He couldn't understand why everyone was sniggering at him in the dressing room and it had to be pointed out to him that he was wearing one black shoe and one brown shoe!

"He also told us once that the day England won the World Cup he was at the evening reception and quickly nipped out to the toilet. He came back in and sat down, looked around and thought 'the bloody lads have gone out on the town and left me behind.' They hadn't... Nobby had gate-crashed a wedding reception next door...

"As a 13 year old, I went to see Scotland play England at Hampden Park in 1966 before the World Cup tournament. There was 134,000 on the terraces that day, and Scotland lost 3-4. My hero Denis Law scored one of the Scotland goals. I loved watching him play, and when he scored I thought that's what I want to do.

"It was the first time I had watched Nobby, and he absolutely ruined my day completely when he headed the ball off the England line near the end!

"I just had to tell him and one day I said to him, Nobby you might not believe this but as a kid I really disliked you. I've never really forgiven you for heading the ball off the line at Hampden Park in 1966! We ended up having a good laugh about it all.

"Seriously, you could not dislike Nobby.

"As a management team, Nobby was the boss but assistant Alan Kelly complemented him really well.

"Tactics wasn't the big thing that it is today. Things were pretty straightforward, plus I'm not so sure that half the players would have understood them anyway!

"We were generally told to play the ball forward as quickly as possible before the opposition had time to set up their defence. These days there is less risk taking, and teams look to keep the ball as long as possible.

"Under Nobby and Kel, our defence was strong and we were a good side who played really decent football."

How does Alex recall his teammates of that glorious promotion year?

Roy Tunks – "A good guy and a great goalkeeper for North End. Commanded the area."

John McMahon – "Cracking bloke, very funny. Good full back, very hard shot."

Danny Cameron, Harry Wilson – "Decent players, very steady and reliable"

Francis Burns – "Superb player, sublime passer of the ball. Passed the ball into feet, or into a bit of space. Never punted ridiculous and hopeful long balls."

Mick Baxter – "Really good player. Good in the air and ground."

Graham Cross – "'Crossy' was a real character around the place. Very good player."

Gordon Coleman – "'Coley' was a real all-rounder. Every team needs a Coley, he could play in any position."

Steve Doyle – "Tough tackler, good player.

Sean Haslegrave – "Division One player with Forest and Stoke City. Very good player, played on the opposite side of midfield to Coley."

Ricky Thomson – "Sometimes, when players have to retire through injury, people say 'he would have been a great player' out of sympathy. But I actually think he would. He was streets ahead of any of us regarding skills, whether in training or in a match. He definitely would have been a great player. I used to like playing alongside Thommo because there was always something likely to happen and as a poacher in the box, I usually got a few chances off him."

Mick Robinson – "A big lad with a big engine, and like with Ricky, often something would come my way from 'Robbo'."

Mick Elwiss – "Never practiced anything with Mick as regards our partnership. We had a few absolutely wonderful years together. He was as strong as an ox, and much more aggressive in his play than me. I wanted to be in the right place in the box at the right time to finish off all his hard work. I think that's how we gelled and got on. Mick always worked hard, had real pride in his performances and was great to play with. To be absolutely fair, I think I made him one or two goals as well...yeah, maybe two!

"We still keep in touch, but these days we talk mainly about ailments!"

And what about Alex Bruce on himself?

"I'll hold my hands up – I know I drove some of my managers mad, and I know I drove some of my teammates mad – especially 'Smudger' and 'Thommo' – who incidentally, *still* let me know that I was the greediest so and so they ever played with!

"You will see players who miss a chance start to hang back and become a bit timid, but you have to be thick-skinned and again, that's what I learned from Malcolm McDonald. You miss sitters, and everyone's saying how did he miss that? You just have to take it and think next time I will get back in again and score."

Alex is a wonderfully modest man, who I think would approve of me saying that he simply wanted to score a lot of goals for Preston North End. And he certainly did! He was a most prolific and consistent goal scorer – in the league alone averaging a goal every 2.3 games, with a total of 157 in 363 appearances.

Strikers like him come along perhaps once in a generation and thank goodness Bobby Seith and Alan Ball Snr. nurtured and developed him in his formative years so he became that clinical, fearless, goal machine. He gave us all so many great memories. What a striker he was!

He was ushered out of Deepdale twice in his career, quite ridiculous when you consider what he brought and gave to Preston North End. We fans knew he never wanted to leave on either occasion – Deepdale was always his home.

As a lifelong North End fan, meeting Alex was a dream come true. When he speaks about his playing days, you sense a deep affection for North End and all of his old teammates.

Alex hung his boots up in 1985 and began a career in leisure management, later becoming head of the leisure department at South Ribble Borough Council.

These days he gives a lot of his time up helping out at the Sporting Memories Foundation units at both Deepdale and the Lancashire Football Association in Leyland which tackle dementia, depression and loneliness through sporting memories.

Alex is everything you want a hero to be, and a credit to his profession.

A very special talent **RICKY THOMSON**

Ricky was yet another of Jimmie Scott's discoveries, arriving at Deepdale from Edinburgh in 1973. He was the North End youngster that everybody could identify as 'going places'.

He had a miserable time with injuries, and just when it seemed that finally there was a clear path ahead of him, he suffered two humdingers that wiped out a very promising career.

He is very good company, and a real character – and yet another ex-North End player who still lives in the area.

"He was the most skilful player at the club. He was in a way, ahead of this time at North End with the ball at his feet," says Alex Bruce. "He could do the tricky stuff like delicately chipping a goalkeeper to score and used to practice that using a heavier type of ball that weighed a ton when it was soaked."

Ricky used to glide over the pitch; he had speed and skill – and as 'Brucie' says, he possessed considerable talent. He could go around defenders like a cool breeze.

"I made my North End debut in the game against Chesterfield on March 31st 1975. Bobby Charlton had decided to retire from playing after making his comeback at the start of the season and replaced himself with me. I kept my place for the next six games, and was substitute in the last two games of the season.

"I was only 17 and when I look back, I think I knew Bobby and Nobby too soon – by that I mean I didn't really appreciate what they had achieved in their careers at the time. There I was trying to take the mickey in training and shove Nobby out of the road. They were World Cup winners for God's sake!

"I wish I knew then what I know about them now, about who they were, what they had done and how they were with people. They were both real gentlemen."

Nobby moved up to chief coach when Harry Catterick arrived, but it got even better when he was appointed manager.

"He was a coach that was in amongst you, taking part, as was Kel. They both got involved and didn't hold back either! Kel was a taskmaster and very involved in all the decision making, even the signings that arrived.

"Nobby gave me latitude. I was a midfield player but under Nobby I was encouraged to attack. It was simple too. No complicated tactics, it was all about getting the ball up the field. I was still on the fringes of the first team in the promotion year.

"I remember once at Deepdale, the match was well underway and 'Taffy' (Stephen Doyle) was substitute. He was sat between Nobby and Kel in the dugout wearing one of those all-in-one type tracksuits they had back then to keep warm. Nobby and Kel were both smokers, and all of a sudden there was a tremendous kerfuffle and when we all turned round one of them had managed to set Taffy's all-in-one alight and everybody was running around trying to extinguish him.

"It was a great time to be at North End. We all got on great together, and still do.

"Playing alongside Alex Bruce and Mick Elwiss taught me a few things, one was never to expect a pass off Brucie in the penalty area. He wouldn't set foot outside of the box. Kel used to shout to him, "chase the full-backs" – no chance!

"I scored some of my goals because I learned to sense when Brucie was going to shoot or when Mickey was going to shield it, go a certain way and cross it.

"Mickey made hundreds of chances for Brucie and I remember scoring a header at Bury in the promotion season from one of Mickey's crosses. I always tried to be around too for when Brucie scuffed a shot so that I could hopefully get the tap-in."

"Alan Spavin had come back to the club and played in that game, but I also remember Mickey having a go at me for losing the ball when I tried to dribble my way out of our penalty area near the end, allowing Bury to equalise."

Like a dog with a bone, Ricky tidies up the loose ends about that particular game with a considered, "... aye, but Brucie did miss a penalty though..."

"I remember being in the player's lounge at Craven Cottage with Nobby

PNE FC

Top: *Ricky fires in a terrific 25 yard shot to score against Burnley at Deepdale*
Middle: *A 'shimmy' leaves Archie Gemmill of Birmingham City floored as Ricky continues his mazy run*
Bottom: *Thommo is far too fast and tricky for the Burnley defence*

after a game there. Who should walk in but George Best, who had come along specially to see his old mate. Nobby introduced me to him and I shook Bestie's hand. He was rumoured to have been drinking heavily at the time, but he looked the fittest, brightest bloke in the place!"

Talk switches inevitably to Ricky's ability to strike a breathtaking goal. He is particularly proud of two – against Queens Park Rangers at Loftus Road, where he brilliantly chipped Chris Woods in October 1979 – and in the previous season against West Ham United in a televised match at Upton Park in November 1978. It really was a sensational goal, driving forward at goal from near the half way line to blast a screaming 30 yard drive past the hapless Mervyn Day.

Just 17 days after that brilliant goal at West Ham the first disaster struck.

He had been a regular first teamer since the start of the season and coming into a night match at Deepdale against Sunderland, had scored three goals in his previous six appearances.

In that fateful match, Sunderland went in front before Thomson scored a superb equaliser in the 42nd minute. Alas, there was still enough time left in the first half for Sunderland defender Shaun Elliott (cousin of North End's Steve), to collide in a tackle with Ricky which resulted in the Scot receiving a broken ankle.

The home crowd booed off Sunderland at the interval, and Elliott in particular for their apparently over-zealous tackling during the first half, but Ricky isn't for apportioning blame.

"To be fair, it wasn't a nasty tackle, my ankle was trapped and I fell over. I made a comeback towards the end of the season and started the 1979/80 season in my usual role.

"I was 22 by then and just getting really started, weighing the job up.

"The second disaster – the injury that finished my career – was an accident on the Lowthorpe Road training ground where my leg went into a pothole, twisted, and wrecked my knee inside.

"At first it was thought that it wasn't serious, but then they said it was cartilage trouble and I had to go into hospital for an operation. But while the operation was in progress, they discovered it wasn't the cartilage that was damaged after all, it was in fact the lining of the knee."

The manager logged the problems in his programme notes of February 2nd 1980.

"Ricky Thomson was due to have the plaster taken off his leg this week after his knee operation but it will be some time before he is back with us in the first team line-up.

"Ricky is a big asset to the club and there is no point in him rushing back to fitness. I would rather he got fully fit in his own time and then is with us for a long time to come."

"I had two operations on it by orthopaedic surgeon Barry Case, and he couldn't do anything to fix it so that I could play again.

"I was only 23, and had spent three of those years injured, not even kicking a ball!"

Ricky's next spell was on civvy street. "I worked for a year or so building greenhouses, and then got a job building swimming pools for rich footballers," he says, laughing at the irony.

But just how good a footballer was Ricky Thomson? What exactly did North End miss out on?

Fortunately, a chance conversation between Eric Potts and Nobby Stiles back in the late Seventies gives us a massive clue.

Potts, who signed for North End early in the 1978/79 season, recalled the exchange when he was interviewed a few years ago by the Lancashire Evening Post.

"We had a young striker called Ricky Thomson, a very special talent. He could do anything on the field, and it was so sad when injury forced him out of the game at such a young age. I'm convinced he would have played for a Manchester United or for a Liverpool.

"During training one day, Nobby turned to me and said, 'Ricky has as much raw skill as George Best'."

That's a big claim to make.

But, just to dispel any doubters, if anybody would have known that, Nobby, with his Manchester United connection, certainly would!

CHAPTER 14

STILES AND KELLY ON...

During the 1977/78 season both Nobby Stiles and Alan Kelly wrote a column for the Lancashire Evening Football Post.

Their articles would appear in alternate issues and gave an opportunity for the management team to air their views on football – be it national or North End issues. They are a very interesting snapshot of the time.

There follows a selection of these columns that relate to North End issues over the 1977/78 season.

STILES ON: BECOMING MANAGER

Lancashire Evening Football Post 20th August 1977

I am looking forward to my first season as team manager and I am very happy to have been given the chance of being in charge of a side like Preston North End.

For some people the grass is always greener somewhere else, but I believe the North End team have very good prospects.

This is not to say I am promising miracles this season, because all that I can promise is hard work.

I have already worked hard for the last few years with Alan Kelly, who has been appointed assistant manager, and we have formed a partnership. I'm sure that if we keep our fingers crossed, we can have a good year.

My approach to football has changed now that I am manager and I know that position will be more difficult than that of chief coach. As a manager, I will have to be much tougher.

I will have to dictate the way I want things to be done and will have to give the players a good talking to now and then.

The big difference is that, when I was chief coach under Harry Catterick, my main task was just to try and get the best out of the lads in a nice way.

My first few weeks in charge at Deepdale have been very hectic, but I am determined not to let the job affect my home life. I am not going out to matches every night because I think this would make me lose my objectivity and the work would become a burden.

I want it to remain enjoyable so I will use my common sense about just how many hours I should put in. Being a manager has always been my ambition since I gave up playing and I think I have gained some useful experience.

In my first year as a coach I still played on occasions, as well as training with the youngsters. Then I had two years as chief coach at Deepdale and this has helped me enormously.

As everyone knows, I had the opportunity of being given the Preston managership two years ago, and I wanted to take the job then.

But I felt that I couldn't because of my friendship for Bobby Charlton who had resigned and I believed that I had to make a decision at the time which gave me peace of mind.

Looking back, I admit that I may have been wrong to turn down the offer, and my refusal was unfortunate for the club in terms of the extra money that has had to be paid out. I agree with all that, but, from my own personal point of view, it has been better for me to have had two extra years working under a manager.

Alan Kelly and I have also worked even more closely during this period than we did before, and we have learned things from each other, so the time has not been wasted. We have already begun our first season in charge and the team have played another Division Three club, Port Vale, in the first round of the League Cup.

We are not through to the second round yet, having lost 2-1 at Vale Park last Saturday, and only having been able to beat Vale 2-1 at Deepdale this week in the second leg. But at least we are still in there with a shout, and will be going all out to win the replay at Stockport on Tuesday night.

We have done a bit better than last year when we were knocked out of the competition at Bury in the first round and there have been times in the two matches when we have looked a good side.

I believe we have to get organised at the back, and I am glad to see that our new first teamers Graham Cross and Harry Wilson are settling down. As for strengthening the side, my first priority is still a big forward, but players of this type are very hard to find.
I was disappointed when Brighton's Sammy Morgan decided to sign for Cambridge United instead of us, but he was only available for £15,000 because he is getting on a bit – and younger players are much more expensive.
I can only stress that I hope young Preston forwards like Ricky Thomson, John Smith and Ian Cochrane can show their ability in the next few weeks and prove me wrong in thinking we need to sign a new player – but they must realise that, as manager, I can't afford to wait very long.
I have already learned that I have got to be brave enough to make decisions that are bound to upset people – and I will not shirk them.

KELLY ON: THE NEW SET UP

Lancashire Evening Football Post 27th August 1977

The new set up at Deepdale can only be judged by the team's performances on the park, and we will have to take risks if we are to win anything.
But manager Nobby Stiles has taken his new job in his stride and he deserves to succeed.
He works hard, has a lot of common sense and is not afraid to bark at the players when necessary to keep discipline.
We will only know if the Preston directors have made the right changes if we win something, but I don't like people talking about "pressure."
Playing football, managing a club, or working in any way in the game does not put anyone under pressure. And those people who talk about being under pressure are just using the word as a get-out.
Pressure is something that you only feel if you haven't got a job. There may be a bit of anxiety in football, but that is all – and it is wonderful to be paid for doing something you love.
As Preston's new assistant manager, I am working closely with Nobby although there have not been that many changes since last season.
The main thing is that Nobby and I make the decisions now instead of former boss Harry Catterick, after having a chat.

We get on well together and discuss everything – and he involves me in all aspects of the club. We attend board meetings together and also have a meeting every Thursday afternoon with chief scout Jimmie Scott and chairman Alan Jones.

We talk about any problems, big or small, and the meeting is useful as we may otherwise forget one or two things.

I also help with the training every day, so I only spend an odd afternoon at the sports shop owned by Alan Spavin and myself at Lancaster, which is now managed by Alan's brother.

We sold our other sports shop in Morecambe some time ago and I devote most of my time to football.

We are fortunate at Deepdale in having a very good scout and he has done a fine job in signing young players over the years and in assessing opposing teams.

But the only way we are going to succeed is by concentrating on doing what we want to do on the field and we bear this in mind all the time. It is good to know how other teams take free kicks, corners and throw-ins, but what we really want is for them to worry about us.

I will be watching the first team when I can, but I will continue to look after the reserves and my priority is to get two or three youngsters through to the senior squad each season.

I would like the Central League side to achieve good results as this would make it easier for the lads to develop confidence, but results are not the main thing at this level and sometimes we play three schoolboys and five apprentices against teams packed with players who have Division One or even international experience.

I believe That we have some very promising youngsters and they are a credit to Jimmie Scott, and to Brian Pilkington and Nick Bailey who work hard on a part-time basis to help them.

KELLY ON: THE RETURN OF SPAVIN

Lancashire Evening Football Post 8th October 1977

Some people were surprised when Preston North End manager, Nobby Stiles and I decided to ask former club captain Alan Spavin to return to Deepdale.

But we were delighted when 'Spav' agreed to re-join Preston this week on a month's trial after finishing his job as the player-coach of Washington Diplomats.

After knowing him so well for many years, I wanted him back as soon as I knew he was available.

We have re-signed him mainly with a view to helping the young kids in the reserve team, but who knows what he will be able to do?

He has never been appreciated as much as he should have been.

Spav joined North End when he was 14 and didn't need asking twice when he was told he could make a contribution again.

He has no plans for returning to the United States and just wants to help the club in any way he can. Although we won't know until we have seen him play in a few games, I think he may be able to force his way back into the first team. I know he is 35, but that is not too old for a midfield man of his type.

Eire's player-manager Johnny Giles is 36 and so too is Liverpool's Ian Callaghan, who recently returned to the England side, while Wrexham's player-manager, Arfon Griffiths is even older.

Spav is a player's player and you have got to be in the same team with him to appreciate what he does for the side.

He is a good passer of the ball, but the main thing about him is that he gets involved all the time.

It may be that he makes more mistakes than other players, but this is simply because he has more of the ball.

A player who only makes the odd mistake is not getting involved enough. This is something that a lot of people don't understand and some spectators used to get on to Spav in certain matches.

But he would still want the ball whether he was having a good time or a bad time and would always be near enough to help other players out even though the crowd thought he wasn't playing well.

I have seen a lot of midfield men lately and he still compares favourably with many of those who could be signed to play in Division Three.

He had a great season back in 1963/64 when Preston reached the FA Cup Final and just missed promotion to Division One, and he was also the outstanding player in the entire section when North End won the Division Three championship in 1971. Now he is as keen as mustard to do well and is fully fit.

He compensates for any lack of pace by his clever use of the ball and is recognised everywhere by his fellow professionals as a fair player. Some people talk about the need to have 'crunchers' in midfield, but this is rubbish.

Spav hustles opposing players and nicks the ball time and time again to illustrate that you don't need to kick anyone up in the air to gain possession.

In the next few weeks, his skill and experience is bound to rub off on our youngsters, and they need someone to bring them on, for several in the reserve team are only 16.

Some were out of their depth playing against Derby County reserves in midweek when Steve Uzelac had 'flu, and another defender Grant Davies was with the Welsh youth team, and when Brian Gardner, a third defender, had to play in midfield. Spav is certain to be a big help in the Central League in the circumstances, but I repeat he will also add depth to the Deepdale senior squad and that he has all the qualities necessary to get back in the first team.

All the lads at Deepdale will have to be on their toes and I am never worried about how old anyone is as long as he shows everyone that he can still play well.

Spav will do this and that is why Nobby and I were so pleased to welcome him 'home' when he returned from America on Tuesday. I am sure he has the ability to prove that we were right.

STILES ON: <u>NEW SIGNINGS</u>

Lancashire Evening Football Post 29th October 1977

I have been delighted with the way Graham Cross, Harry Wilson, Sean Haslegrave and Steve Uzelac, the new players signed by Preston since the end of last season, have settled in at Deepdale.

They are all well liked by the other lads, and this is tremendous. It shows they are the right type of players for Preston and it also proves the set-up is right and that the players already on North End's books are the right type.

All the lads have been great but there are cliques at some clubs and this makes it very difficult for newly signed men. Fortunately, there are no cliques at Deepdale and no one has made things hard for the new signings.

The fact that they have all settled down has shown in their play.

Graham has done particularly well, and Harry, Sean and Steve are all ambitious young players.

Football is a team game and all the lads in our side have been helping each other. We have a good harmony at the club, and although Steve has not been able to get into the first team squad on many occasions, he has worked hard and shown the right attitude.

It has been difficult for me to promote him because both our regular first team centre backs have been doing well, but I had no hesitation in calling him up to the squad when Graham pulled a calf muscle during our 2-1 win over Tranmere at Deepdale on Tuesday night.

Graham is 34 in December, but I can't see his playing career finishing for a long time and I am not even thinking about such a possibility. He and former North End captain Alan Spavin, who returned to the club a few weeks ago at the age of 35 on trial, have proved the point that, if you can still play well, it doesn't matter how old you are.

Both Graham and Alan are very good trainers and are still as keen as ever on the game.

Graham has helped Mick Baxter enormously in the middle of our back four, and has also had a good influence on our other young players.

Apart from his coolness on the field, Graham is great in the dressing room, where he is a complete extrovert.

He has been a really good influence and I have had no problems with him at all.

When we played Brighton last season, we thought he might be a bit slow and that we would be able to take advantage.

But we discovered that Graham reads the game very well and stops attacks before they have even started.

He has done the same for us this season and on reflection I cannot understand why he never played for the full England side.

I have known him for a long time and he was in the Leicester City team beaten 3-1 by Manchester United in the FA Cup Final in 1963 when I was a United reserve.

He also played in many big games against United and was in the England U23 when he was 19 before I gained a place in the team.

I made my debut for United when I was 18, but I was 22 before I gained a regular league place, and was nearly 23 before I was called up to the England U23 squad. Alan Ball junior said that I was the oldest under-23 he had ever seen – and I know what he meant!

But Graham was a regular in that side as a midfield player or defender.

His attitude now is an example to everyone and, touch wood, I am pleased with the performances of all Preston's new players.

They and all the other lads are prepared to work hard and I was delighted when there were no grumbles when I made them all report to Deepdale for special training last Sunday after our defeat at Exeter the day before and the long trip back.
They know that the lesson from that game was that we have got to get our attitude right in away matches.
We have shown that we can beat the best teams in Division Three at Deepdale, but we have got to prove that we can compete at places like Exeter, as well as play good football.
The lads have got the opportunity to prove themselves in the match at Port Vale next Saturday

STILES ON: SELLING MY BEST PLAYERS

Lancashire Evening Football Post 11th February 1978

I want to assure Preston North End's fans that I do NOT want to sell any of the club's best players.
But the position is that I cannot guarantee that Preston will gain promotion to the Second Division at the end of the season and most players are ambitious to play in a higher grade of football.
There have been suggestions this week that First Division Newcastle United are considering making a bid for Mike Elwiss, but no offer has been received yet.
Mike is a fine forward who has done well for Preston and improved 100% since being signed from Fourth Division Doncaster Rovers four years ago.
He saw his teammates Gary Williams and Mark Lawrenson move to Brighton last summer and was naturally disappointed that he had to remain in a Third Division side.
But I told him that I would let him know if Preston received any bids for him – and he has accepted the situation.
Every now and again there are rumours that he may be leaving Deepdale, but my main concern has always been to get him to play well for North End. I don't look too far ahead and Preston's next game is always the most important thing for me.
Wrexham came in for Mike back in September and asked him if he was interested in going there, but he said he was not, and that was the end of the matter.
It will be up to him to decide if he wants to move if another bid comes in,

and he knows that I will be honest with him.
I am working for the future of North End, but I have got to be fair to him and to everyone else at the club.
I am sure most fathers wouldn't stand in the way of their sons if they had the chance to better themselves.
I believe my policy at Deepdale is the right one, and I also think that are not happy should be put on the transfer list.
That's why John McMahon, Danny Cameron and Ricky Thomson were told that they could go when they asked to be listed, but I'm glad that they have all now decided to stay and are no longer on offer.
The Preston players have proved that they are good enough to go up to the Second Division and I want them to continue to show the right attitude.
It would not do any good at all if I stood in the way of one of them, and I will never do that.
Mike Elwiss has kept his feet on the ground and is very happy at Deepdale where he is enjoying his football, but I will not be able to stop him leaving if the right kind of offer comes along because North End are still only a Third Division club.
I can understand supporters worrying about the possible sale of players, and I hope that Mike will stay at Deepdale, but I won't try to force him or anyone else.
It is then up to our youngsters to show that they are good enough to be promoted to the first team if any senior players have to be sold.

KELLY ON: NOBBY STILES

Lancashire Evening Football Post 4th March 1978

Nobby Stiles fully deserves the success he's had as Preston's manager this season. He is completely honest and he does things simply and with common sense.
I have known him for quite a few years because he often used to watch Republic of Ireland international games when I was playing, and he has not changed.
He is married to Katy, the sister of Eire's player-manager Johnny Giles, so I saw a great deal of him even before he was signed by Preston from Middlesbrough as a midfield player.
He was a very good footballer when he was at his peak, and although fans

remember him for playing very hard, what they forget is that he was one of the best passers of the ball in England.
He rarely wasted possession after winning it and it should be recalled that England's vital third goal in the 1966 World Cup Final against West Germany came from one of his passes.
He split the German defence at Wembley with a long pass to Alan Ball junior and Geoff Hurst scored from Ball's centre when the ball bounced over the German line from the crossbar.
People never give him the credit he deserved as a player, and it is unfortunate that they think of him as dirty.
He kept things simple then, and this is how he manages North End now. He does the job in an effective way and has all that it takes.
The Preston players understand what he is talking about and have plenty of respect for him.
He does not look for problems, but if something has to be done, Nobby does it without fuss and no one has any complaints, even though he is firm and strong in disciplinary matters.
We are all very pleased with the way things have gone at Deepdale this season because we now have a good set of players together.
Nobby ran the first team as chief coach last year, when Harry Catterick delegated much of the responsibility, and was appointed team manager when I was made assistant manager just before the start of the present season.
Basically, we discuss everything together and discuss anything that happens at the club, and we are sure that team spirit is very high.
It is to his credit that the reserve players listen for the first team results and give a tremendous cheer if they hear North End have won.
We all talk about the team together and there are never frills or fancy things. Nobby has a great knowledge of football and does everything well. His secret is his ability to make others understand him and not use words like 'motivation' or the other new words that have come into the game lately.
The only thing I can motivate is my car and I am not very good at that sometimes, but I am sure that Nobby will continue to do well as Preston's manager and it is just a pity that North End fans didn't see him at his best as a player.

(chapter continues overleaf)

STILES ON: PFA TEAM SELECTION

Lancashire Evening Football Post 25th March 1978

A lot of Preston fans were disappointed on Sunday when none of the North End players were named in the Division Three team of the year selected by members of the Professional Footballers Association.

Some supporters were even shocked – and I believe they were right to be shocked!

All the Preston first teamers should have been in contention for places in the representative side – and North End remain my Division Three team of the year.

I cannot understand why some of my lads were left out and forwards Alex Bruce and Mike Elwiss should have been automatic selections.

They should also have been selected in the team last year, when our only representative was right back John McMahon.

John lost his place this time, but I don't know why, because he has been playing even better.

Going through our side, I would say that I have not seen a better goalkeeper than Roy Tunks. He is still only young for a 'keeper and works tremendously hard at his game in training with North End assistant manager Alan Kelly.

We have had changes this season in our back four because of injuries, but Graham Cross is still one of the best defenders in the game at stopping attacks before they even start, and that is the sign of a class player. Mick Baxter, who partners Graham in the middle of the defence, has improved tremendously this year and is now one of the best young players in the game.

I have already mentioned McMahon, and I rate Danny Cameron as a very good full back too. He played on the right when McMahon was out and switched to the left when Harry Wilson, another of the best full backs in the division, was ruled out.

In midfield, we have four fine players in Gordon Coleman, who is a good reader of the game, Francis Burns, who is still very skilful, Stephen Doyle, who has tremendous potential, and Sean Haslegrave, who does his job quietly and efficiently.

At the front, we have Ricky Thomson alongside Bruce and Elwiss, and Ricky showed his great skill in our recent win at Swindon. He is still maturing and I believe he will become a very good player.

There is not much more I can say about Bruce and Elwiss except that I see them week in and week out, and know that there are no better forwards in the division.
Alex is a great goalscorer, and Mike is superb at playing balls early and in causing defences all sorts of problems.
I know that all the Wrexham players are good and should also have been in contention and I also think that Danny Westwood of Gillingham, who scored a superb winning goal against us recently, and Bobby Tynan of Tranmere, are both very good players.
But I repeat my lads are as good as anybody in the division, and I think it is now up to them to take the needle and prove some of their opponents are wrong in not rating them more highly.
I hope that being left out of the representative team side will prove a major spur to the Preston players and that they will continue to play as well as they have been doing lately so that promotion will be gained at the end of the season.
If they play well as a team, they play well individually, and prove themselves to everyone.

KELLY ON: STOKOE AND TEAM SPIRIT

Lancashire Evening Football Post 1st April 1978

The only disappointing thing this season for Preston manager Nobby Stiles and myself is that a lot of people have said that the North End team is not good enough for Division Two.
Even North End president Tom Finney had reservations about the club's future when he was interviewed on television recently, but if the Preston side was not good enough, it would not be near the top of Division Three.
Bury manager Bob Stokoe had a real go at the North End team after Preston's 1-1 draw at Gigg Lane on Easter Monday, and Nobby and I were surprised at this because we don't talk about players in other sides and there is no way in which we would slang other teams.
I can only think some of our critics are jealous of what success we have had, and Nobby and I are just trying to do the best we can.
We are also being honest and, if other people can do a better job in running the team at Deepdale, they are welcome to have a go as far as we are concerned.
North End have won games this season because of good team efforts and

not because we are a two-man team as Stokoe said.
If one of the players has not been doing well, someone else has made up for him by playing even better and everyone has kept battling in every game.
Against Bury on Easter Monday, I doubt that many people thought we had much chance when they found out that three centre halves had been ruled out through injury.
But Nobby and I are paid to make the team decisions and Stephen Doyle and Gordon Coleman did magnificently in deputising for Mick Baxter and Graham Cross in the middle of our back four.
Alan Spavin also did well after coming into the team in midfield and the Bury game alone proved that we were right in bringing him back to the club after his spell in America.
If any of our decisions had backfired on us, we would have been in trouble but we believe in getting good skilful players together and are convinced that we have a lot of such players at Deepdale.
They all do their job efficiently and there is a great spirit at the club. That does not mean to say we are satisfied with everything and we know that problems will occur from time to time.
But North End are still in Division Three and there is no point in talking about Division Two yet. In fact, if you take anything for granted you are asking for trouble.
We know that we have not got the time to wait too long in Division Three however, and are determined to get promoted as soon as possible.
I believe that our team is improving all the time and that the lads play simple football with a bit of individual flair added. We have the makings of a very good side, and the more the players play together, the more they will improve.
The support we have been getting in our away games recently is the best I have ever known since I arrived at Deepdale.
The players are absolutely thrilled by this and I can assure everyone that this kind of support helps a team tremendously and makes up for what the knockers say.
Confidence is one of the most important factors in football and our lads are now confident enough to try the extra little things which they wouldn't try if they hadn't been doing well.
Naturally we have had setbacks and we will have more setbacks, but the lads have shown they can recover. Everyone has worked hard this season and everyone at the club wants to do well.
They all help each other on the field and off, and they are great fighters.

They don't want to know about losing and are always trying to do better. They are behind one another – and that is what team spirit is all about.

STILES ON: WINNING PROMOTION

Lancashire Evening Post supplement 'Going Up' 2nd May 1978

The manager usually gets all the credit when a team wins any kind of honour in the Football League, but at Deepdale Alan Kelly and I are partners.

People should not congratulate me on my own, because Alan and I do everything together and consult one another all the time.

From our point of view, we know that promotion has been achieved because everyone at the club has put in a lot of hard work.

The players have been tremendous, and they are all good players who have shown confidence and applied themselves week in and week out.

There is also a backroom team behind every good team and we have been lucky to have Jimmie Scott who has done a great job in giving us fatherly advice and in analysing opposing sides.

Trainer Harry Hubbick is another great character in the dressing room and on the touchline, and our kitman George Warr has also been terrific in doing the little things to keep players happy.

I am bound to leave some people out when paying tributes, but I must not forget assistant secretary Derek Allan, who has made my job so easy for me on many occasions, and coach Nick Bailey who has always been around.

Both Kel and I have made mistakes in our first season in charge of the team, but we have not made as many as we would have done a couple of years ago, and our period spent coaching provided us with a lot of valuable experience.

Now, gaining promotion has been as wonderful as anything that has happened to us in our careers because you are only as good as you have been in your last job.

The players will have no need to feel inferior in Division Two, and I don't think they know what they are capable of yet.

I believe that they have formed the next best team to Wrexham in Division Three and we will have to prove that we can better them next season.

Wrexham set us a standard this time, and we have a good mixture of

youth and experience, with a player like Alan Spavin having contributed a lot off the field and on in his occasional appearances.
I hope all the lads enjoy their success, and return to Deepdale ready to work harder than ever.

DIVISION THREE FINAL LEAGUE TABLE 1977/78

		P	W	D	L	F	A	Pts
1	**Wrexham**	46	23	15	8	78	45	61
2	**Cambridge United**	46	23	12	11	72	51	58
3	**Preston North End**	46	20	16	10	63	38	56
4	**Peterborough United**	46	20	16	10	47	33	56
5	**Chester**	46	16	22	8	59	56	54
6	**Walsall**	46	18	17	11	61	50	53
7	**Gillingham**	46	15	20	11	67	60	50
8	**Colchester United**	46	15	18	13	55	44	48
9	**Chesterfield**	46	17	14	15	58	49	48
10	**Swindon Town**	46	16	16	14	67	60	48
11	**Shrewsbury Town**	46	16	15	15	63	57	47
12	**Tranmere Rovers**	46	16	15	15	57	52	47
13	**Carlisle United**	46	14	19	13	59	59	47
14	**Sheffield Wednesday**	46	15	16	15	50	52	46
15	**Bury**	46	13	19	14	62	56	45
16	**Lincoln City**	46	15	15	16	53	61	45
17	**Exeter City**	46	15	14	17	49	59	44
18	**Oxford United**	46	13	14	19	64	67	40
19	**Plymouth Argyle**	46	11	17	18	61	68	39
20	**Rotherham United**	46	13	13	20	51	68	39
21	**Port Vale**	46	8	20	18	46	67	36
22	**Bradford City**	46	12	10	24	56	86	34
23	**Hereford United**	46	9	14	23	34	60	32
24	**Portsmouth**	46	7	17	22	41	75	31

FIXTURES AND APPEARANCES SUMMARY 1977/78

Date	Opponents	F A	Gate	1	2	3	4	5	6	7	8	9	10	11	12
1977															
Aug. 13 Sat.	Port Vale (LC1) (A)	1–2	4,530	Tunks	McMahon	Wilson	Doyle	Baxter	Cross	Coleman	Brown	Smith	Elwiss	**Bruce 1**	Thomson
16 Tue.	**PORT VALE** (LC1) (H)	2–1	5,816	Tunks	McMahon	Wilson	Doyle	Baxter	Cross	Coleman	Brown	Smith	**Elwiss 2**	Bruce	Thomson*
20 Sat.	Plymouth Argyle (A)	0–0	7,154	Tunks	McMahon	Wilson	Doyle	Baxter	Cross	Coleman	Brown	Thomson	Elwiss	Bruce	Burns*
23 Tue.	Port Vale (LC1R) (A)	2–1	2,201	Tunks	McMahon	Wilson	Doyle	Baxter	Cross	Burns	Brown	Thomson	**Elwiss 1**	**Bruce 1**	Smith
27 Sat.	**ROTHERHAM UNITED** (H)	3–2	5,964	Tunks	McMahon	Wilson	**Doyle 1**	Baxter	Cross	Burns	Brown	Thomson	**Elwiss 1**	**Bruce 1**	Coleman
30 Tue.	Walsall (L.C. 2) (A)	0–0	5,445	Tunks	McMahon	Wilson	Doyle	Baxter	Cross	Coleman	Burns	Thomson	Elwiss	Bruce	Smith
Sept. 3 Sat.	Oxford United (A)	0–1	4,804	Tunks	Cameron	Wilson	Doyle	Baxter	Cross	Coleman	Burns	Thomson	Elwiss	Bruce	Smith*
6 Tue.	**WALSALL (L.C. 2 replay)** (H)	0–1	7,069	Tunks	McMahon	Wilson	Doyle	Baxter	Cross	Coleman	Burns	Thomson	Elwiss	Bruce	Smith
10 Sat.	Carlisle United (A)	1–3	5,743	Tunks	McMahon	Wilson	Doyle	Baxter	Cross	Coleman	Burns	Thomson	Elwiss	**Bruce 1**	Cochrane
13 Tue.	**SWINDON TOWN** (H)	1–1	6,014	Tunks	McMahon	Wilson	Doyle	Baxter	Cross	Coleman	Burns	Thomson	Elwiss	Bruce	**Robinson 1***
17 Sat.	**HEREFORD UNITED** (H)	0–0	5,447	Tunks	McMahon	Wilson	Doyle	Baxter	Cross	Coleman	Burns	Robinson	Elwiss	Bruce	Thomson*
24 Sat.	Colchester United (A)	0–0	4,978	Tunks	McMahon	Wilson	Doyle	Baxter	Cross	Coleman	Burns	Smith	Elwiss	Bruce	Robinson
27 Tue.	Walsall (A)	0–0	5,138	Tunks	Cameron	Wilson	Doyle	Baxter	Cross	Coleman	Burns	Smith	Elwiss	Bruce	Robinson
Oct. 1 Sat.	**CAMBRIDGE UNITED** (H)	2–0	5,319	Tunks	Cameron	Wilson	Doyle	**Baxter 1**	Cross	Coleman	Haslegrave	Smith	Elwiss	**Bruce 1**	Burns
4 Tue.	**SHEFFIELD WEDNESDAY** (H)	2–1	7,627	Tunks	Cameron	Wilson	Doyle	Baxter	**Cross 1**	Coleman	Haslegrave	Smith	**Elwiss 1**	Bruce	Robinson
8 Sat.	Bradford City (A)	1–1	5,815	Tunks	Cameron	Wilson	Doyle	Baxter	Cross	Coleman	Haslegrave	**Smith 1**	Elwiss	Bruce	Burns
15 Sat.	**GILLINGHAM** (H)	2–0	7,212	Tunks	Cameron	Wilson	Doyle	Baxter	Cross	Coleman	Haslegrave	**Smith 1**	**Elwiss 1**	Bruce	Robinson*
22 Sat.	Exeter City (A)	0–2	5,444	Tunks	Cameron	Wilson	Doyle	Baxter	Cross	Coleman	Haslegrave	Smith	Elwiss	Thomson	Burns*
25 Tue.	**TRANMERE ROVERS** (H)	2–1	7,906	Tunks	Cameron	Wilson	Doyle	**Baxter 1**	Cross	Coleman	Haslegrave	Smith	**Elwiss 1**	Bruce	Robinson
29 Sat.	**CHESTER** (H)	2–1	7,550	Tunks	Cameron	Wilson	Doyle	Baxter	Cross	Coleman	Haslegrave	Smith	Elwiss	**Bruce 2**	Uzelac
Nov. 5 Sat.	Port Vale (A)	0–0	4,208	Tunks	Cameron	Wilson	Doyle	Baxter	Uzelac	Coleman	Haslegrave	Smith	Elwiss	Bruce	Burns
12 Sat.	**WREXHAM** (H)	1–3	10,342	Tunks	Cameron	Wilson	Doyle	Baxter	Uzelac	Coleman	Haslegrave	Smith	Elwiss	**Bruce 1**	Spavin*
19 Sat.	Lincoln City (A)	2–2	3,924	Tunks	Cameron	Wilson	Doyle	Baxter	Burns	Coleman	Haslegrave	Smith	Elwiss	**Bruce 2**	Spavin*
26 Sat.	**LINCOLN CITY F.A. Cup (1)** (H)	3–2	6,965	Tunks	McMahon	Cameron	Doyle	Baxter	Burns	Coleman	Haslegrave	Smith	**Elwiss 2**	**Bruce 1**	Spavin
Dec. 3 Sat.	**PORTSMOUTH** (H)	3–1	5,936	Tunks	McMahon	Cameron	Doyle	Baxter	Burns	Coleman	Haslegrave	**Smith 1**	**Elwiss 1**	**Bruce 1**	Robinson
10 Sat.	Shrewsbury Town (A)	0–0	3,764	Tunks	McMahon	Cameron	Doyle	Baxter	Burns	Coleman	Haslegrave	Smith	Elwiss	Bruce	Spavin
17 Sat.	**WREXHAM F.A. Cup (2)** (H)	0–2	11,134	Tunks	McMahon	Cameron	Doyle	Baxter	Burns	Coleman	Haslegrave	Smith	Elwiss	Bruce	Spavin*
26 Mon.	**BURY** (H)	4–0	10,297	Tunks	McMahon	Cameron	Burns	Baxter	Cross	**Coleman 1**	Haslegrave	Thomson	**Elwiss 1**	**Bruce 2**	Spavin*
27 Tue.	Chesterfield (A)	1–0	6,484	Tunks	McMahon	Cameron	Burns	Baxter	Cross	Coleman	Haslegrave	Thomson	Elwiss	**Bruce 1**	Spavin
31 Sat.	Peterborough United (A)	0–1	7,134	Tunks	McMahon	Cameron	Burns	Baxter	Cross	Coleman	Haslegrave	Thomson	Elwiss	Bruce	Doyle
1978															
Jan. 2 Mon.	**PORT VALE** (H)	2–0	10,930	Tunks	McMahon	Cameron	Burns	Baxter	Cross	Coleman	Haslegrave	**Thomson 1**	Elwiss	**Bruce 1**	Spavin
6 Fri.	Tranmere Rovers (3) (A)	0–1	7,254	Tunks	McMahon	Cameron	Burns	Baxter	Cross	Coleman	Haslegrave	Thomson	Elwiss	Bruce	Doyle
14 Sat.	**PLYMOUTH ARGYLE** (H)	5–2	7,065	Tunks	McMahon	Cameron	Burns	**Baxter 1**	Cross	**Coleman 1**	Haslegrave	**Thomson 1**	**Elwiss 1**	**Bruce 1**	Doyle*
Feb. 4 Sat.	**CARLISLE UNITED** (H)	2–1	9,095	Tunks	McMahon	Cameron	Burns	Baxter	Cross	Coleman	Haslegrave	Thomson	Elwiss	**Bruce 2**	Doyle
11 Sat.	Hereford United (A)	0–0	4,791	Tunks	Coleman	Cameron	Burns	Baxter	Cross	Doyle	Haslegrave	Thomson	Elwiss	Bruce	Robinson
21 Tue.	**OXFORD UNITED** (H)	3–2	6,169	Tunks	Coleman	Cameron	Burns	Baxter	Cross	Doyle	Haslegrave	**Thomson 2**	Elwiss	**Bruce 1**	Robinson
25 Sat.	Cambridge United (A)	1–1	5,766	Tunks	Coleman	Cameron	Burns	Baxter	Cross	Doyle	Haslegrave	**Thomson 1**	Elwiss	Bruce	Robinson
28 Tue.	**COLCHESTER UNITED** (H)	4–0	9,225	Tunks	Coleman	Cameron	Burns	Baxter	Cross	Doyle	Haslegrave	Thomson	Elwiss	**Bruce 4**	Robinson
Mar. 4 Sat.	**BRADFORD CITY** (H)	3–1	11,920	Tunks	**McMahon 1**	Cameron	Burns	Baxter	Cross	Coleman	Haslegrave	Thomson	**Elwiss 2**	Bruce	Doyle
7 Tue.	Swindon Town (A)	2–0	10,211	Tunks	McMahon	Cameron	Burns	**Baxter 1**	Cross	Coleman	Haslegrave	Thomson	Elwiss	**Bruce 1**	Doyle
11 Sat.	Gillingham (6) (A)	1–2	9,568	Tunks	McMahon	Cameron	Burns	Baxter	Cross	**Coleman 1**	Haslegrave	Thomson	Elwiss	Bruce	Doyle
18 Sat.	**EXETER CITY** (H)	0–0	9,189	Tunks	McMahon	Cameron	Burns	Baxter	Cross	Coleman	Haslegrave	Thomson	Elwiss	Bruce	Spavin*
24 Fri.	Chester (A)	2–1	7,864	Tunks	McMahon	Cameron	Burns	Baxter	Cross	Coleman	Haslegrave	Thomson	**Elwiss 1**	**Bruce 1**	Doyle
26 Sat.	**CHESTERFIELD** (H)	0–0	10,922	Tunks	McMahon	Cameron	Burns	Baxter	Cross	Coleman	Haslegrave	Thomson	Elwiss	Bruce	Doyle*
27 Mon.	Bury (A)	1–1	9,783	Tunks	McMahon	Cameron	Burns	Doyle	Coleman	Spavin	Haslegrave	**Thomson 1**	Elwiss	Bruce	Cochrane
Apr. 1 Sat.	**PETERBOROUGH UNITED** (H)	0–1	9,695	Tunks	McMahon	Cameron	Burns	Baxter	Cross	Coleman	Haslegrave	Thomson	Elwiss	Bruce	Doyle*
4 Tue.	**WALSALL** (H)	1–0	11,239	Tunks	McMahon	Cameron	Burns	Baxter	Cross	Coleman	Haslegrave	**Robinson 1**	Elwiss	Bruce	Doyle
8 Sat.	Wrexham (SF) (A)	0–0	19,088	Tunks	McMahon	Cameron	Burns	Baxter	Cross	Coleman	Haslegrave	Robinson	Elwiss	Bruce	Doyle
15 Sat.	**LINCOLN CITY** (H)	4–0	11,208	Tunks	McMahon	Cameron	Burns	**Baxter 1**	Cross	**Coleman 1**	Haslegrave	**Robinson 1**	Elwiss	**Bruce 1**	Doyle*
18 Tue.	Sheffield Wednesday (A)	0–1	12,426	Tunks	McMahon	Cameron	Burns	Baxter	Cross	Coleman	Haslegrave	Robinson	Elwiss	Bruce	Doyle*
22 Sat.	Portsmouth (A)	2–0	6,866	Tunks	McMahon	Cameron	Burns	Baxter	Cross	Coleman	Haslegrave	Robinson	**Elwiss 1**	**Bruce 1**	Doyle
25 Tue.	Rotherham United (A)	1–2	5,646	Tunks	McMahon	Cameron	Burns	Baxter	Cross	Coleman	Haslegrave	Robinson	Elwiss	**Bruce 1**	Doyle*
29 Sat.	**SHREWSBURY TOWN** (H)	2–2	16,078	Tunks	McMahon	Cameron	Burns	Baxter	Cross	Coleman	Haslegrave	Robinson	**Elwiss 1**	**Bruce 1**	Doyle*

** Denotes sub. used*
Scorers in heavy type

PRESTON NORTH END FOOTBALL CLUB

1977/78

Back Row left to right: Harry Wilson, Jimmy Brown, Mike Elwiss, Steve Uzelac, Mick Baxter, John McMahon, Michael Robinson

Middle Row left to right: Peter Morris, Ricky Thomson, Danny Cameron, Stephen Doyle, Gordon Coleman, Alex Bruce, John Smith, Grant Davis

Front Row left to right: Francis Burns, Alex Smith, Alan Kelly (Assistant manager), Nobby Stiles (Manager), Harry Hubbick (Trainer), Roy Tunks, Ian Cochrane

ABOUT THE AUTHOR

A North End fan. Can't help it. It won't go away.

Printed in Poland
by Amazon Fulfillment
Poland Sp. z o.o., Wrocław

58701765R00226